D1481986

The Camden House History of German Literature

Volume 3

German Literature of the High Middle Ages

The Camden House History of German Literature

Volume 3

The Camden House History of German Literature

Edited by James Hardin

Vol. 1: Early Germanic Literature and Culture
Edited by Brian Murdoch and Malcolm Read,
University of Stirling, UK

Vol. 2: German Literature of the Early Middle Ages
Edited by Brian Murdoch, University of Stirling, UK

Vol. 3: German Literature of the High Middle Ages
Edited by Will Hasty, University of Florida

Vol. 4: Early Modern German Literature
Edited by Max Reinhart, University of Georgia

*Vol. 5: German Literature of the Eighteenth Century:
The Enlightenment and Sensibility*
Edited by Barbara Becker-Cantarino, Ohio State University

Vol. 6: Literature of the Sturm und Drang
Edited by David Hill, University of Birmingham, UK

Vol. 7: The Literature of Weimar Classicism
Edited by Simon Richter, University of Pennsylvania

Vol. 8: The Literature of German Romanticism
Edited by Dennis F. Mahoney, University of Vermont

Vol. 9: German Literature of the Nineteenth Century, 1832–1899
Edited by Clayton Koelb and Eric Downing,
University of North Carolina

*Vol. 10: German Literature of the Twentieth Century:
From Aestheticism to Postmodernism*
Ingo R. Stoehr, Kilgore College, Texas

German Literature of the High Middle Ages

Edited by
Will Hasty

CAMDEN HOUSE

First published 2006
by Camden House

Camden House is an imprint of Boydell & Brewer Inc.
668 Mt. Hope Avenue, Rochester, NY 14620, USA
www.camden-house.com
and of Boydell & Brewer Limited
PO Box 9, Woodbridge, Suffolk IP12 3DF, UK
www.boydellandbrewer.com

ISBN: 1–57113–173–6

Library of Congress Cataloging-in-Publication Data

German literature of the high middle ages / edited by Will Hasty
   p. cm. — (Camden House history of German literature; v. 3)
Includes bibliographical references and index.
ISBN 1–57113–173–6 (hardcover: alk. paper)
   1. German literature—Middle High German, 1050–1500—History and
criticism.   2. Germany—Civilization—History.   3. Civilization, Medieval.
I. Hasty, Will.   II. Series.

PT191.G47 2006
830.9′0021—dc22

2005024594

A catalogue record for this title is available from the British Library.

This publication is printed on acid-free paper.
Printed in the United States of America.

To a dear colleague and friend, Sidney M. Johnson (1924–2003)

Contents

Part I. The First Flourishing of German Literature

Part II. Lyric and Narrative Traditions

Part III. Continuity, Transformation, and Innovation in the Thirteenth Century

Part IV. Historical Perspectives

Illustrations

All illustrations are from the Codex Manesse.

Acknowledgments

THIS VOLUME BECAME LENGTHIER, both in regard to content and production time, than originally planned. Hence, it is fitting that I gratefully acknowledge not only the contributors' effort and cordial collaboration, but also their patience. I am grateful to the Universitätsbibliothek Heidelberg for permission to reproduce images from the Codex Manesse in this volume. Finally, I would like to thank everyone else who has been involved in the production of the manuscript, in particular Brian Murdoch for his many helpful suggestions during the final editing stage, and Jim Hardin and Jim Walker for their steadfast encouragement and help, and for the opportunity to work with them again on the literature of the High Middle Ages.

W. H.
August 2005

Introduction

Will Hasty

THE EUROPEAN HIGH MIDDLE AGES saw a convergence of oral and written narrative traditions, new philosophical and scientific knowledge, and individual creativity that has been called the "Twelfth Century Renaissance."[1] Beginning in the twelfth century, authors schooled in the *septem artes liberales* (seven liberal arts) turned in greater numbers from Latin to the vernacular languages as their means of literary expression. Literary works from classical antiquity enjoyed a surge of popularity and reached wider audiences as they were transformed into epics in French and German.[2] Poetry originally based on events during the migration period (*Völkerwanderungen:* fifth and sixth centuries) or on conflicts with Saracens in the Carolingian period (eighth century), which may have been transmitted orally through countless generations, also began to take literary form as authors structured it into longer epic narratives involving fanciful versions of historical figures such as Theoderic the Great, Attila the Hun, and William, Count of Orange, and legendary heroes such as Arthur and Roland. Lyric love poetry arose in Provence, spread from there to the kingdoms of France and Germany, providing impetus to already existing indigenous lyric traditions. Contacts with Islamic culture put Western Europe in contact with philosophical and scientific texts from Greco-Roman antiquity that had been preserved in Arabic, and sometimes provided with Arabic commentaries that were quite influential in their own right.[3] The knowledge gained from an intensive preoccupation with these texts contributed to an increasing sensitivity for the natural world and peoples' place in it, opened up new questions for intellectual inquiry,[4] and in turn enriched the flourishing vernacular literatures. Individual authors, often knights who acquired the ability to read and write, emerged to make their own characteristic marks on literary culture, despite the continuing authority of pre-existing narrative traditions and conventions, and the medieval dependence of the vernacular artist/author on the favor, largesse, and tastes of powerful patrons and the noble audiences among whom the authors typically lived and worked.[5]

The Twelfth Century Renaissance is the broader European context for the literary history addressed by the chapters in this volume, the principal aim of which is to familiarize readers with the most significant authors, works, and literary traditions in medieval Germany, during what has come among German literary scholars to be known as the first *Blütezeit,* or "period of flourishing" of literature in the German vernacular, from ca. 1170 to ca. 1270.[6] The use of the term *Blütezeit* brings with it the risk of overlooking or understating the importance of literary developments that may occur between periods of flourishing, but it nevertheless seems appropriate in the case of the German literature of the High Middle Ages, when a vibrant literary culture in the German vernacular emerged in the form of narrative and lyric poetry that continued to shape the cultural horizons of German-speaking peoples to the present day. Seemingly all at once, in the latter twelfth century, German poets are singing of their love, writing didactic and political (gnomic) poetry (*Sangsprüche*), and composing longer and shorter poetic works — epics, romances, courtly legends, and shorter narratives — that are frequently about the quest of an individual, usually a lay-person and a knight, for someone or something — a wife, higher social standing, the Holy Grail — that can be seen as representing the achievement of one's proper position in the world and one's appropriate relationship to God.

The efflorescence of literature in the German vernacular in the High Middle Ages occurred in fertile cultural and literary ground. Since about the middle of the eleventh century, religious authors had again begun producing texts in the German vernacular, after more than a century of silence. The language that these authors employed was so clearly different from the Old High German used in earlier centuries that German language historians have considered it appropriate to speak of a new stage of language development, Middle High German, beginning ca. 1050 and lasting until, very roughly, 1350.[7]

Like Old High German, Middle High German was not a single codified super-regional standard language throughout German-speaking domains. The extremely large corpus of Middle High German texts (in comparison to the small number of surviving texts in Old High German) shows a high degree of dialectal variation. Phonologically Middle High German reflects the reduction of unstressed full vowels in Old High German (as with the word "praised": OHG *lobôta* → MHG *lobete*) and also orthographically marks the fronting of all back vowels followed by original *i* or *j*, which is called "Secondary Umlaut" (a case of which is the word for "would be able to": OHG *mochti* → MHG *möchte*). Consonants were affected by a word-final devoicing of OHG *b*, *d*, and *g* to *p*, *t*, and *k* (OHG: *tag* — *taga* → MHG *tac* — *tage*). With the reduction of unstressed suffixes, the umlauted root vowel became more important as a marker of morphological categories (such as singular and plural), and the general reduction of unstressed syllables in OHG resulted in a weakening of OHG inflectional markings, the function of which was taken over in MHG by the increasing use of articles to mark case and gender. The overall result was a considerably more supple and expressive language than Old High German had been.

Already in the early Middle High German period leading up to the literature covered by the chapters in this volume, one can observe not only a lively literary activity among both religious and lay-noble populations, but also some early signs of some of the problems and concerns that became central during the *Blütezeit*. Particularly the approximation of religious and worldly concerns, the endeavor to mediate between the value placed on a life of action in this world and that placed on a life of prayer, contemplation, and preparation for the afterlife, was a concern that is visible already in the early MHG period. This is the case in the corpus of early MHG religious literature consisting of about ninety works that was produced from ca. 1060 to ca. 1180, which consisted of biblical epics, moral allegorical tracts, commentaries on the Song of Songs, sermons, zoological treatises, minstrel epics, commentaries on the Mass, litanies, laments for sin, and historical literature.[8] This literature includes four works about Christ's act of Redemption by the first woman poet in the German language who is known by name, Frau Ava (d. 1127), who probably came from a noble family and retired to a hermit's cell at the monastery at Melk. Ava's poetry has been regarded as "a natural outcome of her beliefs,"[9] evincing an immediacy of individual spirituality and religious fervor outside of the formal rhetorical trappings of monastic and cathedral schools. This literature also included the *Melker Marienlied*, in which we find many of the epithets that will become traditional in Marian poetry. As the most human of the divine personages,[10] Mary was adored and venerated with an emotional intensity that anticipated and prepared the way for the adoration of beloved ladies in the courtly love lyrics.

Around the middle of the twelfth century, a massive chronicle called the *Kaiserchronik* (Emperors' Chronicle), composed by an anonymous cleric in Regensburg, claimed to relate the history of all the Roman emperors from the foundation of Rome to the present, though it is in fact more concerned with the saints who lived and died under the respective emperors. This text, full of real and imagined episodes, was ultimately designed to present pagan and Christian rulers of the past as examples for those of the poet's own time, and it served as one of the great models for the later vernacular chronicles (such as Rudolf von Ems's *Weltchronik*). This draws attention to one of the important functions of this corpus of early MHG religious literature. Following the Investiture Conflict (which officially ended with the Concordat of Worms in 1122)[11] and coinciding with its ongoing and increasingly insistent claim to temporal power, the Church was interested in influencing the noble laity and in setting down for the laity the proper way to live one's life in this world.

Another corpus of texts that preceded the courtly period covered in this volume, and that shared certain aspects with heroic epics, saints' lives, and romances, without belonging to any one of these genres, was the so-called *Spielmannsepen*, or minstrel epics (*König Rother* [King Rother], *Herzog Ernst* [Duke Ernst], the *Münchener Oswald* [Munich Oswald], *Salman und Morolf*, and *Orendel*), all of which were probably first written down sometime in the second half of the twelfth century. The minstrel epics, though they lack the concern with chivalric adventure and love (*âventiure* and *minne*) that would be central features in much of the later court poetry, were intensely interested in life in this temporal world and in control over it.[12] Almost all of these epics (with the exception of *Herzog Ernst*) are based on a bridal quest, in which the king/hero undertakes to win a wife in a foreign realm. The winning of the bride invariably involved the hero in conflicts with pagan adversaries, and these conflicts, in which the hero's efforts ultimately extend and consolidate the empire politically, also would have carried a religious significance for audiences during the time of the crusades. King Rother fights against heathens and retires to a monastery at the end of his life. Oswald and Orendel become saints. These and other examples from the *Spielmannsepen* show us that these epics, despite their emphasis on worldly action, are frequently not distant from the religious concerns of the saints' lives. In their own way, the minstrel epics show the approximation of religious and worldly concerns, and the presentation of ideal ruler-types, that were also characteristics of early Middle High German religious literature, and thus form part of the fecund literary terrain in which German literature blossomed beginning in the second half of the twelfth century.

Earlier literature in the German vernacular had been, on the whole, a tentative extension of Christian Latin culture. By contrast, the vernacular literary culture of the *Blütezeit*, though it was still heavily indebted to Christian Latinity, was an integral part of broader cultural developments in which traditional and authoritative antique/Christian cultural and literary models were transformed in novel ways. In the vernacular literary culture of the twelfth and thirteenth centuries, we begin to witness new ways of thinking, feeling, and imagining. These new developments do not occur in the manner of a revolution or declaration of independence on the part of a secularized courtly culture, even if some of the manifestations are quite striking. In the prologue of Gottfried von Strassburg's *Tristan*, the story of the adulterous lovers is given added importance by likening it to the bread of the Holy Eucharist.[13] Here Christian imagery is put to a startling new use that lends a religious aura and spiritual depth to a very worldly love. By and large, this is the manner in which innovations occurred in the period under discussion. Traditional religious images and rhetorical devices are neither forgotten nor rejected, but rather endowed with new functions in the framework of narrative and lyric poetry that is intensely interested in this world, as well as in the afterlife.[14]

One of the predominant and recurring ambitions in the German court literature of the High Middle Ages is to be pleasing both to God and to one's fellow man. This ambition involved establishing a difficult balance of values and priorities. Giving too much of oneself to the world brought with it the risk of eternal damnation. In the prologue of his *Gregorius*, the author Hartmann von Aue laments his earlier attachment to worldly honor and warns his audience against the sinfulness of worldly ties and the youthful temptation to believe there will be time enough for penance later on:

> swer durch des helleschergen rât
> den trôst ze sîner jugent hât
> daz er dar ûf sündet [. . .]
> der gedenket anders danne er sol. (7–16)[15]

[Whoever in his youth trusts the scheming of hell's jailer, and, trusting in his youth, sins . . . such a person thinks other than he should.][16]

In a didactic song laden with a clearly religious import, Walther von der Vogelweide addresses the same danger of perdition from the perspective of a wise old man, who informs the world that his debt is paid and that he is leaving her service for good:

> Frô Welt, ir sult dem wirte sagen
> daz ich im gar vergolten habe.
> mîn grôziu gülte ist abe geslagen,
> daz er mich von dem brieve schabe. (100, 24–27)[17]

[Lady World, you must tell the host [= Satan] I am square with him. My great debt is paid off, so he needs to remove me from his list of debtors.][18]

While the religiously inspired thought that all worldly delights have to be categorically rejected was never very far from mind (however formulaic its specific manner of articulation), the courtly authors were simultaneously and intensely invested in worldly life. *Minne* and *âventiure* (love, adventure), the principal worldly themes of the poetry of the medieval *Blütezeit*, show an involvement in and fascination with the sundry challenges of the military life, and with new and gentler forms of social interaction between the genders that may have been taking hold at larger courts.[19] Although borrowing from older literary genres (saints' lives, epic poetry), the new poetry of love and adventure was dynamic and indeterminate to an unprecedented degree, and no doubt owed much of its allure to its open-endedness. It was in the nature of an adventure — perhaps derived from the Latin *advenire* (to come to) — to be unpredictable. An adventure can involve an encounter with nearly anything, from a formidable knight, to a monstrous giant, to a fire-breathing dragon, the only constant being that it requires great courage, strength, and force of will on the part of the knight facing it. Love — in some of its most striking instances adulterous love[20] — is dynamic and unpredictable in a different way, as a feeling one begins to have for another (which is inspired by the other's beauty and often beyond the individual's control) and that one hopes is mutual. However, affection on the part of one's beloved can only be fervently hoped for, never forced. Love involves individual risk. Courtly poetry is full of examples demonstrating that happy, mutual love is fleeting, depends on a confluence of individual characteristics and fortuitous circumstances, and that any endeavor to force one's beloved to return the feeling is foolhardy and misguided at best. Love and adventure as literary manifestations suggest an investment in the world and other people — an investment that incorporates a fascination with the unknown and a tolerance for the unpredictable that was unknown or unacceptable in earlier literary genres and traditions.

If there was a single overriding concern of the courtly poetry of this period, it was establishing a balance between the worldly concerns of love and adventure (and the more dynamic, open-ended relationship to the world and others they involved) and the religious concerns alluded to above (which frequently involved a more fixed and preemptively condemnatory posture towards all things worldly). Authors envisioned such a balance in their poetry very directly. In another of his didactic poems, Walther von der Vogelweide anxiously considers how one should live properly in the world:

> deheinen rât kond ich gegeben,
> wie man driu dinc erwurbe,
> der keines niht verdurbe.
> diu zwei sint êre und varnde guot,
> daz dicke ein ander schaden tuot.
> daz dritte ist gottes hulde,
> der zweier übergulde. (8, 8–14)[21]

[I couldn't give any council, about how one could acquire three things, of which none would be ruined. They are worldly honor and possessions, which often do harm to each other; the third is God's favor, more valuable than the other two.]

Another of the finest and most memorable poetic expressions of this balance is achieved at the end of Wolfram von Eschenbach's *Parzival*, when the significance of this singular romance is boiled down to a simple moral:

> swes leben sich sô verendet,
> daz got niht wirt gephendet
> der sêle durch slîbes schulde
> und der doch der werlde hulde
> behalden kan mit werdekeit,
> daz ist ein nütziu arbeit. (827, 19–24)[22]

[When a man's life ends in such a way that God is not robbed of his soul because of the body's sinning and who nevertheless succeeds in keeping his fellow's good will and respect, this is a useful toil.][23]

This reconciliation of religious and worldly interests, along with other less weighty social and individual ambitions, was pursued with an expressive literary language, as supple as it was forceful, that allowed for a wide array of poetic positions and stylistic approaches. One of the important features of this language was the evident endeavor on the part of many authors to aim for a trans-regional literary language that was largely, though never entirely free of the peculiarities of the regional German dialects. The great variety of individual stylistic variations in this trans-regional poetic idiom can be seen in terms of degrees of adherence to, or divergence from, a compositional standard grounded in the medieval art of rhetoric that involved the elegant correspondence of content and form, subject matter and its poetic expression. The range of stylistic approaches is already visible in the works of the great poets of the *Blütezeit:* Hartmann von Aue represents an exemplary standard, according to the later poet Gottfried von Strassburg, who writes in his *Tristan*:

> wie er mit rede figieret
> der âventiure meine!
> wie lûter und wie reine
> sîniu cristallînen wortelîn
> beidiu sint und iemer müezen sîn. (4621–30)[24]

[How eloquently he establishes his story's meaning! How clear and transparent his crystal words both are and ever must remain!][25]

Gottfried's own ornate style, visible in these verses, is not coincidentally indebted to the same rhetorical standard of compositional clarity and formal elegance that is praised in Hartmann's writing, and it is no coincidence that Gottfried, as Hartmann before him, clearly prided himself on his education in the liberal arts and placed this education on display in his poetry. For poets such as Hartmann and Gottfried and the majority of their literary successors in the thirteenth century, poetry was a learned craft involving the expert adornment and exegesis of the subject matter (that is, the tale, or *âventiure*, as it existed in the sources available to these authors). Gottfried's poetic style, though similar in its clarity and elegance to that of Hartmann, tends to rhetorical flourish and poetic showmanship, somewhat independent of the subject matter proper. This tendency would be further developed by later poets such as Konrad von Würzburg, who would bring the purely formal aspect of poetry as close to *l'art pour l'art* as one finds in the Middle Ages. On the other end of the stylistic spectrum is Wolfram von Eschenbach, who pointedly denies being educated (though his works betray an abundance of knowledge that demonstrate he somehow achieved a high level of learning), and whose literary style often seems like a transcription of living speech — rambling, spontaneous, and sometimes obscure. The power of Wolfram's poetry consists precisely in its independence from the clerical ideal of poetry as rhetorical craft, which enables the poet to convey his material to audiences with an unmatched intensity and immediacy. Rather than from rhetorical learning, Wolfram claims to have the structuring principle for his poetry from a quite different source:

> swaz an den buochen stêt geschriben,
> des bin ich künstelôs beliben:
> nicht anders ich gelêret bin,
> wan hân ich kunst, diu gît mir sin. (2, 19–22)[26]

[I have remained ignorant of what is written in books and am tutored in this way alone: if I have any skill, it comes from my mind.][27]

The period covered by the chapters in this volume begins with the production of the first significant narrative poems by Heinrich von Veldeke and Hartmann von Aue, the first songs by the earliest minnesingers, and the first preserved heroic epics. The beginnings of German court literature thus coincide with the highpoint of the rule of Emperor Friedrich I of the Hohenstaufen dynasty (known by the nickname "Barbarossa"; ruled 1152–90) who, in unstable political times plagued by private wars and feuds, succeeded to some degree in restoring order and stability to the Holy Roman Empire. Basing his reforms on Roman and feudal law, Friedrich succeeded in expanding imperial power in both Germany and Italy.[28] It is tempting to draw parallels between the Whitsun festival in Mainz in 1184, at which Barbarossa's sons Friedrich and Heinrich were knighted, and the courtly festivals of King Arthur as depicted in literature.[29] Political reality and literature here seem to enter an alliance that enabled Barbarossa to bask in the glow of the chivalric authority and security depicted in the literature. Just as in the fictional world of Arthur, political and social stability remained tenuous, because the centralized authority of the emperor could be maintained only against the particular, centrifugal designs and ambitions of the powerful German princes (many of whom themselves were also patrons of literature), among whom the emperor was, in the best of times, closer to a *primus inter pares* than to the absolute monarchs of later centuries. Political and social turbulence, and the violence that went along with it, were never far removed and remained a major concern in literature.

Barbarossa's son Heinrich VI, also a patron of literature and possibly even the composer of some preserved love songs,[30] consolidated and extended the imperial power his father left him, but when he died

Kaiser Heinrich. A miniature from the Codex Manesse (364r).

unexpectedly in 1197 upon his departure on the Fourth Crusade, his son and designated heir Friedrich was only three years old. Old rivalries among the German princes resurged. Philip von Schwaben (Heinrich's brother), originally designated to serve as regent until young Friedrich reached maturity, and his rival Otto von Braunschweig (son of Barbarossa's great nemesis Heinrich der Löwe) were both crowned German king in 1198 (also coincidentally the year in which thirty-seven-year-old Innocent III was elected pope). Struggles between the partisans of Philip and Otto continued during the first decade of the thirteenth century, in which Innocent asserted himself as a powerbroker in German politics by recognizing Otto and excommunicating Philip and his followers in 1201. In the years after 1202, the military and political tide nevertheless turned in Philip's favor. The political schism between the Hohenstaufen party of Philip and the Welf party of Otto remained in place until the murder of Philip by the Bavarian count Otto von Wittelsbach in a private feud in 1208. Otto, now recognized even by Philip's former supporters, was again crowned king in 1208, and in the following year he was crowned emperor Otto IV by Innocent III in Rome. In subsequent years Otto set about to chase his only remaining rival, Friedrich, son of Heinrich VI and grandson of Barbarossa, out of Sicily. The new political contest now was between Otto and young Friedrich, whose supporters elected him emperor in 1211. This contest was not concluded until 1214, when Otto (along with his ally, the English King John) was decisively defeated at Bouvines by Friedrich's ally, the French King Philippe Augustus. In 1215, Friedrich II was crowned German king in Aachen, and in 1220, he was crowned emperor in Rome by Honorius III (1216–27). By many accounts Friedrich II, who was shaped by the "multi-cultural" milieu of his native Sicily (and particularly by the rational-empirical scientific approach fostered in Islamic learning that had taken hold in Sicily), was the first modern political leader. Friedrich spent most of his reign in Sicily, returning only once to Germany in 1235 to put down a rebellion staged by his son Heinrich.

The ostensibly supreme worldly power of the emperors had to maintain itself not only against the ambitions of princes, but also against a papacy that reached the height of its political ambitions under Innocent III (ca. 1160–1216, pope 1198–1216). As early as the time of the so-called Investiture Conflict (1075–1122), emperors and popes had contended over the right to elect and install bishops and abbots, and popes continued in the twelfth and thirteenth centuries to claim ascendancy even in worldly affairs based on the primacy of religious concerns over material ones.[31] The Roman Catholic Church at the beginning of the thirteenth century was an opulent worldly institution that was bent on obtaining and holding worldly power and authority. Medieval lay people who were in a position to do so — which in most cases means the lay nobility — responded to the worldliness of the church in different ways. Some became eremites, others swelled the numbers of the new mendicant orders, the Franciscans and Dominicans, and still others brought their dissatisfaction with ecclesiastical institutions to literary expression. One of the principal functions of the court literature produced in Germany around 1200 was to strike a morally and spiritually fulfilling balance between worldly and religious concerns. The attempt to achieve this balance frequently involved a lay religiosity that was at least as pious and devout as orthodox forms of literary expression.

The events outlined in the above paragraphs, some of which find explicit mention in court poetry (especially in the political poetry of Walther von der Vogelweide), show not only the occasional political instability of this period, but also the importance of strong individual personalities and their continued rule for lasting political stability. Given that a modicum of political stability is a prerequisite for blossoming cultural activity, it seems appropriate to view the Hohenstaufen dynasty as the political foundation of the literary *Blütezeit* explored in this volume. Many of the literary developments that first flourished around 1200 and were continued in the thirteenth century did, of course, not cease with the demise of the Hohenstaufen dynasty and the ensuing period of political and social chaos called the Great Interregnum (1256–73). Despite the continuing cultivation of court literature following models established during the first flourishing, a new chapter of political, cultural, and literary history arguably begins with the coronation of Rudolf I, the first of the Habsburg emperors. The Hohenstaufen dynasty was, in the end, a glorious, tumultuous, and relatively brief chapter in the history of the Holy Roman Empire. Its fame in posterity is probably more literary than political, as its rulers succeeded for a short period in stemming the centrifugal designs of the powerful territorial princes and in creating a courtly-chivalric literary culture based mainly at the larger courts in Germany. The circumstances of the production of the Codex Manesse (also known as the *Große Heidelberger Liederhandschrift*), produced in the first quarter of the fourteenth century by lay and ecclesiastic nobles near Zurich, suggests the direction of developments in the thirteenth and fourteenth centuries, when the cities became increasingly important and began to rival the cultural importance of courts. (The Codex Manesse includes more than a hundred small paintings, or miniatures, of medieval poets, ten reproductions of which can be found on the pages of this volume.)

The organization of this volume endeavors to do justice to a complex literary and cultural period in which we see both the emergence of significant individual authors such as Wolfram, and the cultivation of literary traditions in which the creativity of individual authors is still bound to a great degree to generic and communal considerations of different kinds. Authors provide the starting point of discussion in the first and third sections of this volume. Writers of Christian-Latin literature tended to remain anonymous, consistent with the subordination of the individual to generic and communal traditions that is characteristic of monastic and clerical cultures. With the beginnings of the vernacular poetry of the High Middle Ages, we witness the emergence of the author as a "known quantity" in many of the vernacular genres, though caveats are necessary. In contrast to the situation of modern authors, there is virtually no historical information about the lives of courtly authors such as Heinrich von Veldeke, Hartmann von Aue, Wolfram von Eschenbach, and Walther von der Vogelweide. The modicum of knowledge we have about the authors as individuals and their life circumstances is based on what they say about themselves and each other in their literary works. In some cases, it is difficult to know if we really get to know the authors at all, rather than the different roles they play in their narratives. Despite these caveats, it nevertheless seems appropriate to say that in the court poetry of the *Blütezeit*, the authors themselves emerge for the first time, on a broad scale, as a visible, active, and creative force. In recent years there has been an ever increasing appreciation of the degree to which the vernacular authors of the twelfth and thirteenth centuries did not merely copy, disseminate, and compile already existing authoritative texts (which may have been more characteristic of earlier times), but rather transformed existing narratives in frequently striking ways, by virtue of their own imaginative and expressive capabilities.[32]

The treated authors have been divided into two groups in order to suggest two different stages of literary development during the time covered by this volume. The first section, titled "The First Flourishing of German Literature," includes the significant authors working from ca. 1180 to ca. 1220, whose works could be considered pioneering and continued to be viewed with awe and reverence and to serve as models through the thirteenth century. In the first section, poets and a period of literary and cultural history are examined. Albrecht Classen's chapter on Heinrich von Veldeke and Rodney Fisher's chapter on Hartmann von Aue show how these two pioneering poets established a poetic foundation upon which later generations of poets could build, especially by means of their introduction of the themes of love and adventure to German audiences. Rüdiger Krohn's analysis of the German Tristan-narratives finds in the subject matter of the story itself something quite new for the Middle Ages: a radical conflict between social norms and individual drives that no poet takes farther than these narratives' principal representative in Germany: Gottfried von Strassburg. In their chapter on Wolfram von Eschenbach, Marion E. Gibbs and Sidney Johnson underscore the individual, forceful, idiosyncratic style of this poet's literary idiom, which has been discussed above: the myriad differences that separate his *Parzival*, for example, from its Old French source. Nicola McLelland's chapter on Ulrich von Zatzikhoven's singular Lancelot narrative, which, though probably composed around the first decade of the thirteenth century, evinces characteristics of the so-called "post-classical" romances, shows this work to be quite exceptional in its own way, as an innovative combination of narrative styles and voices. Finally, Will Hasty's chapter on Walther von der Vogelweide explores the innovations this most famous of the medieval German poets brought to didactic poetry and the love lyrics.

Despite the new importance of the author as a creative force in the production of vernacular poetry, authors continued to work in a cultural setting and social milieu in which literary conventions and the demands and expectations of powerful patrons and audiences had an immediate impact on the production of vernacular literature. Some literary traditions, such as the relatively "new" Arthurian romances, lent themselves to a relatively higher degree of creative adaptation and transformation by individual authors, and allowed these authors to achieve a higher degree of visibility (at least via their narrative personae). In other kinds of vernacular literature, traditions, conventions, and communal considerations played a much more important role, and the position of the author, while still important (often in terms of coming up with creative variations on certain set themes), is not as immediately visible as in the romances and much of the narrative poetry.

The second section of this volume, titled "Lyric and Narrative Traditions," focuses on four such literary traditions that shaped German literary history from 1170 to 1270: political and didactic poetry (the *Sangsprüche*), the love songs of the minnesingers (*Minnesang*), heroic narratives, and early mystical writing. In the respective chapters on these corpora of literature, generic and communal considerations form the primary points of departure for discussion.

The tradition of didactic and political poetry, or *Sangsprüche*, the topic of Nigel Harris's chapter, was in the beginning associated with wandering, non-noble bards, who were hired for short-term engagements to present their moral-didactic stanzas. It was left to Walther von der Vogelweide to expand and transform this genre into a courtly art, but it never succeeded in becoming a courtly art of nobility in the same way as the love lyrics (*Minnesang*). In the political and didactic poetry, the space for authorial creativity and innovation seems largely determined by the moral-didactic concerns the poetry brings to expression, and by the interests and demands of powerful patrons. Even Walther, who greatly expanded the range of expressive possibilities of this poetry, had to adapt the content of his *Sangsprüche* to the tastes and whims of his patrons, and could indulge in criticisms of former patrons only when he was safely in the orbit of another. The love lyrics of *Minnesang* were, by contrast, exclusively an art form of nobility. Will Hasty's chapter on the lyrics shows that they adhered closely to set conventions regarding content and form, though there are ample demonstrations of the singer's own individual artistic proclivities within the constraints posed by these conventions. We know the minnesingers by name because they are mentioned by poets in other genres (in his *Tristan*,

Gottfried von Strassburg mentions the minnesingers collectively, before discussing some of their most famous representatives individually),[33] and because they are named in the illuminated manuscripts in which their songs are transmitted, but not because they name themselves in their lyrics, which very rarely occurs.[34] Given the importance of literary conventions and communal considerations in the political and didactic lyrics and in the love songs, and the great number of individual singers (an individual treatment of which would be impossible in a single volume), the chapters on these corpuses of lyrics focus primarily on the most significant generic and communal aspects of these types of literature, and discuss a few representative individual cases in view of these general aspects. It is fitting to discuss the love lyrics of poets such as Heinrich von Veldeke, Hartmann von Aue, and Wolfram von Eschenbach in the chapters dealing with these authors, because their involvement in *Minnesang*, alongside their production of longer epic narratives, provides us with a more complete picture of the versatility and creative talent of these individual poets.

The points of departure for the discussion of the heroic narratives and early mystical literature are also primarily generic and communal. Heroic literature, surveyed in the chapter of Susann Samples, was from its earliest origins a communal art form, and the anonymity of the author was always a set part of the evolving tradition of heroic tales and narratives, even when they began to be fashioned into longer epic works in the course of the twelfth century. The heroic poetry revolves around the great deeds of historical and legendary leaders of peoples ranging from Alexander the Great to Charlemagne. Although by the High Middle Ages all the heroic narratives incorporated at least some Christian elements, the majority of heroic narrative traditions were originally pre-Christian, with their roots in Greco-Roman antiquity (in the case of the Alexander epics) or in ancient Germanic societies in which, as the Roman historian Tacitus tells us, warriors sang songs of their heroes to rouse their spirit when going into battle. The Chansons de Geste maintain the heroic ethos of the pre-Christian epics, but have a religious significance by virtue of their rendering of struggles between Christians and Muslims that occurred in the eighth and ninth centuries. The chapter on the early mystical literature by Sara Poor focuses on some of the overriding common characteristics of this literature — the importance of Bernhard of Clairvaux's commentaries on the Song of Songs, the low German and Dutch urban contexts in which this literature was produced, and, perhaps most important, the fact that the early vernacular mystical writers were women who had to develop their own strategies regarding authorship/authority in a time in which (as today, despite the greater range of possibilities), authorship and authority tend to be male-gendered. This chapter is somewhat exceptional in that, in order to present a complete picture of early mystical writing, it considers texts in Latin, German, and Dutch, some of which combine prose and poetry.

The third section, "Continuity, Transformation, and Innovation in the Thirteenth Century," includes a representative group of significant thirteenth-century authors from ca. 1220 onward, who responded in different ways to the literature of their hallowed predecessors (as which the earlier authors were generally seen, even when the later authors diverged from their predecessors' literary conceptions quite intentionally and sharply, as they often did). Scholars have traditionally distinguished between the earlier "classical" works (those of Hartmann von Aue, Wolfram von Eschenbach, and Gottfried von Strassburg) and later "post-classical" works, and seen the latter as artistically inferior to the former. The distinction between "classical" and "post-classical" has been used by scholars to stress the presence of certain characteristics (such as the bipartite quest of the hero in the Arthurian romances) and their absence in the later "post-classical" works. Recently, scholars have argued that the "post-classical" works quite consciously employ different structural models and literary styles, and that their divergence from the "classical" bipartite model cannot and should not necessarily be seen as aesthetically deficient.[35] While the terms "classical" and "post-classical" continue to turn up in the critical literature and also appear on the pages in this volume, it has become increasingly difficult to use these terms as an aesthetic judgment of superiority or inferiority.

The chapters in this section demonstrate that the later authors, even if their gaze was directed back towards the "first flourishing," often operated quite independently and creatively with the models handed down to them by their revered predecessors. Neil Thomas's examination of Wirnt von Gravenberg's *Wigalois* and Heinrich von dem Türlin's *Diu Crône* focuses on these narratives as critical responses to Wolfram's version of the Grail story. Michael Resler's chapter on Der Stricker, who is somewhat exceptional in that he does not seem to have been a knight, looks at this poet's less elegant, yet nevertheless very spirited and witty narrative style. Elizabeth Andersen's chapter on Rudolf von Ems continues a trend visible in many of the chapters in this section by focusing on the greater scope and diversity of this poet's subject matter, due in large part to his adaptation of Latin literary traditions. An especially striking case among the later poets is Ulrich von Liechtenstein, treated in the chapter by Ulrich Müller and Franz Viktor Spechtler, who with his *Frauendienst* authored what these two scholars regard as the first autobiographical romance in the German vernacular. Much like Der Stricker with respect to the breadth and variety of his literary oeuvre, but much more a stylistic virtuoso, Konrad von Würzburg, as examined in the chapter of Rüdiger Brandt, develops a poetic style that comes close to a modern *l'art pour l'art* position. Finally, Ruth Weichselbaumer's chapter examines the transposition of the courtly chivalric plot structure to the peasant milieu, and the interesting consequences of this poetic experiment, in her chapter on *Helmbrecht*.

The final section includes two chapters that provide different perspectives of the historical situation in which the literature of the *Blütezeit* was produced. William H. Jackson's chapter on violence and constraints on violence not only provides important perspectives for our understanding of many of the narrative works discussed in the other chapters, in which force and its legitimate uses seems often to be a central concern, but it also helps link this literary history to a lively scholarly discussion about chivalry and violence that is currently taking place among historians and literary scholars.[36] The final chapter on medieval mobility by Charles Bowlus paints a picture of political culture in the High Middle Ages that is consistent with the literary and cultural situation described in this introduction. In the High Middle Ages, the world was in motion, both intellectually and spatially.

The poetry covered in the volume is, almost without exception, a poetry of nobility, composed with a view to its "live" performance before audiences at the larger courts of emperors, princes, and bishops, those with the political contacts to acquire source manuscripts and the financial wherewithal to maintain poets and support their craft. Despite critical intentions of various kinds on the part of individual authors and the ongoing importance of conveying some kind of moral if not religious significance, this poetry was largely dedicated to entertainment and tends to depict a world in which noble magnates and their retinues see an ideal image of themselves. The retinues were to a large degree made up of *ministeriales*, legally unfree knights who performed a variety of military and administrative services for their lords.[37] Peasants, who make up the vast majority of the population, rarely appear in this poetry, and when they do, as in the love poetry of Neidhart (in the form of the *gebúren* depicted in his lyrics) or in the *Helmbrecht* of Wernher der Gärtner, it is seldom in a very flattering light. Burghers fare somewhat better: Gottfried's Tristan masquerades in Ireland as the son of a merchant without any very negative aspersions being made about his station, and in Wolfram's *Willehalm*, the burgher Wimar is the only person in Laon who is willing to provide the weary Willehalm with lodging and food. Despite the relatively narrow social milieu in which this poetry was cultivated — when seen in comparison to the entire social range of the medieval world from the highest nobles to the lowest laborers — the secular literary culture that this poetry involved might be regarded as a first, necessary step in the direction of a world and a time in which "culture" will no longer be the possession or prerogative of a single privileged social group (as it had been of monks and clerics in the early Middle Ages). In the thirteenth century, not long after literary culture has taken hold at noble courts in Germany, urban elites, especially in southern Germany, Switzerland, and along the Rhine, adopted and transformed this poetry according to its own interests and priorities, thus beginning a trend that shows no signs of abating in our networked world today: the appropriation and assimilation of idealized knights in armor, their deeds, and their loves.

Even as it represents communal values and interests, the court poetry nevertheless opens up a greater range of exemplary models — and therefore possibilities for identification — for individual men and women. Though they doubtless incorporate characteristics of males as represented in saints' lives and heroic epics, men as represented in the court poetry — in the Arthurian romances, for example — are no longer the perfect heroes of the older literary genres, but rather flawed human beings, who do their best, make their way in an unpredictable world in which one's best is often not good enough, and invariably reach some kind of accommodation with their world, though not always a blessed or even happy one. Just as with the literature of later historical periods, the production of poetry during the first *Blütezeit* was largely the preoccupation of men. In Germany there is no female patron of literature with the stature and fame of an Eleanor of Aquitaine, nor do we see a female poet such as Beatriz de Dia. While direct evidence concerning the role of women in the production of court literature in medieval Germany (in contrast to early mystical writing) is scant, the basic concerns of the poetry — the *âventiure* and *minne* discussed above — give great weight to women and the concerns of women, however mediated these may be by male authorial perspectives and the communal values and interest in which these in turn were grounded. With characters such as Hartmann von Aue's Enite and Wolfram von Eschenbach's Herzeloyde, the court poetry articulates many models of womanhood between the extremes of sinful Eve and the blessed Virgin. In the representation of female as in that of male characters, court poetry experiments with individual, sometimes even quite idiosyncratic variations on set models. This greater scope in the representation of individual contours is one of the important ways in which this poetry can be considered to participate in a renaissance — that of the twelfth century — and to anticipate the more famous one that begins less than two centuries later in Italy.

After lying dormant during the age of Enlightenment, the German court poetry of the High Middle Ages began to experience its own "renaissance" in the latter half of the eighteenth century in the same geographic region where many of the most famous medieval poets lived and worked, with the publication in Zurich of the *Sammlung von Minnesingern aus dem schwäbischen Zeitpuncte* (Collection of Minnesingers of the Swabian Period, 1758–59) by Johann Jakob Bodmer and Johann Jakob Breitinger, and of Hartmann von Aue's *Der arme Heinrich* (Poor Heinrich) and *Iwein* by Christoph Heinrich Myller in the first volume of the *Sammlung deutscher Gedichte aus dem 12. 13. und 14. Jahrhundert* (Collection of German Poems from the Twelfth, Thirteenth, and Fourteenth Centuries, 1784). The interest in the Middle Ages and in medieval poetry increased greatly in the first half of the nineteenth century among the poets, philologists, and scholars associated with German Romanticism. Initially the allure of the Middle Ages and medieval poetry was in their perceived divergence from the rationalistic conception of poetry championed most prominently by Johann Christoph Gottsched, according to which poetry had to adhere to the same "laws" that were seen to underlie all of nature. In contrast to such a narrow rationalistic conception of poetry, early Romantic writers such as Novalis stressed the role of fantasy and imagination, unfettered by any kind of rules, and saw in the Middle Ages a wondrous and unitary time in which the world had not yet been "demystified" by Enlightenment, and divided, separated, and classified according rationalistic "laws." From the early nineteenth century onward, the scholarly and artistic reception of medieval German literature (notably Richard Wagner's adaptation of medieval romances and legends in his music dramas) were shaped, and perhaps even to a great degree sustained, by the idea that the medieval poetry articulated aspects of German national character, even the very spirit of the German *Volk*. This nationalistic (mis)understanding of medieval poetry, which remained particularly interested in separating that which was considered to be specifically German from that which was not,[38] continued into the twentieth century and did not end until the cataclysms of the Second World War and the Holocaust.

For the latest chapter of the scholarly and artistic reception of medieval German poetry — from the mid-twentieth century to the present — there is no single organizing idea or principle. Freed to a large degree from its nationalistic moorings, this reception has gone in many different scholarly and artistic directions, far too many to be addressed in this introduction; and the social role of poetry — and not just of medieval poetry — in the networked world of today is certainly no longer as clear as it once was. A starting point for the understanding of the German poetry of the High Middle Ages has been suggested in this introduction and is borne out in different ways by the chapters in this volume: this poetry marks the beginnings of a secularization of literary culture in particular, and of culture in general, among German-speaking peoples. In this poetry, the divine language of God has begun to be a language of medieval men and women, used to represent the spiritual and worldly things dearest to them. In this important respect, the poetry of the High Middle Ages is not merely part of a renaissance: it is modern.

Notes

[1] Charles Homer Haskins, *The Renaissance of the Twelfth Century* (New York: Meridian Books, 1957).

[2] Such as Virgil's *Aeneid*.

[3] By Avicenna (ibn Sina, 980–1037) and Averroes (ibn Rushd, 1126–98); in his *History of the Arab Peoples* (New York: MJF Books, 1991), Albert Hourani stresses the importance of Neo-Platonism in the philosophies of Avicenna and Averroes,

particularly the concept of the created world as emanations of divinity, which the philosophers particularly associated with light imagery (172–75).

[4] Particularly the question of the relationship of philosophy to religion, of reason to faith and revelation, which formed the basis of Scholasticism in the twelfth and thirteenth centuries, and went hand in hand with the foundation of the first European universities: Bologna 1119, Padua 1222, Naples 1224, Oxford 1214, and Cambridge 1229. In Germany, educational institutions associated with the Dominicans functioned practically as universities around 1300; the first German university was founded in Prague in 1348.

[5] See *Literarisches Mäzenatentum: Ausgewählte Forschungen zur Rolle des Gönners und Auftraggebers in der mittelalterlichen Literatur*, ed. Joachim Bumke (Darmstadt: Wissenschaftliche Buchgesellschaft, 1982) and Joachim Bumke, *Mäzene im Mittelalter* (Munich: Beck, 1979).

[6] The second traditional *Blütezeit* being the age of Goethe in the late eighteenth and early nineteenth centuries.

[7] Robert B. Howell, "The Older German Language," in *A Companion to Middle High German Literature to the 14th Century*, ed. Francis G. Gentry (Leiden: Brill, 2002), 27–52; here 40.

[8] Francis G. Gentry, "German Literature to 1160," in *A Companion to Middle High German Literature to the 14th Century*, ed. Gentry, 53–115; here 88.

[9] Gentry, "German Literature to 1160," 112.

[10] Gentry, "German Literature to 1160," 113.

[11] This will be discussed in more detail below.

[12] See Maria Dobozy, "Spielmannsepen," in *German Writers and Works of the Early Middle Ages: 800–1170, Dictionary of Literary Biography*, vol. 148, ed. Will Hasty and James Hardin (Detroit: Gale, 1995), 268–78.

[13] Gottfried von Strassburg, *Tristan*, ed. Friedrich Ranke, rev. ed. & trans. (modern German) Rüdiger Krohn, vol. 1 (Stuttgart: Reclam, 1984), verses 233–44.

[14] See Walter Haug, *Literaturtheorie im deutschen Mittelalter: Von den Anfängen bis zum Ende des 13 Jahrhunderts: Eine Einführung* (Darmstadt: Wissenschaftliche Buchgesellschaft, 1985), especially chapter 1 (7–24).

[15] Hartmann von Aue, *Gregorius*, ed. Hermann Paul, 13th revised edition by Burghart Wachinger (Niemeyer: Tübingen, 1984).

[16] The translation is from *Arthurian Romances, Tales, and Lyric Poetry: The Complete Works of Hartmann von Aue*, trans. Frank Tobin, Kim Vivian, and Richard H. Lawson (University Park, PA: The Pennsylvania State UP, 2001).

[17] *Die Lieder Walthers von der Vogelweide, vol. 1: Die religiösen und politischen Lieder* ed. Friedrich Maurer (Tübingen: Niemeyer, 1974).

[18] Translations of Walther's lyrics are the editor's.

[19] See the chapter "On the Sociogenesis of *Minnesang* and Courtly Forms of Conduct" in Norbert Elias, *The Civilizing Process*, trans. Edmund Jephcott (Oxford: Blackwell, 2000), 236–56.

[20] As in Gottfried von Strassburg's *Tristan.*

[21] Citing the edition of Maurer.

[22] Wolfram von Eschenbach, *Parzival,* ed. Karl Lachmann (Berlin: de Gruyter, 1965).

[23] Citing A. T. Hatto's translation *Wolfram von Eschenbach, Parzival* (Harmondsworth: Penguin, 1980).

[24] Gottfried von Strassburg, *Tristan,* ed. Friedrich Ranke, trans. (modern German) with an afterword by Rüdiger Krohn (Stuttgart: Reclam, 1984).

[25] Citing A. T. Hatto's translation, *Gottfried von Strassburg, Tristan* (Penguin: Harmondsworth, 1960).

[26] *Wolfram von Eschenbach, Willehalm Buch I bis V,* ed. Albert Leitzmann (Tübingen: Niemeyer, 1963); whatever the ultimate sources of Wolfram's artistry may have been, it is important to realize that his seemingly rougher and more spontaneous poetic language is a conscious stylistic choice, rather than a sign of rhetorical or poetic deficiency.

[27] Citing the translation of Marion E. Gibbs and Sidney Johnson, *Wolfram von Eschenbach, Willehalm* (Penguin: Harmondsworth, 1984).

[28] Michael Frasetto, "Medieval Germany: History of Emperors and Empire, c. 750–c. 1350," in *A Companion to Middle High German Literature to the 14th Century,* ed. Gentry, 1–25; here 18.

[29] Josef Fleckenstein, "Friedrich Barbarossa und das Rittertum: Zur Bedeutung der großen Mainzer Hoftage von 1184 und 1188," in *Festschrift für Hermann Heimpel,* vol. 2 (Göttingen: Vandenhoeck & Ruprecht, 1972).

[30] See the songs attributed to Emperor Heinrich VI in *Des Minnesangs Frühling,* ed. Karl Lachmann, Moriz Haupt, Friedrich Vogt, and Carl von Kraus, 37th rev. ed. Hugo Moser and Helmut Tervooren (Stuttgart: S. Hirzl, 1982).

[31] Maurice Keen, *The Penguin History of Medieval Literature* (Harmondsworth: Penguin, 1991), 135–45.

[32] See, for example, D. H. Green, *The Beginnings of Medieval Romance: Fact and Fiction* (Cambridge: Cambridge UP, 2002).

[33] See Gottfried's *Tristan,* 4751–4820.

[34] Among the principal poets of the *Blütezeit,* Hartmann von Aue is the only one to name himself in the love lyrics.

[35] See, for example, Monika Schausten, *Erzählwelten der Tristangeschichte im hohen Mittelalter: Untersuchungen zu den deutschsprachigen Tristanfassungen des 12. & 13. Jahrhunderts* (Munich: Fink, 1999) and Neil Thomas, *Diu Crône and the Medieval Arthurian Cycle* (Cambridge: D. S. Brewer, 2002).

[36] See, for example, Richard W. Kaeuper, *Chivalry and Violence in Medieval Europe* (Oxford: Oxford UP, 1999).

[37] For a detailed treatment of *ministeriales* as a specifically German social and political phenomenon, see Benjamin Arnold, *German Knighthood 1050–1300* (Oxford: Clarendon Press, 1985).

[38] The "other" was typically defined as French.

Part I

The First Flourishing of German Literature

Heinrich von Veldeke. A miniature from the Codex Manesse (30r).

Heinrich von Veldeke

Albrecht Classen

TWO CLOSELY CONNECTED MYTHS deeply influenced medieval concepts about the origins of the medieval world and its cultural identity. The first myth dealt with the history of ancient Troy and its defeat at the hands of the Greeks, originally described in Homer's *Iliad*, parts of which were later handed down in the sixth century *Historia de excidio Trojae* attributed to the Latin author Dares Phrygius and in the fifth century *Ephemeris belli Trojani* attributed to Dictys Cretensis, which in turn goes back to a Greek source from the first century.[1] The second myth concerned Aeneas and his successful escape from the defeated city. After landing on numerous European shores, according to ancient tradition, Aeneas eventually became the founder of Rome, as Virgil (70–19 B.C.) reported in his *Aeneid* (29–19 B.C.). Aeneas was thus an integral part of the medieval conception of the transferal of imperial authority and glory from the eastern Mediterranean to Western Europe (the *translatio imperii*). The story of Aeneas was reiterated, for instance, in the eleventh-century Middle High German *Annolied* and in the fourteenth-century Middle English *Sir Gawain and the Green Knight*, but many other poets and chroniclers also dealt with this fascinating figure from classical antiquity. One of the most extensive accounts was the Old French *Roman d'Eneas* (more than 10,000 verses), written before 1160, which in turn became the source for the Middle High German *Eneit* by Heinrich von Veldeke.[2]

In his famous *Tristan* romance (ca. 1210), Gottfried von Strassburg praises his predecessor Heinrich von Veldeke as the founder of German courtly literature:

> wie wol sang er von minnen!
> wie schône er sînen sin besneit!
> ich waene, er sîne wîsheit
> ûz Pegases urspringe nam,
> von dem diu wîsheit elliu kam.
> [. . .]
> er inpfete daz erste rîs
> in tiutischer zungen. (4728–39)[3]

[How well he sang of love! How finely he trimmed his invention! I imagine he had his insight from Pegasus's spring, from which all wisdom
comes. . . . [he] grafted the first slip on the tree of German poetry.][4]

Heinrich was one of the first major Middle High German poets to introduce the ideas of courtly love and chivalry into the world of the medieval
German courts. He established the foundation on which a whole generation of new writers built. He obviously had a good command of Latin and
French, though he was a knightly lay person and not a member of the
learned clergy. He was a native of the area around Maastrich/Limbourg
near Hasselt (today in Belgium), and in the 1170s he was in the service of
the counts of Loon, later of a Countess of Cleve, and in the 1180s in the
service of the landgraves of Thuringia. Due to his origin he spoke a form
of a Limbourg dialect, but all his works have come down to us only in the
courtly standard Middle High German, with the exception of several hundred verses in his religious tale of the life and miracles reportedly attributed
to the fourth-century bishop Servatius of Tongeren.[5] This legendary
account (*Servatius*, originally inspired by the sacristan Hessel of the
Maastrich church S. Servaaskerk or St. Servatius) seems to have been his
earliest literary work, dedicated to the Countess Agnes of Loon. Heinrich's
hagiographical narrative comprises 6226 verses and is one of the longest
religious poems in Low German.[6]

Love Lyrics

Heinrich also composed at least forty love songs. In the formal structure
of his songs Heinrich followed the early minnesingers such as Der
Kürenberger and Dietmar von Aist, but thematically he anticipated the
more sophisticated courtly love poetry composed by Heinrich von
Morungen, Friedrich von Hausen, and Reinmar.[7] Heinrich von Veldeke's
lyric poetry cannot be dated precisely, but he seems to have written his
poems throughout his adult life between 1170 and 1190.[8] Recent research
has shown that the difference between a traditional courtly love song and
didactic poetry (*Sangspruch*) is not yet fully developed in Veldeke's lyrics.
Ludger Lieb has demonstrated that Veldeke tends to transform a general
statement about court society into an observation about the nature of
courtly love, and vice versa.[9] Influences by French troubadour and
Provencal trouvère poets on specific songs by Veldeke are difficult to establish and have been posited only in a few cases. Olive Sayce states that he
"clearly had such a wide knowledge of the content and form of Romance
poetry that the imitation of specific poems was superfluous."[10]

Overall, Veldeke developed a highly esoteric concept of courtly love
and avoided any allusion to the physical fulfillment of love. The knight in
his poems is allowed to serve his lady as her wooer and protector, but he

never reveals her name to his audience. This service for unrequited love proves to be the highest ideal for Veldeke, as he does not even expect any concrete reward for his *minne*: "Ich minne die schoenen sunder danc" (I love the beautiful lady without her gratitude; XII; 62,4). In his view, the art of courtly love poetry is predicated on the notion of abstract, esoteric love (see XII; 62,9). This attitude implies that courtly love by itself was not an expression of concrete erotic desire, but an erotic medium for the ritualization and performance of courtly culture. He confirms this obser-vation in a didactic stanza or "Sangspruch" (XXVII; 66,24) in which he argues that well-formulated verses accompanied by music often alleviate melancholy. But he concludes with the admission that all his own efforts to win his lady's favor have been fruitless, which adds an ironic twist to his teaching.

In an interesting intertextual experiment, Veldeke refers to the Tristan narrative (probably Béroul's or Thomas's version) when he points out that he never imbibed a love potion as Tristan did, and yet experienced a much more intense feeling of love than this literary figure (IV; 58,35). In another song, the poet carefully qualifies his love for his lady as ideal, free of any moral blemishes, and far removed from any doubt (V; 59,31). Consequently, many courtiers who do not enjoy the same type of intense love are envious of him, but the poet does not allow this to influence his personal happiness. Veldeke explicitly combines ideal courtly love with honor, and suggests that true love makes it possible for him to compose his songs (VI; 60,13). Not surprisingly, envious people can be found everywhere and deserve to be condemned because they do not understand love and cannot enjoy it for themselves. They therefore do not know the meaning of a courtly culture sustained by love. Their failure to find love rests in their blindness, because, as Veldeke writes, they are looking for proverbial pears in beech trees (VII; 65,11). The poet describes himself lucky in his role as lover, because so many people are envious of him. The more he experiences their envy, he emphasizes, the less he would be inclined ever to abandon his love (IX; 61,9–10).

On a more serious note, the singer admonishes his lady to show mercy and to grant him her love, as he would otherwise succumb to death (XXVIII; 66,32). On the other hand, the lady clearly spells out the dan-gers for women if they carelessly fulfill their wooers' wishes, which could easily lead to their social disgrace (XXX; 67, 9). Veldeke states in another stanza that true courtly love is a matter of loyal service free of any doubt about its usefulness and free of any change of mind with respect to the true value of love service (XXXII; 67,33). In this sense, courtly love in its absolute, esoteric, and selfless nature, constitutes, as Veldeke formulates in "Waer ich unvrô dar nâch, alse ez mir stât" (If I were unhappy thereafter, as things stand with me; XXXIII), the highest form of culture, far removed from earthly desires and peasant-like voluptuousness, or "dorpheit" (see XXXIII; 146,11–14). The true lover does not know any "riuwe" (regret or remorse), that is, never questions the principles of courtly love because it proves to be an infinite source of happiness: "wan blîschaft, diu die riuwe slât" (happiness which slays sorrow; XXXIII; 68,11).[11]

Eneit

Like Gottfried von Strassburg, many medieval German poets sang Heinrich's praise, or referred to his widely-admired epic *Eneit* as a preferred model for their own writing, such as Herbort von Fritzlar (in his *Liet von Troye*, ca. 1190–1210) and the anonymous author of *Mauritius von Craûn* (ca. 1220), both of whom identified him as "Meister"; this label suggested that Heinrich had received a thorough formal training in a church school without having been ordained as a priest. Wolfram von Eschenbach, Reinbot von Durne (fl. middle of thirteenth century), Rudolf von Ems (fl. ca. 1220–54), the anonymous author of *Willehalm von Orlens* (ca. 1240), and the unidentified author of the *Göttweiger Trojanerkrieg* (ca. 1300) also refer to Heinrich as their ideal courtly poet.[12]

Although his *Eneit* still reflects the language of *Frühmittelhochdeutsch* (early Middle High German), a type of pre-courtly language that lacked the intellectual sophistication and elegance achieved in Middle High German, Heinrich successfully introduced the classical legend of the Trojan Aeneas and his foundation of Rome into the world of medieval German chivalry, thus combining the culture of classical antiquity with the world of medieval courts and knighthood.

Heinrich's use of rhymes and rhyme schemes indicates that he intended to reach the largest possible courtly audience by avoiding dialect barriers. Heinrich used the more common Rhine-Frankish and Hessian dialects rather than the West Rhenish dialect of his homeland. His move to Thuringia, where he completed *Eneit*, did not have any impact on his literary language, which closely followed the standard Middle High German spoken at most Hohenstaufen courts in central, southern, and eastern Germany.[13] The *Eneit* is a particularly well-preserved work that has come down to us in thirteen manuscripts, seven of which only in fragmentary form, dating from the late twelfth through the late fifteenth centuries.

In his *Eneit* we find a number of clues about Heinrich's life: he participated at the wedding of Landgrave Ludwig III of Thuringia with Countess Margarete von Cleve in 1174, and he attended the famous court festival in Mainz in 1184 where Emperor Friedrich II's (Barbarossa's) two sons were knighted (347, 13–29). Possibly Count Heinrich Raspe III (d. 1180), brother of Ludwig III, stole Heinrich's *Eneit* manuscript during the wedding celebrations in 1174, and it took the poet nine years to recover it. Count Hermann of the Palatinate (1182–90), who had become Landgrave of Thuringia in 1190 after his brother Ludwig III's death during the Third Crusade, along with Count Friedrich, another brother of Hermann, returned the manuscript to Heinrich and requested him to complete the unfinished romance (353,4–29).[14]

In his *Eneit*, Heinrich demonstrates his extraordinary knowledge of Latin and French, as he closely follows his Old French source, the *Roman d'Eneas*, and various texts from Roman antiquity, particularly Virgil's *Aeneid* and Ovid's *Metamorphoses*.[15] Other sources drawn on by Heinrich were the Old French *Roman de Thèbes* and the *Roman de Troie*, the Middle High German *Kaiserchronik* (1135–50), the *Rolandslied* (ca. 1170), *Annolied* (ca. 1175), the *Strassburg Alexander* (ca. 1170), and Eilhart von Obergs's *Tristrant* (ca. 1170). This combination of sources made it possible for Heinrich to introduce the new value system of courtly love (*minne*) and to enrich the account of Eneas's set course of life as a knight with a strong love interest.[16] He obviously did not feel entirely bound by literary tradition and operated surprisingly freely with the various source materials.[17] For instance, Virgil had opened his account with a report about the goddess Juno's anger at Paris's slighting of her beauty, her jealousy of the entire Trojan race, and her apprehension of a plan that the Fates had determined with regard to Carthage.[18] Heinrich, on the other hand, first focuses on the conquest of Troy by the Greeks where Eneas, not immediately affected or endangered because of the remote location of his palace, deliberates with his family and friends as to whether he should obey the gods' wishes and escape by sea to meet his destiny in Italy. When they discover twenty well-stocked but abandoned Greek ships nearby, they seize them, load them with all their valuables, and quickly depart from the doomed city. Eneas loses his wife in the turmoil but succeeds in having his aged father carried onto the ship. Another major divergence from the classical tradition is found in a new emphasis on Lavinia, Eneas's future wife and daughter of King Latinus, whose hand had originally been promised to Duke Turnus. Heinrich develops a passionate love story between Eneas and Lavinia and also focuses on the mother, who bitterly fights her daughter's marriage with the Trojan hero, favoring Turnus as her future son-in-law.

Even from a formal perspective, the differences between Virgil's *Aeneid* and Heinrich's *Eneit* are remarkable. The Roman author employed a complex book composition, structuring his work in twelve chapters because he most likely addressed primarily a reading audience, whereas Heinrich does not emulate this strategy at all, probably because he expected that his work would be read aloud.[19]

The discussions between mother and daughter about love and the two male competitors represent an extraordinary literary motif and established a tradition later often copied by poets such as Gottfried von Strassburg, the

anonymous author of the *Nibelungenlied*, the Winsbeckin, and the minnesinger Neidhart.[20] The combination of Ovidian love motifs with classical battle scenes and adventure stories represents, as Lee Patterson has
pointed out with regard to the Old French *Roman*, "the *Eneas* poet's
boldest act of revision."[21] To this we can add the considerably reduced role
that the gods play in Virgil's *Aeneid*, as Heinrich had to adapt his text to
the expectations of his Christian audience. The classical epic, however, is
not entirely transformed into a Christian tale of knighthood and courtly
love, since, interestingly, the pagan gods continue to exert an influence on
Eneas's destiny. Still, the protagonist deliberates with his family, friends,
and advisors about the right course of action, and he demonstrates unmis-
takably the behavior of an exemplary Christian ruler and knight who listens to his counselors.[22]

Eneas's difficult journey lasts seven years until he and his men reach
the shores of Carthage. Queen Dido welcomes them and quickly falls in
love with the protagonist. Their relationship, however, cannot last, because
the gods have determined that the protagonist has to move on and journey to Italy to found Rome. There are significant differences in the
description of how the love between Dido and Eneas develops in Virgil's
version, in the Old French work, and in Heinrich's adaptation. The three
authors also raise different questions as to Eneas's culpability with regard
to Dido's suicide and his obligation toward the Carthage queen after their
sexual union, as each author addresses these issues from different perspectives.[23] Heinrich paints a picture of Dido as a woman burning with erotic
passion who cannot live without her lover; when she finally realizes that he
has decided to abandon her, following the gods' call, she wounds herself
mortally and throws herself into a fire. Heinrich's psychological treatment
of this love affair reveals the profound ambivalence of their relationship.
Dido loves Eneas passionately, whereas Eneas never fully commits to her,
keeping the goal of Italy firmly in mind, thus abusing her emotional
attachment to him while he prepares for the continuation of his journey.
Initially, when the two find themselves alone after a thunderstorm, he
forces himself upon her (63, 24–28). Even though the narrator attempts to
assuage his audience's concern about this obvious rape scene: "so daz er ir
hulde / manliche behielt" (so that he preserved her favor through his
manly skills; 63, 26–27),[24] the violent nature of Eneas's treatment of Dido
is obvious: "so der man so schivzet, / daz er sin genivzet, / so liebet ime div
vart" (when the man launches a shot successfully, he will enjoy the hunt;
63, 37–39). Despite her love for Eneas, Dido feels ashamed of having lost
her virginity before her marriage, and to avoid dishonor she publicly
declares Eneas her husband (65, 1–9) despite general disgruntlement and
rancor against the foreigner.

At the moment of the couple's seemingly complete happiness the
gods order Eneas to leave the country and to continue with his interrupted

journey. Without hesitation the protagonist prepares his departure, though he feels sadness for leaving his "wife" behind (67,6). Not surprisingly, Dido displays extreme signs of desperation, as she is the one who is in love. She herself admits that her love is "so harte uber mazen" (so excessively painful, 69, 7), but no pleading and no harsh words can prevent the hero from leaving her. As soon as her lover has departed, Dido falls into a fury, burns all the gifts that Eneas had given to her, and commits suicide, which the narrator comments in unequivocally negative terms: "daz quam von vnsinne. / ez was vnrechtiv minne / div si dar zů twanch" (this resulted from madness. It was wrong love that forced her to do it; 78,3–5).

Eneas will later be accused for having abandoned Dido without any care for her well-being and for having driven her to her death. In Italy, King Latinus's wife Amata — she is named only in Virgil's text, not in any of the medieval versions — argues against him as a potential husband for her daughter Lavinia and reminds her husband of Eneas's evil reputation. Not only does she severely criticize him for the wrongful treatment of the Carthaginian queen, but also for being of too low social status in relationship to Lavinia, for having fled from Troy out of cowardice, and for a general disrespect for women (121,6–123,24). Amata goes so far as to suggest that Eneas would quickly abandon Lavinia after having married her and thus having gained wealth and power through her, as all Trojans are lacking in honor and loyalty (123,16–21). King Latinus resists her barrage of accusations and points out that the gods determined the marriage between Lavinia and Eneas, and that he, Latinus, had been tricked by her in the first place into promising Turnus his daughter's hand in marriage (124,28–125,19).

Divine intervention in human affairs — now in the Christian sense of the word — also plays an important role in Eneas's struggle to fight for Lavinia's hand and for the right to establish himself in Latinus's kingdom against the challenges of Turnus and Amata. Through his father Anchises whom he visits in Hell, Eneas is informed that the gods have decided for him to become the founder of the Roman Empire (107,10–109,20). The description of this descent into the netherworld allows Heinrich to adapt fully the ancient worldview to the Christian concepts of Hell and Purgatory.[25]

The largest section of the *Eneit* deals with the gruesome details of the battle between Turnus's and Eneas's armies. The narrator demonstrates a keen sense of realism in his description of how Turnus besieges Eneas's newly erected castle and yet fails because of the superior fortification created by Eneas himself and because of the bravery and military skills of Eneas's son Ascanius. During the siege Eneas forges an alliance with King Evander, whose son Pallas is then knighted and leads his father's army into battle. The narrator criticizes Turnus for his merciless treatment of his own men as he sends the foot soldiers into battle although he knows too well that they will not be able to breach the defenses and will only find their own death: "Tvrnus tet vnrehte, / daz er die schiltchnehte / zů deme sturme treip. / da uil tot beleip, / wande ez enhalf niht ein bast" (Turnus did wrong in sending the foot soldiers into the attack. Many met their death as nothing could be achieved; 177,25–29).[26] Frustrated, Turnus orders a retreat, and when he discovers the Trojans' ships he has them burned. But in the following night he makes another military blunder, as he allows his men to feast and get drunk. When everybody is asleep, two Trojans, the friends Eurialus and Nisus observe this, sneak out of the fortress into the enemy camp, and slaughter a large number of them before they themselves are discovered and killed. The narrative also contains much detailed information about siege machinery, weapons, and attack strategies that reflects Heinrich's personal experience as a knight. The battle is predominantly individualized through the specific focus on the heroes and their friends along with whom they die fighting against the enemy. The author also drastically emphasizes the death of great numbers of warriors, obviously drawing from the tradition of the Chansons de Geste with its many battle scenes leading to the death of thousands of Christians and Saracens.

Heroism and glorification of the protagonist naturally play the most important role in Heinrich's *Eneit*. He finds his most congenial companion in the young Pallas, who accomplishes almost impossible tasks. But in the end Pallas meets his death in combat with Turnus, whom he almost overpowers, but who manages to kill him when he is already on the ground, knocked down by a mighty blow from Pallas's sword. In a parallel event, Turnus loses the glorious Queen of the Amazons, Camilla, in the fight against the Trojans, which clears the field for the two main opponents who finally agree to end the mass battle and to determine the winner in single combat. This duel demonstrates that both heroes possess the same strength and skills and cannot overcome the other until the gods intervene and make Turnus's sword break. He continues to fight, however, with rocks and a broken shaft of a lance, proving his outstanding fighting abilities and untiring bravery.[27] Eneas eventually defeats Turnus, and in response to Turnus's pleas for mercy is about to take pity on him. But when Eneas recognizes a ring he had given to Pallas on Turnus's finger (which Turnus had taken from the dead Pallas's finger), Turnus's pleas fall on deaf ears: "des waz dir nehein not, / daz du sein vingerlin trůge, / den du in meiner helfe slůge. / es waz ein bosiv girshait, / des sage ich dir die warheit" (there was no need for you to wear the ring of him who provided me with help. This was evil greed, I tell you truly; 331, 28–32). Eneas brutally beheads Turnus and in so doing ends the battle.[28] Otherwise, as the narrator emphasizes, Turnus had been a model knight, shining in his heroism, bravery, and military might, excelling through his wisdom and moderation, loyalty and honesty. He characterizes him most positively and emphasizes that he would have killed Eneas if the Gods had not determined his destiny differently:

> milte vnd erhaft,
> in adilar seines gûtes,
> ein lewe seines mûtes,
> ein ekkestain der eren,
> ein spiegel der herren.
> er het einen wohlgetanen lip,
> vil liep waren im div weip.
> si waren ouch im holt,
> daz waz seiner tugent scholt.
> er het in seiner iugende
> auzerwelter tugende
> wol zehen seiner genoze teil,
> wan daz chlageleich vnheil,
> daz er dez tages veige was
> vund daz der herre Eneas
> seinen leip danne solte tragen.
> Turnus hete anders in erschlagen. (332,10–26)

[generous and honorable, an eagle with regard to his property, a lion with regard to his courage, a cornerstone of honor, a model for all lords. He was beautifully built, loved women, and was loved by them as a consequence of his virtues. He possessed, in all his youth, extraordinary strength of character, probably ten times more than his peers. There was only the lamentable tragedy that he died that day and that Lord Eneas kept his own life.]

Wolfram later followed this model in his treatment of the fight between Willehalm and the Saracen Arofel, and in both cases the reader is curiously left with a strong feeling of injustice committed against the defeated opponent.[29]

One of the most intriguing aspects in Heinrich's *Eneit* is the conflict between the queen and her daughter, and the latter's attempt to understand the meaning of love. Amata repeatedly tries to influence Lavinia to love Turnus: " 'tohter, so minne Turnum!' " (daughter, love Turnus!; 261,16). Despite the emotionally charged scene, the discussion contains pronounced elements of comedy as Lavinia seems not to know the meaning of *minne* at all, and misunderstands her mother's metaphoric words by interpreting them verbatim. For instance, when Amata encourages her to give her heart to the duke, Lavinia wonders how she herself could survive without this organ (261,20). When the mother tells her that *minne* will teach her all about love (261,26), the daughter asks, " 'durch got, wer ist div minne?' " (by God, who is love?; 262,27). After the mother has defined love as an all-encompassing power, Lavinia insists that it is entirely unknown to her (262,40), and then states that she would rather get sick from a fever than feel *minne*, for which there is no known medicine (263,4–5). When the mother discusses love as a sweet torture, Lavinia expresses her hope never to be affected by it, a topos that later poets such as the *Nibelungenlied* author and Wolfram also integrated into their own works.[30]

The queen elaborates her theory of love in great detail and particularly emphasizes the dialectics of love. Although it would bring much pain, the ultimate happiness resulting from love would be worth it: " 'ia ist ez michel senfticheit' " (it is a wonderful feeling; 265,36). At this point Lavinia still does not seem to understand. Even when her mother threatens her with death and torture if she ever were to love Eneas and become his wife, she does not accept the teaching, but instead obstinately claims that her mother can easily forbid her that for which she does not have any interest: " 'ich engiwan es nie willen' " (I never had any intention; 266,13). This remark, however, irritates Amata even more, as she realizes that all her rhetorical strategies have been for naught, as love cannot be taught through words: "do sweich dv frove stille, / in zorne giench siv hin dane / vnde sach die tochter ane / vil vngutliche, / div kuneginne riche" (the lady stopped talking and angrily went away; the mighty queen looked at her daughter full of wrath; 266,14–18). Ironically, soon thereafter the innocent and naive Lavinia catches sight of Eneas and immediately falls in love with him, hit by a metaphorical arrow shot by Lady Venus (267, 24–25). Eneas soon becomes aware of her as well, and similarly develops strong feelings of love for the princess. She spends a painful night experiencing all of love's tribulations. The author has Lavinia reflect upon the nature of love at great length, developing an entire discourse on this emotion, as can also be found in Andreas Capellanus famous *Art of Courtly Love* (ca. 1185–90, in Latin),[31] and offering us concrete descriptions of the physical and emotional effects of love on the individual. Not surprisingly, the next morning her mother immediately realizes what has happened to her daughter. When embarrassed Lavinia finally writes Eneas's name on a wax tablet, another rhetorical battle begins in which Amata claims that Eneas is a homosexual: "er geminnite nie wib" (he never loved a woman; 282,38). Moreover, she warns Lavinia of the existential danger resulting from homosexuality, as humanity would simply die out within a hundred years if all men were given over to it: "div werlt muse schiere zergan / innerhalp hundert iaren" (283,8–9). She also reminds her daughter of how unfaithfully Eneas had treated Dido and exerts tremendous pressure on her daughter to comply with her wishes, but she cannot change the young woman's mind. In her frustration she threatens and abuses her badly until Lavinia faints. The more Amata tries to influence her daughter, the more Lavinia is determined to pursue her love for Eneas at all costs. She contacts him by means of a letter, particularly as she is convinced that her mother's charge against Eneas as a homosexual cannot be true: "man weiz des wol die warheit, / daz der herre Eneas / ie vil vnschvldich was / vmbe solhe missetat" (the truth is well known that Lord Eneas is innocent of such wrong behavior; 286, 10–13).

With Eneas's victory and Turnus's death the two lovers finally marry and enjoy the rest of their life together, establishing a new family that then becomes the foundation of the new Roman Empire. Before the wedding Lavinia's mother dies of grief after having hurled new threats and insults at her daughter, maligning her own husband Latinus, and announcing her preparedness to commit suicide. Lavinia, however, declares her unwavering love for Eneas and warns Amata of the shame she would bring upon herself if she killed herself.

Heinrich succeeded in composing an innovative courtly romance based on classical mythology and Ovidian ideas of love. At the same time *Eneit* offers a global perspective on the history of Troy, Carthage, and finally Rome, which then leads to the birth of Christ and the salvation of mankind (352, 6–10). In light of these elements and the later poets' admiration of Heinrich's accomplishments, it is justifiable to identify the *Eneit* and Heinrich's courtly love poems as the crucial foundation from which classical Middle High German literature could rise.

Notes

[1] Horst Brunner, "*Von der stat Roya vrsprung, päwrung, streyten und irer zerstorung.* Literarische Formen der Vermittlung historischen Wissens an nichtlateinkundiges Publikum im Hoch- und Spätmittelalter und in der frühen Neuzeit," *Der Deutschunterricht* 41, 1 (1989): 55–73.

[2] Heinrich von Veldeke, *Eneasroman. Die Berliner Bilderhandschrift mit Übersetzung und Kommentar*, ed. Hans Fromm. *Mit den Miniaturen der Handschrift und einem Aufsatz von Dorothea und Peter Diemer* (Frankfurt am Main: Deutscher Klassiker Verlag, 1992), 745–54. The text will be quoted from this edition; all translations are by A. C. An English translation of the Old French text is *Eneas: A Twelfth-Century French Romance*, trans. with an introduction and notes by John A. Yunck (New York, London: Columbia UP, 1974).

[3] Gottfried von Strassburg, *Tristan, Nach dem Text von Friedrich Ranke neu herausgegeben, ins Neuhochdeutsche übersetzt, mit einem Stellenkommentar und einem Nachwort von Rüdiger Krohn* (Stuttgart: Reclam, 1980), here 106.

[4] Gottfried von Strassburg, *Tristan*, first complete translation, with the surviving fragments of the *Tristran* of Thomas and an introduction by A. T. Hatto (London: Penguin, 1960).

[5] Gabriele Schieb, *Heinrich von Veldeke* (Stuttgart: Metzler, 1965), 2–6.

[6] John R. Sinnema, *Henrik Van Veldeke* (New York: Twayne Publishers, 1972), 54–66.

[7] See Günther Schweikle, *Mittelhochdeutsche Minnelyrik. I. Frühe Minnelyrik. Texte und Übertragungen, Einführung und Kommentar* (Stuttgart, Weimar: Metzler, 1993), 414–29, and Stephen J. Kaplowitt, "Heinrich von Veldeke's Song Cycle of 'Hohe Minne,'" *Seminar* 11 (1975): 125–40.

[8] Heinrich's lyrics are quoted from *Des Minnesangs Frühling*, ed. Hugo Moser and Helmut Tervooren, *I: Texte*, 37th revised edition (Stuttgart: S. Hirzel, 1982), 97–149; Roman numerals refer to the ordering of the melodies in this edition, and Arabic numerals designate Lachmann's ordering of the verses. Translations of the lyrics are by A. C.

[9] Ludger Lieb, "Modulationen: Sangspruch und Minnesang bei Heinrich von Veldeke," *Zeitschrift für deutsches Altertum* 119 (2000): 38–49; cit. 42. Sonderheft: *Neue Forschungen zur mittelhochdeutschen Sangspruchdichtung*.

[10] Olive Sayce, *The Medieval German Lyric, 1150–1300: The Development of Its Themes and Forms in Their European Context* (Oxford: Clarendon Press, 1982), 114.

[11] Günther Schweikle, *Die mittelhochdeutsche Minnelyrik. I: Die frühe Minnelyrik. Texte und Übertragungen, Einführung und Kommentar* (Darmstadt: Wissenschaftliche Buchgesellschaft, 1977), 414–49.

[12] *Dichter über Dichter in mittelhochdeutscher Literatur*, ed. Günther Schweikle (Tübingen: Max Niemeyer, 1970), nos. 7, 9, 10, 12, 34, 35, 37, 38, 43, 61.

[13] Thomas Klein, "Heinrich von Veldeke und die mitteldeutschen Literatursprachen: Untersuchungen zum Veldeke-Problem," in Thomas Klein and Cola Minis, *Zwei Studien zu Veldeke und zum Strassburger Alexander* (Amsterdam: Rodopi, 1985), 1–121; here 69–71.

[14] Rodney W. Fisher, *Heinrich von Veldeke: Eneas. A Comparison with the Roman d'Eneas, and a Translation into English* (Bern, Frankfurt am Main: Peter Lang, 1992), 2; Bernd Bastert, "*Dô si der lantgrâve nam:* Zur 'klever Hochzeit' und der Genese des Eneas-Romans," *Zeitschrift für deutsches Altertum und deutsche Literatur* 123 (1994): 253–73; Tina Sabine Weicker, "*Do wart daz buch ze Cleve verstolen:* Neue Überlegungen zur Entstehung von Veldekes *Eneas*," *Zeitschrift für deutsches Altertum* 130, 1 (2001): 1–18.

[15] Marie-Luise Dittrich, *Die 'Eneide' Heinrichs von Veldeke. I. Teil: Quellenkritischer Vergleich mit dem 'Roman d'Eneas' und Vergils 'Aeneis'* (Wiesbaden: Steiner, 1966).

[16] Renate Kistler, *Heinrich von Veldeke und Ovid*, Hermaea, Germanistische Forschungen, N.F. 7 (Tübingen: Niemeyer, 1993), 232–37.

[17] Elisabeth Lienert, *Deutsche Antikenromane des Mittelalters*, Grundlagen der Germanistik 39 (Berlin: Erich Schmidt Verlag, 2001), 78.

[18] Virgil, *The Aeneid*, trans. into English prose with an introduction by W. F. Jackson Knight (Baltimore: Penguin, 1956).

[19] Wolfgang Brandt, *Die Erzählkonzeption Heinrichs von Veldeke in der* Eneide: *Ein Vergleich mit Vergils 'Aeneis,'* Marburger Beiträge zur Germanistik 29 (Marburg: Elwert, 1969), 191–204.

[20] Ann Marie Rasmussen, *Mothers and Daughters in Medieval German Literature* (Syracuse: Syracuse UP, 1997), especially 32.

21 Lee Patterson, *Negotiating the Past: The Historical Understanding of Medieval Literature* (Madison: U of Wisconsin P, 1987), 177.

22 Ingrid Kasten, "Herrschaft und Liebe: Zur Rolle und Darstellung des 'Helden' im *Roman d'Eneas* und in Veldekes *Eneasroman*," *Deutsche Vierteljahresschrift* 62 (1988): 227–45.

23 Rodney W. Fisher, *Heinrich von Veldeke*, 9.

24 Fisher offers the somewhat misleading translation: "he did with her what he wanted, and gallantly received her favour." This obscures the fact that Eneas indeed rapes Dido.

25 Lienert, *Deutsche Antikenromane*, 83; see also Hans Fromm, "Die Unterwelt des Eneas: Topographie und Seelenvorstellung," *Philologie als Kulturwissenschaft: Studien zur Literatur und Geschichte des Mittelalters. Festschrift für Karl Stackmann zum 65. Geburtstag*, ed. Ludger Grenzmann (Göttingen: Vandenhoeck & Ruprecht, 1987), 71–89.

26 See William C. McDonald, "Turnus in Veldeke's *Eneide*: The Effects of Violence," in *Violence in Medieval Courtly Literature: A Casebook*, ed. Albrecht Classen, Routledge Medieval Casebooks (New York and London: Routledge, 2004), 83–95.

27 In Wolfram von Eschenbach's *Parzival*, the protagonist's sword also breaks into two pieces at the end of a long battle against his brother Feirefiz, who then graciously ends the fight, crediting his opponent with the victory, although he himself still has his sword intact, and asking for the opponent's name. Thus he opens the communicative channels preparing peace and brotherly love between them. By contrast, the fight between Turnus and Eneas ends in the death of the former because he had robbed Pallas of his ring.

28 Andreas Kraß, "Die Mitleidfähigkeit des Helden: Zum Motiv der *compassio* im höfischen Roman des 12. Jahrhunderts (*Eneit* — *Erec* — *Iwein*)," *Wolfram-Studien* XVI: *Aspekte des 12. Jahrhunderts. Freisinger Kolloquium 1998* (Berlin: E. Schmidt, 2000), 282–304; here 287–91.

29 See Lienert, *Deutsche Antikenromane*, 92.

30 Albrecht Classen, "Wolframs von Eschenbach *Titurel*-Fragmente und Johanns von Würzburg *Wilhelm von Österreich*: Höhepunkte der höfischen Minnereden," *Amsterdamer Beiträge zur Älteren Germanistik* 37 (1993): 75–102.

31 Andreas Capellanus, *The Art of Courtly Love*, with introduction, translation, and notes by John Jay Parry (New York: Columbia UP, 1960/1990).

Hartmann von Aue. A miniature from the Codex Manesse (184v).

Hartmann von Aue

Rodney Fisher

A LTHOUGH ONE OF THE BEST KNOWN and most widely studied poets of the German Middle Ages, Hartmann von Aue presents the modern scholar in search of biographical details with the usual problems: there are no firm dates, no contemporary historical records of his name, no precise pointers, even within the works themselves, to personal circumstances or family connections.[1] By his own proud boast, he was a knight with a good education, an unusual distinction for the warrior class. The place name "Au" and compounds of it are far too common to be localized with any degree of confidence. There is some consensus that the southwest of the German-speaking empire is where Hartmann lived, and since he appears to imply a close link between the Swabian hero of *Der arme Heinrich* and the aristocratic family with whom Hartmann himself was in service, the old duchy of Swabia is most likely Hartmann's homeland. Hartmann is considered a pioneer, with Heinrich von Veldeke, in adapting medieval courtly narratives for a German public. His works, in the generally accepted order of their completion, are: *Erec*, an Arthurian romance for which Hartmann's major source was probably the French *Erec et Enite* of Chrétien de Troyes; *Gregorius*, a much shorter narrative which traces the miraculous career of an exceptionally talented aristocrat from incestuous beginnings to papacy, and which is based on an anonymous French tale *La vie du pape saint Grégoire; Der arme Heinrich,* the account of a high-born and apparently blameless hero's brush with the dreaded disease, leprosy; and *Iwein,* another Arthurian romance adapted from Chrétien's medieval French version. In addition, Hartmann wrote the *Klage* (also known as his *Büchlein*), a sort of treatise on love in the form of a disputation between the lover's heart and body, for which no direct source is known; and a corpus of perhaps eighteen songs in the *Minnesang* or troubadour tradition.[2]

A rough time frame for his works can also be established, partly by reference to the work of other poets who are likely to have followed in his footsteps in popularizing courtly narratives. Gottfried von Strassburg's *Tristan* (1210) includes a famous passage reviewing some of the poets known to him, with high praise for Hartmann which one assumes is genuine, but unfortunately Gottfried does not say whether he was acquainted with what is thought to be Hartmann's last work, *Iwein,* nor even whether Hartmann was still alive at the time. That Wolfram von Eschenbach knew

Hartmann's *Iwein*, however, is more plausible, and this suggests a date of around 1200 for that work. Hartmann's earlier works are presumed to date from the 1180s. Further pegs on which to hang a biography are provided by Hartmann's corpus of songs. Although it is notoriously hazardous to equate any author with the "I" who speaks in the works, one can be fairly confident that when in his lyrics Hartmann challenges contemporary knights to uphold their crusaders' ethical obligations, or urges them to follow his example and place crusading goals above romantic ones, the poet is genuinely convinced of the spiritual message being promulgated, although whether the crusade in question is that of 1189–90 or of 1197–98, or whether he himself took part in it, is not certain. Much has also been made of the death of Hartmann's much loved feudal overlord, an event which on the poet's own evidence caused him to commit himself so enthusiastically to the crusading cause. Although it has never been proved beyond doubt, some scholars have argued that Hartmann's overlord could have been no less a personage than the emperor Friedrich Barbarossa, who died in 1190 while on the Third Crusade.[3]

Like any of the few contemporaries equipped with some formal education, Hartmann was acquainted with basic theological concepts, and may even, like his hero Gregorius, have excelled in a monastery school. But he was also a knight in service with an aristocratic overlord whose interests presumably determined Hartmann's choice of subject matter and his treatment of it. Further, his works were written for various court circles, some of which would have appreciated the more spiritual dénouement of *Gregorius*, while an audience composed largely of knights and courtly ladies would have been eager to hear about the tales of love and chivalry narrated in more leisurely fashion in the longer romances *Erec* and *Iwein*. In short, it is hazardous to infer from Hartmann's works anything that might have been determined by personal experiences, since his creative freedom was constrained by several factors: the typically medieval respect for sources, the need to accommodate his patron's preferences, the need to take account of a particular public, and finally, the conventions of the particular genre with which he was working.

Certain constants can be discerned running through all Hartmann's works. He appears to have been concerned about balance, in both his poetic style and his understanding of human relationships.[4] As an illustration of the former, consider the following passages from his *Heinrich* and *Gregorius* respectively. The first is part of the narrator's introductory description of Heinrich's many good qualities, which are listed in chiastic formulations that reinforce the sense of harmony and perfection in the hero's world, soon to be abruptly disturbed by his illness:

> er was ein bluome der jugent,
> der werltvreude ein spiegelglas,
> staeter triuwe ein adamas,

ein ganziu krône der zuht.
er was der nôthaften vluht,
ein schilt sîner mâge,
der milte ein glîchiu wâge . . . (60–66)

[He was a flower of youth, of worldly pleasure a mirror, in loyal depend-
ability a diamond, a real crown of good breeding. He was for those in
need a refuge, a shield for his kinsfolk, in generosity an even balance . . .]

The passage consists of a series of metaphors in noun form (flower, mirror,
diamond and so on), with dependent phrases that relate the metaphors to
Heinrich's world. The style is particularly appropriate here because the
rhythmic pattern lulls the hearer into a sense of enduring well-being, just
as the hero himself appears to be convinced of his own self-sufficiency.
Compare this with a passage from *Gregorius* which prepares the audience
for a harrowing description of the hero's appearance after years of deprivation, but which, in its carefully balanced antitheses, underlines the gulf
between physical and spiritual states, between the human and the divine
view of things:

sus vunden sîe den gotes trût,
einen dürftigen ûf der erde,
ze gote in hôhem werde,
den liuten widerzaeme,
ze himele vil genaeme. (3418–22)

[Thus they found God's loved one: a miserable wretch on earth, to God
one most highly exalted, for humans a repulsive figure, for Heaven most
pleasing.]

Hartmann is an "intellectual" poet, one who loves to develop arguments
through balanced word play and dialectical analysis.

Hartmann shows a surprisingly modern attitude to the need for balance between the sexes, an attitude that he seems to uphold at times in
opposition to contemporary practice. A brief survey of Hartmann's lyric
production may illustrate the point. Of the eighteen songs attributed to
him in manuscripts, two are of uncertain authorship (12 and 18).[5] Of the
rest, there are some that are characteristic of the troubadour fashion ema-
nating from Provence and France that at the end of the twelfth century
began to dominate German love songs as well. Typical of this fashion are
stanzas in which the performer plays the role of a male lover elated or frustrated at the experience of loving an aristocratic lady who is in the difficult
position of not being able to respond publicly, because of the social
conventions at court. The singer's high praise of this lady functions as
"service" in the feudal sense, for which he might reasonably (and legally)
expect some "reward," normally some sign of recognition, occasionally

something more openly erotic. Any real or imagined positive response elicits joy, a failure to respond, or outright rejection, elicits self-doubt and lament (hence the term *Klagelied*), but often also a determination to persevere in the face of adversity.

Hartmann's song No. 10 is a good example of this attitude; the singer accepts the fact that the public distance he has to maintain between himself and his lady is no reason to lose faith in the ultimate worth of women, who are responsible for the edification of men generally:

> nieman sol ir lobes gedagen.
> swaz wir rehtes werben,
> und daz wir man noch nien verderben
> des suln wir in genâde sagen.

[No one should withhold praise of women. Whatever good we men achieve, including the fact that we're never entirely lost, all this we owe to them.]

Or take Song 3, in which the singer announces his intention of taking his "service" elsewhere, but refuses to indulge in the disloyalty of blaming the lady for his lack of success: dûhte ich si sîn wert, / si hete mir gelônet baz. (If she had thought me worthy of it, / she would have rewarded me better).

By way of contrast, there are several songs from a lady's perspective: 9, 14, and 16. In the first of these the speaker bitterly laments the treachery of a man whom she ironically describes as "as free of deceit as the sea is of waves"; in 14, a song of surprising intimacy, a woman declares her determination to commit herself body and soul, in spite of advice from friends, to the lover who will keep her warm through the long winter nights; and 16, frequently seen as the lament of a widow for her dead spouse, is a moving expression of the despair felt by a woman surrounded by the joys of spring or summer which she cannot appreciate because of the loss of her partner. Such images of women are more reminiscent of the earlier love song tradition in Germany, although in terms of his techniques Hartmann is clearly acquainted with contemporary Provençal and French models.

If most of Hartmann's songs suggest whole-hearted acceptance of the ideals of courtly love, and of *Minnesang* as an appropriate medium for them, there are some that appear to question basic assumptions of the fashion. Foremost among these is No. 15, sometimes referred to as the "Unmutslied" (song of discontent). Apart from the fact the performer identifies himself by name (a rare enough phenomenon in *Minnesang*), the song objectifies the whole elaborate ritual of paying court to ladies, in a manner that suggests the superficiality and brittleness of the convention.

If scholars have sometimes questioned the seriousness of this song, there can be no doubting Hartmann's conviction in his crusading songs. The genre functions frequently as the platform for a typically medieval conflict of loyalties: on the one hand the secular attraction in the form of love for a woman (however stylized the expression of that love may be), and on the other, the spiritual commitment to demonstrate one's love for God by embarking on a crusade. Both forms of service could of course be seen in terms of feudal obligations, so that the resulting dilemma was one likely to appeal to a culture much given to theorizing and casuistry concerning the phenomenon of love. Hartmann appears in his three crusading songs to have nothing but scorn for those who prevaricate; for him the crusader had no choice but to fulfill his promise to God. His most famous song on the subject (number 17) begins as a conventional re-statement of the feudal and ethical obligations that love imposes on those under her sway, and develops into a direct challenge to fellow knights to follow the singer's example and seek the everlasting reward which only God's love can bring. In this plea for spiritual commitment to crusading Hartmann thus highlights two crucial tenets of feudal relationships which the contemporary doctrine of love did not fully satisfy: the certainty of reward for service, and the idea of reciprocity between partners.

The fascination of poets and their public for the phenomenon of courtly love is clear in Hartmann's early work, the *Klage*, which dramatizes the universal conflict between body and soul, as found in medieval Latin allegorical disputation poems (compare also Hartmann's *Gregorius*, 2667–83 and *Der arme Heinrich*, 681–735) in a new secular context, so that the heart appears as the sensitive party in matters of love, teaching the body restraint, constancy and the many other virtues which make of courtly love something pleasing in God's eyes. Hartmann's talent for rational psychology is remarkable in this youthful exercise in dialectics, as is his mastery of form: a final section consisting of fifteen stanzas addressed to the anonymous "lady" follows a pattern in which the stanzas are regularly reduced by two verses from the original thirty-two, down to the last stanza of four verses.

Erec

The romance *Erec* is considered the first example in German of a genre already popular in France, the courtly romance. It survives in only one manuscript, datable to the early sixteenth century and already missing the opening verses and some sections later; in addition there are some earlier fragments surviving which partly fill the gaps. Since it deals with the exploits of a knight belonging to the circle of King Arthur, *Erec* is more specifically an Arthurian romance, a narrative in which Arthur appears, however much on the periphery, as the inspiration for all who aspire to chivalry. Hartmann based his narrative on the version written by Chrétien de Troyes (perhaps written 1165–70), and the superficial reader of both versions might conclude that Hartmann simply translated his source into German.[6] Nothing could be further from the truth. Comparative studies over many years have consistently demonstrated that Hartmann's work is an adaptation of Chrétien's, rather than a translation. Like most medieval poets he was obliged to reproduce the known plot, some basic elements of which his audience may well have heard already. But his German public would have had a rather different interpretation of legal, social, and ethical nuances than Chrétien's public,[7] and more important, Hartmann's narrative style and his understanding of motivation are so distinctive as to make of his *Erec* a new romance.

Hartmann's *Erec* tells the story of a young knight, the son of a king, who is publicly humiliated near Arthur's court by an unknown knight and has to ride out in pursuit of the knight in order to repair his damaged reputation and recover his honor. In order to engage the unknown knight in combat, the unarmed Erec makes a bargain with an impoverished old knight: in return for the knight's armor and weapons, Erec will marry the knight's beautiful young daughter Enite. Inspired by her beauty, Erec defeats his adversary, whose name turns out to be Iders, and he later brings his bride-to-be back to Arthur's court. They arrive at an opportune moment: Arthur has hunted down the white stag and now has to confer a kiss upon the most beautiful lady at court. Upon Enite's arrival, the possibility of dissent about which lady is most deserving is gone. Arthur kisses Enite, and the wedding of Erec and Enite and a tournament follow. Erec returns with his wife to his homeland, becomes king, but then experiences a crisis as he falls into disrepute when he neglects his knightly endeavors and duties, entirely absorbed as he is by love for his wife. When he discovers the shame into which he has fallen, he takes his wife with him into the wilderness on a series of dangerous challenges that structurally form the second cycle of adventures in this romance. Enite, commanded by her husband to remain silent, repeatedly breaks this commandment at the risk of her own life. The adventurous challenges are punctuated by a return to Arthur's court in the middle, and the battle against the knight Mabonagrin at the end. In the end, Erec has again proven his valor and reconstituted his honor, while Enite has demonstrated her great loyalty to her husband.

The hero Erec was known to the twelfth century primarily in connection with two motifs which were already linked in Chrétien's version and which form the axis around which the narrative is built: first, Erec's loss of warrior honor because of his infatuation with his wife Enite and his overindulgence in marital comforts; and second, his demand that his wife remain silent on their hazardous journey, regardless of what she might see or hear. The first of these motifs Hartmann adopted with little modification; his Erec spends so much time in bed with his beautiful wife that society finds no pleasure in attending his court and criticizes him for his indolence (his offence is *sich verligen*, frittering away one's reputation in bed). His obsession with Enite thus has important consequences for courtly society, which is deprived of the "sparkle," the "joy" which the good host should provide: "in schalt diu werlt gar. / sîn hof wart aller vreuden bar . . ." (Everybody criticized him, his court became devoid of all pleasure, 2988). The criticism is all the more unwelcome for being communicated by Enite, a fact that explains the second motif, Erec's subsequent insistence on his wife's silence. Psychologically, it seems as if the warrior-hero associates his fall from grace with the messenger, the wife who informs him of it, sees the beautiful woman as a problem, as it were, and responds by imposing silence and other hardships on her. In Chrétien's version and presumably in the earlier Celtic sources[8] the hero's treatment of his wife is a test designed to establish whether Enite is loyal enough to disregard his command and break her silence when physical danger threatens.

But Hartmann's version presents some minor modifications that give this central scene of the hero's humiliation and departure on his journey of rehabilitation a different twist. On being informed by Enite of society's criticism of him Hartmann's hero gives no indication that he accepts the criticism, unlike Chrétien's version, in which Erec states: "you (Enide) are right and those who reproach me are right" (2572). Hartmann reinforces this image of a hero whose mind is disoriented and unable to face the truth when his narrator tells us that although Erec might rant and rave about it, he is genuinely in need of Enite's warnings because his armor restricts his hearing and his vision (4150–65). Thus, whereas one might accurately speak of the hero "testing" his wife's loyalty in Chrétien, whose Erec can see danger for himself but nevertheless waits for his wife to speak (2957), there can be no question of a test in Hartmann when Erec is really unaware of his surroundings. For Hartmann's audience, as for a modern reader, Erec's limited consciousness (and conscience) no doubt suggests that he is at this point far from being in control, and hence a long way from rehabilitation.

Before analyzing events after this crisis it is worth looking briefly at the first third of the work which traces the process by which the hero makes a name for himself, as that process gives us an insight into the mind later shocked into total self-isolation. Although we lack the opening verses of Hartmann's version, which may well have provided valuable information on the German poet's principles in adapting Chrétien's narrative for his own (or his patron's) purposes, the plot is intact: the hero suffers a slight to his honor and sets out to gain satisfaction by challenging the knight responsible, Iders, whom he defeats in an encounter which establishes Erec's warrior credentials. A "love interest" is already present in the form of the beautiful Enite, at first simply the partner necessary for Erec's challenge to Iders, but in the course of events the object of his desire and love, and a fitting bride in a magnificent wedding celebration provided by

King Arthur. During the combat with Iders, and then in the brilliant victories in tournaments, the crucial interplay between deeds of knighthood and love is apparent: the hero draws strength from his loving partner, whose support inspires him to win honor in combat. Precisely this interrelationship is upset in the subsequent crisis, when Erec loses honor and prestige because his love prevents him from testing his warrior qualities in combat.

Certain features of the plot up to this point merit further comment. At her first appearance, the beautiful Enite who is later to captivate almost every male who sees her, is in abject poverty, forced by circumstances to act as groom to Erec's horse, however much the hero may protest at the inappropriateness of her service. Further, she is virtually excluded from dialogue; indeed, until the later crisis when she must reveal to Erec his loss of honor, the only words accorded her are "herre, daz tuon ich" (My lord, I'll do so, 322). Erec, on the other hand, appears somewhat brash, quick to feel embarrassment (there are far more references to his "shame" than there are in Chrétien), but reacting in a positive way to real or potential slights to his honor by pursuing public recognition as a knight. By the time he can return to his own court at Karnant he is fêted as a paragon of Arthurian and courtly ideals, possessing wisdom, good looks, strength and generosity. The subsequent loss of his reputation must appear all the more crushing to a young knight used to acclaim from all quarters, but it is significant that for once, he appears to feel no shame.

The narrator gives us no inkling of his motivation, but in imposing "dise kumberlîche spaehe" (this burdensome whim, 3103) of silence on Enite Erec seems to try to revert to the circumstances of their first meeting, her quiet acceptance of his authority, which is then reinforced with her inappropriate service as groom for horses. Whether Erec is rational enough to impose these hardships as some sort of punishment, wrongly concluding that she is responsible for his disgrace, or whether he feels her sexuality is the source of his problem and needs to be suppressed — hence his insistence not only on her silence, but also on her keeping her distance from him by riding ahead while traveling and eating and sleeping apart — is not clear. What is clear is that in spite of raging outbursts of frustration, culminating in almost demented fury ("sîn zorn wart grôz und ungemach / und unsenfter dan ê" [his rage became extremely disturbing, harsher than before, 4263]), his will is continually thwarted, on the one hand by Enite's concern for his physical safety, which overrides her obligation to obey him, and, more important, by external forces, such as the need to give away some of the horses and thus alleviate Enite's burden (3576–79). That Erec's abuse of his wife's station is evidence of his own state of disorientation is clear also from the narrator's comment (3460–71) that, no matter what hardship Enite might endure, she enjoyed the protection of *vrou Sælde* (Lady Providence) and *diu gotes hövescheit* (God's courtliness), the latter a concept which may well have been a novel idea in a society conditioned to assuming worldly values such as courtliness could jeopardize one's hopes of salvation.

In the hands of master story tellers such as Chrétien, Hartmann, and their followers, the courtly romance organizes external episodes of plot in a pattern that illustrates the inner world of characters, their psychological state. It has long been recognized, for example, that the narrative *Erec* is structured so that the episodes after the hero's crisis follow a double cycle, with a return to the Arthurian circle forming a sort of axis.[9] Before that return, Erec's encounter firstly with robbers, second with a count bent on seizing Enite, and thirdly with King Guivreiz, reflect a progression from crude violence (robbers) through misguided aristocratic love (the Count) to royal chivalry. Immediately after being lured into a premature meeting with the Arthurian circle, Erec's journey takes him through a duplicate, but intensified cycle: pure violence in the form of giants, misguided aristocratic love leading to marriage by force (Count Oringles) and a second encounter with Guivreiz which results in Erec being defeated.

The second cycle shows the hero gradually regaining his awareness of responsibility, and this turn is clearly marked in Hartmann's version in a number of ways: 1) The central motif, Erec's insistence on his wife's silence, disappears without comment. 2) In the encounter with giants, Erec *chooses* to become involved, rather than allowing events to dictate involvement, and further, he responds to the sound of a woman's voice, whereas he had previously sought to silence Enite's warnings. 3) Likewise in this first episode of the new cycle, the hero who had previously appeared to shun communication with the outside world now tries to engage in dialogue with the giants, as an alternative to combat. 4) As justification for not wanting to join the Arthurian circle, Erec stresses first that he is determined to avoid *gemach* (leisure, 4978) and secondly that he cannot radiate *vreude*, the mood of joy which life at court demands (5052–67); both these terms echo the earlier crisis, when Erec's devotion to leisure had deprived his court of pleasure.[10] 5) Perhaps most significant of all, Erec's victory over the giants reveals that he now has the support of that God of courtliness who had previously protected Enite from Erec's own unjustified punishment.

These and other nuances in Hartmann's text point to subtle changes in the hero's self-awareness by the time he sets out on the second cycle of adventures, changes which lead to his recovery from a death-like state in the Oringles episode, in response to the sound of Enite's long-suppressed voice, his admission of defeat at the hands of Guivreiz, and his reconciliation with Enite after begging her forgiveness. Whereas the first cycle had seen him physically victorious, but mentally disoriented, this sequence of physical and psychological setbacks paradoxically demonstrates his moral readiness to meet the final challenge in his return to honor, the contest with Mabonagrin, whose isolation from society and destruction of courtly joy caricature Erec's own position earlier. In defeating him Erec becomes the champion ordained by God to restore courtly joy, demonstrating the worth of the responsible knight in maintaining social harmony, a message Hartmann no doubt hoped would be taken to heart by the unrulier elements in his audience.

Gregorius

What sort of audience might have appreciated Hartmann's narrative *Gregorius* can of course only be guessed at, but the plot and the tone surely suggest a more diverse one, or at least one for whom the celebration of chivalric values is of less importance than for those who listened to his *Erec*. Gregorius is the product of an incestuous relationship between a brother and his sister, who are advised to surrender the infant Gregorius to God's protection by sending him out to sea. He is found by fishermen and given to an abbey, where he becomes a brilliant pupil. On learning that he is a foundling, however, he persuades the abbot to let him seek his fortune as a knight. He then arrives unwittingly in his mother's territory, and is able to rescue her from an unwanted suitor, before marrying her. On learning to his horror that he has unknowingly committed incest,[11] he seeks God's forgiveness in a life of deprivation, chained to a rock in the wilderness; here he survives miraculously for seventeen years, until God, amid numerous indications of the hero's sanctity, chooses him to be pope.

Sometimes referred to as a "courtly legend," because it is set in an aristocratic world but with a hero who has many of the characteristics of a medieval saint, *Gregorius* must have been a popular narrative; it survives complete in six MSS and in five further fragments. Of course the hero is again high-born, since the audience would expect nothing less, and Gregorius is also successful as a knight. But Hartmann's chief concern in this work is one relevant to Christians of all social strata: the need for strong religious faith in the face of events that might undermine that faith. That his hero is an aristocrat who becomes a knight is, however, not incidental. Not only does this capture a specific audience; it also means that the test to the hero's faith is all the more difficult, given the fact that he must turn his back on glittering success in the world, as well as in the abbey. When finally elevated to the papacy, Gregorius is thus in an ideal position to judge his fellow man, having experience of both the secular and the spiritual worlds.

Given its clear theological message, it is surprising that *Gregorius* has given rise to widely different interpretations.[12] One reason for this is the severity of Gregorius's self-imposed penance for a sin committed in ignorance: after seventeen years of exposure to the elements on a barren rock he is still reluctant to believe the papal envoys that God could consider him as a potential pope. Because contemporary practice would not have demanded such penance, some modern interpretations have argued that Gregorius must have contributed to his sinful state, for example by deciding to leave the safe confines of the abbey where his upbringing had prepared him for a spiritual career. The argument with his spiritual father, the abbot, which leads to this decision, thus became, in some scholars' minds, the fateful turning point where the hero chooses a secular career as knight-errant and thus exposes himself to danger in the world. Hartmann's narrative was even seen as a warning against secular pursuits in general, including the aristocratic courtly and chivalric culture so celebrated in *Erec*.[13]

More recent studies take a more balanced view. The following points should be borne in mind: 1) If Gregorius is at fault in leaving the abbey, he nowhere acknowledges this fault, as he surely would do as a first step on the road to penance. Nor, incidentally, does his mother acknowledge any of the mistakes sometimes imputed to her, such as inadequate penance for her earlier incest with her brother. It is precisely the feeling that they are "innocent" sinners which heightens the danger of their losing faith in God. The reaction of both characters to the realization of their "sin" in marrying, is one of bewilderment that they could have been led to this in spite of their good intentions. 2) The penance which Gregorius suggests for his mother does not differ markedly from that given after her first incest, and does not recommend rejection of her worldly status. He thus confirms what she herself believes: her previous penitent attitude had been the right one. 3) The severity of the penance Gregorius imposes on himself is surely a mark of his heroic stature; he has excelled at everything in his earlier life, is now destined for the papacy, and therefore should not be judged by normal standards. He is superhuman particularly in his sensitivity to sin, which makes him also an exemplary pope. 4) The spiritual way of life Gregorius rejects on leaving the abbey is by no means idealized. The brotherhood are not above making fun of an uneducated fisherman's speech, the abbot shows a skill bordering on usury in increasing the assets left Gregorius by his mother, and he tries to keep Gregorius at the abbey with temptations of power, influence, comfort (*guot gemach!*) and a rich marriage (1468–73, 1654–74). Moreover, the circumstances that provide Gregorius with the opportunity to become pope reflect poorly on the established Church: Rome is riven with strife between various claimants who seek the office for the wealth and prestige it offers (3146–54).

For Hartmann, then, there is no "right" path that involves rejecting the world and embracing a spiritual way of life. It is more likely that Hartmann's intention is to show how a superior individual, one who makes good decisions and acts in accordance with what he believes to be

God's will, can be faced with a state of unwilled sinfulness which will test his faith and prove him worthy of the highest office.

Der arme Heinrich

Hartmann's *Der arme Heinrich* numbers only some 1500 lines of rhymed four-stress couplets, and the text presents some difficulties; there are three late manuscripts and three fragments, one of which was discovered only in 1964. The hero is a knight of high birth and exceptional qualities whose world is destroyed when he contracts leprosy. He is told the only cure is the blood of a virgin who is willing to die for him. Realizing the impossibility of finding such a girl, Heinrich is resigned to a humiliating and premature death, and after giving away his worldly possessions he retires to an estate. There the farm manager's daughter overhears the details of his plight and, revealing a spirituality and reasoning far greater than one would expect from an eleven year old, is able to persuade her parents and Heinrich that her sacrifice would benefit all of them. Only when the girl is about to die under the physician's knife in Salerno does Heinrich change his mind and decide to leave his fate up to God. On the way back home he is miraculously cured; he is restored also to his former prestige, and in gratitude, marries the girl.

All of Hartmann's works involve the main characters in a crisis that tests them, of course, and their reaction to that test is as much a part of Hartmann's purpose as their responsibility for the crisis, their "guilt." This is especially true of Heinrich, the hero of this tale which, for modern readers at least, remains Hartmann's most popular narrative. Earlier attempts to read into the narrative an anti-courtly message, namely that Heinrich's problem is some obsessive concern for worldly status, which God punishes with leprosy, are now mostly regarded as simplistic. Of course the hero is again high-born and a glittering paragon of worldly success, who himself comes to confess that his affliction is a just response from God for his failings, but this confession represents the hero's own interpretation of events, an interpretation which, as we shall see, is in several respects flawed. Heinrich's birth, character, and accomplishments, so splendidly enumerated at the beginning of the work, are again exactly what one would expect in a hero to be used as model before a courtly audience, whose members can thus identify all the more readily with the shock Heinrich feels when he is tested by the loss of the world he knows. But that world itself is not the problem; like Gregorius, Heinrich is a hero whose experience is relevant not just to the aristocratic élite, but to mankind in general.

What Heinrich must learn is a new way of seeing, one that distinguishes between how one is perceived by one's peers, and how one is perceived by God, the difference between outward appearance and the heart within.

The prestige he enjoys initially has, understandably, not prepared him for the loss of "image" which leprosy brings. The affliction is hence a fitting one, causing him to become repellent in the eyes of the very society in which he formerly shone:

> manne unde wîbe
> wart er dô widerzæme
> nû sehet wie genæme
> er ê der werlte wære,
> und wart nû als unmære . . . (122–26)

> [To both man and woman alike he now became repulsive. Just consider how pleasant he had previously been in the world's eyes, and now became just as worthlesss . . .]

The onset of the disease is described in terms of its repellent effect on others, and in the course of his confession Heinrich bitterly laments how even the lowest ranks of society now turn their eyes away. Yet the confession includes a partial realization that there is more than one form of seeing, when Heinrich admits that he had previously not "looked to" God as the source of his blessings (392, 401).[14] The new perception Heinrich needs, however, involves looking at himself from the outside, so to speak; hence the crucial scene in the physician's chambers in Salerno is carefully structured so that Heinrich must make an effort to use his eyes to view the girl who is about to die on his behalf, and whose physical beauty, in contrast to his own deformed and disease-ridden body, paradoxically enables him to look through the surface to accept God's will (1241–56). That such "insight" is pleasing to God is confirmed immediately afterwards in the term *cordis speculator* ("viewer of the heart," 1357) for Christ, who intervenes to cure Heinrich.

The danger of despair, a central issue in *Gregorius*, is also touched on in this work. In the course of his confession Heinrich laments that his foolishness has destroyed his chance of spiritual salvation; God, the lofty gatekeeper (of paradise) has shut Heinrich out forever. Here, too, the final scene in Salerno highlights a limitation in Heinrich's earlier view of things. The metaphor of the gatekeeper occurs again (1358), merged with the metaphor of *cordis speculator*, to underline the infinite compassion of Christ in seeing into and entering the hearts of any who demonstrate that same compassion.

The nameless heroine who provides Heinrich with the opportunity to see things with fresh eyes is an interesting figure, particularly in a work written for an aristocratic public. Although of much inferior social status, she dominates the narrative for lengthy periods, and is allowed one final outburst in Salerno which serves as the last test of Heinrich's new-found perspective: she reminds him of the worldly status which Heinrich seems to be forfeiting, and of the new threat to his image in society if he breaks his

promise to her, all of which the hero accepts with the equanimity he previously lacked. Since she is disdainful of all worldly values she has been seen
as a saint-like figure and as a positive model for Heinrich, but this view
overlooks the fact that the hero himself does not hear her tirade against the
world, however miraculously mature and theologically sound her argument
may be. She needs this spiritual wisdom to convince her parents that she is
capable of choosing to die for Heinrich, who is completely unaware of her
religious fervor until her outburst after he has already "seen the light."

Iwein

With his *Iwein* (ca. 1200) Hartmann returns to the Arthurian romance
and to Chrétien de Troyes as his source. To judge from the relatively high
number of manuscripts that have survived, and from the number of later
poets who seem to be acquainted with it, *Iwein* was probably Hartmann's
most popular work in his own day. The plot follows a similar pattern to
that of *Erec*, with a hero who initially accepts a challenge which had proved
too much for a fellow Arthurian knight, Kalogrenant: Iwein defeats and
kills Askalon in combat and thus establishes his reputation as a warrior of
distinction. At the same time he acquires a beautiful wife in Askalon's
widow, Laudine, who thus completes the idyll by providing love to go with
his undoubted prowess as knight. A crisis sees him deprived of both, and
temporarily of his sanity as well, and there follows a chain of adventures
that enables him gradually to rehabilitate himself.

The nature of Iwein's crisis is not so self-evident, since the narrator does
not directly comment on the hero's offence as he does in *Erec*, nor is that
offence something that attracts the condemnation of society. Indeed, no less
a figure than Gawein, the Arthurian knight generally regarded as the
embodiment of chivalry, is responsible for persuading the newly married
Iwein to avoid the perils of self-indulgence which had cost Erec his honor,
by following him to the tournaments where he can continue to prove his
warrior credentials, and it is ironically Gawein again who so encourages
Iwein in his pursuit of chivalric honors that the latter forgets the promise he
had made to his wife Laudine not to absent himself from her for more than
a year. The crisis thus raises questions about chivalry itself, and suggests that
deeds of knighthood need to be balanced with an awareness of personal
responsibility. Laudine sends her confidante Lunete to publicly rebuke Iwein
and renounce him, whereupon he loses his sanity and all trappings of honor.

In fact, however, Hartmann's public would have already been encouraged to re-examine their understanding of chivalry in the episode which
initially launches Iwein on his pursuit of honor: Kalogrenant's account of
his unsuccessful challenge to Askalon includes a meeting with a wild man
of the forest, to whom Kalogrenant must explain his pursuit of honor

in terms which reveal the potential irresponsibility of knightly combat. That Iwein himself is later reduced, in his period of insanity, to the same "uncivilized" state as the wild man (he is forced to live in the wilderness), and becomes, as the wild man had been, "gelîch eim môre" in appearance (like a moor, 3348), illustrates once again the medieval poet's skill in linking episodes of the narrative to suggest a deeper meaning: Iwein must shed the outward trappings of civilized courtly and chivalric society, his clothing, manners, speech, even his mental faculties, before he can begin to reconstruct a model of behavior which takes into account the needs of others, rather than the knight's personal drive for prestige.

Thus the adventures that follow Iwein's crisis and recovery all show the hero at the service of others. Various heroic acts of liberation culminate in a final scene in which he and his wife seek mutual forgiveness and are reconciled. As in *Erec*, it is possible to see in the sequence of victories a pattern that throws light on Iwein's earlier immaturity. There is an intricate interplay between actual deeds of chivalry on the one hand, and promises of help on the other. Thus, Iwein's promise to champion his wife's confidante Lunete cannot be fulfilled until after an adventure involving the giant Harpin, and his undertaking to help the younger of two countesses in a further trial by combat is in danger of being unfulfilled because of yet another intervening adventure, the liberation of three-hundred ladies held hostage by two giants as virtual slave labor. What Iwein must learn then, is how to manage his obligations, how to balance the calls on his chivalry in terms of timing, precisely the issue which had destroyed the trust between himself and his wife earlier.[15]

It is significant, too, that there is again an axis midway through the hero's journey of rehabilitation, similar to Erec's unwilling return to the Arthurian circle, when Iwein meets the wife from whom he is officially estranged, and who at this point does not "recognize" him. Iwein's shame at his disgrace will not allow him to identify himself; he prefers to be known by his companion the lion, who has been variously interpreted as a symbol of God or Christ, of justice, or of loyalty. By the end of his travels Iwein can dispense with the lion's assistance, although anonymity still plays a part in the final combat with his good friend Gawein. Although neither emerges officially as the victor, Gawein acknowledges that he has been championing an unjust cause and deserves defeat, and at the same time he publicly identifies "der rîter mittem leun" (the knight with the lion) as the warrior Iwein (7752–62).

Although this public rehabilitation is followed by Iwein's private reconciliation with his wife Laudine, however, there are enough inconsistencies to suggest that Hartmann was not entirely successful in reconciling the Arthurian world of chivalric prestige with the current culture of courtly love. If in earlier rejecting Iwein for his offence, Laudine had appeared as the proud mistress endowed by Love with authority over the male lover, she inexplicably submits to a plea for forgiveness in the final scene, nor can the reconciliation itself appear entirely convincing, when it is brought about by manipulation of a promise. Further, the Iwein who himself had earlier declared that he was not to blame for losing his wife's favor, now admits the opposite. Like the narrator's belated and unmotivated reference in *Erec* to the hero's "test" of his wife's loyalty (6781), such inconsistencies may be due to the fact that Hartmann and his contemporaries felt bound to pay lip service to conflicting versions of the tales, some of them transmitted in the traditional oral fashion, but all needing to be taken into account in this emerging art form of courtly literature.

Hartmann was already considered by his near-contemporary Gottfried von Strassburg to be an example fit to be followed by the finest poets. To have one's style lauded by the stylist *par excellence* Gottfried must be seen as high praise indeed, but it is interesting that Gottfried also admires Hartmann's ability to imbue his narratives with a deeper meaning. Although his longer romances were not among those adapted by the great popularizer of medieval themes in the nineteenth century, Richard Wagner, his shorter works *Gregorius* and especially *Heinrich* proved very influential as inspiration for writers and dramatists from the Romantic period on, among them Gerhart Hauptmann, Ricarda Huch, Thomas Mann, and, most recently, Tankred Dorst.

Notes

[1] A good introduction to Hartmann, with relevant scholarship, is Christoph Cormeau and Wilhelm Störmer, *Hartmann von Aue: Epoche–Werk–Wirkung* (Munich: Beck, 2nd ed. 1993). Two more recent surveys are Will Hasty, *Adventures in Interpretation: The Works of Hartmann von Aue and Their Critical Reception* (Columbia, SC: Camden House, 1996), and Petra Hörner, ed., *Hartmann von Aue: Mit einer Bibliographie 1976–1997* (Frankfurt am Main: Lang, 1998).

[2] Hartmann's works are cited here from the following editions: *Erec*, ed. Christoph Cormeau and Kurt Gärtner (Tübingen: Niemeyer, 1985); *Gregorius*, ed. Friedrich Neumann (Stuttgart: Reclam, 1963); *Der arme Heinrich*, ed. Ursula Rautenberg (Stuttgart: Reclam, 1993); *Iwein*, ed. Benecke/Lachmann/Wolff (Berlin: de Gruyter, 1968); *Lieder*, ed. Ernst von Reusner (Stuttgart: Reclam, 1985). English translations of all Hartmann's narratives are available in *The Narrative Works of Hartmann von Aue. Translated by R. W. Fisher* (Göppingen: Kümmerle, 1983). All translations are by R. F.

[3] See Günther Schweikle, "Der Stauferhof und die mhd. Lyrik, im besonderen zur Reinmar-Walther-Fehde und zu Hartmanns *herre*," in Günther Schweikle, *Minnesang in neuer Sicht* (Stuttgart/Weimar: Metzler 1994), 67–88; on the chronology of Hartmann's works see also Jean Marc Pastré, "Le Gregorius, la croisade et la chronologie des oeuvres de Hartmann von Aue," *La croisade: realites*

et fictions; notes du colloques d'Amiens, 18–22 mars 1987, ed. Danielle Buschinger (Göppingen: Kümmerle, 1989), 183–92.

[4] See Helmut De Boor, *Die höfische Literatur: Vorbereitung, Blüte, Ausklang,* 5th ed. (Munich: Beck, 1962), 73.

[5] Reusner's designations of Hartmann's songs with Roman numerals is based on the same designations in the standard edition of the songs in *Minnesangs Frühling,* ed. Karl Lachmann, Moriz Haupt, Friedrich Vogt, and Carl von Kraus, 37th rev. ed. by Hugo Moser and Helmut Tervooren (Stuttgart: Hirzel, 1982).

[6] For an assessment of the relationship between Hartmann and his source, see the introduction of Michael Resler's translation of Hartmann's *Erec* (New York: Garland, 1987).

[7] The sociological background of Hartmann's works is well treated by W. H. Jackson, *Chivalry in Twelfth-century Germany: The Works of Hartmann von Aue* (Cambridge: Brewer, 1994).

[8] For the relevance of Celtic sources to this and other motifs in the romances, see Dagmar Ó Riain-Raedel, *Untersuchungen zur mythischen Struktur der mittel-hochdeutschen Artusepen* (Berlin: E. Schmidt, 1978).

[9] Hugo Kuhn, "Erec," in Hugo Kuhn, *Dichtung und Welt im Mittelalter* (Stuttgart: Metzler, 1959), 130–50.

[10] See Sylvia Ranawake, "Erec's *verligen* and the Sin of Sloth," in *Hartmann von Aue, Changing Perspectives: London Hartmann Symposium, 1985,* ed. Timothy McFarland and Sylvia Ranawake (Göppingen: Kümmerle, 1988), 93–116.

[11] A unifying and important element in the tale is the tablet sent out to sea with the infant Gregorius and containing vital information about his noble but sinful origins. The hero is confronted with it in his argument with his spiritual father the abbot, consults it and weeps over it while married to his mother, and loses it while hastening to begin his penance; when he miraculously recovers it unscathed after seventeen years it is regarded as a sign that Gregorius is indeed a man chosen by God for a higher purpose.

[12] See, for example, Hildegard Nobel, "Schuld und Sühne in Hartmanns Gregorius und in der frühscholastischen Theologie," *Zeitschrift für deutsche Philologie* 76 (1957): 42–79.

[13] The most detailed interpretation along these lines, with compendious references to theological literature, was that of Ulrich Ernst, "Der Antagonismus von *vita carnalis* und *vita spiritualis* im *Gregorius* Hartmanns von Aue," *Euphorion* 72 (1978): 160–226, *Euphorion* 73 (1979): 1–105. But see also the more recent review of interpretations by Oliver Hallich, *Poetologisches, Theologisches: Studien zum Gregorius Hartmanns von Aue* (Frankfurt am Main: Lang, 1995).

[14] See also David Duckworth, "Heinrich and the Godless Life in Hartmann's Poem," *Mediaevistik* 3 (1990): 71–90.

[15] A recent study argues that Iwein must acquire discernment, the ability to find the right answers amid conflicting moral demands; see Sabine Heimann-Seelbach, "Calculus Minervae: Zum prudentiellen Experiment im *Iwein* Hartmanns von Aue," *Euphorion* 95 (2001): 263–85.

Gottfried von Strassburg. A miniature from the Codex Manesse (364r).

Gottfried von Strassburg and the Tristan Myth

Rüdiger Krohn

B EHIND THE MYTH OF TRISTAN AND ISOLDE is an Occidental tradition of thinking according to which marriage and love are mutually exclusive. This tradition was already formulated in a provocative way by Andreas Capellanus around 1200 in his theoretical treatise on love, *De amore libri tres*,[1] and it was given a broader cultural and socio-historical legitimacy in 1939 by Denis de Rougemont.[2] Nowhere has the contradiction between the universally binding demands of society and the autonomously postulated desire of the individual been so sharply formulated as in the Tristan romances. Each of these romances depicts in its own way the story of the adulterous love of Tristan and Isolde, which begins when they unintentionally drink a magical love potion, and the lovers' subsequent ongoing deception of Isolde's husband King Marke and indeed of the entire court; in most of the extant romances this story is preceded by the story of Tristan's parents, also one of illegitimate and ultimately unhappy love, and followed by that of Tristan's relationship with Isolde White Hands, whose rivalry with Tristan's true love (Isolde "la blonde") ultimately leads to the lovers' tragic end. Each romance endeavors in its own way either to soften the scandal of an idealized adultery into an eruption of demonic forces, as these slumber for example in the love potion, or to formulate it provocatively as a sovereignty of the senses, which cancels the laws of collective order and even renders such laws unjust. The alarmingly timeless power of the material lies in its "doppelte Wahrheit" (double truth),[3] which is provocatively developed as the contradiction between the demands of love and those of society. No work went further in radicalizing this conflict between norms and drives than Gottfried von Strassburg's *Tristan*. Because it renders the destructive power of sexuality as the reason for the tragedy of Tristan and Isolde, Gottfried's poem has occasionally been seen by scholars as a work that belongs more to modern times than to the Middle Ages.[4]

It is precisely the modern readers who have had their own significant problems on moral grounds with Gottfried's *Tristan*. The beginnings of the academic discipline of *Germanistik* were shaped by patriotic efforts to unearth the sunken treasures of the old German past. Results of this effort in epic poetry were the *Nibelungenlied* and the works of Hartmann von Aue and Wolfram von Eschenbach, but the first scholars of *Germanistik*, with conspicuous accord, avoided Gottfried's romance, clearly influenced by the condemnation of the great philologist Karl Lachmann, who in 1820 had valued "die gehaltene, verständig geschmückte Darstellungsweise" (controlled, judiciously adorned style) of this work, but nevertheless issued the following consequential criticism with regard to the subject matter: "anderes, als Üppigkeit und Gotteslästerung, boten die Haupttheile seiner weichlichen unsittlichen Erzählung nicht dar" (the principle parts of his soft immoral story offered nothing more than voluptuousness and blasphemy).[5] This split between great admiration for Gottfried's formal artistry and the aesthetic refinement of his depiction, on the one hand,[6] and indignant rejection of his supposed immorality on the other, shaped the reception of his *Tristan* through the nineteenth and twentieth centuries.[7]

To understand Gottfried's importance in the development of the Tristan material (*Stoff*) in German literature, it is helpful to place him in the tradition from which he draws and which he transforms with his fragmentary romance. Despite the difficulties in reconstructing the origins and later development of the Tristan myth, a model has developed in the critical literature[8] that posits the Celtic origins of the material,[9] and on this foundation further posits three (by no means proven) stages in the development of the Tristan material.[10] First, an archaic Celtic stage that tells the story in two independent plot lines, *immram* (a maritime voyage into the unknown, that is, Tristan's first trip to Ireland to heal his poisoned wound) and *aithed* (a narrative of refuge taking, that is, the forest life of the lovers); next, an older epic, which by introducing the love potion and linking the originally independent parts of the narrative represents the Ur-version proper of the later Tristan story; and, finally, an (again postulated) later continuation, which adds the story of Tristan's parents to the beginning and does not have the story end with the forest life, but rather with the return of the lovers to court, their separation, and the Isolde White Hands episode. In this third version of the material scholars have wanted to see that *estoire* that presumably served as the original version on which the later Tristan stories were based and which is mentioned twice by the Norman Béroul in the preserved fragments of his twelfth-century romance.[11] Unfortunately, neither the dating of his work, which is characterized by a simple sequence of episodes and a heroic manner of epic depiction, has been established with certainty, nor is it known whether there were other, similar written or oral versions of the material besides Béroul's. Consequently, there is no concrete evidence about the degree to which the early German courtly poet Eilhart, in his *Tristrant*, may have followed Béroul, and possibly also other related sources.[12]

Some scholars have argued that the poet Eilhart was the *ministerialis* Eilhardus de Oberch (or one of his relatives), who is documented in the village of Oberg between 1189 and 1209.[13] This man was connected to the Welf court in Brunswick, a plausible and inviting connection with regard to the history of the Tristan material, because it suggests that Eilhart may have come to the Tristan story by way of Mathilde, the wife of the Welf prince Heinrich der Löwe (and daughter of the English Queen Eleanore of Aquitaine).[14] The Tristan romance of Thomas of Britain also enjoyed great popularity at about the same time and also served as Gottfried's source.

Eilhart explains at the beginning of his romance that it is about *man-heit* and *minnen* — heroic deeds and love.[15] This action-oriented romance arranges the episodes, in which Tristant overcomes all obstacles for the sake of his love to Isolde and thanks to his cunning and courage, into a highly suspenseful series of adventures. Because it seems frequently to be aimed above all at entertainment, scholars have long been critical of Eilhart's effort, which they viewed exclusively in its function as a prede-cessor to Gottfried.[16] Only gradually and recently have scholars begun to appreciate the unique literary and innovative value of *Tristrant*.[17] Eilhart tailors his rendition of the heroic deeds of the protagonist to the tastes of audiences schooled on the sensational events of the heroic epics, and he takes steps to remove the stain of adultery from the lovers and to portray their forbidden love in the best possible light. This goal was served by the reference to the overpowering influence of the love elixir in the traditional material. In Béroul's version, the influence of the potion lasts three years, and Eilhart extends this to four years, after which the effects abate, but never entirely cease. The exculpating power of the elixir justifies the trans-gression of the lovers, but it also manifests the destructive erotic power to which the lovers are subjected without any possibility of resistance: "sô grôz was die minne / undir in âne iren dang: / daz hâte gemachit der trang" (so great was the love between them in spite of themselves — the love potion had done that).[18]

Scholars have considered Eilhart's *Tristrant*, along with Béroul's romance, as belonging to a presumably more primitive, rough-hewn *ver-sion commune*, while Thomas and Gottfried's versions are generally con-sidered representatives of a finer and more elegant *version courtoise*. This differentiation, which has always also been an aesthetic judgment, is no longer supported by some recent scholars, such as Danielle Buschinger,[19] who has placed Eilhart's version in the tradition of the *adaptation cour-toise*. The view of Eilhart's archaic manner of depiction as a sign of a regressive, pre-courtly narration has also been brought into question by the insight that the author may intentionally have employed techniques of oral narration, thus feigning orality as a stylistic strategy.[20] The small num-ber of manuscripts is not reflective of its enthusiastic reception in the Middle Ages. It is significant that the continuators of Gottfried's fragment return to Eilhart as a source, and that the anonymous New High German prose romance of which no fewer than sixteen prints are preserved from between 1484 and 1664 was mainly influenced by the first German version of the Tristan material.[21]

It is difficult to know if Gottfried von Strassburg knew Eilhart's version of the story. Gottfried clearly distances himself from some of the earlier versions (131–34), and Eilhart's may have been among them. While it is difficult to know which predecessor(s) Gottfried is criticizing, the source that he is following is indisputable. No one, he says in the prologue, has told the story as correctly as Thomas:

> der âventiure meister was
> und an britûnschen buochen las
> aller der lantherren leben
> und ez uns ze künde hât gegeben. (150–54)

[who was a master-romancer and had read in books the lives of all those princes of the Britons and made them known to us.][22]

Little is known about this Thomas who names himself twice in his *Tristan* (which is also preserved only in fragments). The appellation "von Britanje" helps little, for it can designate the British Isles as well as Brittany. He presumably worked in the second half of the twelfth century for an Anglo-Norman audience at the court of Henry II (Plantagenet), whose literary taste was largely shaped by his wife, Eleanore of Aquitaine, but this assumption is based above all on the fact that Thomas praises the English capital London in his work and that he gives his hero Tristan the cross of the Angevin house.[23] The dating of his *Tristan* is also uncertain, but it is likely that it was composed around 1170 or even earlier.[24] That would mean that is arose possibly at the same time as Eilhart's first German version, which throws an interesting light on the temporal proximity of two fundamentally different versions of the traditional material.

Thomas clearly adapted the Tristan material to the finer tastes and the literary "Erwartungshorizont" (horizon of expectations) of a courtly audience. He endeavors to achieve psychological depth, avoids unrealistic details, and softens contradictions that result from the competing strands of pre-courtly Tristan narratives. Especially the depiction of the forest life is given new meaning. Whereas the episode was depicted in the versions of Béroul and Eilhart as a time of bitter privation and hard suffering, Thomas (and more explicitly Gottfried) render this exile of the lovers as a time of idyllic harmony and idealized happiness.[25] The most striking and consequential change that Thomas makes in the traditional material concerns the effects of the love elixir: with him (as also with Gottfried), the effects are not temporary, but permanent. In this way, the exculpatory function of the temporary condition of Tristan's love is removed, and the elemental, socially destructive force is given greater weight. In this way, Thomas (and subsequently Gottfried) places himself in opposition to the value system of the courtly romances, and this opposition is significant enough to raise doubts about the "courtly" character of Thomas's *Tristan*.[26] This is even truer for Gottfried's poem, which transforms the material in an entirely different way,[27] due to the significant touches that the Middle High German poet has added to his source (as a comparative view of the recently discovered Carlisle fragment of Thomas's *Tristan* shows: in the crucial scene involving the love potion and the play on words with *lameir*, the obvious differences between Thomas's and Gottfried's version indicate that the German author stresses the idea of mutuality in his conception of love more than his French predecessor). Whether the sharpening of the inherent conflict rests on an anti-courtly sentiment on the part of the poet has remained a matter of debate in the critical literature. Gottfried's *Tristan* diverges from the norms and expectations of its time even as it remains indebted to them in important respects, thus revealing its position between the traditional spirit of the Middle Ages and the turn towards a new idea of the world that is characteristic of the Renaissance. This impressive project gives Gottfried, despite the narrow and somewhat obscure oeuvre attributed to him, a singular place in the literature of the High Middle Ages as the poet who gave the Tristan material its "klassische Form."[28]

Gottfried's poetic oeuvre is not voluminous in comparison with other epic poets of the *Blütezeit*, such as Hartmann von Aue and Wolfram von Eschenbach. Whether it is due to poor transmission of his works or to limited productivity of the poet, posterity knows and praises only his fragmentary *Tristan*. Whether he also composed lyric poetry (as other epic poets of his day) remains uncertain. Rudolf von Ems mentions in his *Alexander* (after 1230) that "der wîse meister Gotfrit" (wise master Gottfried) wrote a didactic poem called "daz glesîn gelücke" (glass fortune),[29] and such a poem is indeed included in the Codex Manesse. Though Ulrich von Liechtenstein is named there as the author, scholarship has arrived on the basis of internal and external criteria at the conclusion that the strophe in question is to be attributed to Gottfried (along with the preceding strophe in the same Ton or melody).[30] Both strophes about *valsch* (falsity), *anderunge* (change), and the transitoriness of happiness can be read as a melancholy motto of the story of Tristan and Isolde, and a textual passage such as "Vröide gît den smerzen" (joy gives pain) expresses the idea of the unavoidable mixture of happiness and suffering that the author in the prologue of his romance makes the distinguishing attribute of true love.[31] Gottfried there describes the ideal lovers for which his romance is aiming, as people who are prepared to accept the togetherness of joy and pain that is inherent in love, because,

> swem nie von liebe leit geschah,
> dem geschah ouch liep von liebe nie.
> liep und leit diu wâren ê
> an minnen ungescheiden. (204–7)

[He who never had sorrow of love never had joy of it either! In love, joy and sorrow ever went hand in hand!]

Gottfried differentiates these chosen people from the incompetent masses of those, "diu keine swaere enmüge getragen / und niwan in vröuden welle sweben" (who are unable to endure sorrow and wish only to revel in bliss, 53–54), with which he may well mean the courtly world and its orientation towards superficial distraction. With a high degree of linguistic virtuosity and a cascade of oxymora he sets off from this the audience that he imagines for his work as,

> ein ander welt [. . .]
> diu samet in eime herzen treit
> ir süeze sûr, ir liebez leit
> ir herzeliep, ir senede nôt,
> ir liebez leben, ir leiden tôt,
> ir lieben tôt, ir leidez leben. (58–63)

[another world, which together in one heart bears its bitter-sweet, its dear sorrow, its heart's joy, its love's pain, its dear life, its sorrowful death, its dear death, its sorrowful life.]

The life, social position, and personality of Gottfried remain obscure, though some information can be gleaned from his own work and from references to him in the works of contemporaries and successors. The dating of *Tristan* is also uncertain. Literary references, the references to known poets in his *Literaturexkurs* (literary excursus, 4621–4820) and, above all, the polemical references to Wolfram von Eschenbach (as which they have been almost unanimously understood in the critical literature) which run through the romance, make a dating around 1210 to 1215 likely. But even this dating is by no means certain, for it is based on the uncertain, relative chronology of German court poetry in general.[32] Also, the connection between the episode of the ordeal and its commentary in *Tristan*, and the trials of heretics in Strasbourg in 1212, remains unproven.[33] This link would suggest a somewhat later dating, possibly after the Lateran council of 1215, at which the legal institution of the trial by ordeal was forbidden. A dating of *Tristan* after 1212 is supported by the thesis that there are intentional parallels between the rise of the extraordinary titular hero and the life of the charismatic Hohenstaufen emperor Friedrich II, who put an end to the rule of the Welfs in Germany in 1212.[34]

Gottfried's provenance as living in or having been born in Strasbourg is based solely on his name, which is used by a number of poets and also appears in the manuscripts A and C. The transmission of the unfinished *Tristan*, which with eleven "complete" manuscripts and fifteen fragments is relatively well preserved, also points in this direction, for a large number of the oldest manuscripts are from Alsace or even from Strasbourg itself,[35] even if the work appears to have been circulated beyond the southwest German region.[36] The localization of the author in Strasbourg is also supported by the city's geographical proximity to France with its intellectual and artistic climate and culture of nobility, which runs through Gottfried's work. No chronicle, no official record documents the historical existence of Gottfried.

It was in the production of literature that authors took notice of each other, to praise or to criticize, to accept or reject. It is to such literary references among authors that we owe the clues as to Gottfried's social standing. In contrast to the other great epic authors of the time, he was never given the title *hêr*, which would indicate he belonged to the ministerial class or was a knight. Rather, he is always only mentioned as *meister*, quite conspicuously in the second half of the thirteenth century in a list of authors by Konrad von Stoffeln: "meister Gotfrit und hêr Hartman / von Eschenbach hêr Wolfram."[37] But this designation alone permits no conclusions about social position.[38] It could designate a burgher, a master of some trade, or an especially gifted career poet. It could also designate a man who has studied the *septem artes liberales* and achieved the academic title of *magister*. We can therefore assume that Gottfried was not a member of the nobility and it is likely that the title of *meister* refers to the high level of the author's education, which is also supported by the author's knowledge of literature, his erudition, and his formal artistry. He was familiar with areas such as theology, mythology, music, law, and philosophy, as well as with questions of chivalric practice and courtly living. He was familiar with the ideals of antiquity and his own time, and also with the intellectual controversies of the High Middle Ages, which makes it quite possible that he obtained this knowledge in a Latin school, possibly even at one of the significant universities of the Middle Ages (such as Paris[39]) in close contact with intellectual circles. Because *meister* can also be used as a title for teachers at cathedral and monastery schools, an activity of Gottfried as instructor (*magister puerorum*) has also been considered, without conclusive results.

It is undisputed that *Tristan* demonstrates traces of early scholastic thinking that can be traced to contemporary intellectual developments in France.[40] Indications of heretical ideas have led some scholars to consider that Gottfried sympathized with the heresies of his time (above all with the Cathars).[41] The adulterous betrayal of King Marke by his minion Tristan and his wife Isolde, the thoroughly un-medieval insistence of the lovers on their own individual fulfillment, the denial of the courtly ethos that was otherwise binding in contemporary literature, and the softening of the conventional chivalric values by means of the ambivalent use of central concepts (such as *êre*, *triuwe*, and *edel* — honor, loyalty, nobility),[42] all of this distinguishes this work markedly from the literary culture of its time, which was determined by the rules of an ideal Arthurian world, by the laws of heroic manhood, and the de-sensualized rituals of a happily ascetic love service for ladies. Gottfried employs his deep and considerable knowledge with cool detachment, masterful calculation, and great artistic discipline. Although Wolfram victoriously claims to be a knight and thus sets himself apart from unchivalric "intellectuals" who were exclusively poets, Gottfried never presents himself in any way as a representative or proponent of the feudal life or society that provides the basis of the "classical" romances of Wolfram and Hartmann.

There is reason to believe that Gottfried belonged to circles of cultivated city-dwellers. The thorough education revealed in *Tristan* supports the assumption that Gottfried numbered among the more prosperous, ambitious burghers, who on the one hand based their own norms and values on those of the courtly culture of nobility, but on the other hand sought to replace inherited ideals with their own view of the world. This may be the reason why the author manifests a conspicuous and at times sharp restraint when it comes to the typical set pieces of courtly poetry, as found for example in the Arthurian romances: the sumptuous, evidently highly popular depictions of splendid knightly deeds, the magnificent tournaments, the pompous processions, the clash of swords and armor, the frequent battles that lacked any meaning beyond heroic self-assertion. It was in such an affirmative literary stylization of the world and reality that courtly-aristocratic audiences loved to see themselves glorified. By means of such stylizations, courtiers hoped to find helpful orientation and affirmation in the formation of a new social and cultural identity. To be sure, Gottfried's romance does occasionally move in the direction of such expectations, but more frequently it undermines them and gives traditional conventions new contours and significance. His aim seems to be a pragmatic instrumentalization of force, and the replacement of violence by calculation: military conflict serves concrete political purposes, feuds follow concrete economic or political interests, heroism is directed toward rational ends, battles are decided by prudence and cunning. In this way, the ideal world of Arthurian poetry that was so popular with contemporary audiences is given a realistic accent that it did not previously have. The spirit of a new time, urban virtues of cleverness and mercantile sobriety, can no longer be expressed in the chivalric conception of heroic manly deeds aiming only at honor and fame.

This is especially evident in those passages in which Gottfried intentionally distances himself from his source (to the degree the latter can be reconstructed) — as in the prologue, which is certainly Gottfried's own work, in which he not only conceives his aesthetic program with unparalleled rhetorical brilliance, but at the same time undertakes to delimit himself from an exclusively courtly reception and its characteristic horizon of expectations. His work is directed toward the "edele herzen" (noble hearts, 47), an intellectual elite that is pointedly set off from "ir aller werlde" (the world of the many, 50), which — as indicated above — accepts the necessary connection between *liep* and *leit*, and which is endowed by the author with a heightened aesthetic and ethical sensibility. Regardless of the lively scholarly discussion about whether Gottfried's controversial concept of the *edele herzen* intentionally refers to the mystical idea of the *anima nobilis*, whether it goes back to the antique ideal of a nobility of intellect and virtue (*nobilitas cordis*) that is taken up by Christianity and transmitted into the Middle Ages, or whether the concept can be seen as analogous to the romance term *gentil cor* — it is noteworthy that the author uses the normally quite conventional term *edel* in a way that is not bound exclusively to social class and as a designation of an *inner* nobility. Gottfried turns to a select audience, which although it may be courtly, very likely also included burghers of a somewhat refined mental and intellectual status, those *edele herzen* who, without belonging to nobility, nevertheless corresponded to Gottfried's definition of the new cultural and social ideal.

Gottfried's narrative strategy can be seen against the backdrop of social developments in the early thirteenth century, especially in the city of Strasbourg, in which the middle class was ever more involved in political developments.[43] These socio-historical developments were consciously brought to ambivalent expression in *Tristan*, both in the language and in the accents placed on the content of the story. The work is, despite the numerous qualifications mentioned earlier, a courtly romance, in which the urban upper class was supposed to be able to recognize itself. Correspondingly, Gottfried always makes opportunities for identification in those parts of his story that involve merchants[44] — the occupation to which many of his urban audiences would have belonged. Their admirable manner of living is repeatedly emphasized, even in cases such as the one involving Tristan's abduction by Norwegian merchants. Tristan himself claims to be the son of a merchant (at Marke's court and in Ireland) and amazes the courtiers with the cultivated practices of the merchant class. The author thereby implicitly equates the figure of the prosperous, educated burgher with that of the courtly, aesthetically refined aristocrat, and embarks on a path that shortly thereafter Rudolf von Ems will take in *Der guote Gêrhart* (ca. 1220–25). The question about the identity of the "Dieterich" that is contained in the acrostic of Gottfried's work might be addressed in this broader social context.[45] If this name, about which scholars have long puzzled, refers to the Dietherus cellerarius,[46] who is documented in the monastery of St. Thomas, then this would be a further important support for the thesis that this romance, despite its indebtedness to the traditional material and manner appropriate to the genre, is significantly beholden to the ideas and norms of the prosperous burgher class that was becoming increasingly influential in cities such as Strasbourg. However, to infer a decidedly anti-courtly posture in *Tristan* or to read the romance primarily as the radical testimony of an awakening urban identity would be to misapprehend the conditions under which Gottfried wrote. He could scarcely afford an all-too sharp criticism of the feudal principle.[47]

Not only the propagators of chivalric culture, the *ministeriales* and the lower nobility, employed literature as a manner of determining their own intellectual, political, and cultural standpoint: the prosperous burgher class likewise sought new models of identification and orientation, which it found in the aristocratic culture and in which it found its own social ambitions already expressed. The new upper class ennobled itself by means of the appropriation of a feudal manner of thinking and living. In the interest of this audience, Gottfried could not be bound to a strictly anti-courtly position. But the appropriation of the traditional culture of nobility, which was the broader project of the author and his envisioned audience, occurred by way of the rejection of elements of the originally foreign catalogue of norms that were not reconcilable with the life conditions and beliefs of the new urban upper class.

A central problem for the interpretation and classification of Gottfried's *Tristan* is the changed function that the author gave to the love elixir. Thomas had already suggested that the love of the pair had already begun before the drinking of the elixir. The originally magical power of the drink is displaced by its symbolic meaning. Gottfried, in turn, intentionally leaves the question about the beginning of love undecided, and the continuous intensive scholarly discussion about this can only confirm the success of Gottfried's tactic.[48] Clear indications about the origin of the love are absent, and in the author's abstinence in the clarification of this central question for the understanding of his work lies the revolutionary potential of his version. The effect of the elixir, which in earlier works had aimed apologetically at exculpation, here remains unclear — and at times contradictory. It seems that Gottfried intentionally wishes to leave his listeners in doubt. It is unmistakable that fate has made Tristan and Isolde a perfect pair, destined for one another. Their love consequently seems merely the logical fulfillment of this predestination, the compulsory realization of a foreordained plan, regardless of how this realization is accomplished. In this way the elixir loses its function as the immediate, unique cause of love, and it manifests only marginally the eruption of the demonic into the world of the pair — as when the previously calm water, after Brangaene has thrown the elixir overboard, is transformed into a "tobenden wilden sê" (wild and raging sea, 11695) that symbolizes the irresistible power of the magical mixture. In this key episode, Gottfried depicts love, which is repeatedly personified elsewhere in the romance, as the highest life principle of his figures and thus underscores the elemental power of their passion independent of all demonic influences. This is not a matter of justifying the sensual with some transcendental principle. Rather, Gottfried invokes the primacy of feeling over social demands. The latter are not questioned as values, but they are nevertheless subordinated to love.

A higher destiny is made concrete in a visible way in the elixir, which to this point in the depiction was only hinted at. In their courtly perfection, Tristan and Isolde are love heroes who are quite clearly made for each other. In their undisturbed harmony, the idea of exemplary love is realized. The elixir is necessary as an epic formulation of the overpowering attraction between the two, but also to meet the moral expectations of the courtly audiences by means of superficial dependence on the narrative tradition. The scandal of adulterous love is also relativized by means of the suggestive defamation of its witnesses: the unsympathetic councilors Melot and Marjodo, just as the court as a whole, appear as negative figures, according to the literary tradition of *minnefeinde* (enemies of love), whose meanness manages, by comparison, to cast a positive light on the illegitimate behavior of the lovers. Even the deceived King Marke is so strongly discredited in his weakness and indecision that his moral and legal right to Isolde is implicitly placed in doubt. At the very least, this insinuates the legitimacy of the adulterous relationship.[49]

The strategy of exculpation is also served by Gottfried's depictions of the love episode in the grotto. In a departure from the earlier versions of the Tristan material which depict this time in the forest as one of want and need, Gottfried (like Thomas before him) describes it as a *wunschleben*, superficially a time of untroubled happiness. This lovely idyll in which Tristan and Isolde can apparently dedicate themselves to love after being exiled from Marke's court is related to contemporary cathedral architecture, which Gottfried expounds according to the scheme of tropological-mystical hermeneutics.[50] In this way Gottfried's conception of love appears as an exaltation of love in which the love grotto seems a religious temple — a symbolically laden concretization of the "kingdom of the heart."[51] In his detailed allegorical depiction of the love grotto the author gives every detail of the cave spiritual meaning and thus places the scene of Tristan and Isolde's illegitimate love in the compensatory framework of religious exegesis. This technique culminates in the stylization of the pair to "Minne saints" by means of implicit parallels between the crystal bed that is at the center of the grotto and the religious altar upon which the lovers are portrayed in the manner of an *unio mystica,* and thereby morally exculpated.[52]

At the same time the apparent ideality of the idyll of love is overshadowed by the implication of threats that cast a shadow on the happiness of the lovers and thus make the episode, despite the enumeration of ideal conditions and occupations appear a "beschädigte Utopie" (damaged utopia).[53] Consequently, their love remains imperfect without the necessary authentication and recognition of the court. The court thus has to be replaced. It is the forest birds, trees, and love itself who serve the solitary pair better than "Artûses tavelrunden / und alle ir massenîe" (King Arthur's Round Table and all its company, 16900–1). The emphasis that Gottfried places on the validity of these substitutions for the Round Table only serves to make their insufficiency more evident. The deficiency of their happiness is also revealed by the *senemaere* (love tales) performed by the lovers to pass the time. The ideal, Arcadian ambience of the episode forms an ominous contrast with the couple's preference for sad stories taken from antique mythology about passions ending in death, which typologically anticipate the future fate of the two.[54] In view of doubts such as these, which Gottfried places throughout his depiction of the lover's happiness at the grotto and with which his guiding principle, that joy and pain are inseparable in love, is strengthened, it is not surprising when Tristan and Isolde give up their deficient happiness in the grotto and return to court, when Marke, deceived once again, calls them back: "daz dûhte die gelieben guot / und wurden in ir herzen vrô [. . .] / durch got und durch ir êre" (This met with the lovers' approval, and they were glad of it in their hearts [. . .] for the sake of God and their place in society, 17694ff.).

In the depiction of love between Tristan and Isolde, Gottfried again pursues a double strategy that confirms the ambivalent character of his work: by spiritualizing the love of the pair, he removes it from the domain of moral judgment, but at the same time he makes it evident that the happiness of this love is imperfect because it is not affirmed by courtly society. The provocative claim of Tristan love to realization even against the dictates of society, which Gottfried both sets forth and takes back, bursts the framework of the literary tradition to which the author was indebted. This precarious tightrope walk ends with a fall: the romance remained unfinished, perhaps because its composer saw the paradox into which his conception was leading and in recognition of its foreseeable failure broke off his work. Another speculation that has occasionally been made is that Gottfried's *Tristan* remained incomplete because of its all too ambitious conception, though it could simply be that Gottfried's death prevented the work's completion, as his continuators Ulrich von Türheim and Heinrich von Freiberg both state in their prologues.[55] His romance breaks off just after 20,000 verses in the middle of a monologue, in which Tristan, in a conflict of feeling and conscience between the blond Isolde and Isolde White Hands, seeks a justification for his action. Despite being a fragment, there was a rich transmission of this work. Of the eleven manuscripts that contain the complete torso of the poem, two are from the thirteenth and one from the fourteenth, and the remainder from the fifteenth century. The fifteen fragments also belong to the thirteenth century.[56] It is revealing that — with a single exception — the manuscripts of Gottfried's text are followed by one of the two continuations produced in the thirteenth century: first that of Ulrich von Türheim (ca. 1235–43) and then that of Heinrich von Freiberg (1280–90).[57] This transmission synthesizes the version in such a way that, in the layout of the manuscripts, there is no difference between Gottfried's text and those of his continuators. This suggests that audiences of the completed romance understood the entire text as a single coherent artwork. The assumption in older scholarship that the continuations should be judged in comparison to Gottfried's achievement, and thus dismissed as inferior, has been revised in favor of the conviction that the works of both Ulrich and Heinrich should be evaluated on their own merits.[58]

The continuation of Ulrich, 3731 verses in length, was composed under the patronage of the imperial cupbearer Konrad von Winterstetten. On the one hand, Ulrich's continuation documents changing audiences' expectations, which increasingly preferred entertaining narrative segments, such as those Ulrich found in his principle source, Eilhart von Oberge. On the other hand, Ulrich endeavored — at least on the surface — to continue with Gottfried's problematic idealization of the adulterous pair, at the same time warning against the destructive consequence of their love.[59] Ulrich explicitly rejects the "unreht leben" (wrongful life) of Tristan and has his hero express this perceptive insight in a monologue:

> Tristan, la den unsin
> unde tu die gedanke hin,
> die dir din heil verkerent
> und gar din ere unerent.[60]

[Tristan, abandon the folly, and rid yourself of thoughts that spoil your salvation and sully your honor.]

Ulrich depicts Isolde White Hands contrastively with the blond Isolde as the ideal wife who tolerates Tristan's adultery with selfless humility. The conflict between love and honor can, based on Ulrich's moral and theological perspective, only be decided in favor of marital fidelity. Ulrich's conception is exemplified by the fate of Kaedin, who during an elicit rendezvous with Kassie is killed by her jealous husband Nampotanis. This instance of Tristan-like love clearly evokes the sad example of Tristan himself.[61] At the end of Ulrich's continuation, which is clearly based on Eilhart's *Tristant* with its glorification of the lovers and its exculpation of them owing to the magical power of the potion, Ulrich returns to the narrative tradition before Gottfried. At the same time, he takes up the early tendency to sanitize the lovers, when he pleads in the concluding commentary that both might accept both sinners, who by means of their fateful suffering and their sorrowful death have done penance for their sins, and whose love has proven their "groze triuwe" (great fidelity). The pair has an especially effective advocate in King Mark himself who — in a noteworthy divergence from Eilhart — dedicates the remainder of his life to the service of the lovers, and has them buried there. The miracle of rose and vine, in which the idealization of their wrongful love is symbolized, is again taken from Eilhart.

Heinrich von Freiberg's continuation, 6890 verses in length and composed under the patronage of the Bohemian noble Reimund von Lichtenburg, reaches back not only to Eilhart's early version (as had Ulrich's), but also to that of Ulrich.[62] Although Heinrich's work was clearly superior to that of Ulrich with respect to its narrative complexity, by no means did it replace it. Both continuations were transmitted side by side, and Ulrich's poem was even given a slight preference.[63] In Heinrich's work, the influence of Christian morality is even stronger than it had been with Ulrich. To be sure, he follows the model of Gottfried initially, whom he regards as an exemplary poet in his introduction, and he praises the lovers because of their constant *triuwe*. Heinrich stylizes Tristan as the courtly love-knight of Isolde, for whom he performs a series of exemplary heroic deeds; and he condemns — just as Gottfried had done — the enemies of love (*minnefeinde*) who oppose the pair's realization of love. The case of the fateful love of the pair rests for Heinrich not only in the love potion, but also in a particularly unfortunate constellation of the stars.

Yet, Heinrich von Freiberg leaves no doubt that he finds the adulterous love of the pair objectionable. Just as Ulrich had already done, Heinrich has his hero characterize his relationship to Isolde in quite negative terms: "du sundest sere wider got: / der tuvel der hat sinen spot / mit dir getriben alze vil" (you sin grievously against God, the devil is mocking you all too much).[64] When Tristan turns to Isolde White Hands, the author depicts (again as Ulrich had done before him) the hero's wife with all attributes of exemplary virtue. The ideality of this marriage underscores the reprehensibility of the lovers' passion. Again, Kaedin comes to a tragic end by following Tristan's example. It is clear that Heinrich takes an evaluative position regarding the struggle between love and marriage that is based on religious moral ideas and that implicitly questions the lovers' claim to individual happiness. In Heinrich's work, Tristan's love is a "Krankheit zum Tode" (sickness to death) that is triggered by a destructive infection of love, and which ends with Kaedin and also with Tristan in "Liebestod."[65]

In the end what has remained is the legend of an ultimately futile effort, which nevertheless succeeded in articulating a utopian goal of individual fulfillment. The happiness of what is probably the most famous pair of lovers in world literature, stands paradigmatically for the eternally endangered yearning for love against all the obstacles of world and society: Tristan and Isolde.

—Translated by Will Hasty

Notes

[1] "Dicimus (. . .) amorem non posse suas inter duos iugales extendere vires"; *Andreae Capellani Regii Francorum De Amore Libri Tres,* ed. E. Tojel (Copenhagen: In Libraria Gadiana, 1892), 153; see also the English translation of Andreas's text by P. C. Walsh (London: Duckworth, 1982).

[2] Denis de Rougemont, *L'Amour et l'Occident* (Paris: Plon, 1939); see also the perceptive observations of Peter von Matt, *Liebesverrat: Die Treulosen in der Literatur* (Munich: Hanser Verlag, 1989) and Daniel Rocher's essay "Denis de Rougemont, la 'légend' de Tristan et le roman de Gottfried von Strassburg," in *La Légend de Tristan au Moyen Âge,* ed. Danielle Buschinger (Göppingen: Kümmerle, 1982), 139–50.

[3] Kurt Ruh, *Höfische Epik des deutschen Mittelalters,* vol. 1 (Berlin: E. Schmidt, 1977), 50.

[4] Peter Wapnewski, "Liebe als Literatur im Mittelalter," *Lexikothek: Spektrum der Literatur,* ed. Bettina and Lars Clausen (Gütersloh: Bertelsmann Lexikon-Verlag, 1975), 89.

[5] Karl Lachmann, *Kleinere Schriften,* vol. 1 (Berlin: Reimer, 1876; reprint Berlin: De Gruyter, 1969), 159.

[6] See Rüdiger Krohn, "Gottfried von Strassburg," *Deutsche Dichter: Leben und Werk deutschsprachiger Autoren,* vol. 1: *Mittelalter,* ed. Gunter E. Grimm and Frank Rainer Max (Stuttgart: Reclam, 1989), 233. The present essay is indebted to this article and also to the "Nachwort" of my edition of Gottfried's *Tristan, Gottfried von Strassburg: Tristan, nach dem Text von Friedrich Ranke neu herausgegeben, ins Neuhochdeutsche übersetzt, mit einem Stellenkommentar und einem Nachwort von Rüdiger Krohn,* 3 vols. (Stuttgart: Reclam, 1985) — the edition of Gottfried's work cited in this essay.

[7] For more information on this relationship, see Waltraud Fritsch-Rössler, *Der "Tristan" Gottfrieds von Straßburg in der deutschen Literaturgeschichtsschreibung (1785–1985)* (Frankfurt am Main: Lang, 1989).

[8] Started by Gertrude Schoepperle, *Tristan and Isolt: A Study of the Sources of the Romance,* vol. 2 (New York: Franklin, 1960).

[9] See W. J. McCann, "Tristan: The Celtic Material Re-examined," in *Gottfried von Strassburg and the Medieval Tristan Legend,* ed. Adrian Stevens and Roy Wisbey (London: Institute of Germanic Studies, 1990), 19–28, and *The Growth of the Tristan and Iseut Legend in Wales, England, France and Germany,* ed. Phillipa Hartmann et al. (Lewiston: Mellen, 2003).

[10] Following Ranke, *Tristan und Isold* (Munich: Bruckmann, 1925).

[11] *The Romance of Tristran by Béroul: A Poem of the Twelfth Century,* ed. Alfred Ewert, vol. 1 (London: Bristol Classical Press, 1967), verses 1267 and 1789.

[12] On Eilhart's dependence on Béroul, see Alois Wolf, *Gottfried von Straßburg und die Mythe von Tristan und Isolde* (Darmstadt: Wissenschaftliche Buchgesellschaft, 1989), 62–91.

[13] For information on the life and work of this poet, see the introduction in Hadumond Bussmann's edition *Eilhart von Oberg, Tristrant: Synoptischer Druck*

der ergänzten Fragmente mit der gesamten Parallelüberlieferung (Tübingen: Niemeyer, 1969), vii ff.

[14] On the significance of Eleanor for the dissemination of the Tristan material, see Rita Lejeune, "Rôle littéraire d'Aliénor d'Aquitaine et de sa famille," *Cultura neolatina* 14 (1954): 31–36; see also Alison Weir, *Eleanor of Aquitaine: By the Wrath of God Queen of England* (London: Jonathan Cape, 1999), especially 136–38.

[15] Citing the edition of Eilhart's work by Franz Lichtenstein (Hildesheim: Olms, 1973), verse 52.

[16] See René Wetzel, "Der Tristanstoff in der Literatur des deutschen Mittelalters: Forschungsbericht 1969–1994," in *Forschungsberichte zur germanistischen Mediävistik* 5/1, ed. Hans-Jochen Schiewer (Frankfurt am Main: Lang, 1996), 192.

[17] See the recent study by Monica Schausten, *Erzählwelten der Tristangeschichte im hohen Mittelalter: Untersuchungen zu den deutschsprachigen Tristanfassungen des 12. und 13. Jahrhunderts* (Munich: Fink, 1999).

[18] This strategy of rehabilitation is also visible in the lyric poetry, for example in the verses of Heinrich von Veldeke: "Tristan muose sunder sînen danc / staete sîn der küneginne, / wan in daz poisûn dar zuo twanc / mêre danne diu kraft der minne" (Tristan had no choice but to be faithful to the queen; the poison compelled him in this more than love's power). Quoted from *Des Minnesangs Frühling: Bearbeitet von Hugo Moser und Helmut Tervooren, 36. neugestaltete und erweiterte Auflage* (Stuttgart: Hirzel, 1977), 108; see also Volker Mertens, "Intertristanisches: Tristan-Lieder von Chrétien de Troyes, Bernger von Horheim und Heinrich von Veldeke," in *Germanistik und Deutschunterricht im historischen Wandel,* ed. Johannes Janota (Tübingen: Niemeyer, 1993).

[19] Danielle Buschinger, *Le "Tristrant" d'Eilhart von Oberg,* 2 vols. (Lille: Service de reproduction des thèses, 1974).

[20] See Schausten, *Erzählwelten der Tristangeschichte im hohen Mittelalter,* 91ff.

[21] *Tristrant und Isalde,* ed. Alois Brandstetter (Tübingen: Niemeyer, 1966).

[22] English translations are from *Gottfried von Strassburg: Tristan. With the Surviving Fragments of the "Tristran" of Thomas,* trans. A. T. Hatto (London: Penguin, 1960).

[23] Thomas, *Les Fragments du Roman de Tristan. Poème du XIIᵉ siècle,* ed. Bartina H. Wind (Geneva: Droz, 1960); here the *Fragment Douce,* 1379ff.

[24] For the dating, see Bartina H. Wind, "Nos incertitudes au sujet du *Tristan* de Thomas," *Mélanges Frappier* (Geneva: Droz, 1970), 1129–38.

[25] On the transformations of this motif in the history of the material, see Wolfgang Spiewok, "Varianten der Waldleben-Episode in der Tristan-Rezeption," in *Tristan-Studien: Die Tristan-Rezeption in den europäischen Literaturen des Mittelalters,* ed. Danielle Buschinger (Greifswald: Reineke-Verlag, 1993), 139–44; especially 142–43.

[26] Erich Köhler, *Ideal und Wirklichkeit in der höfischen Epik: Studien zur Form der frühen Artus- und Graldichtung* (Tübingen: Niemeyer, 1970), 267. Köhler concludes that the distinction between *version commune* and *version courtoise* is erroneous, insofar as Thomas's *Tristan* is "antihöfisch."

[27] See Wolf, *Gottfried von Straßburg und die Mythe von Tristan und Isolde,* 91.

[28] Ranke, *Tristan und Isold*, 178.

[29] *Dichter über Dichter in mittelhochdeutscher Literatur*, ed. Günther Schweikle (Tübingen: Niemeyer, 1970), 86.

[30] Printed in *Des Minnesangs Frühling*, 431–32.

[31] For the interpretation of both strophes, see Karl Stackmann, "*Gîte* und *Gelücke*. Über die Spruchstrophen Gotfrids," in *Festschrift Ulrich Pretzel* (Berlin: E. Schmidt, 1963), 191–204.

[32] Werner Schröder, "Zur Chronologie der drei großen mittelhochdeutschen Epiker," *Deutsche Vierteljahrsschrift für Literaturwissenschaft und Geistesgeschichte* 31 (1957): 274 and 283.

[33] See Marc Chinca, *Gottfried von Strassburg, Tristan* (Cambridge: Cambridge UP, 1997), 9–10.

[34] See Rüdiger Krohn, "*Dietherus cellerarius*. Mutmaßungen über den Gönner Gottfrieds von Straßburg," in *Verstehen durch Vernunft: Festschrift für Werner Hoffmann*, ed. Burkhardt Krause (Vienna: Fassbänder Verlag, 1997), 238–46.

[35] See Hans-Hugo Steinhoff, *Gottfried von Straßburg, "Tristan." Ausgewählte Abbildungen zur Überlieferung* (Kümmerle: Göppingen, 1974), v–ix and René Wetzel, *Die handschriftliche Überlieferung des "Tristan" Gottfrieds von Strassburg: Untersucht an ihren Fragmenten* (Freiburg/Schweiz: Germanistica Friburgensia, 1992), 52–56.

[36] Thomas Klein, "Ermittlung, Darstellung und Deutung von Verbreitungstypen in der Handschriftenüberlieferung mittelhochdeutscher Epik," in *Deutsche Handschriften 1100–1400*, ed. Volker Honemann and Nigel F. Palmer (Tübingen: Niemeyer, 1988), especially 124–28.

[37] Schweikle, *Dichter über Dichter in mittelhochdeutscher Literatur*, 59.

[38] The different meanings of *meister* are explored by Gerda Sälzer, *Studien zu Gottfried von Straßburg* (Dissertation, Bochum, 1975), 73–84; see also Siegfried Grosse, "Der Gebrauch des Wortes *meister* in Gottfried's *Tristan*," in *Sprache, Literatur, Kultur: Studien zu ihrer Geschichte im deutschen Süden und Westen. Wolfgang Kleiber zu seinem 60. Geburtstag*, ed. Albrecht Greule and Uwe Ruberg (Stuttgart: Steiner, 1989), 291–99.

[39] With great certainty C. Stephen Jaeger posits: "He surely studied in France at the humanist cathedral schools, and while there is no historical certainly [*sic*] on this point, the text of the poem offers strong proof that that is the case"; *Medieval Humanism in Gottfried von Strassburg's "Tristan und Isolde"* (Heidelberg: Winter, 1977), xiii.

[40] See Hans Fromm, "Gottfried von Straßburg und Abaelard," in *Arbeiten zur deutschen Literatur des Mittelalters*, by H. F. (Tübingen: Niemeyer, 1989), 173–90; Tomas Tomasek also discusses reflections of early scholastic philosophy in Gottfrieds poem (*Die Utopie im "Tristan" Gotfrids von Straßburg* [Tübingen: Niemeyer, 1985], 216–19).

[41] This view is especially significant in the interpretation of Gottfried Weber, *Gottfried von Straßburg: Tristan und die Krise des hochmittelalterlichen Weltbildes um 1200*, 2 vols. (Stuttgart: Metzler, 1953).

[42] See Tomasek, *Die Utopie im "Tristan" Gotfrids von Straßburg,* 51–69.

[43] See Otto Langer, "Der 'Künstlerroman' Gottfrieds — Protest bürgerlicher 'Empfindsamkeit' gegen höfisches 'Tugendsystem'?" *Euphorion* 68 (1974): 1–41.

[44] On this aspect see Danielle Buschinger, "L'image du marchand dans les romans de Tristan en France et en Allemagne," *Tristania. A Journal Devoted to Tristan Studies* 10 (1984/85): 43–51 and Tomasek, *Die Utopie im "Tristan" Gotfrids von Straßburg,* 248–55. While the acrostic is distributed throughout Gottfried's work, most of the letters are concentrated in the prologue, where the name "Dieterich" is spelled.

[45] On the acrostic that runs the entire length of the romance, see Bernd Schirok, "Zu den Akrosticha in Gottfrieds *Tristan*: Versuch einer kritischen und weiterführenden Bestandsaufnahme," *Zeitschrift für deutsches Altertum und deutsche Literatur* 113 (1984): 188–213 and Gesa Bonath, "Nachtrag zu den Akrosticha in Gottfrieds *Tristan*," *Zeitschrift für deutsches Altertum und deutsche Literatur* 115 (1986): 101–16.

[46] On the discussion of this thesis and its consequences for the interpretation of the romance, see Krohn, "Dietherus cellerarius," 227–46.

[47] See Tomasek, *Die Utopie im "Tristan" Gotfrids von Straßburg,* 41–89.

[48] This discussion is summarized by Reiner Dietz, *Der Tristan Gottfrieds von Straßburg: Probleme der Forschung (1902–1970)* (Göppingen: Kümmerle, 1974), 89–105.

[49] See Rüdiger Krohn, "Erotik und Tabu in Gottfrieds *Tristan*: König Marke," in *Stauferzeit: Geschichte, Literatur, Kunst* (Stuttgart: Klett-Cotta, 1979), 362–76; especially 367ff.

[50] First interpreted in this way by Friedrich Ranke, "Die Allegorie der Minnegrotte in Gottfrieds Tristan," in *Gottfried von Straßburg,* ed. Alois Wolf (Darmstadt: Wissenschaftliche Buchgesellschaft, 1973), 1–24.

[51] Will Hasty, *Adventure as Social Performance: A Study of the German Court Epic* (Tübingen: Niemeyer, 1990), 119.

[52] The term "Minneheiligen" is used by Helmut de Boor in his "Die Grundauffassung von Gottfrieds Tristan," in *Gottfried von Straßburg,* ed. Alois Wolf (Darmstadt: Wissenschaftliche Buchgesellschaft, 1973), 25–73; on the mystical influence on Gottfried's text, see Julius Schwietering, "Der Tristan Gottfrieds von Strassburg und die Bernhardinische Mystik," in *Philologische Schriften* (Munich: Fink, 1969), 338–61.

[53] Karl Bertau, *Deutsche Literatur im europäischen Mittelalter,* vol. 2: *1195–1220* (Munich: Beck, 1973), 957.

[54] See Ulrich Ernst, "Gottfried von Straßburg in komparatistischer Sicht. Form und Funktion der Allegorese im Tristanepos," *Euphorion* 70 (1976): 1–72; 48ff.

[55] Whether Gottfried consciously broke off his romance or died before its completion is a question that has received much attention in the critical literature; see Christoph Huber, *Gottfried von Straßburg: Tristan* (Berlin: E. Schmidt, 2000), 120–28.

[56] On the transmission see *Gottfried von Straßburg, Tristan: Ausgewählte Abbildungen zur Überlieferung,* ed. Hans-Hugo Steinhoff (Göppingen: Kümmerle, 1974).

[57] Schausten, *Erzählwelten der Tristangeschichte im hohen Mittelalter,* 200–7 and Wetzel, "Forschungsbericht," 226–32.

[58] On the medieval reception of Gottfried's work, see Burghart Wachinger, "Zur Rezeption Gottfrieds von Straßburg im 13. Jahrhundert," in *Deutsche Literatur des 13. Jahrhunderts,* ed. Wolfgang Harms and Leslie Peter Johnson (Berlin: E. Schmidt, 1975), 56–82 and Klaus Grubmüller, "Probleme einer Fortsetzung. Anmerkungen zu Ulrichs von Türheim Tristan-Schluß," *Zeitschrift für deutsches Altertum und deutsche Literatur* 114 (1985): 338–48.

[59] See Grubmüller, "Probleme einer Fortsetzung. Anmerkungen zu Ulrichs von Türheim Tristan-Schluß," 348.

[60] Citing the edition of Ulrich's work by Buschinger and Spiewok (*Ulrich von Türheim, Tristan und Isolde (Fortsetzung des Tristan-Romans Gottfrieds von Straßburg), Originaltext (nach der Heidelberger Handschrift Pal. Germ. 360), Versübersetzung und Einleitung von Wolfgang Spiewok in Zusammenarbeit mit Danielle Buschinger* [Greifswald: Reineke-Verlag, 1992]); the English translations are by the editor.

[61] See Strohschneider, "Gotfrid-Fortsetzungen, Tristans Ende im 13. Jahrhundert und die Möglichkeit nachklassischer Epik," *Deutsche Vierteljahrsschrift für Literaturwissenschaft und Geistesgeschichte* 65 (1991): 70–98; 82.

[62] Wolfgang Spiewok, "Zur Überlieferung der Tristan-Fortsetzung Heinrichs von Freiberg," in *Tristan-Studien: Die Tristan-Rezeption in den europäischen Literaturen des Mittelalters,* ed. Danielle Buschinger (Greifswald: Reineke-Verlag, 1993), 148–52.

[63] See Margarete Sedlmeyer, *Heinrichs von Freiberg Tristanfortsetzung im Vergleich zu anderen Tristandichtungen* (Frankfurt am Main: Lang, 1976), 261.

[64] Heinrich von Freiberg, *Tristan: Mit Einleitung über Stil, Sprache, Metrik, Quellen und die Persönlichkeit des Dichters,* ed. Alois Bernt (Halle: Niemeyer, 1906); a recent edition of Heinrich's text with modern German translation is Heinrich von Freiberg, *Tristan und Isolde (Fortsetzung des Tristanromans Gottfrieds von Straßburg),* ed. Danielle Buschinger, trans. Wolfgang Spiewok (Greifswald: Reineke, 1993). The cited verses (209–11) are from the latter edition.

[65] See Silke Grothues, *Der arthurische Tristanroman: Werkabschluss und Gattungswechsel in Heinrichs von Freiberg Tristanfortsetzung* (Frankfurt am Main: Lang, 1991), 166.

Wolfram von Eschenbach. A miniature from the Codex Manesse (149v).

Wolfram von Eschenbach

Marion E. Gibbs and Sidney M. Johnson*

WOLFRAM VON ESCHENBACH BELONGS TO the great quartet (along with Hartmann von Aue, Gottfried von Strassburg, and the anonymous author of the *Nibelungenlied*) of medieval German narrative poets at the turn of the twelfth and thirteenth centuries, but he is as distinct from them as they are from one another. It is the nature of that distinctiveness that will concern us here, together with the enduring regard in which he is held. The number of manuscripts of his two major works attests to his popularity in the Middle Ages (87 MSS and fragments of *Parzival*, 76 of *Willehalm*). In the late thirteenth century he became a literary figure himself in the *Wartburgkrieg*, the literary evocation of an imagined contest of singers at the court of Hermann von Thüringen. The *Meistersinger* of the fifteenth and sixteenth centuries honored him as one of the founders of their art. His *Parzival* was printed, in early New High German form, in verse, as late as 1477, but shortly thereafter his works disappeared from view for over two hundred years, until interest in them arose again and some were republished from the original Middle High German manuscripts. Serious scholarly interest in them began around the beginning of the nineteenth century, and the now enormous mass of critical writing on Wolfram has grown steadily since that time.

A small town in Middle Franconia claims to be the birthplace of Wolfram von Eschenbach and, despite the lack of documentary evidence and rival claims of other places in southern Germany, since 1917 it has borne the official designation "Wolframs Eschenbach." Wolfram was probably born about 1170 and died some time after 1220. There is good reason to believe that at some point he was at the court of Hermann von Thüringen, a famous patron of literature in the early thirteenth century, whose court was focused in the mighty Wartburg near Eisenach, far to the north, where many of the literary figures of the age crossed paths. As with almost all the medieval German poets, almost nothing is known with certainty about Wolfram's life. In his works he tells us so many things about himself — he is poor, has a daughter, is "illiterate" — that he, or his narrative persona, is very much present, participating in the events he narrates. It seems likely that this sophisticated author, who possessed a wide range of knowledge in such matters as astronomy, medicine, warfare, geography, and history, chose to adopt the pose of an unlettered, impoverished knight.

The scope of Wolfram's work is striking, encompassing lyric poetry and epic narrative. In both genres there is a marked admixture of the dramatic, in essence, though not, at this early stage of German literature, in form. Four distinct works or work complexes constitute his remarkable oeuvre: *Parzival*, *Willehalm*, the two fragments usually called *Titurel* and a small group of "songs." All of Wolfram's works were probably written in the first two decades of the thirteenth century, but the chronology is open to argument. No one would doubt that *Parzival* is earlier, possibly by as much as twenty years, than *Willehalm*, where Wolfram refers to his *Parzival* as a completed work. *Titurel* probably belongs to the later period; the Songs, most difficult of all to place, may have been composed over a long period, some of them preceding *Parzival*, others after it, and in what order it is impossible to establish, though successive critics have attempted to do so.

Parzival

By the time Wolfram began writing, the early works of Hartmann von Aue were current. The German audience had been introduced to the Arthurian romance and to chivalrous values through *Erec* (ca. 1185). Hartmann's *Gregorius* had tackled the central issue of guilt and redemption and presented it by means of the story of a saintly figure. Both works were composed in rhymed couplets, and Wolfram adopted this form for his *Parzival*.[1] Like Hartmann's *Erec* and *Iwein*, the principal source for Wolfram's work was a romance by Chrétien de Troyes, his unfinished *Perceval* or *Li conte du graal*, in all possibility curtailed by his death (ca. 1180–90). Wolfram used Chrétien's work for his Books III to XIII, but also completed and greatly expanded the original, adding an introduction and conclusion.

What distinguishes Wolfram's *Parzival* both from his French source and from the Arthurian romances of Hartmann — apart from myriad differences in style and perception of the material — is his handling of the narrative in an individual, often idiosyncratic, way. The central action of *Parzival* is the hero's search for the Grail, a recurrent theme in European literature, but one that gains in substance and subtlety in the hands of Wolfram. The author creates many new characters, whose histories he often pursues independently from his main story, and even when he adopts characters from his source, such as Gurnemanz, Sigune, Condwiramurs, he extends their significance within his story. He adds the parental history, exploring the themes of lineage and inheritance, so important to his concept of the dynasty of the Grail and his ideas on chivalry. Parzival's father, Gahmuret, is not only an attractive subsidiary hero, the focus of knightly adventures and poignant love affairs, but he is also portrayed as a much more worldly, experienced figure than his son, who begins his chivalric career in the world as a completely inexperienced young man. The characterization of Gahmuret is one of the important ways in which the poet underscores how much Parzival will have to learn in his adventures. In contrast to the French source, Wolfram introduces the exotic world of the East, where Gahmuret spends much of his active life and where he dies. In the figure of Belakane, Gahmuret's first wife, Wolfram touches on the theme of the Saracen world: although she disappears at the end of the first Book, when she is left to grieve for her departed husband and to nurse her newborn son in sorrow, her presence echoes, through the re-emergence of that son, in the closing stages of the poem, completing the framework of the broader, Christian-Saracen world into which Wolfram has set the principal action of the poem. There is a scope in this concept unimagined in the work of Chrétien and in the Arthurian romances of Hartmann, both of whose romances move in a more limited sphere.

However, the Arthurian world plays an immensely important role in *Parzival*. Wolfram devotes almost half of his narrative to the exploits of Gawan, who, with his more conventional morality and as the focus of a series of familiar Arthurian adventures, represents a sharp contrast to Parzival. Gawan is the norm, against whom the extraordinary Parzival can be measured, but his story is told with enormous panache, in a narrative characterized by complexity and sharp twists and turns of plot. One of Wolfram's achievements is to maintain a clear distinction of style and language in his handling of these two central characters, whose careers run parallel in many respects and yet lead to very different goals: Gawan's to the conventional peak of the exemplary Arthurian knight, and Parzival's to the unique office of Grail King.

Wolfram's *Parzival*, unlike his Old French source and his own *Willehalm* and *Titurel*, is indisputably complete, a rounded work with all the ends tied up. This is a huge achievement, because he clearly worked with so many different strands in this poem of almost 25,000 lines. Karl Lachmann, in the first critical edition (1833), divided the poem into sixteen sections ("Books"), which correspond to the divisions, marked by illuminated letters, in the leading manuscript (designated "D" and located in St. Gall). Within these divisions, the major part of the work falls into thirty-line sections, a practice Wolfram appears to have adopted in the course of *Parzival* and then throughout *Willehalm*. Such sectionalization, with corresponding breaks, almost certainly has implications for any assumptions about how the work was performed, although too little is known for sure about the matter, beyond the near certainty that the poem was delivered before a live and possibly participating audience.

The structure of *Parzival* lends itself to linear representation, following the division into these sixteen Books. An important aspect of the work is the interrelationship of events, the many repetitions and echoes, the sense of an accumulation of circumstances and, not surprising given the essential theme of the poem, the awareness of the negative superseded by the positive, of success balancing failure, and, ultimately, of the triumph of good over evil. The optimistic tone of the work is already evident in the first verses of the prologue, which, despite their complexity of imagery and references, suggest both the broad scope of this work — it will cover domains of courtly-chivalric and religious experience — and the possibility of a happy conclusion based on courage and perseverance:

> Ist zwîvel herzen nâchgebûr
> daz muoz der sêle werden sûr.
> gesmæhet und gezieret
> ist swâ sich parrieret
> unverzaget mannes muot,
> als agelstern varwe tuot.
> der mac dennoch wesen geil,
> wande an im sint beidiu teil,
> des himels und der helle.
> der unstæte geselle
> hât die swarzen varwe gar
> und wirt ouch nâch der vinster var:
> sô habet sich an die blanken
> der mit stæten gedanken. (1–14)

[If vacillation dwell with the heart the soul will rue it. Shame and honor clash where the courage of a steadfast man is motley like the magpie. But such a man may yet make merry, for Heaven and Hell have equal part in him. Infidelity's friend is black all over and takes on a murky hue, while the man of loyal temper holds to the white.]

At the heart of the work is the story of Parzival's progress toward his destined goal, but this is but one story among many. The realm in which Parzival moves is only one of the areas with which Wolfram is concerned, and, in peopling his poem with a somewhat bewildering cast of many, he pursues also myriad subsidiary stories and delves into other histories. It is his achievement, unique in medieval German literature, to handle a mass of material with a keen eye for detail, yet never to lose sight of his essential theme. Thus, the following basic account of the contents of *Parzival* disguises a highly complex inner structure:

• Book I: Wolfram's prologue, together with a spirited defense of his style and some playful jibes at his critics, tells us that his hero is not yet born. He proceeds to the story of Parzival's father, Gahmuret. This younger son, disinherited on the death of his own father, occupies the first two Books, with the account of his chivalrous adventures, notably in the service of the Saracen Baruc, and his two marriages. The first Book ends with Gahmuret's desertion of his Saracen wife Belakane, her grief and the birth of their checkered son, Feirefiz.

- Book II: Gahmuret falls in love with Queen Herzeloyde, wins her hand, but insists that she allow him to go off at regular intervals in search of adventure. With this proviso, they enjoy a happy marriage, until he dies in a Saracen land, responding to a call for assistance from the Baruc. Herzeloyde is left to bear their son, Parzival.
- Book III: Parzival grows up in the forest, where his mother hopes to protect him from the dangers that led to his father's death by keeping him ignorant of the very word "knight." Inevitably, he meets a group of knights who introduce him to the word and the concept, and he insists on leaving in pursuit of his innate way of life. Herzeloyde dies as soon as he leaves her. He meets Jeschute, and his cousin Sigune, comes to Arthur's Court, where he reveals both his inherent chivalry and his ignorance, and slays the Red Knight Ither. At the castle of Gurnemanz, he learns much about the techniques of chivalry and a certain amount about social behavior and, in coming to know Liaze, his host's daughter, he glimpses the relationship achievable between man and woman.
- Book IV: He meets Condwiramurs, saves her from danger and marries her. Theirs is a seemingly perfect love, but he grows restless and asks her permission to go off to see his mother and in search of adventure.
- Book V: After a second encounter with Sigune, he finds his way to the Grail Castle, Munsalvæsche. Here he witnesses strange and overwhelming events which touch him deeply but about which he does not ask, in the belief that this reticence is in accordance with correct behavior. He leaves the Castle, puzzling over the experience but unaware that he has failed in his special task — the posing of a question about the suffering of his host that would have healed that suffering. The Book ends with his second meeting with Jeschute, which enables him to put right the wrong he had done her earlier.
- Book VI: On a snow-covered plain at dawn, he has a mystical experience, when three drops of blood in the snow remind him of his wife and lead him to a paean of praise for God the Creator. Following his first meeting with Gawan, he comes again to Arthur's Court, and is invited to join the Round Table. Amid the rejoicing at this high point in his knightly career, he is devastated by the arrival of Cundrie, the messenger of the Grail, who accuses him of irredeemable wrong-doing on account of his silence at the Grail Castle at the crucial moment when the question needed to be asked, and reproaches him in public for lacking in compassion and loyalty. Angry, he turns on God and rejects His aid as he departs on his journey to try to rectify his mistake. This Book is important for the introduction of Gawan, whom Wolfram sets beside Parzival as a man who is likewise accused of a terrible offence, in his case against chivalry, and who also sets out to right his wrong.
- Books VII and VIII are devoted to Gawan's adventures, with only passing references to Parzival. Gawain becomes embroiled in the battle at

Bearosche, fighting as the knight of the little girl Obilot on the side of her father Lyppaut. The Book ends with reconciliation and the prospect of an harmonious outcome for Obilot's older sister Obie and her lover. Book VIII is a semi-comic episode, tinged with serious overtones, with Gawan drawn into a passionate encounter with Antikonie and forced to defend his position in a most undignified way, hurling pieces of a chess-set from a tower at the crowd below baying for justice.

- Book IX is centrally placed, both structurally and thematically. It contains three deeply spiritual and decisive encounters for Parzival: his third meeting with his cousin Sigune, now a hermitess; his brief conversation with the Pilgrim and his two daughters; his sojourn with the hermit Trevrizent, his maternal uncle. The two weeks he spends with Trevrizent are crucial for him. He learns much, about the nature of God, the origins of the Grail and his own relationship to it, his family ties, and the obligations they bring to him. He leaves Trevrizent at the end of the Book better equipped to go on his spiritual journey, but geographically lost in his search for the Grail.

- Books X, XI, XII and XIII are again devoted to the very different adventures of Gawan, now in pursuit of his great love, Orgeluse. These adventures have as their focus *Schastel merveile*, the Wondrous Castle, and the Arthurian Court, where Parzival and Gawan meet again in Book XIV. Two tests of Parzival's chivalry, with Gramoflanz and then with Gawan, prepare the way for the ultimate test, against his half-brother Feirefiz in Book XV. Meanwhile, Book XIV ends with rejoicing, marriage for Gawan and Orgeluse, but, for Parzival, the recognition that his task remains unfulfilled and that he does not belong in this environment.

- Books XV and XVI see the conclusion of Parzival's journey, both literally when he is summoned to Munsalvæsche by Cundrie and, more abstractly, with his ability now to pose the question which releases the Grail King Anfortas from his anguish and ensures his own succession. The combat with Feirefiz ends in a draw and sets the seal on his chivalric reputation. The reunion with Condwiramurs after the healing of Anfortas places the final piece in the puzzle of his achievement. Wolfram anticipates a future in which Feirefiz, married to the Grail Bearer, spreads the message of Christianity in the East, and the twin sons of Parzival and Condwiramurs continue the task of protecting the Grail and extending its influence.

At the heart of Wolfram's dense narrative is Book IX, which tells of Parzival's spiritual turmoil and sets him on the path of resolving that turmoil. It also contains much of Wolfram's most detailed and individual explanation of what the Grail meant to him and thus its place in Parzival's progress. In a work full of original and often quite striking details, the most concentrated focus of Wolfram's delight in innovation is his conception of the Grail. Traditionally a vessel, often indeed *the* vessel in which the blood of Christ was collected on the Cross, the Grail that Parzival seeks and finds is explicitly a stone. Defined at its first mention simply as "ein dinc" (a thing, 235, 23),[2] it accrues many properties, both physical and abstract, as more and more is revealed, before Parzival finally attains its kingship by the simplest expression of concern for a suffering fellow human being when he poses the question that heals his uncle Anfortas (795, 24–25). In building up his singular concept of the Grail and arriving at a picture that distinguishes it from any tradition, Wolfram adopts features from many areas of myth and superstition, orthodox religion and, not least, his own vivid imagination. Following the rebellion of Lucifer, the neutral angels were sent to the Grail on the earth. We do not know what happened to them later, but they left, and the Grail family has had the task of guarding the Grail ever since (471, 26–28). The Grail dispenses food and drink as requested (238, 13–17); it is invisible to the unbaptized, as we discover only very late in the poem, when the Saracen Feirefiz can see the Grail Bearer, but not the object she is carrying (810, 7–13; 813, 9–22); a dove places a wafer on it on Good Friday to renew its powers (469, 29–470, 20); a person cannot die in the week following the sight of it (469, 14–17); it can be borne only by a pure virgin (235, 25–30); inscriptions appear on it from time to time, announcing matters of importance to the Grail community, but, once read, these messages vanish (470, 23–30).[3]

This is an extraordinary mixture of strange properties, but overriding them is the injunction to purity, in those who serve the Grail and partake of its own purity: "der stein ist immer reine" (the stone is always pure, 471, 22), says Wolfram, using the same adjective as he uses to describe the select body which guards it (469, 4). In Wolfram's clearly developed thesis, purity is a manifestation of humility (*diemuot, diemüete*) and inseparable from the virtue which is pre-eminent in his analysis of human qualities, that *triuwe* (love, loyalty) which, in Wolfram's ultimate definition, is the very essence of God: "wan got selbe ein triuwe ist" (for God Himself is Love, 462, 19).

There is another important aspect of the Grail: its international, political implications. The Grail sends out rulers to lands that are in need of a ruler, male or female. It recruits its candidates as young children who are called to the Grail to receive their training. The parents are happy to give up their children, who will attain salvation by being trained at the Grail. This information, when it is given to Parzival by Trevrizent during their discussions in Book IX, causes an angry outburst from him, since, as he sees it, such young people are blessed in this way, while he, for all his striving, appears to be denied salvation (470, 21–472, 11). The women, like Herzeloyde, are sent out openly, but the young men must go covertly and are prohibited from answering questions about their origins (494, 5–495, 6). With this information, Wolfram anticipates the fate of Parzival's son, Lohengrin, who succumbs to the repeated questioning of his wife (826, 10–20). Theoretically at least, the Grail is able to influence political situations throughout the world.

Wolfram's version of the Grail demonstrates his fondness for the exotic and his pleasure in mystifying his audience. He claims to have learned about the Grail from an intermediary, Kyot, a singer from Provence, who had read the story of Parzival in Arabic and then told it in French:

> Kyôt la schantiure hiez,
> den sîn kunst des niht erliez,
> er ensunge und spræche sô
> dês noch genuoge werdent frô.
> Kyôt ist ein Provenzâl,
> der dise âventiur von Parzivâl
> heidensch geschriben sach.
> Swaz er en franzoys dâ von gesprach,
> bin ich niht der witze laz,
> daz sage ich tiuschen fürbaz. (416, 21–30)

[Kyot laschantiure was the name of one whose art compelled him to tell what shall gladden no few. Kyot is that noted Provençal who saw this Tale of Parzival written in the heathenish tongue, and what he retold in French I shall not be too dull to recount in German.]

This famous scholar found a book in Arabic, cast aside in Toledo. Having learned to read Arabic earlier, and as a Christian, he was able to understand the secrets of the Grail, something Oriental scholars were unable to do. A certain Flegetanis, who stemmed from Solomon on his mother's side, wrote the book, but he was a heathen like his father, who worshipped a calf. Flegetanis knew all the courses of the planets and had read in the stars of a "thing" named the "Grail" that had been left on earth by a host of angels. Later Christians who were especially worthy to perform that service cared for the Grail. Kyot tried to find the true story about these guardians in Latin writings, the chronicles of Britain, France, and Ireland, and finally found the story about the Grail family in Anjou (453, 5–455, 24). The question of Kyot occupied scholars during the first part of the twentieth century, but it is now generally accepted that he is a figment of Wolfram's invention, a substantial example of his characteristic delight in keeping his audience in suspense.[4] He creates something intentionally outlandish to attest to the truth of his story and only at the end of the work acknowledges his true source, though still with a backward glance at his spurious Kyot (827, 1–4). It is hardly surprising that Wolfram tried, however playfully, to suggest a source for a work that has so many diverse threads to it and moves in areas unimagined in Chrétien's unfinished romance.[5]

Although the Grail, with its complicated history, its fascinating properties and strange rituals, is undoubtedly the prime example of Wolfram's interest in the exotic, there are other elements in his *Parzival* that illustrate this predilection. These may be seen in a variety of forms in many of his minor characters, whether the character is modified from one in the source or stems from Wolfram's own invention. An important example is Sigune, Parzival's cousin, cradling the body of her unrequited lover when Parzival first meets her (138, 16–23), sitting in a linden tree, still holding the corpse of her now embalmed knight the second time (249, 11–20), and an incluse immured in a cell with the corpse of Schionatulander in a casket on the third occasion (435, 19–30). Finally, after Anfortas has been released from his suffering and Parzival, Condwiramurs and their twin sons are returning to the Grail Castle, Parzival pauses on his journey to visit Sigune, only to find her dead (804, 21–805, 2), whereupon he has her buried alongside Schionatulander. Her outstanding *triuwe* is embodied in her extraordinary life and death. The figure of Sigune, who assumes a significant role in the course of Parzival's journey, reflecting his own uneven progress, is an outstanding example of Wolfram's use of his source, for, in Chrétien's poem, the corresponding figure, unnamed and identified only as Perceval's *germaine cousine*, appears only once, more or less in passing.

While Sigune is distinguished by her life as a penitent, Parzival's half-brother Feirefiz — as far as we know, Wolfram's own invention — is marked by his extraordinary appearance. His skin is spotted black and white, the result of his having been born of the union of Parzival's father with Belakane, the black, Saracen queen. In Book I, Wolfram delights in the exotic life of the East, describing the development of love between the two amidst all the luxury of that fabled part of the world, and the unhappy ending of that idyll. When the mature Feirefiz returns in Book XV, Wolfram can hardly find words to describe him and his richly decorated clothing and armor. He revels in naming the precious stones that decorate Feirefiz's shield and points out *ecidemon*, the fabulous, pure animal, given to him as his coat of arms by Queen Sekundille. As if his personal appearance were not enough to mark him out, Feirefiz comes with twenty-five armies from such disparate places that no army understands the language of the other. And there are seemingly no limits to the exotic names in the long list of kings and princes and their lands that Feirefiz has conquered (770, 1–30).

As we have seen, the broad outline of the contents of *Parzival* suggests a linear development, with the core of the poem the progress of the young Parzival to his destined status as Grail King. Yet there are other ways of seeing this structure, for it is framed by the story of Gahmuret and his son Feirefiz, and contains the parallel narrative devoted to Gawan. Already one can identify three separate areas: the Grail kingdom, the Arthurian world, and the broad reaches of the Saracen world. It is a major achievement that Wolfram shows the distinctions among these three, while showing also their interrelationship. Significant single themes unite them: chivalry, religion, love and kinship. Although each area has its own central figure, these are linked, by the bonds of blood and friendship, but also by more abstract qualities that they share as human beings.

Parzival can be seen from the point of view of his genetic inheritance. His father was devoted to fighting and traveled the world to find adventure in the service of the most powerful ruler. On his mother's side, Parzival is related to the Grail family, those entrusted with protecting the Grail whose chief familial trait is loyalty to its assigned task and to God. Both traits are combined in Parzival, and it is interesting to note that Wolfram refers to Parzival as "Gahmuret's child" when Parzival is in a situation where manly courage and knightly skill are required of him, whereas he is called "Herzeloyde's child" in other circumstances, where his faithfulness to the Grail and to God is most prominent and most needed.

At a crucial point in his progress, when he has just met the pilgrims, the Grey Knight and his beautiful daughters, and been deeply moved by their devotion and their compassion, Parzival is stirred by thoughts of God and at last undergoes a spiritual change that will make him susceptible to the influence of his maternal uncle, the hermit Trevrizent. Wolfram emphasizes the connection explicitly:

> hin rîtet Herzeloyde fruht.
> dem riet sîn manlîchiu zuht
> kiusch unt erbarmunge:
> sît Herzeloyd diu junge
> in het ûf gerbet triuwe,
> sich huop sîns herzen riuwe.
> alrêrste er dô gedâhte,
> wer al die werlt volbrâhte,
> an sînen schepfære,
> wie gewaltec der wære. (451, 3–12)

[Herzeloyde's child rides on. His manly discipline enjoined modesty and compassion in him. Since young Herzeloyde had left him a loyal heart, remorse now began to stir in it. Only now did he ponder Who had brought the world into being, only now think of his Creator, and how mighty He must be.]

Parzival is destined by birth to become the next Grail King. What takes him so long is his inability to understand his relationship to God, and Wolfram has underscored this early on when he described his hero as being "*træclîche wîs*" (sluggish in gaining insight through experience, 4, 18).

That Parzival is a knight, by birthright and by inclination, is important, and he progresses towards a true understanding of his chivalrous calling. Passing through many trials and tests, and even failure, he joins with the central figures in Arthurian literature, in the works of Chrétien and Hartmann, and elsewhere in German medieval literature, in such narratives as Heinrich von dem Türlin's *Diu Crone*, Wirnt von Gravenberg's *Wigalois*, and Der

Stricker's *Daniel von dem blühenden Tal*, and many more. The identification of many common factors in such literature runs the risk of diminishing it, however, and what is remarkable about the abundance of chivalrous romance in German is its variety and the potential it showed for individual treatment. Nowhere is this potential more fully realized than in *Parzival*, where the man who is the knight *par excellence* is also first and foremost an exemplary human being. He eventually reaches the successful culmination of his Grail quest by means of error and misjudgment, alleviated by personal effort and the Grace of God. There is a sharp contrast between the careers of Parzival and Gawan. Parzival spends most of his early career seeking an answer to the question that he asked his mother before leaving her: " 'Ôwê muoter, waz ist got?' " ("Alas, mother, what is God?" 119, 17). In his desire to become the best knight, he sins, unwittingly and repeatedly, and he cannot achieve his destiny by virtue of his own strength alone. Once he realizes this and confesses his sinful nature to his uncle, Trevrizent, he is ready humbly to accept God's grace. For Gawan, God is no "problem," and he seems to expect God's help as needed. He does get into difficult situations and becomes involved in some hair-raising adventures, but, by adhering to the ideals of knighthood, he succeeds, in the more limited sphere that is his rightful domain. He serves several purposes in the narrative: as a foil to Parzival, to provide a certain amount of light relief, and to demonstrate the courtly norm, from which Parzival so significantly departs.[6]

In his depiction of Parzival Wolfram achieves a remarkable fusion of the norm and the unique. Parzival's behavior strikes chords with the modern reader as, doubtless, with the medieval audience. This is a man who stumbles and falls, as he makes his often clumsy way through his early life. In his ignorance and inexperience he leaves a trail of suffering behind him: his mother dies immediately after he leaves her, Jeschute must confront the accusations of her husband, Ither lies slain and the ladies weep for him, Gurnemanz and Liaze and their whole household are disappointed by his departure. Above all, Anfortas is not healed by the guest who has been so enthusiastically heralded and so warmly welcomed: the Grail kingdom is, if anything, more bereft than ever when Parzival has passed that way, yet not fulfilled the expectations of his visit. When Sigune learns of his failure to express concern for the suffering of Anfortas, her anguish is increased to the level of total despair and she bitterly rejects the possibility that he could ever make amends (255, 24–29).

Parzival is a man beset by doubts. Even in his apparently blissful marriage with Condwiramurs, he senses a lack of something that he can express only in his desire to see how his mother is faring, though the listeners know that she is long since dead, or — less tangibly — in his craving for adventure. In the context of chivalry, the *âventiure* which he seeks is quite simply the testing of his knightly vocation, but, more abstractly, and given the fact that he transcends his immediate, restricted identity to become the representative of any man or every man, it assumes a much broader significance as a challenge, the fulfillment of a personal destiny.

In this context, it becomes relevant that the question which lies at the heart of Parzival's achievement and precipitates his accession to the Kingship of the Grail, is no mystical expression of a search for identity, still less the factual questions required of Chrétien's hero ("Why does the lance bleed? Whom does the Grail serve?" 3552–53; 3568–69). The expression of concern for a fellow human being — " 'hêrre wie stêt iwer nôt?' " ("My lord, how is it with your suffering?" 484, 27) — Trevrizent's formulation of the missing question — is revised by Parzival when the time comes. What he actually asks is, if anything, even more direct: " 'œheim, waz wirret dir?' " ("Uncle what is the matter with you?" 795, 29). The concern is there, right enough, but Parzival's inclusion of the address to his maternal uncle speaks volumes for his now complete awareness, both of his place in the whole of humankind and of his specific responsibility towards his family.

Willehalm

Wolfram's second major work, arguably unfinished, is based on an Old French Chanson de Geste and has stood in the shadow of *Parzival*, at least until fairly recently, when it began to receive the attention it has always deserved. We are dealing here with heroic poetry, anonymous tales of Charlemagne, Roland, Guillaume, and the other paladins, not courtly *âventiure*, and Wolfram is quick to note the difference when he says:

> swâ man sluoc od stach,
> swaz ich ê dâ von gesprach,
> daz wart nâher wol gelendet,
> denne mit dem tôde gendet:
> diz engiltet niht wan sterben
> und an vreuden verderben. (10, 21–26)[7]

[Whatever I recounted earlier about fighting with sword or spear, of hacking and thrusting, ended in some way other than in death. *This* fighting will settle for nothing less than death and loss of joy.]

His immediate source was a Chanson de Geste from the Guillaume d'Orange cycle entitled *La Bataille d'Aliscans*. It describes two great battles between Christians and Saracens, in the first one of which Guillaume (Willehalm) loses his entire army, but returns with fresh forces to defeat the enemy decisively and put them to flight in a second battle.

The initial reason for the battles is quite clear. In the course of earlier combat Willehalm had been taken prisoner by the Saracens and, during his captivity, become acquainted with Arabel, daughter of the great ruler Terramer and wife of the Saracen King Tybalt. They fell in love; she converted to Christianity, changed her name to Giburc and escaped with him. As Wolfram's tale begins, Terramer, Tybalt, and an immense army have just arrived at Aliscans and started to attack Willehalm near his fortress at Orange, in order to regain Giburc. Willehalm loses all his men but evades the Saracens, slipping away from Orange and leaving Giburc to defend the castle, while he goes to Munleun (Laon) to seek help from King Loys (Louis the Pious), son of Charlemagne. As in the source, Willehalm is ultimately successful in gaining the king's help; the Christian forces gather at Orange, and the second battle begins. Wolfram's work breaks off abruptly, just at the moment of victory, leaving several narrative strands untied.

Willehalm is a very different kind of work from *Parzival*. It does not show the linear development that we have seen in *Parzival* but is based rather on a number of larger problematic themes that recur throughout the poem. It seems appropriate, therefore, to consider some of these larger complexes, rather than go into detail about the events of the poem. Although this poem is, on the surface, like its source, it becomes obvious that it is not just a Christians versus Saracens tale from which the Christians emerge victorious. After all, Willehalm is St. William, the patron saint of knights (3, 12–17; 4, 2–18), who, according to legend, founded and entered a monastery after defeating the Saracens and who can be relied upon to help knights in need. There is no question that Christianity is the true religion, but in the figure of Giburc contradictions appear that problematize that assumption. She belongs to *both* sides, as indicated by her very name: Arabel-Giburc. She is related by birth to the Saracens, yet she is a Christian, married to Willehalm. In a moving speech on the eve of the second battle, she explains her feelings to Heimrich, Willehalm's father, and stresses her sense of having to pay a price herself and watch the suffering of those about her because she has espoused the Christian faith.

Yet Giburc is unswerving in her faith in the Christian God. While Willehalm is away raising a new army, two discussions of religion take place, and these are an important aspect of Wolfram's re-conception of the old material. The first is Terramer's lament over his great losses and his expression of his inability to believe in the Christian God who has caused them, and of his wish to dishonor Jesus by inflicting unheard-of misery and a disgraceful death on Arabel (107, 14–108, 22). This reflects in part the Saracen view of Christianity. The second is in the form of a debate on religion by Giburc, standing on the battlements with her besieging father below, and it affirms the Christian point of view (215, 10–221, 30). Giburc stresses the power of God the Creator and Sustainer, through whose sacrifice on the Cross mankind has been redeemed from sin and saved from eternal damnation. Her words are, in a way, a Christian catechistic text. Terramer scoffs that the Holy Trinity could surely have saved the one from his shameful death on the cross at the hand of his own people if it were so powerful, and Giburc replies that even if the Saracen gods were stronger, her love for Willehalm would not allow her to change her mind. We sense that the talking has been going on for some time when Wolfram states that Terramer was using now threats, now cajolery to persuade Giburc to recant, and indeed we hear him presenting her with a choice of three methods of execution (109, 22–28).

The problem of religion goes even deeper just before the second battle, when Giburc stands up at the end of the council of war, during which the Christian leaders have recounted atrocities by the Saracens and affixed crosses to their armor. She expresses the view that the Saracens are also children of God and that we were all heathens once. In the course of Giburc's long speech before the council, she touches on other aspects of man's relationship with God and pleads for compassion for the Saracens from the Christians in two significant passages: "Hœrt eins tumben wîbes rât / schônt der gotes hantgetat" (Pay heed to the advice of a foolish woman: spare the creatures of God's hand! 306, 27–28), she urges, and a bit later she argues that, whatever the Saracens may have done to them, the Christians should bear in mind that Christ forgave those who took His life and have pity on the enemy in the event of victory (309, 1–6). And almost at the end of the text, Wolfram's narrator abruptly strikes a similar note in the aftermath of the Saracens' defeat:

> die nie toufes künde
> empfiengen, ist daz sünde?
> daz man die sluoc alsam ein vihe,
> grôzer sünde ich drumbe gihe:
> ez ist gar gotes hantgetât,
> zwuo und sibenzec sprâche, die er hât. (450, 15–20)

> [Is it a sin to slaughter like cattle those who have never received baptism? I say it is a great sin, for they are all creatures of God's Hand, and He maintains them, with their seventy-two languages.]

Wolfram's attitude towards the Saracens in *Willehalm* is a development of attitudes already found in *Parzival*. There Gahmuret has no problem in overcoming his initial aversion when he witnesses the grief of Belakane as she recounts the death of her lover Isenhart (*P* 28, 10–19). The Baruc of Baldac may not know the significance of the Cross but he respects its role in the faith of his friend Gahmuret when he places it on the elaborate tomb he has erected in his memory (*P* 107, 7–10). Feirefiz may be black and white checked, and he may call on a disparate array of Saracen gods in time of need, but he is still the only match for Parzival when it comes to combat, and, more than that, it is he whom Parzival chooses to accompany him to the Grail (*P* 784, 25).

The image of the Saracens themselves is another large issue in *Willehalm*. Terramer has assembled his huge army at the request of the Baruc of Baldac, the spiritual leader of the Saracens, who worship their gods Mahmet, Apollo, Tervigant, and Kahun, and whose images are carried into battle on wagons. If one counts one language for one country, then Terramer has troops from sixty of the seventy-two lands on the earth. In only twelve is Christian baptism observed (73, 7–14). Like their languages, the Saracens are a diverse assemblage of peoples, and Wolfram seems to have had many sources, including his own imagination, for his description of them. Some wear armor like the Christians, others wear turbans instead of helmets; at least one group is led by Gorhant from Ganjas, and these are covered with horny skin; they fight on foot with steel maces and have no human voice, but howl like hunting dogs or low like cattle (35, 10–28). The Saracen knights on horseback are usually described as being splendidly armed with exotic helmet decorations, like Cliboris of Tananarke (409, 19–30), who has a ship on his helmet and other precious stones hanging on gold threads which give the impression of sparks flying and who is killed, and "swamped" by a wave of blood flooding his "ship" (411, 6–10). Wolfram's infatuation with the sound of exotic names and places, already evident in *Parzival*, is even more pronounced in *Willehalm*. Terramer's order of battle in Book VIII is a case in point.

The concept of chivalry among the Saracens and the Christians is something of a problem. Both sides are fighting for Love and the reward of women. Each side is defending its faith, and there is little difference so far as this life is concerned. The Christians, however, are fighting for the reward of salvation in the next. The Saracens have no such hope. Nevertheless, the Saracens are at least as chivalrous as the Christians. They have the same desirable qualities: knightly reputation, generosity, honor, loyalty, noble upbringing, courage. The Saracens' fixation on Love is greater than their worship of their gods. In fact, the gods are mere idols, and they defend them, but the secular reward of Love has become almost a religion of Love for the Saracens and a motivation for their chivalry.

The praise Wolfram gives to two Saracens who are killed in the first battle shows how problematic this depiction of the Saracens can be. Willehalm, moved by revenge for the martyr-death of his nephew Vivianz in the first battle, has a chance to spare the life of mighty Arofel, Giburc's uncle and brother of Terramer. Instead, he chooses to cut off his head, whereupon Wolfram comments that this was a day of loss for Love ("da erschein der minne ein vlüstec tac," 81, 20) and that Christian ladies should to this day be mourning that Saracen man (81, 21–22). The second example is King Tesereiz, a nephew of Terramer, of whom Wolfram observes that any knight who possessed his qualities would receive the love of ladies as a reward for his lofty deeds. On the death of Tesereiz, Wolfram exclaims that the ground upon which this noble Saracen died would be sweet as sugar, and thus provide bees with their nourishment, within the radius of a day's ride from that spot. That comes very close to the "odor of sanctity" at the death of a Christian saint like Willehalm's nephew, the martyred Vivianz.[8]

A third problematic complex involves family relationships, but the scope of this work means that it extends to the political situation and the role of the Holy Roman Empire in the second battle. First we should note that, as in *Parzival*, almost all the participants are related in some way. On the Christian side there is Willehalm and his family, including, by marriage, King Loys, from whom Willehalm eventually secures help in raising an army to fight the Saracens and free the embattled Giburc. On the Saracen side is the huge family of Terramer with his twelve sons and various other relatives. The marriage between Arabel-Giburc and Willehalm is the connecting link, or, perhaps more correctly, the point of dispute, and the first battle is fought ostensibly to reclaim Giburc for the Saracens, or to kill her as revenge for her defection. Much of the bitterness and pain on both sides is caused by the loss of many relatives in the first battle, as Willehalm states and restates in the period between the two battles. The narrator himself comments critically on the dispute in an aside, when he says that Terramer was foolish to treat so badly the man whom his daughter loved and that he, Wolfram, would make every effort to keep the friendship of his daughter's chosen husband (11, 19–24). The remark, trivializing as it may seem to be, hints at some of the problematic aspects of family relationships in *Willehalm*.

From the beginning of the work, Willehalm and his brothers have a family problem. Their father, Heimrich, disinherited all of them in favor of a godchild and advised them to seek their fortune at the court of Charlemagne. This they do and become powerful lords in the politics of the Empire, but apparently they have had only sporadic contact over the years with their parents, or with one another for that matter. Exactly what effect this has had on family relationships is not quite clear, but the relationship of the various members of the family may be at the root of Willehalm's uncertainty about whether he can raise a new army with the help of his brother-in-law, the King.

Willehalm's main problem is to get help to rescue Giburc and avenge the death of his many relatives in the first battle. He arrives at Loys' court, where the king is preparing for a festival. Willehalm's father, mother and four brothers will soon arrive, but Willehalm is not welcomed. In fact he is shunned. This arouses his anger, because, as a margrave, he had been entrusted with the march (Provence) to protect the land from Saracens attack, and he had done so successfully for seven years without asking for help (146, 4–11). His uncourtly appearance in Laon disturbs the pleasure-loving atmosphere inside. His sister, the Queen, recognizes him, knows why he is there and orders that he be locked out. On the next day, Willehalm goes into the castle and sits down with his sword across his knees, threatening the cowardly king and waiting in uncertainty for his father to arrive. When his father, mother and brothers arrive, the King duly receives them, and Willehalm gambles that this is his opportunity to make his point before the King, hoping that his family will support him. He reminds him of what he owes him, implying that he (the King) has repaid him ill for his service (145, 17–30).

Although Willehalm's brothers attempt to mollify him and even the King quickly offers whatever help he can, it is the Queen who causes an angry disruption, when she points out what they may lose in helping her brother (147, 7–10). Willehalm forgets himself, seizes her crown from her head and hurls it to the ground, snatching her by her braids. Only the intervention of his mother, Irmschart, prevents him from cutting off her head. The Queen flees to her chamber, leaving the court stunned by this uncontrolled display by one who, as the King is quick to point out, is a vassal. Willehalm, close to despair now, believes that his family will not support him, but his father assures him that they will do so, when he appeals to him in the name of the Trinity to acknowledge him as his son (149, 19–26). Despite the shock of this episode, it appears that, for the time being at least, family relationships on the Christian side are less problematic than they appeared to be.

However, the related theme of the Empire has not yet been addressed. After the Queen has fled, Willehalm recounts before the court the extent of his losses in the first battle, reporting that all of the family members who had fought on his side have either been killed or taken prisoner. They join him in lamentation for their loss and the immense pain he has suffered, especially through the deaths of the young knights Mile and Vivianz, as well as for his anguish in leaving Giburc besieged in Orange. Yet Willehalm again goes too far when he slanders his sister, calling her a prostitute and saying that Tybalt, Giburc's first husband, had been her knight for a long time. Then he goes on to assert that he has deprived Tybalt of his wife more out of revenge than for her own sake, an extraordinary statement which tells us much about Willehalm's distraught state, but also underlines the problematic relationship between Willehalm and his sister, thus, indirectly, with the Empire (153, 1–30).

A dramatic change in the atmosphere at the court is brought about by the intervention of Willehalm's lovely niece, Alyze. The Queen, her mother, returns and begs the King to offer generous support to Willehalm for the sake of the Empire and for Loys's own honor, but the King is not easily mollified after the insults he has suffered. A further example of Willehalm's violent behavior occurs after the magnificent banquet, when he appeals to the King as defender of the Empire, saying that Terramer's attack is an attack on the King himself and upbraiding him when he again hesitates, for betraying his birthright as the son of Charlemagne. The King's dilemma is apparent: how to respond to the affront he has received yet still give aid to Willehalm. Loys is persuaded eventually to give his support, when the Queen addresses him as "Roman King" (180, 7) and makes reference to the "Roman Emperor Charles" (180, 28) and Heimrich and his family likewise raise the issue above the personal, by urging him to show that he has inherited his father's courage and to strive for the honor of the Empire (182, 23). This is a work in which personal and public issues both play a part, and one of Wolfram's major achievements is to suggest the relationship between them, whether in the broad political perspectives that he presents, or, on the battlefield, in the attention that he pays to individual participants within the vast depiction of the conflict.

Another central issue, which can be described as a problematic complex, is concerned with the young giant Rennewart, and it also has to do with family relationships and, since Rennewart is a Saracen, with religion. Rennewart is Giburc's long-lost brother — a fact that emerges only gradually and then by a build-up of innuendo — who had been abducted as a child by merchants and sold to King Loys. Unable to persuade Rennewart to accept baptism, he has assigned him to the demeaning role of kitchen boy. Willehalm watches as some young squires torment Rennewart, and, sensing that the boy must be of noble Saracen lineage, persuades the King to allow him to assume responsibility for him.

Rennewart is a mass of contradictions. He is a Saracen who cannot accept Christianity. He is angry with his family for having abandoned him, as he believes, and he is willing to fight against the Saracens on the Christian side. His innate nobility means that he wants desperately to escape from his demeaning circumstances at the French court, not least because he is in love with the Princess Alyze, but dares not reveal his love until he has established his reputation as a knight. As in the source, the young giant is an entertaining, carnivalesque buffoon, who provides comic relief for the listeners with his exaggerated, uncourtly actions, preferring to fight with a huge club, which he keeps forgetting. He prefers the kitchen as a sleeping place; he eats and drinks to excess. His familial resemblance to Giburc is hinted at but never completely disclosed. For all his rough ways, he assumes the role of leader in the second battle after he has managed to force the French knights to return to Orange when they were attempting to desert. He becomes a hero and the Christians' victory is largely attributable to him.

Yet, at the end of the second battle, when Wolfram's text breaks off, Rennewart has disappeared, so that there is no satisfying resolution to this problematic, contradictory figure. Indeed, his fate is a crucial aspect of the final problem for discussion here: the ending or lack of ending of *Willehalm*. In *Aliscans* there is closure. Rainoart, after having practically achieved the victory by himself, fighting and wounding his father, returns to Guillaume for the victory celebration, is baptized and marries Aelis. There is no such closure in *Willehalm*, and some would maintain no satisfactory conclusion at all. Others believe that Wolfram intended it that way, arguing that Willehalm's immense suffering and loss resulting from the battle is the whole point. What more can be said? Wolfram has told us that he will speak of such suffering, the inevitable legacy of faith (4, 25–29). When Willehalm turns the bodies of the Saracen kings over to King

Matribleiz to be buried at home according to their religion and frees the captive kings, it is a gesture of respect for Saracen nobility, not a concession that their religion has validity for Willehalm, or indeed for Wolfram. Willehalm is willing to deal with Terramer at any time in the future, but he will certainly not forsake Christianity, or Giburc. He has given up too much for that already.

Some feel that Wolfram was unable to finish his poem, because he had diverged so far from his source that he could not realistically follow it to its conclusion. Most scholars, however, attribute the lack of closure to Wolfram's death, or to the loss of support following the death of his patron Hermann von Thüringen. The lengthy continuation by Ulrich von Türheim (see below) was an attempt in his day to satisfy natural curiosity. And the lack of a satisfactory conclusion has not kept scholars even today from advancing a plethora of studies — far too many to be discussed here — which comprise a large part of the scholarly research on *Willehalm*, in which the lack of an ending is central to the interpretation. Christopher Young gives what is probably the most thorough summary of positions, especially for the most recent scholarship.[9]

The Songs

In both *Parzival* and *Willehalm* Wolfram adapts his French source to a very different literary environment and manipulates it in a thoroughly individual way. In his poetry, too, he takes up the established mode of *Minnesang* and gives it a personal twist which ensures that, though his output in this area is relatively slight, the Songs are individually remarkable and reflect a further dimension of this versatile poet.[10]

Of the seven songs that survive, five belong to the category of dawnsong, a sub-genre familiar to medieval Europe but given a special power by Wolfram.[11] At the heart of this type of love song is the illicit relationship between a man and a woman, whose stolen time together must end at dawn. Considering the extent to which his narrative works reveal his understanding of human reactions, and what we have described as "problematic complexes," it is not surprising that Wolfram exploits to the full this situation, in which the fulfillment of love is tinged with the awareness of danger, and joy barely triumphs over sorrow. His subtle presentation of the differing responses of the man and the woman is juxtaposed to the intervention of a third person, who, though necessarily peripheral to the relationship, becomes embroiled in it. This is the watchman (*wahtære*), a figure who may have been introduced by Wolfram, and who is certainly used by him to extraordinary effect, to express the rights and wrongs of this illicit love, which flies in the face of society. The lovers know what a high price they would pay if they were discovered, yet their inevitable parting is too hard to contemplate, and the watchman is torn between his compassion for them and his concern for their well-being which has been entrusted to him. He has a professional duty to announce the day, and, though he may delay a little for their sake, it is a question of his honor as well as of theirs.

One of the dawn songs — "von der zinnen wil ich gên" (I will go down from the battlements) — more than any other focuses on the watchman, who is the speaker in the first two of the three stanzas, torn between his awareness of his own responsibility and his understanding of the tragic dilemma he is witnessing in the lovers.[12] In another masterly song — "sîne klâwen durch die wolken sint geslagen" (Its talons are thrust through the clouds) — Day itself is portrayed as a great monster, as it claws its way through the sky, or, in more human terms, as it peeps in at the window, approaching ever closer until it breaks in and forces the departure that the lovers have resisted. Once more, it is left to the watchman to announce the coming of day and articulate the threat it brings, pleading with the lady to release her lover and responding to her pleas that they be allowed to stay together a little longer. The urgency of the situation, which involves all three people, is intensified by the relentless approach of day and the passion of the inevitable leave-taking.[13]

The Songs are indeed remarkable for their evocation of passionate love in which the physical is not denied, and for the suspense and drama of an intensely human situation. This is not the somewhat artificial playing with the idea of adulterous love of the minnesingers, but the presentation of a dilemma in which the two protagonists are deeply vulnerable. Although he understands the lovers' suffering, and appears not to doubt the power of the love which gives rise to it, Wolfram does not really pass judgment either way. In the song beginning "Der helden minne ir klage" (The lament of secret love), he does, however, seem to advocate another, better way of loving, within marriage and thus without the threat of discovery at daybreak. Yet it is hard to be sure about this message, and some critics see the song as a parody of the conventional *Minnesang*, while others take it rather at its face value, as an affirmation of marriage and its place in the social framework. The latter view is not surprising, given that the state of marriage lies at the heart of both *Parzival* and *Willehalm*.

Wolfram is full of surprises, however, and parody is not altogether alien to him. The two songs that do not belong to the group of dawn songs show him using the language and imagery of *Minnesang*, and something resembling its basic stance, but manipulating all these in a thoroughly original way. He achieves a distance from the convention, which might lead one to suspect a deliberate attempt at parody.

The remaining song attributed to Wolfram is also a strange mixture, beginning as it does with a powerful evocation of springtime — "ursprinc bluomen, loup ûz dringen" (The shooting up of flowers, the pushing out of leaves . . .) — and, against that background, linking the singer with the nightingale. Yet then, almost as though checking himself after this exuberant opening, Wolfram drifts into a much more conventional mode for the remaining three strophes, in which he addresses his lady in language familiar from his predecessors: *güetlich wîp, guot wîp, werdez wîp* (gentle woman, good woman, noble woman). The stance that he now adopts is the traditional one of devoted service, unto death if necessary, and of submission in the face of grief and even anger.

In sum, it is important to note that this poet who is known above all as a powerful narrator was capable of attaining heights of lyrical expression, unsurprising in view of the capacity he shows in both *Parzival* and *Willehalm* to evoke tender, idyllic scenes. Equally, his lyric has a distinct kinship with drama and narrative, particularly in its powerful yet succinct presentation of a very human dilemma.[14]

Titurel

The interrelationship of narrative, drama in its broadest sense, and lyric finds its ultimate expression in the two fragments usually known as *Titurel* because Titurel, the old Grail King in *Parzival*, is named in the first line of the first fragment.[15] Some critics, however, would prefer to call them *Sigune and Schionatulander*, after the central characters. This work completes the picture of Wolfram's remarkable œuvre, and it could be argued that it supplies a key to it and to the understanding of Wolfram's special position within the literature of his age. This may seem to be an extravagant claim, since it is probably the least well known of Wolfram's works and in many respects cannot be compared with the two vast narratives, *Parzival* and *Willehalm*. Its striking form — a four-lined strophe of considerable metrical complexity — distinguishes it from his other two narrative works which are composed in the rhymed couplet form adopted for most German narratives of the Middle Ages and gives it even at first sight a special distinction.[16]

The very first strophe makes an immediate impact that is sustained throughout the fragments. Already there is the contrast of old age and youth, the bitter-sweetness that comes with the passage of time, and already the power of the unique strophic form is evident. The lines of unequal length, bound together in a sustained rhyme scheme, and the frequent enjambments ensure that the poem moves with extraordinary grace as it tells of the juxtapositions in human fortunes. The subject matter is an elusive story of tragic love and the quest for a prized goal. It, too, is very much Wolfram's own invention. Here he depends, not on a French precursor, but on a line apparently thrown away in his own *Parzival*, where Sigune, the first cousin of Parzival, laments her lost love, the dead knight cradled in her arms, and offers the incomprehensible explanation: " 'ein bracken seil gap im den pîn' " (A hound's leash caused him his suffering, 141, 16).

Incomprehensible in *Parzival* and not fully explained in *Titurel*, the hound's leash, with its elaborate decoration of embroidery and encrusted jewels, is the focus of the beautiful fragment, an outstanding example of Wolfram's delight in extravagance and detailed description of the exotic. Wolfram shows again his sensitivity to the power of love and his awareness of human ambition, which can lead to recklessness. He takes up themes that pervade his other narratives: the legacy that passes from one generation to another, family allegiances and the tragic potential of chivalry. The Wolfram of the Songs plays again with the language of *Minnesang*, as Sigune speaks of her burgeoning love for the young Schionatulander (114–21), but he is fully conscious, too, that love demands a high price and that the threat of society and circumstances looms. The approach of daybreak was described with enormous power in the Songs, but with no less power does Sigune picture herself watching across the waves for the return of her beloved (118).

The scene which opens the first fragment links it firmly to *Parzival*, as King Titurel, the old man "grayer than the mist" (240, 30) whom Parzival glimpsed in the room beyond the great hall at Munsalvæsche, hands over the rule of the Grail to his son Frimutel. The fascination with the complexity of the Grail and the insistence that it rests in the guardianship of a selected dynasty, lead him to base this story of young love, doomed to tragedy, in a context familiar to his audience. His account of the meeting and growing love between Sigune and Schionatulander causes him to return to the story of Herzeloyde's love for Gahmuret, but his purpose this time is less to tell of Parzival's parents than of the separation of lovers of the younger generation and the bitter-sweetness of their pain.

Tantalizingly, the second fragment breaks off when Schionatulander is again about to depart, this time on the quest for the hound's leash that Sigune so desires and that he hopes may secure her love for him. The leash to which, in *Parzival*, Sigune had attributed the death of her lover becomes a symbol of knightly endeavor, yet exactly how remains untold.

Fascinating though this delicate torso is to the modern reader, it probably caused considerable exasperation to the medieval audience, with its craving for a good tale well told, leaving no ends untied. Far from answering questions, Wolfram's *Titurel* raises new issues. The obvious question of the connection between the hound's leash and the death of a knight in full armor remains unanswered, as Schionatulander races off in pursuit of the hunting dog with its leash inscribed with tales of tragic love. All we know is that the young couple has made a kind of pact and that perhaps, but only perhaps, Schionatulander will gain the love of Sigune if he brings this exotic object back to her. What adventures he encounters along the way lie beyond the close of Wolfram's second fragment. This beautiful and enigmatic little work may have been a sketch for a long poem of epic grandeur or, a more "modern" notion, may have been *designed* as a fragment, artistically as elusive as the love it treats with such poignancy. It completes our picture of the work of Wolfram von Eschenbach and aptly underlines our central thesis of the range and originality of this remarkable poet.

We have looked at Wolfram from our modern perspective, and with the benefit of many generations of scholarly work, but it is probably safe to say that even in the Middle Ages people had an awareness of his uniqueness and his rare poetic gifts. Those praising Wolfram outnumbered his critics, and the number of manuscripts of his works attests to their popularity. Even during his lifetime he was frequently imitated and some set out to continue his apparently unfinished works.

The obvious candidates for such "completion" were *Willehalm* and *Titurel*. Two people turned to *Willehalm* in the middle of the thirteenth century and added to it: Ulrich von dem Türlin with his *Willehalm*, known also, less confusingly, as *Arabel*, and Ulrich von Türheim, who composed a lengthy continuation usually called *Rennewart*.[17] Their works appear in the manuscripts both individually and, in some cases, together with Wolfram's *Willehalm*, as an enormous trilogy. Later generations were thus able to hear the story of the youth of Willehalm, his upbringing at the court of Charlemagne, his captivity in Todjerne, where he meets and falls in love with Arabel and elopes with her, events told in retrospect by Wolfram, and then, after the central events related in Wolfram's poem, to learn of the fate of Rennewart, his investiture, and his marriage to Princess Alyze. When Ulrich von Türheim goes on to tell of the death of Alyze in giving birth to the giant-like Maleser, the abduction of the child and the withdrawal of the grief-stricken Rennewart into a monastery, he goes beyond the task of adding an ending to Wolfram's masterpiece, though one may be sure that the medieval audience enjoyed the exciting narrative, and were then more than content to hear of Willehalm's new encounter with the Saracen forces, led now by the son of Terramer. Ulrich shows a certain understanding, too, of Wolfram's emphasis on the spiritual life of Willehalm when he concludes his narrative with his death in the monastery he himself had founded.

The *Jüngerer Titurel* (ca. 1270–75)[18] bears a very different relationship to the original fragile fragments and is a literary phenomenon that speaks both for the taste of its age and the esteem in which Wolfram was held. Despite much disparaging criticism in the post-medieval period, it is actually a *tour de force* of some significance, though probably best viewed quite separately from Wolfram's *Titurel*. At the same time, it must be remembered that this was not how the Middle Ages viewed it.[19] The author, now identified quite simply as Albrecht, would have his audience believe that he is Wolfram von Eschenbach, and he appears to have satisfied his audience with this grotesque subterfuge. The large number of manuscripts (eleven of them complete and forty-five fragments) suggests a work that was well received, and it would seem that, throughout the medieval period, this vast narrative which covers many and quite diverse areas and includes elaborate descriptions of the Grail temple, eclipsed the tiny fragments which had inspired it and much of which Albrecht actually includes within his own poem.

Possibly one final example best demonstrates the perspective from which these "continuators" were working. Although not strictly speaking a "continuation," the anonymous poem *Lohengrin*, usually dated somewhere in the 1280s,[20] is clearly dependent on Wolfram's *Parzival*. Lohengrin is the son of Parzival and Condwiramurs, and, whereas the fate of his twin-brother Kardeiz is decided by the fact that he is heir to the Grail throne, his future is less prescribed than his brother's. Instead, as a part of the careful tying-up of the strands of his narrative in this poem, Wolfram anticipates the course of his life in the closing stages of the final Book of *Parzival* and thus provides, in embryo, a story taken up by an unknown author in the later twelfth century. In the nineteenth century the work evolved into the famous opera by Wagner. The crucial inspiration comes in Wolfram's lines 824, 27–28, which refer to Lohengrin as having been brought to Brabant from Munsalvæsche by a swan. Parzival's second son thus becomes identified with the Swan Knight, who marries the Queen of Brabant and warns her never to ask where he came from. Their love is doomed, for her curiosity will get the better of her, and he will be forced to leave her. It is entirely consistent with the whole picture of Wolfram and his oeuvre that he should hint at another story even as he is closing his great poem, and understandable that a later author should seize on it in the desire to honor his revered predecessor, arguably *the* outstanding poet of the German Middle Ages.

Notes

* Sadly, when the greater part of this chapter had been written, but before it could be completed, my friend and colleague Sidney Johnson died. This final version is dedicated to him, in affection and deep respect, and gratitude for many years of collaboration. M. E. G.

[1] Karl Lachmann, *Wolfram von Eschenbach*, 6th ed. (Berlin: de Gruyter, 1926), contains all of Wolfram's works, frequently re-issued complete or in separate texts — all quotations here are from the Lachmann text. The most recent text of *Parzival* is by Eberhard Nellmann, *Wolfram von Eschenbach: Parzival*, 2 vols. (Frankfurt am Main.: Deutscher Klassiker Verlag, 1994), with a verse translation into modern German by Dieter Kühn. Translations into modern German prose include that by Wolfgang Spiewok (*Parzival*, translated into modern German prose, with a *Nachwort* [Stuttgart: Reclam, 1981]). The most accessible English prose translation is that of Arthur T. Hatto (Harmondsworth: Penguin, 1980), which is followed by a useful "Introduction to a Second Reading." The English translations of *Parzival* cited below are those of Hatto.

[2] Wolfram's text is cited here, as in the critical editions, with two numbers; the first refers to the number of the thirty verse group (discussed above), the second to the specific verses in that group.

[3] Joachim Bumke, *Wolfram von Eschenbach* (Stuttgart, Weimar: Metzler, [6]1991, 141–46; [7]1997, 107–13).

[4] For a recent treatment of Kyot as a creation of Wolfram, see D. H. Green, *The Beginnings of Medieval Romance: Fact and Fiction, 1150–1220* (Cambridge: Cambridge UP, 2002), 78–82.

[5] See Sidney M. Johnson, "Doing his Own Thing: Wolfram's Grail," in Hasty, ed., *A Companion to Wolfram's "Parzival,"* 77–93.

[6] See Martin H. Jones, "The Significance of the Gawan Story," in Hasty, ed., *A Companion to Wolfram's "Parzival,"* 37–76.

[7] Several editions of the text are available, aside from Lachmann's. We cite from Joachim Heinzle, ed. *Wolfram von Eschenbach: Willehalm. Nach der Handschrift 857 der Stiftsbibliothek St. Gallen. Mittelhochdeutscher Text, Übersetzung, Kommentar* (Frankfurt am Main: Deutscher Klassiker Verlag, 1991). Translations into English are taken from Marion E. Gibbs and Sidney M. Johnson, *Willehalm* (Harmondsworth: Penguin, 1984, repr. 1992).

[8] John Greenfield, *Vivianz: An Analysis of the Martyr Figure in Wolfram von Eschenbach's "Willehalm" and in his Old French Source Material* (Erlangen: Palm & Enke, 1991).

[9] A recent useful study is Christopher Young, *Narrativische Perspektiven in Wolframs "Willehalm"* (Tübingen: Niemeyer, 2000).

[10] Texts of the songs are in Lachmann's edition and in Hugo Moser and Helmut Tervooren, eds., *Des Minnesangs Frühling I: Texte* (Stuttgart: S. Hirzel, 1977), but other editions are also important, especially since they include translations: Peter Wapnewski, *Die Lyrik Wolframs von Eschenbach. Edition, Kommentar, Interpretation* (Munich: Beck, 1972); the Middle High German songs with an English translation are contained in Marion E. Gibbs and Sidney M. Johnson, eds. and trans., *Wolfram von Eschenbach: "Titurel" and the "Songs"* (New York: Garland, 1988). Texts and translations are from this edition.

[11] A. T. Hatto, ed., *Eos: An Enquiry into the Theme of Lovers' Meetings and Partings at Dawn in Poetry* (London, the Hague, Paris: Mouton, 1965); particular reference to German literature, 428–72.

[12] See Cyril Edwards, "Von der zinnen wil ich gen: Wolfram's Peevish Watchman," *Modern Language Review* 84 (1989): 358–66.

[13] L. Peter Johnson, "*Sîne klâwen*: An Interpretation," in *Approaches to Wolfram von Eschenbach*, ed. Dennis Green and L. Peter Johnson (Frankfurt am Main: Lang, 1978): 295–334.

[14] See Karl Heinz Borck, "Wolframs Tagelied '*den morgenblic bi wahtaers sange erkos*': Zur Lyrik eines Epikers," in *Studien zur deutschen Literatur: Festschrift für Adolf Beck zum 70. Geburtstag*, ed. Ulrich Fülleborn and Johannes Krogoll, Heidelberg: Winter, 1979, 9–17, and Peter Wapnewski, *Die Lyrik Wolframs von Eschenbach: Edition, Kommentar, Interpretation* (Munich: Beck, 1972).

[15] Text in the Lachmann edition.

[16] A helpful reference work is Joachim Heinzle's *Stellenkommentar zu Wolframs "Titurel." Beiträge zum Verständnis des überlieferten Textes* (Tübingen: Niemeyer, 1972). An English translation of *Titurel* is in the above-cited edition and translation of *Titurel* and the Songs by Marion E. Gibbs and Sidney M. Johnson.

[17] Ulrich von dem Türlîn's text is found in Werner Schröder, ed. *Arabel Studien*, 6 vols. (Wiesbaden: Franz Steiner, 1982–1993); the edition of Ulrich von Türheim's work is by Alfred Hübner, *Ulrich von Türheim: Rennewart, aus der Berliner und Heidelberger Handschrift* (Berlin: Weidmann, 1938).

[18] Werner Wolf, ed., *Albrechts von Scharfenberg Jüngerer Titurel* (Berlin: Akademie Verlag, 1955), vol. 1; 1964, vol. 2, 1; 1968, vol. 2, 2; continued by Kurt Nyholm (Berlin: Akademie Verlag, 1985 and 1992).

[19] For a comparison of Wolfram and Albrecht, see Linda B. Parshall, *The Art of Narration in Wolfram's "Parzival" and Albrecht's "Jüngerer Titurel"* (Cambridge: Cambridge UP, 1981).

[20] Thomas Cramer, ed. *Lohengrin* (Munich: W. Fink, 1971).

Ulrich von Zatzikhoven's *Lanzelet*

Nicola McLelland

*L*ANZELET, A WORK OF 9444 LINES in the four-beat rhyming couplets of German courtly romance, is based, according to the narrator, on a *welschez buoch* (9324–41), a French written source brought to Germany by a hostage for Richard the Lionheart in 1194, Hûc de Morville. The author of the German work, Ulrich von Zatzikhoven, was probably a cleric who lived not far from Lake Constance in what is today Switzerland. K. A. Hahn's edition (1845, reprinted 1965) is based on the two nearly complete manuscripts which survive, W (fourteenth century) and P (fifteenth century), both from the Alemannic dialect area (today's south-west Germany and Switzerland) and on fragments from two others. Hahn does not take into account the two more recently discovered fragments, G[k] and B, and his critical apparatus is incomplete and inconsistent, but his remains the only edition available.[1] The dating of the work is controversial. A dating of 1200 to 1203 assumes based on textual parallels that Ulrich drew on Hartmann's *Erec* but not his *Iwein*, and knew at least some of the early books of Wolfram's *Parzival*.[2] *Lanzelet* is certainly rather derivative, drawing on several traditions. The influence of two early courtly works, Eilhart von Oberg's *Tristrant* (ca. 1175–80) and Heinrich von Veldeke's Aeneas romance (ca. 1185), is evident in virtually every line of a monologue on the nature of irresistible love (4373–4406),[3] but Ulrich's vocabulary is indebted to the tradition of heroic epic too — the hero is often referred to not just as a *ritter* (knight), but as a *recke, wîgant, helt* and *degen*, all terms meaning warrior or hero, and most familiar from heroic verse (though later romance writers will use them too). Ulrich also has a fondness for formulaic and well-worn proverbial phrases. The narrator's view of the overthrow of Lanzelet's father at the start of the work is one of many such examples: "dô wart diz wort bewaeret: / er belîbet dicke sigelôs / swer die sîne verkôs" (There the saying was proved: he who disdains his men is often defeated, 130–32). Yet Ulrich's combining such different styles and narrative voices is itself innovative — and the resulting work seems to have met with a respectable measure of success among medieval audiences and later medieval authors who make reference to Lanzelet's exploits.

Ulrich von Zatzikhoven's version of the Lancelot matter relates the career of Lanzelet du Lac as he sets out, a young unknown, from the kingdom of a sea-fairy who has brought him up since his infancy, when his father Pant was killed in a rebellion against his tyrannical rule. Lanzelet enjoys repeated successes in his adventures, twice incidentally winning a maiden (the Galagandreiz daughter and Ade) and thus control over their respective lands, but each is left behind as Lanzelet continues his quest for his name. He ultimately triumphs in single combat with Iweret, "dem besten ritter der ie wart" (the best knight who ever was, 329). As a reward for this victory, he is told his name and kinship (a device that connects the work with the tradition of the Fair Unknown). He also wins Iweret's daughter, Iblis, and her lands, and she remains his faithful queen for life. Her fidelity is confirmed by a *Mantelprobe*, a test by coat, at Arthur's court — only she can don the magic fidelity-testing coat with impunity. Lanzelet himself, however, soon finds himself trapped with the Lady of Pluris, who claims him for herself after he succeeds in an *âventiure* that she instituted to select a husband. He is only rescued by his friends from Arthur's court. He subsequently leads expeditions to rescue Ginover from an abductor (though Ulrich makes no mention of the adulterous love for Guinevere for which Lancelot in Chrétien de Troyes's *Charrette* is best known), and then to free Erec and Walwein (Gawein) from the clutches of a sorcerer. Unlike his father Pant, Lanzelet rules wisely with his wife Iblis over their inherited lands. They live to see their four children take over their four kingdoms, and die in old age on the same day.

Ulrich's *Lanzelet* was long neglected as one of the "lesser" Middle High German romances, but over the past three decades it has received greater critical attention. First, it is noteworthy for its deliberate variation of narrative voices within and between episodes — a technique reminiscent of the heteroglossia identified by Bakhtinian approaches to Wolfram von Eschenbach's *Parzival*.[4] To create such variation in narrative style, Ulrich draws on motifs and plot elements from outside what modern scholarship has tended to consider the "classical" Arthurian romance tradition. This suggests a greater fluidity between the courtly romance, heroic epic, the *Schwank* (short comedic tale), and fairy-tale traditions (genre distinctions imposed retrospectively) than is often acknowledged. The static perfection of Ulrich's hero — who certainly grows up, but does not develop, for he is already flawless — points forward to later works such as Wirnt von Gravenberg's *Wigalois* (ca. 1205–35), Der Stricker's *Daniel* (ca. 1220–25), and Heinrich von dem Türlin's *Diu Crône* (1220–25), where the protagonists are likewise already perfect at the outset. The later episodes focus on the need to respond collectively to collective danger, as the very existence of the Arthurian court as a whole is threatened. *Lanzelet* is also in part an exploration of the nature of good and bad lordship — Lanzelet becomes as good a king as his father was bad.[5] The work has even been read as a kind of textbook about good and bad practice for young nobles.[6] Finally, Ulrich's female characters invite feminist analyses — the aggressive sexuality of Lanzelet's multiple partners poses a threat to the patriarchal order,[7] as does the dominant role of the mother-figures (the hero's mother, Clarine, and foster-mother, the sea-fairy) in shaping Lanzelet's destiny and assuring his *saelde* (a term which arguably embraces both good fortune and the qualities that attract it).[8]

These are features that make *Lanzelet* significant in the context of Middle High German literature. It has been forcefully argued by Pérennec that *Lanzelet* also deserves a place in French literary history, for it still owes much to the French literary context in which its source emerged, in which ancestral *enfances* were written to justify the dynastic succession of noble families.[9] For Pérennec, the biographical and circular structure of *Lanzelet* and the importance of kinship relations reflect the typical exile-and-return schema of the French *enfances* — and like the *enfances*, the work reveals a preoccupation with dynastic succession to lordship.

Lanzelet did not fare well at the hands of critics of the nineteenth and first half of the twentieth century. The work was dismissed for its uneven style and viewed as a poor compilation of already familiar elements. It was not until the 1970s that it enjoyed a rehabilitation, though ironically this rested on the discovery of a two-part structure supposedly like that familiar from Hartmann's romances: in *Lanzelet*, a search for identity is followed in the second half by a progressive accession to social responsibilities. In the first half, it was suggested, the hero earns the right to learn his name through victory in a series of increasingly difficult individual combats, as well as by winning his queen, Iblis. In the second half it was suggested that he earns his place in the Arthurian world by undertaking adventures for the collective good, rescuing first Ginover, then Erec and Walwein from imprisonments and returning them safely to the court. Only then is he ready to take on his destined place in society — to reclaim his kingship by inheritance in Genewis, from which he was exiled as an infant, and to take on the rule of the lands he won by defeating Iweret, the father of his wife Iblis.[10] The identification of this bipartite structure — and particularly its parallels to the two-part structure of *Erec* and *Iwein* — made *Lanzelet* more palatable to many scholars, but the parallel mistakenly implied a Hartmannesque moral development where there is none. Lanzelet's search for his name does not reflect any kind of development toward knightly identity or Arthurian worth — he is explicitly seen as a perfect knight from the start. His only setback before learning his name is a temporary conversion to utter cowardice in the enchanted castle of Schatel le Mort, and even this only reflects his exceptional courage in the outside world — a spell dictates that the bravest outside the castle becomes the most craven within its walls.

We find in the prologue strong support for the view that Lanzelet does not undergo any edifying moral crisis or development. The prologue is carefully structured, but unlike other Arthurian romance prologues of its time, it fails to point to any edifying, improving purpose of the work.[11] Instead, it is built around a contrast between the *boese* or *zagen* (cowardly, morally weak) and the *frume* (courageous, morally strong) in the world. Against this background, we need not look for a Hartmann-style hero who learns from his mistakes. Instead, the whole work can be seen as an emphatic affirmation of *vrumecheit / manheit* (courage). The central episode is the defeat of Iweret, as a result of which Lanzelet both wins Iblis and learns his name. This episode is a stylistic showpiece, in which courtly love (a prophetic dream of the beloved, a *locus amoenus*, lovers' dialogue, the overpowering force of love, nods to Ovid) and courtly accoutrements (a palace, a pavilion, luxurious furnishings and armor) are dwelt on in great detail. Yet even here, love is portrayed as a spur to *manheit* (4584–86).

The high courtly narrative style of the central episode is not typical of the work as a whole, and this perceived "unevenness" has been much criticized. But there is another way of looking at the work. The episodes on either side of the central showpiece fall into a symmetrical structure and are all re-statements of Lanzelet's outstanding *manheit*, or courage, presented in a number of different narrative styles. To give two of the clearest instances, Lanzelet's first exploit is the frenzied killing of Galagandreiz in a knife-throwing contest, after the latter's daughter has virtually forced herself upon the unsuspecting but willing hero:

> er leit si an dem arm sîn
> und kuste si wol tûsent stunt.
> in wart diu beste minne kunt,
> diu zwein gelieben ie geschach.

[He laid her on his arm, and kissed her a good thousand times. They experienced the best love that ever two lovers had. (1096–99)]

When the father Galagandreiz bursts into the bedchamber,

> diu juncfrowe sich verbarc
> under ir friunt den jungen degen
> und wolte dâ sîn tôt gelegen.

[The maiden hid under her friend, the young warrior, and would fain have lain there dead. (1140–42)]

As these extracts show, the entire episode has many comedic features. At the same time, the humor of the episode also highlights Lanzelet's courage compared to his two companions who reject the daughter's advances from fear and who "waeren wundergerne dan" (would dearly have wished to be elsewhere, 1171) when the furious father challenges Lanzelet. In the next episode, at Limors, Lanzelet defeats a giant, then two lions, and finally the lord of Limors himself, Linier, even though by this third battle our hero is already much weakened by loss of blood. The bloody battles are portrayed with the intense seriousness familiar from Germanic heroic epic, and Lanzelet's ultimate victory against such odds takes on a truly heroic dimension. Once again, his courage contrasts with the cowardice of Linier, who requires all to approach his castle unarmed and who only faces Lanzelet after the latter has already survived two bloody encounters. The third occurrence of the motif of winning a maiden, in the central episode, is again utterly different. Now the approach of the father, Iweret, is in high courtly style: "dô kom ir vater zuo geriten / ûf eime stolzen rosse grôz / [. . .]" (There came her father riding up on a great proud steed, 4408–89). With his fine apparel and armor "er schein ein engel, niht ein man. / [. . .] ze einer hübscheite / fuorte er sîdîn mouwen" (He seemed an angel rather than a man. [. . .] As a courtly adornment, he wore silken sleeves, 4430, 4432–33). Altogether, then, Ulrich presents three episodes, in each of which the hero wins a maiden and is offered the rule over her lands. Each demonstrates his great courage, but each is narrated in a quite different style — humor in the manner of the *Schwank*, heroic earnest and high courtly style. There is no linear character development; rather the hero exhibits perfect *manheit* in a manner befitting the style of each episode. Courage is not just force of arms, however, but also moral strength — Lanzelet's final, crowning adventure does not involve combat at all, but is simply to plant a kiss on the hideous mouth of a dragon (in the Middle Ages a terrifying symbol of sin and evil, associated with Satan). His moral bravery releases the enchanted maiden Elidia from her imprisonment in dragon's form.[12]

The nature of Lanzelet's successive relationships with women has received much critical attention — beginning with condemnation of their supposed "uncourtliness." Recently interest has shifted to how these female characters *control* the hero and his destiny. Each of the three maidens is the instigator of their relationship with Lanzelet: the Galagandreiz daughter comes to his bedside after being rejected by two other more experienced knights; Ade sees his valor fighting the defending army of Lîmors and rides out to rescue him; and Iblis comes to the fountain in Behforet to meet him after seeing him in a prophetic dream. Meyer sees here the expression of threats to the patriarchal order from unbridled female sexuality.[13] Nor is it only Lanzelet's lovers to whom Ulrich gives a controlling role. Lanzelet's mother Clarine — whose fate was not clear after the rebellion which killed his father — returns to the plot toward the end of the work, and although she remains a minor figure, it is only after he is reunited with her that Lanzelet is acclaimed as king in his own lands and in those of Iblis too. Lanzelet also has a sea-fairy for a foster-mother, who brings him to her all-female realm where he is educated; it is this mother figure too who first withholds and then ultimately reveals the hero's name and background which he needs to participate fully in Arthurian society; and it is her enchantment that holds Lanzelet captive and powerless in Schatel le Mort until its lord Mabuz decides he needs Lanzelet's help in the outside world. The mother of the squire Johfrit de Liez, whom Lanzelet encounters soon after leaving the sea-kingdom, also takes a hand in his education, organizing a tournament for his benefit. Women are repeatedly the agents of Lanzelet's destiny, instrumental in assuring his *saelde* or good fortune. Perhaps most complex of all is the role of the queen of Pluris — both a lover and a controlling figure like the sea-fairy. Though Lanzelet has already won Iblis as his lady, when he succeeds in the *âventiure* instituted by the queen of Pluris to find a new lord, she usurps the role of the controlling male. She disarms him, and, thus emasculated, he is obliged to remain with her as her spouse against his will: "dô muose aber briuten / der wîpsaelige Lanzelet" (then woman-blessed / woman-lucky Lanzelet had to marry again, 5528–29). Only a ruse with the help of his Arthurian companions rescues him.

Lanzelet remains in many ways an awkward text. It contains features traditionally viewed as "post-classical" (social as well as individual adventures; no development of the hero; no single harmonious style throughout), yet its date is too early to fall into that tidy category. It is clear, however, that renewed critical interest in it over the last thirty years has borne fruit, opening up new perspectives — of which the theme of dynastic succession to lordship, the variation in narrative patterns, and the key roles of the female characters are perhaps the most promising lines for future enquiry.

Notes

[1] Ulrich von Zatzikhoven, *Lanzelet*, ed. K. A. Hahn (Frankfurt: Brönner, 1845; rpt. with afterword and bibliography by Frederick Norman, Berlin: de Gruyter, 1965). A recent parallel translation into modern German has made the text more accessible: Wolfgang Spiewok, *Ulrich von Zatzikhoven: Lanzelet mittelhochdeutsch / neuhochdeutsch* (Greifswald: Reineke-Verlag, 1997). The romance has also been translated, though not always accurately, into modern English and, more reliably, into modern French: Ulrich von Zatzikhoven, *Lanzelet: A Romance of Lancelot*. Translated from the Middle High German by K. G. T. Webster. Revised with additional notes and an introduction by Roger Sherman Loomis (New York: Columbia UP, 1951), and René Pérennec, "Ulrich von Zatzikhoven. Lanzelet. Traduction en française moderne, accompagnée d'une introduction et de notes" (Diss. Paris, 1970). Translations of Ulrich's verses in this chapter are by N. M. On the manuscript tradition see Rosemary Combridge, "Der Lanzelet Ulrichs von Zatzikhoven im Kreuzfeuer der Editionsprinzipien," *Methoden und Probleme der Edition mittelalterlicher Texte* (Beiheft zu *Editio*), ed. Rolf Bergmann and Kurt Gärtner (Tübingen: Niemeyer, 1993), 40–49. For a summary of evidence of the work's reception, see McLelland, *Ulrich von Zatzikhoven's Lanzelet* (see note 2), 27–30.

[2] For a full discussion of the question of authorship and date, see Nicola McLelland, *Ulrich von Zatzikhoven's Lanzelet: Narrative Style and Entertainment* (Cambridge: Brewer, 2000), 17–27.

[3] See Pérennec, "Ulrich von Zatzikhoven. Lanzelet" (see note 1), 103.

[4] See, e.g. A. Groos, "Dialogic Transcriptions" in *Chrétien de Troyes and the German Middle Ages*, ed. M. Jones and R. Wisbey (Cambridge: Brewer, 1993), 257–76, and A. Stevens, "Heteroglossia and Clerical Narrative" in the same volume, 241–55. For detailed analysis of the variation of styles in *Lanzelet*, see McLelland, *Ulrich von Zatzikhoven's Lanzelet* (see note 2).

[5] W. H. Jackson, "Ulrich von Zatzikhoven's *Lanzelet* and the Theme of Resistance to Royal Power," *German Life and Letters* 28 (1974–75), 285–97.

[6] Ulrike Zellmann, *Lanzelet: Der biographische Roman als Auslegungsschema dynastischer Wissensbildung* (Düsseldorf: Droste, 1996).

[7] Kathleen J. Meyer, "*Lanzelet* and the Enclosure of Female Sexuality," in *New Texts, Methodologies, and Interpretations in Medieval German Literature* (Kalamazoo Papers 1992–1995), ed. Sibylle Jefferis (Göppingen: Kümmerle, 1999), 159–72.

[8] See Elisabeth Schmid, "Mutterrecht und Vaterliebe: Spekulationen über Eltern und Kinder im Lanzelet des Ulrichs von Zatzikhoven," *Archiv für das Studium der neueren Sprachen und Literaturen* 229 (1992), 241–54; also McLelland, *Ulrich von Zatzikhoven's Lanzelet* (see note 2), 223–33.

[9] René Pérennec, "Artusroman und Familie: 'daz welsche buoch von Lanzelete,'" *Acta Germanica* 11 (1979), 1–51.

[10] This rehabilitation began with Ernst Soudek, "Die Funktion der Namensuche und der Zweikämpfe in Ulrich von Zatzikhovens *Lanzelet*," *Amsterdamer Beiträge zur älteren Germanistik* 2 (1972), 173–85, followed by Kurt Ruh, "Der Lanzelet Ulrichs von Zatzikhoven, Modell oder Kompilation?" in *Deutsche Literatur des späten Mittelalters*, ed. Wolfgang Harms and L. Peter Johnson (Berlin: Erich Schmidt, 1975), 47–55, and Helga Schüppert, "Minneszene und Struktur im *Lanzelet* Ulrichs von Zatzikhoven," in *Würzburger Prosastudien: Untersuchungen zur Literatur und Sprache des Mittelalters. Kurt Ruh zum 60. Geburtstag*, ed. Peter Kesting (Munich: Fink, 1969), 123–38.

[11] See James Schultz, "Lanzelet: A Flawless Hero in a Symmetrical World," *Beiträge zur Geschichte der deutschen Sprache und Literatur* 102 (1980), 160–88, and McLelland, *Ulrich von Zatzikhoven's Lanzelet* (see note 2), 35–49.

[12] On this episode, see Rick Chamberlin, "*Got hât liut unde lant von manegem wunder gemaht*: An Example of the Marvellous as Allegory in Ulrich von Zatikhoven's Lanzelet," *Michigan Germanic Studies* 24 (1999), 8–17.

[13] Meyer, "*Lanzelet* and the Enclosure of Female Sexuality" (see note 7), 161.

Walther von der Vogelweide. A miniature from the Codex Manesse (124r).

Walther von der Vogelweide

Will Hasty

O N THE BASIS OF THE NEW ACCENTS he was able to give to the love lyric-
tradition, and the new foundation he provided for didactic poetry
(the *Sangsprüche*, or gnomic poetry) with his verses on religious, social,
and political topics, Walther von der Vogelweide was one of the most innovative and productive lyric poets of the German High Middle Ages.[1]
Walther's lyric poetry could be discussed in the chapters about the love
lyrics and didactic and political poetry elsewhere in this volume, but the
important role he played in shaping these lyrical genres and in establishing
new thematic and formal relationships between them warrant a separate
treatment of his literary career. A separate treatment is further justified
because he also composed a religious lay, or *Leich*, thus demonstrating his
mastery of three genres during a time when most poets concentrated on
one, and because he was highly significant for later literary developments
in the Middle Ages.

Details about Walther's life are, for the most part, as difficult to make
out as those of other medieval poets.[2] Questions begin with the name "von
der Vogelweide," which has brought forth a wide variety of interpretations:
some scholars construe "Vogelweide" (literally: aviary) as a place-name,
while others see in it a metaphorical expression of Walther's career as a
singer. The view of the minnesingers as sweetly-singing birds is known to us
from Gottfried von Strassburg's famous literary review in which the lyric
poets are cast as nightingales, and Walther as their leader: "ich wæne, ich sî
wol vinde, / diu die baniere füeren sol: / ir meisterinne kan ez wol, / diu
von der Vogelweide" (I believe I can find the nightingale to carry their
banner; their master can do it well, the one from Vogelweide; *Tristan*,
4796–99[3]). A rough outline of Walther's personal and artistic development,
based on passages in his poetry and in the works of other medieval poets,
has gained wide currency in the scholarly literature. This outline is largely
dependent on the assumption that some historical information can be gleaned
from poetic works, in which role-playing, or self-stylizations in the form of
different poetic personae, is a predominant element. Yet it seems likely that
many of the poetic roles as developed by Walther, particularly in the didactic and political poetry (for example in the references to contemporary political figures and developments, and perhaps in the so-called *Alterslieder*,
songs of old age), allow us to catch glimpses of the poet's own life.

Walther's place of birth is not known (Würzburg or Feuchtwangen in Franconia, South Tirol, and the Austrian region around Vienna are among the places that have been proposed by different scholars),[4] but it is fairly certain that much of Walther's youth and probably the first part of his literary career were spent in Austria; in his so-called *Alterselegie* he sings "ze Œsterîch lernde ich singen unde sagen" (In Austria I learned to sing love songs and perform *Sangsprüche*),[5] at the court of Prince Friedrich I in Vienna. During this presumed early phase of Walther's career, he seems to have composed songs of *hohe minne* in the mold of Reinmar,[6] and at some point later it is thought that a poetic "feud" between Walther and Reinmar came about, reflections of which may be visible in some of Walther's songs.[7] Probably after the death of Prince Friedrich in 1198, Walther seems to have left Vienna.[8] Making his way as an itinerant poet from one lord and patron to another (indications of which we seem to see above all in the political and didactic poetry), Walther possibly came into contact with erotic themes of the Latin minstrel lyrics (*Vagantenlyrik*) and began to develop his songs of "niedere Minne" (love for women of lower social standing).[9] Later on, it is assumed, Walther endeavored without success to return to the court at Vienna.[10] Around this time, he may have experimented with his new conception of love, endeavoring to balance his conception of *niedere Minne* with the standard model of *hohe minne*. A final stage posited for the development of Walther's lyrical career is the time close to the end of his life when he composed the so-called *Alterslieder*. Possibly from the beginning of his poetic career, and quite probably no later than his first departure from Vienna, Walther was composing didactic and political poetry (*Sangsprüche*) as well as love songs. This view of Walther's life story has achieved an almost legendary status, and it continues to enjoy wide currency in the scholarly literature, although some scholars recently have pointed out that there is little hard evidence to support it.[11]

Walther's poetry demonstrates a familiarity with theology, themes and motifs from Latin poetry (including the *Carmina Burana*),[12] and with the rhetorical theory and practice of the monastic and cathedral schools, so it is probable that he received a clerical education, possibly during his youth in Vienna or its vicinity.[13] Earlier scholars believed Walther belonged to a family of lesser nobility, but was forced by adverse circumstances to become a wandering minstrel. More recently, some scholars have favored an alternative view: Walther was not noble by birth, but managed by means of his art to carve out a place for himself among nobles at court.[14] Whatever his social rank may have been, Walther seems to have enjoyed a special status among the people with whom he lived and worked. Such a special status is indicated by the fact that Walther composed both love poetry and political and didactic poetry, whereas previous to Walther *Minnesang* was an art practiced by members of nobility (even if the legally unfree ministerials may have predominated among them), while the *Sprüche* had traditionally been composed by non-noble, itinerant poets. Despite the inevitable concessions that had to be made to conflicting demands and interests of his different lords and patrons (particularly regarding imperial politics in the didactic and political poetry), Walther's lyric poetry with all its poetic personae are the products of a proud and resourceful individual who expanded the poetic possibilities of the genres in which he worked. He found new ways to express concerns ranging from the joy and pain of love to the admirable and not-so-admirable qualities of princes, emperors, and popes during a turbulent period in Germany's history.

Until a few decades ago it was assumed by many scholars that Walther's love songs could be grouped according to the poet's evolving conception of love. This evolving conception, in turn, fits well into the traditional view of Walther's life and career as sketched out above. Increased scholarly recognition of the importance of recurring formal and thematic elements in *Minnesang*, combined with the lack of external historical evidence to corroborate the posited phases of Walther's life, has led most recent scholars to question, if not reject, a biographical foundation for any chronological or conceptual grouping of his songs.[15] Instead, the focus has shifted to new accents and perspectives that Walther succeeds in giving to the love lyrics. The scholarly estimation of the impact of Walther's love songs on the development of the German love lyrics has become somewhat more conservative than it once was (Bumke says that he was "kein Revolutionär" (no revolutionary),[16] and Schweikle says that it was not Walther, but rather Neidhart, who was the first poet to break away completely from the model of *hohe minne*).[17]

In some of Walther's songs, such as 109,1,[18] we see many of the aspects of the *hohe minne* model that were present in the lyrics of Reinmar and other earlier poets. In this song, the singer looks forward hopefully and happily to the possibility of his love's fulfillment, but conventional aspects of the *hohe minne* paradigm are the subordinate position of the singer to his lady, "Mich fröit iemer daz ich alsô guotem wîbe / dienen sol ûf minneclîchen danc" (I will always be happy that I must serve a lady for love's reward), the element of force that is visible in this relationship, "mich betwanc nie mê kein wîp alsô" (no woman has ever compelled me in this way), and the fact that the ultimate fulfillment of love remains uncertain at best, as the end of the song suggests: "Endet sich mîn ungemach, / sô weiz ich von wârheit danne / daz nie manne an liebe baz geschach" (If my torment ends / then I'll truly know that no man ever fared better with love). Some of the verses of this song are consistent with the idea that the value of love rests not in its fulfillment, but in the singer's ability to find some positive meaning in the absence of its fulfillment, which is to say in the service itself. Despite the conventional elements, the *trûren* and *ungemüete* (sorrows, discontent) of the singer, the song as a whole depicts the singer's love optimistically. It has been encouraged by a greeting from his lady: "mich mant singen ir vil werder gruoz" (Her noble greeting commands me to sing) and also, though this remains less clear, by an encouraging look in his direction: "Dur ir liehten ougen schîn / wart ich alsô wol enpfangen" (I was heartily received by the brightness of her eyes). While such optimistic signs from the beloved belong to the standard repertoire of the love lyrics, in the broader context of Walther's lyrics this song points in the direction of others in which the relationship between the singer and his lady is on a much more equal footing.

Among Walther's other love songs, "standard" types such as the *Wechsel* (Exchange) and the *Botenlied* (messenger song) are represented (214, 34, presents a combination of these two types). While the term *Mädchenlieder* has become somewhat controversial, because it implies a conscious artistic program and a coherent type of song on the part of the poet that may not have existed as such, Walther composed a number of songs traditionally bearing this designation that depicted the role of the beloved woman and thus the entire love relationship in a very different way, a representative example of which is "Herzeliebez frouwelîn" (Beloved lady of mine; 49, 25), which follows the conventional formal structure of the *Kanzone*, in which each of the strophes consists of two rhymed couplets called *Stollen*, and a culminating group of rhymed verses called the *Abgesang*. In the first strophe, it is striking that the singer addresses his beloved directly rather than singing about an unreachable, distant lady, as is the rule in songs about *hohe minne*. The reason for this unusual approach of the singer becomes more evident in the second stro-phe, in which the position of the beloved is established, albeit indirectly: "Si verwîzent mir daz ich / sô nidere wende mînen sanc" (they chide me that my song is directed too low, 49, 31–32). The imagery of the song from this point forward makes no explicit references to the characteristics of the beloved, but certain implications seem clear, on the basis of verses such as these: "Sie getraf diu liebe nie, / die nâch dem guote und nâch der schoene minnent, wê wie minnent die?" (love has never come to those who love for the sake of wealth and beauty — alas, do people such as this really love? 49, 35–36). These verses, which receive emphasis by virtue of their position in the *Abgesang* of the second strophe, are followed by a dis-cussion of the relationship of *liebe* and *schoene* in the third strophe (love takes precedence over beauty, because love can make a woman beautiful, but beauty cannot make a woman worthy of love). In the third strophe, Walther's words to his beloved, "Du bist schoene und hast genuoc" (You are beautiful and have enough), when seen in the broader context of this song, are the clearest indication that his beloved is of lower social standing than the lady one finds in songs of *hohe minne* (even if it must be conceded that the love lyrics are never precise or explicit about the social status of the involved personae). In this song Walther seems to be rejecting the lady of *hohe minne* (whose quintessential characteristics are *guot* and *schoene*), and therefore the kind of love that remains forever unfulfilled, because the beloved lady remains forever distant. The striking and unconventional use of the more encompassing word *liebe* rather than the more conventionally courtly term *minne* to designate love marks these pronounced changes in the depiction of the beloved and the love relationship.

Similar characteristics can be found in other songs. In "Nemt, frowe, disen kranz" (Take, my Lady, this wreath; 74, 20ff.), the setting is not a courtly, but rather a pastoral one, and the forlorn and frequently colorless pining of the singer of *hohe minne* is correspondingly replaced by sensuous images of love's fulfillment: "Die bluomen vielen ie / von dem boume bî uns nider an daz gras" (the blossoms fell down from the tree to us on the grass, 75, 19–20) and of dance: "Waz obe si gêt an disem tanze?" (What if she is at this dance?). In this song, as in the one discussed above, the beloved woman is set apart from the lady of *hohe minne* in a manner that suggests her lower social status, when she accepts the wreath the singer gives to her: "Si nam daz ich ir bôt / einem kinde vil gelîch daz êre hât" (she accepted what I offered her, just like a child of honor). Next to the depiction of the beloved woman as someone of relatively (i.e. to the lady of *hohe minne*) lower social status (therefore somewhat closer to the social status of the singer?) is the idea of a love that is both mutual and fulfilled. In the immediately following verses, the maiden bows to the singer in gratitude, who then suggests that the reward he will receive from her may yet be more substantial: "daz wart mir ze lône. / wirt mirs iht mêr, daz trage ich tougen (I received this [i.e. the curtsey] as a reward; if I receive anything else, this will remain a secret). There is the suggestion in the fourth strophe of this song that love's fulfillment is a dream: "Seht dô muost ich von fröiden lachen. / do ich sô wünneclîche / was in troume rîche" (See, I had to laugh for joy, since in this dream I was so rich in happiness). The importance of earlier minnesingers, and also of the earliest love lyrics (particularly the early *Tagelieder*, or dawn songs) for the formulation of Walther's songs about "niedere minne," suggests that the new direction Walther gives to the discussion of courtly love is a continuation rather than a radical break from earlier currents in the medieval German love lyrics.

Walther's main contribution to the German love lyric was to increase the range of roles that could be adopted by the singer and his beloved, and to lend the depiction of the experience of love new immediacy and vibrancy. The following poem, in which Walther reflects on the nature of *minne*, might be seen as exemplary of the new life that Walther was able to infuse into the lyric conventions of his time:

> I. Saget mir ieman, waz ist minne?
> weiz ich des ein teil, sô wist ichs gerne mê.
> Der sich baz denn ich versinne,
> der berihte mich durch waz si tuot sô wê.

Minne ist minne, tuot si wol;
tuot si wê, so enheizet si niht rehte minne.
sus enweiz ich wie si danne heizen sol.

II. Obe ich rehte râten künne
waz diu minne sî, sô sprechet denne jâ.
Minne ist zweier herzen wünne,
teilent sie gelîche, sost diu minne dâ.
Sol abe ungeteilet sîn,
sô enkans ein herze alleine niht enthalten.
owê woldest dû mir helfen, frouwe mîn!

III. Frouwe, ich trage ein teil ze swaere,
wellest dû mir helfen, sô hilf an der zît.
Sî abe ich dir gar unmaere,
daz sprich endelîche, sô lâz ich den strît
Unde wirde ein ledic man.
dû solt aber einez rehte wizzen, frouwe,
daz dich lützel ieman baz geloben kan.

IV. Kan mîn frouwe süeze siuren?
waenet si daz ich ir liep gebe umbe leit?
Sol ich si dar umbe tiuren
daz siz wider kêre an mîne unwerdekeit?
Sô kund ich unrehte spehen.
wê waz sprich ich ôrenlôser ougen âne?
den diu minne blendet, wie mac der gesehen?

(69,1–69,28)

[I. Tell me someone what *minne* is. I know a little bit, but I would like to know more. He who can consider the matter better than I should tell me why it is so painful. *Minne* is *minne* if it feels good. If it hurts, it should not really be called *minne*. In this case, I don't know what it should be called.

II. If I can correctly guess what *minne* is, then tell me I'm right: *minne* is the joy of two hearts. If they share equally, *minne* is there. But if it is not equal, then a single heart alone cannot contain it. Alas! If you would only help me, my Lady.

III. Lady, I'm bearing a too heavy load. If you want to help me, help me soon. But if you want nothing of me, then say it and I'll let go of the struggle and be a free man. But you should know my Lady, that there is no one who can praise you better than I.

IV. Can my Lady sour what is sweet? Does she believe I will give her affection in exchange for pain. Should I raise her up, so that she can stress my unworthiness? I would have to be blind to do this. Alas, what am I — without eyes or ears — saying? He who is blinded by love — how can he see?]

This song, in the form of a canzona, presents what amounts to a reflection on the true nature of *minne*, followed by the application of the results of this reflection to the singer's specific situation. It contains the standard complaints and calls for the lady's help to end the singer's suffering that are set pieces of *hohe minne*, but such conventions recede to a large degree behind the almost dispassionate consideration of *minne* that occurs in the first two strophes. Although this song does not abandon the distance from the beloved lady that is characteristic of *hohe minne*, the reflection on love's true nature arrives at the conclusion that *rehte minne* (right love) must bring joy, not pain, and it must be shared (i.e. mutual). The third and fourth strophes carry forward with this conception of the true nature of love, maintaining something of the reflective detachment of the first two strophes. Though obviously with little evident success, the lady is called upon to share the burden of love, the assumption being that her doing so would return *minne* to its true nature by making it mutual and by transforming pain to joy. Following the standard *hohe minne* model, the song ends with little hope: the singer claims he would have to be blind to continue tolerating the present situation of painful, and thus wrong *minne*, and in the final verses everything seems to be placed in doubt when the singer laments that love's power may indeed have already left him deaf and blind. Although the song is an example of the *hohe minne* type, it is an unusual one that manifests — by way of the postulation of love as something that should bring joy and be mutual — a view of love similar to that which one finds in Walther so-called *Mädchenlieder*. Unusual also is its dispassionate, reflective tone, which makes this particular example as much a commentary on love as a love song proper, thus bringing the love lyric genre in close proximity to the other reflective, critical genre in which Walther excelled: the *Sangsprüche*.

In the genre of *Sangsprüche*, Walther's contribution is even more pronounced than in the love lyrics, as he was the first to develop this vernacular genre so that it included reflections on a variety of different topics, ranging from general issues of faith and morality, the constitution of the courtly culture of his day, and contemporary social and political developments. Corresponding to these different topics we see a variety of different roles adopted by Walther's lyrical "ich" in the *Sangsprüche*, many of which connect what appear on the surface to be individual or personal sentiments with concerns of broad social and political significance. In the so-called *Alterselegie*, perhaps Walther's best-known poem,[19] the trials of old age, in particular the painful sense of alienation from the world (liute und lant dar inn ich von kinde bin erzogen, / die sint mir worden frömde als ob ez sî gelogen [the people and the land in which I was raised from childhood have become strange to me as if it were all a lie, 124, 9–10]) are associated with unsettling current events that have, in their own way, been the source of unhappiness and alienation: "uns sint unsenfte brieve her von

Rôme komen" (we have received severe letters from Rome, 124, 26). It is possible that the correspondence in question involves the excommunication of Emperor Friedrich II by Pope Gregory IX, in which case the journey overseas that Walther mentions in 124, 49 (möht ich die lieben reise gevaren über sê [if I might take the blessed trip overseas]) might refer to the Crusade of 1227 to 1228, though this is disputed.[20] A similar association of old age and spiritual concerns, though without such explicit political references, is visible in other *Sprüche*, for example in those of the so-called *Alterston*,[21] in which the singer's earlier activity as a minnesinger is viewed critically from the perspective of an older and wiser man. Although the reference to old age is not clear, the dialogue between the singer Walther and *Frô Welt* (100, 24–101, 21) presents a similar distancing of the former minnesinger from the pleasures of the love and the worldly life in which he was so intensely involved.

In contrast to the religious-spiritual concerns of *Sprüche* such as these, the three strophes of the so-called *Reichston*, or imperial song are more strictly secular and political. In the first strophe Walther depicts himself in a contemplative pose, seated on a stone, with legs crossed, elbow on knee, and chin couched in palm of the hand — the manner in which he is depicted in the illumination of him in the Codex Manesse. In the first strophe the singer expresses what appears to be a strictly individual concern: he has found it impossible to reconcile the different priorities associated with possessions, worldly honor, and God's favor. In the other strophes of the *Reichston*, the lack of individual coherence is associated with a chaotic time in which human events are out of kilter. In contrast to the beasts in the natural world, in which the struggle for supremacy is regulated to some degree by the rule of law and natural hierarchy, there is no order in the empire. The political context of this song becomes most evident in the third strophe, which refers to the involvement of the pope in the political struggles following the death of Emperor Heinrich VI, during a time when Heinrich's son Friedrich was too young to assume the throne and a struggle for supreme imperial power occurred between Philip von Schwaben and Otto von Baunschweig. In this song, and many others, one of Walther's abiding positions becomes clear: as one might expect from a poet whose patrons were the imperial elite, Walther remains critical of the powerful and wealthy Roman Church's involvement in German politics during this unsettled time in the early thirteenth century. It is tempting to consider that Walther's own religiosity may have been close to that of the *klôsenaere* (hermit) mentioned at the end of this *Sprüch*.

Such a lay religiosity seems also have made a mark on Walther's *Leich* (religious lay), a praise of the Trinity and the Virgin, which is a single musical composition in versicles, short verses modeled on liturgical practice in which verses sung by the priest are followed by a response from the congregation (*Responsionen*). In the *Leich* Walther alludes to the importance of *riuwe* (remorse, regret), and the fact that he does not mention *bîhte* and *buoze* (penance, confession) — the normal ecclesiastical consequences of *riuwe* — would be consistent with the kind of lay religiosity that one finds in many of Walther's *Sprüche*. Such a lay religiosity has also been posited for Wolfram von Eschenbach, and was more generally characteristic of a time in which many lay people rejected ecclesiastical institutions as too worldly.[22]

Much of Walther's political poetry suggests his own restless wandering from one powerful patron to another, even as it expresses the troubled political situation of his time. Based on references to these figures in his political poetry, scholars have assumed that Walther worked at some time or another at the courts of Philip von Schwaben, Otto von Braunschweig, and Friedrich (Friedrich II — the grandson of Friedrich I "Barbarossa"), all at one time or another rivals for the German kingship and imperial title in the early thirteenth century. The fact that Walther frequently changed his views of these men, and consequently his political affiliations, is not surprising for a wandering poet who was dependent on the favor and good will of his patrons. Not surprisingly, one of the major themes in Walther's political poetry concerns his patrons' largesse, or lack thereof. In the political poetry, a pattern becomes visible:[23] Walther begins with praise; when adequate reward for his efforts remain outstanding, criticism begins; he concludes with often biting ridicule of lords he has left. An example of the latter is the *König Friedrichs Ton* (26, 33ff.), or song of King Friedrich, in which Walther, now apparently safely in the service of Friedrich, tells us that he first wanted to measure Otto according to his tall physical stature; but that soon after he began to measure Otto's size according to the measure of honor, and found him to be much smaller than a dwarf (26, 33ff.). Only the relationship to Friedrich, perhaps his last patron, seems to have ended in a better way. The insecurity of Walther's itinerant life seems to have come to an end when he was granted a fief by Friedrich, an event that Walther celebrated in the *Friedrichston* with the famous verses: "Ich hân mîn lêhen, al die werlt, ich hân mîn lêhen: / nû enfürhte ich niht den hornunc an die zêhen / und wil alle boese hêrren dester minre flêhen" (I have my fief! Listen one and all! I have my fief. Now I must no longer fear the chill of winter, and I will no longer have to ingratiate myself to miserly lords, 28, 31–33).

In Walther's political and didactic poetry we again observe a consummately versatile poetic voice, one which finds new ways to give artistic expression to experience despite the constraints of the taste of audiences and patrons and by the authority of literary conventions. At the same time, this poetry ranged widely over the major political and literary concerns: papal involvement in German politics, the respective qualities of the pretenders to the German throne, the difficult position of the individual during a time of political and religious uncertainty, religious faith in spite of this uncertainty, the need for a spiritual renewal associated with the resolve to renounce one's previous sinful life and to embark on a crusade (though there is no evidence that Walther ever actually participated in one) and, finally, a critical commentary on contemporary literature.

As we already know from Gottfried, Walther was a famous poet in his own time. Walther was also mentioned by name by Wolfram, and he was named and cited by many later medieval poets such as Rudolf von Ems, Ulrich von Liechtenstein, Der Marner, Reinmar von Brennenberg, and Hugo von Trimberg.[24] As early as the twelfth century Walther became a mythic figure and literary character, as we see, for example, in the *Wartburgkrieg*, in which Walther appears as one of the contestants in the poetic competition depicted in this work.[25] Centuries later, the memory of Walther and his poetry was still intact, when many of the other poets and works of the *Blütezeit* were completely neglected. In the fifteenth and sixteenth centuries, the *Meistersänger* considered him one of the twelve old masters, and in the seventeenth century the poet and author of the first German poetic, Martin Opitz (1597–1639) mentions Walther as an example of ingeniousness in older German poetry. In the eighteenth century familiarity with Walther's work increased: the Swiss poet-critics Johann Jacob Bodmer (1698–1783) and Johann Jacob Breitinger (1701–76) published selections of Walther's lyrics from the Codex Manesse, thus providing a foundation for later scholarly preoccupation with the medieval writer.[26] The nineteenth century paid the greatest amount of attention to Walther, not only because of the philological tendencies of the early part of the century, which devoted serious scholarly analysis to German medieval literature, but also because modern readers saw in his poetry an early expression of German nationalism. The image of Walther as a medieval advocate of German virtues and as a defender of the "fatherland" against the encroachments of the Roman Church, in which capacity he appeared to be a cultural forebear of Martin Luther, remained popular until the cataclysm of National Socialism. Following the Second World War, there were calls for a reassessment of Walther and his poetry. This effort to achieve this more measured appraisal continues to the present day.[27]

Notes

[1] The exact number of strophes cannot be known because of the possibility of false attribution: see Joachim Bumke, "Walther von der Vogelweide," in *Kindlers Neues Literatur Lexikon*, vol. 17, ed. Walter Jens (Munich: Kindler Verlag, 1988), 398–403; here 399.

[2] Walther is one of the few German poets of the period who is mentioned in a historical record outside of literature: in a record of the travel expenses of bishop Wolfger von Erla, it is noted that five shillings (or 150 denars) were given to *walthero cantori de vogelweide* for the purchase of a fur coat on November 12, 1203. While the word *cantor* may certainly mean "singer" and thus refer to Walther's

means of livelihood, the spectrum of meaning of this term extends into the religious domain, where it designates someone who has benefited from a clerical-religious education. It is possible that Walther is mentioned (as "dominus Walterus") in another historical source as a messenger (*nuntius*) who was sent from Emperor Otto IV to Bishop Wolfger von Erla on June 30, 1212. However, given the frequency of the name Walterus, it is questionable that our Walther is meant; see Manfred Günter Scholz, *Walther von der Vogelweide* (Stuttgart: Metzler, 1999), 11–13.

[3] Citing *Gottfried von Straßburg, Tristan*, ed. and trans. (modern German) Rüdiger Krohn, vol. 1 (Stuttgart: Reclam, 1984); contributor's translation.

[4] Scholz, *Walther von der Vogelweide*, 5.

[5] Translations of Walther's lyrics are by W. H.

[6] Because the love songs tend today to be understood as *Rollenlyrik*, it has become much more difficult to associate certain songs or kinds of songs with specific moments in a given singer's career.

[7] For example, in regard to the song beginning "Ein man verbiutet âne pfliht" (111, 22), in which Walther, employing the melody or *Ton* of Reinmar's "ich wirbe um allez daz ein man," criticizes Reinmar for praising his lady above all others; many scholars continue to hold to the idea of a "feud," while others more recently have argued that there is actually scant evidence for a full-blown feud and that it is more likely that there was quite simply an understandable poetic rivalry between the two. There is considerable evidence for another rivalry, if not feud, between the older Walther and Neidhart; among other indications of such a tension (on which see Hermann Reichert, *Walther von der Vogelweide für Anfänger*, 2nd ed. [Vienna: WUV-Universitätsverlag, 1998], 153–60); Walther's song 64, 31 contains criticisms of Neidhart's lyrics, particularly the placement of *minne* in a village setting.

[8] That Walther left because of a feud with Reinmar remains speculation; it seems more likely that he did not receive support, after the death of Prince Friedrich from Friedrich's successor, Leopold VI; see Reichert, *Walther von der Vogelweide für Anfänger*, 48–49.

[9] As Bumke points out ("Walther von der Vogelweide," 400), Walther may have already been familiar with Latin poetry by virtue of the clerical education he had clearly received.

[10] Hubert Heinen, "Walther von der Vogelweide," *Dictionary of Literary Biography*, vol. 138: *German Writers and Works of the High Middle Ages*, edited by James Hardin and Will Hasty (Detroit: Gale, 1994), 161.

[11] Bumke, "Walther von der Vogelweide," 399.

[12] In fact, strophes attributed elsewhere to Walther are included the famous Codex Buranus; see Heinen, "Walther von der Vogelweide," 159.

[13] Scholz, *Walther von der Vogelweide*, 4–5.

[14] See Bumke 399 and Scholz 10–11.

[15] Bumke, "Walther von der Vogelweide," 399.

[16] Bumke, "Walther von der Vogelweide," 400.

[17] Günther Schweikle, *Minnesang*, 2nd ed (Stuttgart: Metzler, 1995), 90.

[18] Walther's lyrics are cited from *Die Lieder Walthers von der Vogelweide*, vol. 1: *Die religiösen und politischen Lieder* and vol. 2: *Die Liebeslieder*, ed. Friedrich Maurer (Tübingen: Niemeyer, 1967–69); here and elsewhere we use Lachmann's numbering of Walther's verses.

[19] Reichert, *Walther von der Vogelweide für Anfänger*, 185.

[20] Scholz, *Walther von der Vogelweide*, 169.

[21] See especially 67, 8–31.

[22] See Walther's criticism of the practice of simony in the *Leich*, 6, 38–42.

[23] Reichert, *Walther von der Vogelweide für Anfänger*, 138.

[24] Scholz, *Walther von der Vogelweide*, 172.

[25] Scholz, *Walther von der Vogelweide*, 172.

[26] Scholz, *Walther von der Vogelweide*, 173.

[27] See Scholz, *Walther von der Vogelweide*, who suspects different ideologies behind the more recent views of Walther as a plebian, a political agitator, etc. (175–76).

Part II

Lyric and Narrative Traditions

Didactic Poetry

Nigel Harris

IT IS POSSIBLE TO ARGUE THAT almost all medieval poetry is didactic. Even authors of works such as courtly romances or other essentially secular narratives sought to provide not only amusement, excitement or aesthetic stimulation, but also instruction, edification, and moral improvement. Moreover, most creators and recipients of medieval literature would probably have seen no contradiction between the twin aims of teaching and entertaining, but would have regarded the two as ultimately indivisible.

Within this broad consensus, however, there was ample room for differences of priority and approach. In many works, the didactic element seems, to the modern reader at least, to be decidedly limited, or at least subordinated to a desire to divert and titillate. For other poets again (one thinks of Gottfried von Neifen [fl. ca. 1235–55] and Ulrich von Winterstetten [fl. ca. 1241–80]), the communication of an edifying message appears to have been less important than sophisticated experimentation with language and form. Moreover, many medieval authors (such as those of the great romances), while obviously concerned to educate, challenge, or influence their audiences, tended to do so using subtle, indirect means — such as imagery, structural patterns, the actions and dialogue of characters, and occasional narratorial comments.

All these approaches to literature can be legitimately differentiated from that adopted by the works to be discussed in this chapter. These works have in common — apart from their use of verse form — a clear didactic purport, the communication of which seems to have been their authors' primary objective; and they address their audience in a more or less direct way, often employing techniques such as unequivocal assertion, explanation, exhortation, or admonition. They vary enormously in length, in form, in style, and in subject matter; but they all operate within the bounds of medieval Christian orthodoxy; and, with very few exceptions at either end, they all can all be dated between approximately 1170 and 1260.

Probably the best known genre within Middle High German didactic poetry is the so-called *Spruch*. This catchall term has often been used to refer, in effect, to all lyric poems that cannot reasonably be described as love songs. As such, it is an imprecise concept, and a somewhat misleading one. The most common meaning of the noun *Spruch* in modern German is "adage" or "proverb"; moreover its self-evident relationship to the verb *sprechen*, "to speak," arguably implies that the poems it designates were intended to be spoken, rather than sung (contrast the term "Minne*sang*," used of love poetry). Neither of these implications is wholly aberrant, but neither is particularly helpful. In a broad sense, certainly, *Sprüche* belong to the category of "wisdom literature," and not a few of them base their argument on an aphoristic or sententious statement of some kind. Many *Sprüche*, however, were highly developed and complex poetic structures, and dealt with topics far removed from the subject matter characteristic of proverbs. Moreover, they were definitely sung: the *Jenaer Liederhandschrift*, a fourteenth-century song manuscript from Northern Germany, alone contains some ninety-one melodies intended to accompany didactic lyrics.[1] These melodies are for the most part decidedly simple, and were probably designed, after the manner of what we would call recitative, to be more clearly subordinate to their words than was the case with many *Minnelieder*. Nevertheless, we are dealing here with songs; and not least for this reason we shall refer to the German didactic lyric by the still questionable, but convenient and increasingly familiar term *Sangspruch*.[2]

A full and coherent history of the German didactic lyric within our period would be impossible to write, and it is worth dwelling briefly on two of the reasons why. The first concerns the surviving *Sangspruch* manuscripts.[3] Almost certainly, there are enormous gaps in the manuscripts transmitted to us, especially for the first half of our period. Peter Johnson has calculated that, of the authors of Middle High German love songs who can be named and dated with any confidence, some twenty poets predate Walther von der Vogelweide; in the area of didactic poetry, however, only two do so (depending, of course, on how one categorizes and attributes the authorship of certain songs).[4] This is a remarkable difference, and one that should make us wary of drawing unduly ambitious conclusions, not least when assessing the extent of the innovations made by Walther to a genre of whose earlier stages we have such little trace. This paucity of manuscript evidence might be the consequence of simple chance (many manuscripts may have been lost); but it also tells us something about the nature of our genre. Unlike the more obviously sophisticated *Minnesang*, it probably originated in pre-literary (or sub-literary) forms of oral poetry which, by definition, were not written down; and in many cases also *Sangsprüche* apply their truths to specific events or situations, a characteristic that might also have militated against their being copied for posterity.

A second cause of frustration for the would-be historian of the *Sangspruch* is the fact that, even more so than with other genres, we have very few extra-literary sources of information about the relevant authors, their dates, or the circumstances of their lives. In part, again, this is doubtless a matter of chance; but it surely also reflects the fact that, so far as we can tell, didactic lyrics in German were composed chiefly by traveling professional poets of low social status, artists who inevitably left even fewer traces of their careers in historical documents than did the aristocratic amateurs who produced love songs. In fact, one of the clearest distinctions between the German didactic lyric and love lyric seems to have been that, at least initially, the two genres were associated with different social groups. This factor might indeed help us explain the relative dearth of surviving *Sangsprüche* from the period before Walther: poets who perceived *Minnesang* as the only form of lyric poetry fit for a courtly gentleman to compose might have consciously avoided working in the more apparently popular tradition.

With the above caveats firmly in mind, we must now essay some generalizations about the principal characteristics of the medieval German didactic lyric, and then outline some developments that it underwent during the period under discussion. We shall consider first the themes it typically treats. Tervooren is right to suggest that *Sangsprüche* seek above all to reply to Walther's question as to "wie man zer welte solte leben" (how one should live in the world).[5] In the medieval context this is primarily a religious issue, and it is therefore hardly surprising that much didactic poetry should be religious in character, addressing matters such as the Trinity, the Passion, Mary (an especially common subject as the thirteenth century progressed), the need for repentance, and the falseness and transience of this world. Alongside these specifically religious themes, and arising out of them, was a wide range of moral and ethical ones. Many songs deal, for example, with vices and virtues, not least the courtly qualities of honor, loyalty, moderation and, above all, generosity: one must not forget that many poets were dependent on the largesse of aristocratic patrons. This latter fact presumably accounts in part also for the large number of lyric poems that either praise or denounce the behavior of rulers, and for the development of more specifically political poetry, in which contemporary events and figures are discussed sometimes in an oblique manner, but at other times in uncompromisingly direct terms.

Two further common types of *Sangspruch* fit less seamlessly into the category of didactic verse, but still fall within the purview of this chapter. The first of these are songs in which the poet describes, and often bemoans, the circumstances of his own life — his poverty, the vicissitudes of travel, or unfair treatment at the hands of patrons, or indeed of other poets. Such songs concern us here not only because they do not constitute love poetry, but, more importantly, because their semi- or pseudo-autobiographical utterances are generally made in the context of broader and less subjective discussions of moral categories or timeless truths. Much the same could be said of the second of these types, namely songs that offer insights and instruction *about* love (and to that extent are didactic), rather than describing feelings or experiences *of* love. These songs are also generally more akin to *Sangsprüche* than to *Minnelieder* with regard to their form.

There is, of course, no single formal pattern that all medieval German didactic lyrics follow. Even so, one can legitimately generalize about certain structural characteristics that many of them share. The earliest *Sangsprüche* we have, such as those attributed to Herger, employ a simple stanzaic form generally involving four-foot rhyming couplets but culminating in a six-foot last line in which a climactic *pointe* is often expressed. Individual stanzas tend to be self-contained, but capable of forming loosely connected groups with others on broadly similar themes. The scanty manuscript evidence suggests that individual authors tended to use only one poetic-melodic form (or *Ton*) for all the stanzas they composed, which as such presumably functioned as what we would call their "signature tune." From the time of Walther von der Vogelweide on, this practice began to change: *Sangsprüche* typically adopted, along with *Minnelieder*, the tripartite stanzaic form known as the Romance canzona, and along with it more complex rhyme schemes. Moreover, again in line with developments in the *Minnesang*, didactic poets started to compose a range of different *Töne*. This latter tendency, however, remained less marked in *Sangsprüche* than in *Minnelieder* (Reinmar von Zweter[6] wrote some 234 stanzas in the same *Ton*); and formal differences between the two genres persisted especially in the matter of the relationships between individual stanzas. *Minnelieder* were on the whole coherent poetic structures, whose stanzas were closely linked in both form and content; many *Sangsprüche*, however, continued to consist of single strophes, combinable into sequences, as the occasion arose, with others of the same form and more or less compatible content. In other words, *Sangsprüche* remained, even by medieval standards, remarkably open and flexible configurations.

The previous paragraph has already touched on some of the developments within the *Sangspruch* tradition that occurred within our period, and it is now time briefly to consider some further ones. Inevitably, we can concentrate only on a few significant authors, the earliest of whom is the poet generally called Herger. The standard anthology *Minnesangs Frühling*[7] ascribes to him twenty-eight stanzas. These stanzas, however, are attributed in the relevant manuscripts, along with some thirty-two others, to a poet named Spervogel. The name Herger occurs only once in these stanzas (26, 20), in the phrase "Mich müet daz alter sêre,/wan ez Hergêre/alle sîne kraft benam" (age distresses me a great deal, because it took from Herger all his strength). There would be no reason to assume that the man mentioned here wrote this or indeed any other poem, if it were not for the fact that the Spervogel strophes fall into two distinct types: roughly half correspond to the "early" strophic form described above, and in other respects also have a somewhat archaic feel, whereas the others have a different *Ton* and a markedly more courtly flavor. In short, we seem to be dealing here with two distinct poets; and it has simply become customary to refer to the older one as Herger.

His oeuvre is a fascinating one. Its twenty-eight stanzas can be arranged into five groups of five and one of three — the links between the constituent parts of which are stronger in some cases than in others. In the first of the five-strophe sequences (25, 13), Herger mourns generous deceased patrons and praises their successors, while bemoaning his inability to bequeath riches to his own sons; then (26, 13) he discusses the tribulations of life as a traveler dependent on others' bounty; he relates a series of fables featuring dogs and wolves (27, 13); he adumbrates some central religious doctrines in a sequence (28, 13) linked by the ideas of heaven and hell; and in a particularly loosely connected group (29, 13), he warns somewhat obliquely against avarice, lechery, pride and anger. Meanwhile, in the sole surviving triad (30, 13), he discusses, in theologically simple terms, Christ's death and resurrection, their consequences for mankind, and the ultimate superiority of God over all human praise:

> Crist sich ze marterenne gap,
> er lie sich legen in ein grap.
> daz tet er dur die goteheit.
> dâ mit lôste er die cristenheit
> von der heizen helle.
> der getuot ez niemer mêr.
> dar an gedenke, swer sô der welle.

> An dem osterlîchen tage
> dô stuont sich crist von dem grabe.
> künic aller keiser,
> vater aller weisen,
> sîne hantgetât er lôste.
> in die helle schein ein lieht:
> sô kom er sînen kinden ze trôste.

> Wurze des waldes
> und erze des goldes
> und elliu abgründe
> diu sint dir, herre, künde,
> diu stênt in dîner hende.
> allez himelschlîchez her
> daz enmôhte dich nicht volloben an ein ende.

[Christ gave himself up to suffering. He allowed himself to be laid in a grave. He did this because of his divinity. In this way he saved Christendom from hot hell. He will never do it again. May whoever wishes think on that.

On Easter Day Christ rose from the grave. King of all emperors, father of all wise men, he saved his creation. A light shone into hell — thus he came to console his children.

Plants of the field and ores of gold and all the depths are known to you,
Lord; they are in your hand. All the heavenly host could not praise you
properly or fully.]

Notably absent from Herger's spectrum of poetic themes are the courtly
virtues and contemporary politics, and in that respect as well as others, his
work can be seen as typifying an early phase of the *Sangspruch* tradition.
A hint as to its date is provided in 25, 13, in which Walter von Hausen
(d. 1173) is spoken of as dead.[8]

We have already seen that the number of didactic poets known to us
from the time before Walther von der Vogelweide is rather small. Apart
from the Herger/Spervogel corpus, we have only five anonymous and
apparently separate stanzas, whose vocabulary and poetic techniques make
them appear likely to predate even Herger, and whose themes have much
in common with his; and four *Sangsprüche* attributed with varying degrees
of plausibility to Gottfried von Strassburg, which treat of covetousness and
greed, the fragility of fortune, poverty, and (at great length) Mary. One
might also follow Haustein in adding to this list half a dozen strophes that
appear within the works of twelfth-century *Minnesänger*,[9] but even if one
does this, Walther's didactic lyrics appear to represent — on the basis of
the evidence we have — an abrupt and revolutionary leap forward.

Since Walther is discussed in detail elsewhere in this volume, we need
only pause here to identify the main ways in which his poetry contributed
to the development of the German didactic lyric more generally. One can
point to three innovations above all. First, Walther broke down the divide
between didactic poetry and love poetry simply by writing a great quantity
of each — and, as we have seen, by introducing to the *Sangspruch* strophic
forms previously associated with *Minnesang*. Second, he broadened the
scope of didactic poetry by commenting frequently and explicitly on current affairs, most notably the events of the interregnum of 1198–1212.
Finally, Walther presented himself, or at least the paradigmatic "I" who
dominates so many of his poems, in a radically new way. Earlier authors of
Sangsprüche, while not entirely eschewing personal or subjective elements
(one recalls Herger's laments about his own situation), nevertheless used
the first-person pronoun sparingly, and seem to have viewed themselves not
least as vessels for the communication of generally accepted truths. With
Walther, however, things are different. His poetic "I" is certainly indebted
to the conventional verities, but makes us almost constantly aware of his
own personality, creativity, and values, as he casts himself in a variety of leading roles: as teacher, prophet, observer, God's messenger, or wise coun-
selor. This is a significant development; one is even tempted to wonder
whether the marked increase in the production of didactic poetry that
occurred in the wake of Walther's career might not have resulted in part
from his consistent upgrading of the role and status of the poetic voice.

Certainly we know of many more didactic poets from the years between, say, 1225 and 1285, than from any previous period. The careers of most of them are impossible to date with any certainty, but most would agree with Heinzle[10] that, within this arbitrary period of sixty years, two generations can be discerned. The first was dominated by the Rheinlander Reinmar von Zweter (fl. ca. 1227–48) and the Austrian Bruder Wernher (fl. ca. 1217–51);[11] and the second by Konrad von Würzburg (fl. ca. 1257–87) and Der Meissner (fl. ca. 1270–1300). Straddling the two generations was the Swabian Der Marner,[12] first traceable in 1230–31, and described by Rumelant von Sachsen (fl. 1273–86) as old, sick, and blind when he was murdered at some point after 1267.[13]

Our inevitably brief discussion of the history of the *Sangspruch* roughly between the death of Walther and that of Der Marner will focus on ways in which the former's three principal innovations were carried forward. The first of these, the practice of composing both didactic and love lyrics in canzona form, was continued by many later poets, such as Ulrich von Singenberg (first quarter of thirteenth century), Der Marner, Meister Alexander (ca. 1250),[14] and Friedrich von Sonnenburg (fl. ca. 1250–75);[15] and so was Walther's judicious balance between the older tradition of poets composing in only one *Ton*, and the Romance-inspired courtly tradition of each song having its own poetic-melodic structure. Just as Walther had composed numerous *Töne*, but used several of them many times, so Bruder Wernher seems to have used a total of nine *Töne* for seventy-six strophes, Der Marner fifteen for eighty-one, and Der Hardegger (second quarter of thirteenth century) four for fourteen. The great exception here is Reinmar von Zweter, whose 260 stanzas employ just two very similar *Töne*.

Reinmar was, however, with Wernher, the most notable successor to Walther in the composition of political poetry. Like their great predecessor, these two poets evince special concern with the question of the Empire, its correct governance, and the proper distribution of power between emperor and pope. Reinmar, indeed, explicitly asserts (213–14) the traditional doctrine of the two swords, according to which the pope should have authority in spiritual matters, and the emperor in secular:

> Ein meister der hât uns geslagen
> zwei swert, diu zwêne künege   wol mit êren möhten tragen,
> gemachet volliclîch   von hôher kunst, unt sint uol vollekomen,
> Gelîche lanc, gelîche breit,
> ze trôste unt ouch ze helfe   der vil edeln Cristenheit;
> si sint unschedeclich   unt mugen den getriuwen wol gevromen.
> Stôle unde swert sint si genennet beide;
> si bedurfen niht wan einer scheide;

> an in sich nieman mac versnîden
> wan der dâ lebet sunder vorht:
> erst listic, der si hât geworht;
> ir beider slege mac man vil gerne mîden. (213)

[A master has forged for us two swords, which two kings might indeed bear with honor. They have been made in their entirety with high art, and are utterly perfect, of equal length and breadth, and intended for the consolation and help of noble Christendom. They cause no harm, and are well able to serve faithful people. They are called stole and sword; they only need one scabbard between them; and no-one can injure himself on them save a person who lives his life without fear. The man who made them is highly skilled, and people will fervently wish to avoid their blows.]

Elsewhere, both Reinmar and Wernher express support for the Emperor Friedrich II and/or his son Heinrich VII (Reinmar 136, 138, 140; Wernher 61), and condemnation of the worldliness and political machinations of Pope Gregory IX (Reinmar 125–32, 141, 223; Wernher 2, 44). Again like Walther, however, their support for the imperial cause was not wholly consistent: Reinmar also censured the Emperor (143, 146–47, 169), while Wernher pleaded the cause of Duke Friedrich II of Austria in the latter's dispute with the emperor in 1236–37 (Wernher 7, 37). The reason for these changes is doubtless to be sought, as with Walther, in the differing opinions held by various patrons.

At the very end of our period, 1256–73, there was a notable rise in the quantity and importance of political poetry, as many poets commented on another imperial interregnum (see Marner XIV, 4; Sigeher 2–3; Kelin III, 6 (p. 127) and III, 10 (p. 138).[16] After 1273, however, it seems that that the political lyric declined in importance; and we must anyway be wary of over-estimating its importance for the development of the *Sangspruch* as a whole. After all, only approximately forty of Reinmar's 260 stanzas and twenty-three of Wernher's seventy-six could plausibly be described as political;[17] both also wrote on many other themes, with a particular emphasis in Reinmar's case on honor and its implications (see especially 56–78), and in Wernher's on death and the need to prepare for it (see 3f., 9, 15f., 24, 28f., 76).

The long-term effect of Walther's third innovation, the prominent role of the poetic "I" and the increased self-awareness and self-confidence this suggests, is difficult to assess with any clarity. Nevertheless, one can discern in the work of some later poets from within our period an arguably increased emphasis on their own worth, learning and authority. This tendency, which was to become still more marked in the later Middle Ages, manifested itself in various ways. The title *meister*, master, implying erudition, experience, and the consequent right to teach, was used by poets to refer both to themselves and to their colleagues (see Marner XIII, 3, XIV,

18; Kelin III, 11, p. 140). Moreover, the term *kunst*, meaning art, but also knowledge and skill, was used to designate their poetic activity, interpreted as God-given, and in need of protection against those, including fellow poets, who despised or abused it (see Wernher 70; Marner XI, 3, XIII, 3; Sonnenburg 18f., 55; Kelin I, 8, p. 77 and II, 3, p. 90). In line with this one sees some vernacular poets displaying a knowledge of learned (that is to say, clerical) culture, and employing literary devices derived from it. Der Marner, for example, draws material from classical mythology (XIV, 13) and from the *Physiologus* tradition (XV, 15); and such "learned" techniques are adopted as the definition and exploration of specific concepts (see Reinmar 78, 80, 172, 184; Wernher 53; Sonnenburg 19, 23f., 34, 38, 40, 42, 44; Sigeher 13), allegorical interpretation (Reinmar 8f., 99f.; Marner XV, 15; Alexander 5f., 17–21; Wernher 7, 73), or the use of exempla (Reinmar 103, 171, 179, 193; Marner XV, 11). None of this means that, at least until the fourteenth century, vernacular didactic poets could be considered scholars in any real sense, or indeed that they had *direct* access to Latin sources (though Der Marner may well have written five poems in Latin).[18] It does, mean, however, that, in spite of its origins in popular oral literature, the *Sangspruch* tradition came increasingly to share in the culture of learned Latinity and to assume its authority — a fact of which at least some of its practitioners were aware and proud.

The world of Latin learning looms still larger over the other kind of vernacular didactic verse texts in circulation in high medieval Germany. Alongside the didactic lyric there existed a wide range of longer works, generally employing rhyming couplets and — as far as we can tell — not usually intended to be sung, which similarly sought primarily to edify, and which treated numerous subjects that are already familiar from our survey of the *Sangspruch*. Less so even than the didactic lyric, however, these lengthier texts defy clear categorization, or designation by a generally applicable generic term,[19] and it is therefore possible for us to focus only on a small number of important works, and to mention in passing a few others to which they bear obvious similarities.

Of the longer didactic works from our period, Freidank's *Bescheidenheit* has more in common than most with the *Sangspruch* tradition. It is a massive compendium consisting, in its standard edition,[20] of roughly 5,000 lines, which was written probably in the 1220s or 1230s by a professional poet from Swabia. *Bescheidenheit* here does not mean, as it would in modern German, "modesty," but something like "knowledge/understanding of how to behave properly."[21] The breadth of coverage which this title accurately implies is impressive indeed. As one might expect, the work begins (in most manuscripts) by discussing God, and then Mary, the Mass, the human soul, and salvation (1, 1–24, 5). Later sections include a rather unsystematic treatment of the vices and virtues, beginning with pride (28, 15–30, 20); and Freidank expatiates also on good and evil

(127, 4–134, 5), wealth and its lack (40, 9–43, 23), and wisdom and folly (78, 1–86, 9), before returning to a cluster of religious themes such as the Antichrist, the Ten Commandments, death, and the Day of Judgement (172, 10–180, 7). Like many authors of *Sangsprüche*, he also combines discussion of such all-encompassing generalities with comment on contemporary political realities, notably the venality and moral decay of Rome (148, 4–154, 17), and the Crusade of 1228–9 (154, 18–164, 2). *Bescheidenheit* further shares with many didactic lyrics a fundamentally open structure. Its rhyming couplets often themselves constitute self-contained statements which, in their pregnant succinctness, bear witness to the influence of proverbial lore. Longer poetic units are, however, also employed; and the work's various components are organized in the more than 130 surviving *Bescheidenheit* manuscripts in numerous ways, some more obviously logical than others. One suspects indeed that the work may never have had a fixed, finished form. It does, however, have a pervasive tone of religious seriousness, evident both when Freidank is discussing basic Christian doctrines, and when he is concerned with the practicalities of daily living. This tone is set from the outset of the work, with its many biblical overtones:

> Gote dienen âne wanc
> deist aller wîsheit anevanc.
> Swer umbe dise kurze zît
> die êwigen fröude gît,
> der hât sich selber gar betrogen
> und zimbert ûf den regenbogen.
> Swer die sêle wil uil bewarn,
> der muoz sich selben lâzen varn.
> Swer got minnet als der sol,
> des herze ist aller tugende vol.
> Swer âne got sich wil begân,
> der mac nicht staeter êren hân.
> Swer got niht fürhtet alle tage,
> daz wizzet, deist ein rehter zage.
> Swelch mensche lebt in gotes gebote,
> in dem ist got und er in gote. (I, 5–II, 3)

[To serve God unwaveringly, that is the beginning of all wisdom. Anyone who forgoes eternal joy in favor of this short time (on earth), has deceived himself utterly and is building on shaky ground (literally, the rainbow). Whoever wishes to save his soul must lose himself. Whoever loves God as he should, his heart will be full of all virtue. Whoever wishes to live his life without God cannot have constant honor. Whoever does not fear God, he is — you should know — a true coward. Whoever lives according to God's command, God is in him and he in God.]

Freidank's manifest concern to raise the theological and spiritual awareness of his audience is shared by several other authors of longer didactic texts from our period. A notable example is Der Stricker (fl. 1220–50), who, along with many works of a largely secular orientation, composed numerous others on religious themes. Prominent among these are disquisitions on the Holy Spirit and his gifts (*Vom Heiligen Geist*, 948 lines), the Mass (*Die Messe*, 1202 lines), and the Devil (*Processus Luciferi*, 764 lines).[22] Worthy of mention also is a substantial commentary of 4889 lines on the Lord's Prayer (and on innumerable matters arising from it) written between 1252 and 1255 by Heinrich von Kröllwitz.[23] Heinrich shares the predilections of many of his contemporaries for Mary (see for example 537–719) and for allegory (a good fifth of his text, lines 1159–2100, is devoted to a point-by-point interpretation of twelve precious stones connoting aspects of God's kingdom); his work, like those of Der Stricker and indeed Freidank, is patently indebted to patristic and medieval Latin theologians without constituting a direct translation of any identifiable single text. That such translations were made also in the High Middle Ages is, however, exemplified by Lamprecht von Regensburg's *Tochter Sion* (4312 lines, ca. 1250), a version by a German Franciscan of a Latin treatise from the (Cistercian) school of Bernard of Clairvaux. Lamprecht's work is notable for its thoroughgoing use of allegorical personifications, and for combining teaching on the Christian virtues and on the transience of this world with an exposition of the mystical union that is possible between God and the Christian soul — referred to, in the title and elsewhere, as the "daughter of Sion." As such it is as good an example as any of the popularization and vernacularization of Latin theology in the thirteenth century.

The medieval sense of the ultimate indivisibility of religious and ethical perspectives is plain not only in works such as these, but in the monumental moral compendium *Der welsche Gast* (The Visitor from the Romance Lands, 15,405 lines), avowedly written over a ten-month period in 1215–16 (see lines 12882, 12932–33, 12371–72) by Thomasin von Zerclaere, a cleric at the court of Wolfger von Erla, Patriarch of Aquileia (the same man who, as Bishop of Passau, had given Walther von der Vogelweide a coat).[24] The work's title actually refers to its author, who remarkably, given the generally high quality of his German verse, was a native Italian speaker. Thomasin's target audience is a large and diverse one, consisting of the various groupings within courtly society, but with particular emphasis on young aristocrats. His themes are correspondingly wide-ranging, encompassing, for example, rules for correct behavior at court and towards ladies (especially in Book I), the Seven Liberal Arts (Book VII), and the conflict between empire and papacy (Book VIII, in which Thomasin bemoans the baleful influence of Walther in setting a thousand men [!] against the pope — 11871–77). Above all, however, *Der welsche Gast* is a treatise on the virtues, and one which makes copious use of exempla drawn not just from biblical and classical literature, but also from contemporary politics, and from a fascinating range of high medieval narratives, by such recent authors as Chrétien de Troyes, Hartmann von Aue, and Gottfried von Strassburg:

> iuncherren suln von Gawan
> hören, Clies, Ereck, Iwain,
> und suln rihten ir iugent
> gar nach Gawanes rainer tugent.
> volget Artus dem chunich here,
> der treit iu vor vil guoter lere.
> und habet ouch in iuwern muot
> den chunich Karln den helt guot.
> lat niht verderben iuwer iugent,
> gedenchet an Alexanders tugent.
> an gefuoge volget ir Tristande,
> Saigrimos, Kalogriande. (1653–64)

[Young gentlemen should hear stories about Gawain, Cligès, Erec, and Iwein, and should direct their youth entirely according to Gawain's pure virtue. Follow Arthur, the noble king, who gives you very good teaching. And be mindful also of Charlemagne, the good hero. Do not let your youth go to rack and ruin, but think of Alexander's virtues. As to propriety, follow Tristan, Segremors, and Kalogrenant.]

Thomasin focuses especially on *staete* (constancy, especially Books II–IV), *milte* (generosity, Book X), and *mâze* (the all-embracing quality of moderation, Book VIII), as well as on *reht* (law and justice, Book IX).[25] His discussion of these and other moral categories makes it plain that, in his view, the practice of virtue has implications not only for this life but also for the next. *Unstaete* (inconstancy) was, after all, the sin of Adam, and hence responsible for the Fall (3192f.); and, correspondingly, the practice of virtue will ensure our presence in Heaven (6336f., 6853–58). In this respect and in others (such as, for example, his advocacy in Book IX of the spiritual advantages of poverty) one is aware that the "welsche gast" is one who surveys German aristocratic society not merely as a foreigner but also as a pastorally concerned representative of the clergy.

Not the least of Thomasin's objectives was, as we have seen, to provide young German knights with appropriate moral and spiritual instruction. A similar impulse is observable in various works from our period in which a father is presented as giving advice to his son. Notable among these are a mid thirteenth-century Austrian poem of 508 lines known as *Der magezoge* (The Tutor), which, besides giving practical advice, stresses the importance of loving God and one's neighbor;[26]

twenty-one predominantly seven-line strophes, again probably from the mid-thirteenth century, in which King Tirol advises his son Fridebrant on how to act as a ruler;[27] and several German versions of the pragmatic and worldly-wise Latin *Disticha Catonis*, the earliest of which can be dated to approximately 1250.[28] Perhaps most interesting of all, however, is a sequence of fifty-six stanzas dating from roughly 1210–20 and attributed to *Der Winsbecke* (the man from Windsbach), a small Franconian town not far from the stomping-ground of Wolfram von Eschenbach, with whose works the author was obviously familiar.[29] In the form of its stanzas (ten four-footed lines in a canzona structure), in the often loosely associative way in which these are combined, and not least in the presence in a fifteenth-century manuscript of an accompanying melody, *Der Winsbecke* is in many ways close to the *Sangspruch* tradition; and the lessons the father teaches are also staples of the didactic lyric. He begins by stressing the importance of loving God (1–5) and respecting the Church (6–7), and then discusses women and how to treat them (8–21), knighthood and honor (22–23), control of the tongue (24–25), and such virtues as *mâze* (31) and *scham* (46). In the final stanza (56), he sums up by reiterating the primary importance of three qualities — love of God, truthfulness, and *zuht* (an untranslatable term meaning something like "virtuous and civilized self-control"):

> Wirt gotes minne nimmer vrî,
> wis wârhaft, zühtic sunder wanc;
> manc tugent ir vluz nimt von den driu;
> behalt si wol, hab immer danc. (56, 7–10)

[Never depart from God's love, be truthful and always full of "zuht"; many virtues flow from these three qualities. Keep them well, and always be thankful.]

Seven of the fourteen *Winsbecke* manuscripts contain an additional, probably roughly contemporary text, consisting typically of forty-five stanzas in the same *Ton*, in which a mother (*Die Winsbeckin*) advises her daughter, especially about love.[30] She enjoins moderation, constancy, modesty, generosity, and high spirits (see 5f., 13, and indeed 11, in which Hartmann's Lunete is cited as a role model); and she is able to convince her initially unenthusiastic daughter of the overriding importance of love. *Die Winsbeckin* also culminates in a three-point summary (43–45): the girl should bear no envy or malice toward other virtuous women, should seek to please the wise and honorable, and, again, should pursue *zuht*.

It was, of course, not only women who were given advice about love in medieval didactic literature. Discourses on love, aimed not least at men, were widespread especially in the fourteenth and fifteenth centuries; and already in the thirteenth century there were some important examples of the genre. Probably the best known of these (though it had only limited influence in the Middle Ages) is the work by Hartmann von Aue sometimes known as *Die Klage* (The Lament), sometimes as *Das Büchlein* (The Little Book), and now most commonly as *Das Klagebüchlein* (1914 lines).[31] This is often reckoned to be an early work of the great narrative poet, and hence dated at around 1180. It is cast as a dialogue between the poet's heart and his body, and as such is reminiscent in some respects of classical dialogues between the body and the soul. Its principal didactic meat is to be found in the second half, after the recalcitrant, lazy body has finally agreed (lines 1120–25) to follow the advice of the heart — which, perhaps surprisingly, almost invariably represents the voice of reason. Along with reason (*sinne*) and effort (*arebeit*) it is again the pursuit of virtue that is presented as essential, not just for success in love and happiness in this life, but also for the attainment of eternal bliss. Special emphasis is placed on generosity, humility, and *zuht* (1303), chastity and modesty (1315), and *manheit* (manly bravery, 1317). These qualities, placed in a heart that is free from malice (1322), will facilitate success with ladies (1336–38), and will capture the love both of God and of the world (1346). The erotic impulse can, therefore, according to Hartmann, be channeled in such a way as to promote both civilized behavior and spiritual fulfillment; and as such his disquisition on love is in effect also a work on ethics and theology.

Much the same could be said of one of the few works that are demonstrably indebted both to the *Winsbecke* stanzas and to the *Klagebüchlein*, namely Der Stricker's *Frauenehre* (The Honor of Ladies, 1902 lines).[32] Here too instruction about courtly love is combined with a broad-based treatment of the virtues, albeit in the context of a rather more loosely constructed work whose tone is less subjective and whose purport is rather different. Der Stricker is more concerned than Hartmann to praise women, both in their own right and as benefactresses of men: women are portrayed in particular as sources of virtue, honor, and joy (see for example 569–76, 641–43, 803–9). As such, their influence on men is frequently expressed in quasi-religious terms, most notably in the work's opening section (204–301), which dwells on the *gnade* (grace) shown by women toward men, and in the extraordinary statement at its very end, in which women are described as constituting "der ander got der werlde" (the world's second God, 1894).

A different approach is evinced by the *Frauenbuch* (Book of the Ladies) by the Austrian ministerial Ulrich von Liechtenstein (d. 1275).[33] This discourse on love, consisting of 2134 lines and completed — or so one can deduce from lines 2127–29 — in 1257, is, like Hartmann's, predominantly a dialogue. In this case, however, the speakers are a knight and a lady, and their subject is a perceived decline in courtly values and high spirits, for which each holds the other's sex primarily responsible. Their civilized dispute is eventually settled by a third voice, that of the author (1828). His nostrum for society's ills is an essentially conservative one: the lady is declared victorious (2003f.), and her sex is to be praised, served, and honored as the source of all good; nevertheless women in turn are to be "undertân," subject, to men. Such a paradoxical expression of the Pauline doctrine of female subordination cast in (for 1257) somewhat old-fashioned courtly terms is perhaps an apt final example of the attempt to reconcile the demands of God with those of the world that underlies many of the works we have discussed:

> Ich sprach: "vrou, ich muoz des jehen,
> waz ich ie vrouwen hân gesehen,
> dar zuo aller hande wîp,
> der guot, der leben und ouch ir lîp
> muoz sîn den mannen undertân,
> dâ von muoz ich iu zuo gestân.
> diu wîp müezen beide tuon unde lân
> an allen dingen swaz wir man
> wellen und vns denket guot.
> swelch wîp des niht güetlîchen tuot,
> diu muoz es tuon, daz ist alsô. . . . (1931–41)
>
> . . . Mîn munt iu spricht:
> wîp sint alsô tugentrîch,
> daz ir deheiniu endelîch
> immer niht daz begât,
> des si von rehte laster hât.
> si sint reine, si sint guot.
> si sint tugentlîch gemuot,
> si sint wandelunge vrî,
> in sint hôhe tugende bî,
> daz al der welte vreude stât
> an in. waz ieman saelden hât,
> daz muoz von guoten wîben komen." (1982–93)

[I said: "Lady, I must say that all the ladies and all the kinds of women I have seen must be subject to men in their worldly goods, their lives, and also their bodies. For this reason I must assist you. In all things women must do whatever we men wish and consider to be good. Any woman who does not do this with a good grace must (be forced to) do it. That is how it is. . . . I tell you (addressing the knight), women are so virtuous that in the end none of them will do anything which rightly puts her to shame. They are pure, they are noble, they are virtuous in their thinking, they are free from fickleness, they possess noble virtues, so that the joy of all the world depends on them. Whatever happiness one has must come from good women."]

Two very general reflections suggest themselves as we conclude. One is that, in spite of the enormous cultural significance, potential for inter-disciplinary study, and literary stimulation offered by many of the works we have mentioned, they tend to remain neglected both in scholarship and on university syllabi. The following endnotes document, for example, the extreme age of some of the still-standard editions, and the paucity of translations into English (or indeed modern German); and much analytical work also remains to be done, particularly on the longer texts. Our second general reflection is the perhaps obvious one that, for all their remarkable diversity, many of the texts we have looked at exemplify the desire to unite, integrate, and harmonize that was common to so much high medieval culture. We see this in the constructive combination of aristocratic, popular and learned perspectives; of French, German, and Latin traditions; of religious and secular attitudes; of words and music; and, not least, of edification and entertainment. In Horace's much quoted phrase from *De arte poetica*, poets wish either to do good or to delight ("aut prodesse volunt aut delectare poetae"). Many of our texts demonstrate that they can also do both.

Notes

[1] There is a facsimile edition of this manuscript: *Die Jenaer Liederhandschrift. In Abbildungen, mit einem Anhang: Die Basler und Wolfenbütteler Fragmente*, edited by Helmut Tervooren and Ulrich Müller (Litterae 10, Göppingen: Kümmerle, 1972).

[2] This designation is used in the excellent standard survey of the didactic lyric: Helmut Tervooren, *Sangspruchdichtung* (Sammlung Metzler 293, Stuttgart: Metzler, 2nd revised edition 2001) — hereafter referred to as Tervooren; also in the monumental *Repertorium der Sangsprüche und Meisterlieder des 12. bis 18. Jahrhunderts*, edited by Horst Brunner and Burghart Wachinger (16 vols., Tübingen: Niemeyer, 1986–2001). This is the most important resource for the study of medieval didactic poetry, along with: *Die deutsche Literatur des Mittelalters: Verfasserlexikon*, 2nd edition, edited by Kurt Ruh et al. (11 vols. to date, Berlin: de Gruyter, 1978–present).

[3] These are listed and surveyed in Tervooren, 10–19.

[4] L. Peter Johnson, *Vom hohen zum späten Mittelalter: Die höfische Literatur der Blütezeit. Geschichte der deutschen Literatur bis zum Beginn der Neuzeit* II/1 (Tübingen: Niemeyer, 1999), 188–89.

[5] Walther von der Vogelweide, *Werke, Gesamtausgabe. I: Spruchlyrik*, edited with translation [into modern German] and commentary by Günther Schweikle (Stuttgart: Reclam, 1994), 8, 10 (72); Tervooren, 49. All English translations are by N. H.

[6] 229 of these are printed in: *Die Gedichte Reinmars von Zweter*, edited by Gustav Roethe (Leipzig: Hirzel, 1887). Subsequent references to Reinmar's works are based on this edition, and, as with other authors, consist of the poet's name

followed by the number of the stanza (and, *where it is helpful*, page number) as given in the stipulated edition.

[7] *Des Minnesangs Frühling*, edited by Hugo Moser and Helmut Tervooren (38th edition, Stuttgart: Hirzel, 1988). By convention, stanzas from this anthology are referred to by the page and number of their first lines as these appeared in the first edition.

[8] See Joachim Bumke, *Geschichte der deutschen Literatur im hohen Mittelalter* (Munich: dtv, 4th edition, 2000), 89.

[9] Jens Haustein, *Marner-Studien*, Münchener Texte und Untersuchungen 106 (Tübingen: Niemeyer, 1995), 239. Hereafter referred to as Haustein.

[10] Joachim Heinzle, *Vom hohen zum späten Mittelalter: Wandlungen und Neuansätze im 13. Jahrhundert. Geschichte der deutschen Literatur bis zum Beginn der Neuzeit* II/2 (Königstein/Taunus: Athenäum, 1984), 125.

[11] Anton E. Schönbach, *Beiträge zur Erklärung altdeutscher Dichtwerke, III–IV: Die Sprüche des Bruder Wernher I–II* (Sitzungsberichte der Kaiserlichen Akademie der Wissenschaften in Wien, philosophisch-historische Klasse, vols. 148 and 150, Vienna: Gerold, 1904). Hereafter referred to as Wernher.

[12] *Der Marner*, edited by Philipp Strauch (Quellen und Forschungen 14, Strasbourg: Trübner, 1876). Hereafter referred to as Marner.

[13] See *Minnesinger: Deutsche Liederdichter des 12., 13. und 14. Jahrhunderts*, edited by Friedrich Heinrich von der Hagen, 4 vols. (Leipzig: Barth, 1838), vol. 3, 53 (Rumelant I, 9).

[14] Edition (as "Der wilde Alexander"): *Deutsche Liederdichter im 13. Jahrhundert*, edited by Carl von Kraus, revised by Gisela Kornrumpf, 2 vols. (Tübingen: Niemeyer, 1978), vol. 1, 1–19. Hereafter referrred to as Alexander.

[15] *Friedrich von Sonnenburg*, edited by Achim Masser, Altdeutsche Textbibliothek 86 (Tübingen: Niemeyer, 1979). Hereafter referred to as Sonnenburg.

[16] Edition of Sigeher (fl. 1250–70): *Meister Sigeher*, edited by Heinrich Peter Brodt, Germanistische Abhandlungen 42 (Breslau: Marcus, 1913). Edition of Kelin (third quarter of thirteenth century): Wolfgang von Wangenheim, *Das Basler Fragment einer mitteldeutsch-niederdeutschen Liederhandschrift und sein Spruchdichter-Repertoire (Kelin, Fegfeuer)* (Bern: Lang, 1972).

[17] See the corpus edited by Ulrich Müller, *Politische Lyrik des deutschen Mittelalters*, 2 vols., Göppinger Arbeiten zur Germanistik 68 and 84 (Göppingen: Kümmerle, 1972).

[18] The attribution has generally been regarded as genuine, but is challenged by Haustein, 111–23 and 240f.

[19] The only fully recommendable survey of medieval German didactic literature remains that of Bernhard Sowinski, *Lehrhafte Dichtung des Mittelalters*, Sammlung Metzler 103 (Stuttgart: Metzler, 1971).

[20] Freidank, *Bescheidenheit*, edited by Heinrich Ernst Bezzenberger (Halle: Waisenhaus, 1872). Parts of the work have been edited and translated into modern German by Wolfgang Spiewok (Reclam: Leipzig, 1985).

[21] This version is suggested in Marion E. Gibbs and Sidney M. Johnson, *Medieval German Literature: A Companion* (New York: Garland, 1997), 426.

[22] All three are edited in Ute Schwab, *Die bisher unveröffentlichten geistlichen Bispelreden des Strickers* (Göttingen: Vandenhoeck & Ruprecht, 1959), 49–117.

[23] *Heinrich's von Krolewiz úz Missen "Vater Unser,"* edited by Georg Christian Friederich Lisch, Bibliothek der gesammten deutschen National-Litteratur 19 (Quedlinburg/Leipzig: Basse, 1839).

[24] Thomasin von Zerclaere, *Der welsche Gast*, edited by F. W. von Kries, Göppinger Arbeiten zur Germanistik 425/1 (Göppigen: Kümmerle, 1984).

[25] These four qualities also form, apparently coincidentally, the main subject-matter of the surviving parts of the earliest vernacular collection of instructions for young aristocrats, Wernher von Elmendorf's translation of the Latin *Moralium dogma philosophorum* (ca. 1170). See Wernher von Elmendorf, edited by Joachim Bumke, Altdeutsche Textbibliothek 77 (Tübingen: Niemeyer, 1974).

[26] *Kleinere mittelhochdeutsche Erzählungen, Fabeln und Lehrgedichte. III: Die Heidelberger Handschrift cod. Pal. germ. 341*, edited by Gustav Rosenhagen, Deutsche Texte des Mittelalters 17 (Berlin: Weidmann, 1909), 21–29.

[27] *Winsbeckische Gedichte nebst Tirol und Fridebrant*, edited by Albert Leitzmann, revised by Ingo Reiffenstein. Altdeutsche Textbibliothek 9 (Tübingen: Niemeyer, 1962), 82–87.

[28] Leopold Zatočil, *Cato a Facetus. Zu den deutschen Cato- und Facetusbearbeitungen. Untersuchungen und Texte* (Opera Universitatis Masarykianae Brunensis Facultas Philosophia 48, Brno UP, 1952), 29–51.

[29] *Winsbeckische Gedichte*, 1–32. I am not considering here the "Fortsetzungen" (continuations) printed on pp. 33–45, on the grounds that these are probably later additions made by a different author. The events of Book I of Wolfram's *Parzival* are alluded to (and Gahmuret named) in stanza 18.

[30] *Winsbeckische Gedichte*, 46–66. Translation into modern German by Albrecht Classen, *Frauen in der deutschen Literaturgeschichte: Die ersten 800 Jahre. Ein Lesebuch*, Women in German Literature 4 (New York: Lang, 2000), 74–90. Most scholars would, however, question Classen's view (71–72) that this text was actually written by a woman.

[31] Hartmann von Aue, *Klagebüchlein*, edited, translated [into English] and with an introduction by Thomas L. Keller, Göppinger Arbeiten zur Germanistik 450 (Göppingen: Kümmerle, 1986). There is a further English translation, by Frank Tobin, in *Arthurian Romances, Tales, and Lyric Poetry: The Complete Works of Hartmann von Aue*, translated with commentary by Tobin, Kim Vivian, and Richard H. Lawson (University Park, PA: Pennsylvania State UP, 2001), 1–27.

[32] Klaus Hofmann, *Strickers "Frauenehre." Überlieferung — Textkritik — Edition — literaturgeschichtliche Einordnung* (Marburg: Elwert, 1976).

[33] Ulrich von Liechtenstein, *Das Frauenbuch*, edited and translated by Christopher Young., Universal-Bibliothek 18290 (Stuttgart: Reclam, 2003).

Minnesang — The Medieval German Love Lyrics

Will Hasty

O NE OF THE EARLIEST VERNACULAR REFERENCES to love songs in
Germany is contained in *Von des tôdes gehugede* (remembrance of
death), a poem written ca. 1160 by a layman poet named Heinrich, who
was associated with the monastery of Melk. The poem articulates the
memento mori theme so common in religious and lay literature of the
Middle Ages, by means of which one was brought to think of death and
thus of the instability of life and all worldly things. In this poem, a beautiful woman is instructed to behold the decomposing corpse of a man who
during his life was her lover. The effects of the ongoing decomposition are
described with images that juxtapose the man's current physical state
with his former happy life as a courtier, and also as a lyric poet, who praised
"der frowen hôchvart" (The proud bearing of ladies).[1] The specific reference
to love songs is associated with the consideration of the man's tongue,
"dâ mit er diu troutliet chunde / behagenlîchen singen" (with which he
could sweetly sing songs of love), but which now lies motionless.[2]

Heinrich's reference to love songs, besides its value in documenting
the existence of a love song tradition during a time that preceded most of
the love lyrics that have come down to us in written form, provides a socio-
cultural perspective from which to assess the significance of the emergence
of *Minnesang* in the High Middle Ages. The love of ladies (and of knights,
in the many stanzas depicting a woman's perspective) that is seen negatively in Heinrich's poem and that will be — despite Heinrich's admonitions — tirelessly and multifariously expressed in the preserved love songs
during the century following *Von des tôdes gehugede*, represents one of the
foundations of the secularized courtly culture that emerges in Germany in
the latter decades of the twelfth century. In this courtly culture, and particularly in the preoccupation with the love of ladies (or knights), the decision has been made to situate oneself as comfortably as possible in this
imperfect transitory world.[3] Although echoes of the *memento mori*-theme
reverberate through courtly culture in Germany, this culture is nevertheless irrevocably dedicated to worldly concerns such as love, and nowhere
so explicitly and intensely as in the love lyrics, or *Minnesang*.

If we turn back to the beginning of the love lyric tradition in Germany and endeavor to learn something about its development and its relationship to other domains of medieval life by trying to establish its origins, we are faced with many interesting possibilities, but little that is certain. The adoration of the beloved lady shows parallels to Marian poetry, and scholars have also stressed similarities between *Minnesang* and the Latin poetry of the goliards (wandering scholars who wrote and performed ribald or satirical songs in Latin; the poetry contained in the *Carmina Burana* manuscript includes some Middle High German lyrics, notably by Walther von der Vogelweide).[4] While it seems likely that there was a relationship of influence between the Latin lyrics and the vernacular love lyrics, the two corpuses are quite different in many of their forms and themes (the Latin lyrics dealing with love, for example, tend to deal with it in a much more openly erotic manner than the vernacular love lyrics, which tend to allude to sexuality only very vaguely). Another possibility is that the origins of the love lyric tradition in Germany, at least at the very beginning, were indigenous.[5] The earliest poet whom we know by name is called Der von Kürenberg, who lived along the Danube like the other early singers and whose verses were composed in a unique long line that looks similar to the verse form of the *Nibelungenlied*. These early lyrics lack indications of the relationship of service and reward that will be the hallmark of the *hohe minne* model that will later entrench itself after the German reception of Provencal and French lyrics. Thus, it seems possible that the very earliest love lyrics in the German vernacular may have been based on indigenous popular lyrics, though such an assumption remains conjectural.

One thing that can be said with certainty about the origins of love lyrics in the German vernacular is that they were highly dependent both formally and thematically on Provencal and French lyrics during a crucial, early formative stage around 1180. Poets along the Rhine river such as Heinrich von Veldeke and Friedrich von Hausen came into contact with Romance poetry and in emulation of it (which sometimes involved using the same verse forms and melodies, the results of which were called "contrafactures")[6] first developed the *hohe minne* model that would become the foundation of future German lyrics. Provencal and French influences are thus inseparable from the origins of *Minnesang*, though the German lyrics, however indebted to Romance antecedents they may be, develop in directions that are connected to social and political structures specific to Germany. Recent scholarship is no longer nearly as interested in the question of origins as scholars of the nineteenth century, and this may well have something to do with a more general scholarly endeavor to comprehend medieval artistic practice as a dynamic process involving multiple and mutual relationships of influence.

The earliest love poetry in the German vernacular was composed along the Danube river not long after the middle of the twelfth century by poets

Der von Kürenberg. A miniature from the Codex Manesse (63r).

such as Der von Kürenberg, Dietmar von Aist, Meinloh von Sevelingen, and the barons of Regensburg and Rietenburg. The lyrics of Der von Kürenberg demonstrate an early phase in the development of the German lyrics in which the influence of Romance forms and content is not yet manifest. Besides the archaic verse form already mentioned,[7] the concerns of the world in which the figures of Kürenberg's poetry move is very much that of (lesser) German nobility. Der von Kürenberg's verses, replete with horses, armor, and birds of prey, are evocative of a noble life of considerable appetites on the part of both men and women. At times his verses seem to convey male fantasies of voracious female desire, as when the singer tells of the time he stood at the bedside of his lady, but did not dare wake her, which is followed by the lady's response: " 'des gehazze got den dînen lîp! / jô enwas ich niht ein eber wilde,' sô sprach daz wîp" ("May God curse you for that [i.e. not waking me], I wasn't a wild boar!," thus spoke the woman; 8, 11–12).[8] In another stanza, a woman standing on a castle wall hears Der von Kürenberg singing and resolves that if she is not able to have him, he will have to depart from the land (8, 1–4); the knight's response to this (in a stanza that is transmitted separately in the manuscripts but regarded as his response to the lady's resolve in the form of a *Wechsel* by some scholars)[9] is to call for his horse and armor in preparation for departure. *Minne* — which in this instance clearly has a strongly erotic aspect — cannot, it would seem, be forced on someone against his will: "diu wil mich des betwingen, daz ich ir holt si. / si muoz der mîner minne iemer darbende sin" (She wants to force me to be her servant; she'll have to learn to get along without my love; 9, 31–32). Striking in verses such as these is the depiction of the woman as the aggressive initiator of love, and of the man as reserved in the one example, defiant in the other, but in both cases seeming to avoid amorous bonds. The singer in these instances is capable of resisting the power of love and retains his freedom of movement, which stands in stark contrast to the situation of the singer in the songs of *hohe minne* (love of highborn ladies), which will be discussed below.

Already in the songs of the earliest singers, we see some of the themes and concerns that will remain set parts of the lyric repertoire of *Minnesang*. The association of *minne* and *hoher muot* (high spirits) is present at the culmination of one of Der von Kürenberg's stanzas (10, 17–20), in which the singer tells of a knight who courted a good lady, the thought of which makes his spirits soar. In a dawn song by Dietmar von Aist (cited below) we shall see that the idea of love-service, a main characteristic of *hohe minne*, has already begun to make its mark on some of the early Danubian poets. In the 1180s the basic parameters of the future development of *Minnesang* were set by a group of poets living and working along the Rhine and standing in relationships of allegiance to the imperial Hohenstaufen:[10] Heinrich von Veldeke, Friedrich von Hausen, and Rudolf von Fenis. These poets came into contact with Provencal and French lyrics, began to transform them for their German audiences, and from this time forward the love-service of *hohe minne*, with its challenges, trials, tribulations, and occasional small rewards, will be the predominant kind of song. The songs themselves, besides beginning to consist of multiple stanzas (in contrast to the more archaic tendency towards single stanzas among earlier singers), become formally more complex. These innovations were carried forward and embellished by poets such as Albrecht von Johannsdorf, Hartmann, Heinrich von Morungen, and Reinmar, in the last decades of the twelfth century, and by Wolfram von Eschenbach and Walther von der Vogelweide in the first decades of the thirteenth.

In songs about *hohe minne*, which scholars typically call *Werbelieder*, we usually find the singer lamenting the distance that separates him from his beloved, who occupies a position of status and power that is superior to that of the singer, though this position is never explicitly defined in political or social terms. The ideal characteristics of the lady, which go along with this superior position that she occupies, are *schoene, güete*, and *staete* (beauty, goodness, and constancy). These qualities of the lady have inspired the love of the singer and hold him in love's thrall as he endeavors to win (a token of) her love, but they also, paradoxically, seem to be qualities that serve to keep the beloved irrevocably distant from the singer. To use the imagery of Rudolf von Fenis, the singer is like a man who is stuck half way up a tree and finds that he can neither proceed upward nor climb back down (80, 5–8); he is doomed simply to hang on as best he can and hope for the best. The songs about *hohe minne* tend to be more like laments than serious entreaties to the beloved ladies for their love. The singers typically discuss their qualifications to receive their ladies favor — their long years of loyal *dienst*, or service (which itself frequently involves the valued quality of *staete*), which has remained without *lón*, or love's reward, whereby the exact nature of the love service and the expected reward are seldom clearly specified. Yet despite the singers' reiteration of their qualifications to receive love's reward, the lyrics tend to make it clear that they do not seriously expect this to happen. The involvement of the singers in *hohe minne* is often framed in the lyrics as a cause for regret. A stanza from the lyrics of Friedrich von Hausen (52, 7–16), one of the first German poets to develop the *hohe minne* model in emulation of Romance antecedents, can be regarded as exemplary of the singer's attitude about his position in *hohe minne*:

> Hete ich sô hôher minne
> mich nie underwunden,
> mîn möhte werden rât.
> ich tet ez âne sinne.
> des lîde ich ze allen stunden

nôt, diu mir nâhe gât.
mîn staete mir nu hât
daz herze also gebunden,
daz sî ez niht scheiden lât
von ir, als ez nu stat.

[If only I had not involved myself in so high a love, there might be some
help for me. I wasn't in my right mind. Now because of this I suffer a constant pain within. As things stand now, my own constancy has bound my
heart and will not let it depart from my lady.]

The situation of Rudolf and Friedrich in the above-mentioned lyrics seems
pretty hopeless, but the state of affairs in *hohe minne* is not always so bleak.
In some verses the singers seem to suggest that their love service, even if
there seems to be no serious possibility that it will ever earn love's reward,
nevertheless has a value all its own. Monks are (or at least should be) made
purer by their ascetic suffering; figures such as Erec, Iwein, and Parzival in
the courtly romances improve themselves in the ascetic rigors of their adventures. Similarly, the singer who remains loyal to his beloved, whose perfection simultaneously qualifies her and makes her eternally remote, can be
improved by his love-service and the sacrifice it has involved. This improvement is typically articulated as an increased sense of worth in the singer in
the form of *hoher muot* (joy, high spirits), as if some small part of the lady's
perfection were being transmitted to the singer despite the distance separating them. A song that is frequently cited as an example of this is Albrecht
von Johannsdorf's "ich vant si âne huote" (I found her without a guard; 93,
12–94, 14), in which the singer describes how he has the opportunity to
have a discussion with his beloved lady. The singer reveals his love to his lady
and asks her to end his suffering, while the lady evades the attempted seduc-
tion and questions the singer's sanity. The song ends with the singer asking
his lady pointedly whether his singing and service for the lady will bring him
any success at all, to which the lady replies: "'âne lôn sô sult ir niht
bestân.' / 'wie meinet ir daz, frouwe guot?' / 'daz ir dest werder sint unde
dâ bî hôchgemuot'" ("You shall not remain without reward." / "How do
you mean that, good lady?" / "That you are thereby of greater value, and
high-spirited besides."). However ironic this specific case may be, scholars of
Minnesang long thought that a self-improvement or ennoblement on the
part of the singer, who learned to persevere despite the apparent impossibility of achieving his goal, was the main point in *hohe minne*. Although ves-
tiges of this idea are still current in literary histories and anthologies, in
recent decades scholars — pointing to the scarcity of references in the lyrics
to anything resembling self-improvement, and also to the predominance of
lyrics in which the negative, plaintive attitude prevails — have increasingly
distanced themselves from the idea that self-improvement represents a more
or less explicitly articulated program underlying the lyrics of *hohe minne*.[11]

her friderich von husen.   ·xxviii·

Friedrich von Hausen. A miniature from the Codex Manesse (116v).

Although there is a high degree of thematic and structural uniformity in songs about *hohe minne*, singers did frequently succeed in giving the depiction of their relationship to the lady (as the apparently unreachable embodiment of beauty and goodness) their own individual imprint. One of the more striking individual lyric voices is that of Heinrich von Morungen, in whose song "In sô hôher swebender wunne" (in such a high transport of joy; 125, 19–126, 8) the singer relates the joy resulting from a word from his beloved lady, "daz dem herzen mîn sô nâhe lac" (that went close to his heart; 126, 4), a joy that borders on an ecstatic, almost mystical experience (which is reinforced by the employment of words — *sêle, saelic* [soul, blessed] — which, in a context other than this one, would have a religious significance). While Heinrich is known especially for his musicality, light imagery, and the sensual quality of his verses, and for the manner in which he depicts love and his beloved lady as demonic powers, Reinmar has become widely known as one of the foremost representatives of *hohe minne* as fruitless suffering. The difficulties associated with *hohe minne* seem to function almost as an excuse for Reinmar to engage in a public dissection and analysis of his hopeless desire, what Schweikle calls an "Ästhetisierung des Leids."[12] The singer who is generally credited with developing the different possibilities of the lyric language as it existed before him to their fullest potential was Walther von der Vogelweide, who began as a student of Reinmar in Vienna composing songs of *hohe minne*, but who then distanced himself from this prevalent kind of song. Drawing on both early indigenous lyrics and Latin love poetry, Walther succeeded in creating a lyrical oeuvre with a great variety of new perspectives and themes, significant among which is *niedere minne* (literally: low love), which endeavored to replace the fruitless love of noble ladies with a love for women of more humble background that could be mutual. Even though he diverged pointedly from the *hohe minne* model in some of his songs, Walther — in contrast to some of his successors — remained loyal to the idea of *minne* as a courtly value, and *Minnesang* as a courtly art form of nobility (*Gesellschaftskunst*).

From about 1180 forward, *hohe minne* has become the dominant concern in most of the songs, but there is a great variety of poetic perspectives and themes that play off of the *hohe minne*-model and seem to achieve their effect by undermining it in different ways. One of the perspectives the singers can adopt is that of the lady. In the songs of *hohe minne*, the lady is often abstract and remote, but she can also be depicted with a higher degree of individual nuance as indifferent, scornful, and even cruel (despite simultaneously and paradoxically continuing to possess those ideal qualities that make it impossible for the singer to separate himself from her). This depiction of the lady from the male perspective of the minnesingers (all of whom, as far as we know, were men), gives way in some of the lyrics to verses that are placed in the mouths of female figures. In these stanzas

and verses, the lady receives a voice of her own (even if this is also the creation of the male poets), and when this occurs we see something other
than the lady who is elsewhere so indifferent and cruel. In some of the earliest lyrics, a woman expresses her desire for her beloved.[13] Some of this
female desire remains in the later lyrics,[14] despite the fact that women's
voices from the Rhenish poets onward seem to be more reflective and concerned with social constraints than the seemingly freer voices of the female
voices in the earliest songs. We often see a woman figure who is caught
between the demands of her lover for a reward of love and the watchful
eyes of people at court, who are always on the lookout for a scandal and
would be only too happy to find one (which is one of the ways in which
the lyrics obliquely suggest that the love relationship is adulterous).
Sometimes the lady curses the social obstacles that stand between her and
her lover. Before she will forget about her beloved in deference to the
court, a lady in one of Friedrich von Hausen's stanzas declares that she will
change the course of the Rhine river so that it flows into the Po (49, 4–12).
In one of Reinmar's songs, the lady expresses her concerns about her loss
of reputation if she accedes to the entreaties of her lover, which she casts
as a kind of social death ("Des er gert, daz ist der tot" [What he really
desires is death, 178, 29]).

Another of the roles in which the singers can present themselves in
Minnesang is that of the crusader. In the so-called *Kreuzlieder*, or crusade
songs, the lyrical language is developed in a different direction by playing
the love of ladies off against the love of God. Whether the poets — whose
primary duties were military and administrative in most cases — who composed these songs really went on crusades remains a matter of conjecture,
though it seems likely that many of them did. However lyrical role and life
experience may have fallen together or diverged in the case of the crusade
songs, it is clear that the self-stylization as crusader permitted *minne* to be
discussed in different ways. In the context of a crusade song, the beloved
lady is no longer the only *summum bonum*, as which she tends to appear
in the songs of *hohe minne*, but rather has to contend for this status against
another absolute love, that of the crusader for his God. The result is typically depicted as a struggle of conflicting allegiances within the poet. We
see this in Friedrich von Hausen's "Mîn herze und mîn lîp diu wellent
scheiden" (My heart and my body want to part, 47, 9–40), in which the
singer's heart wants to remain dedicated to his lady, even though he has
taken the vows of a crusader that will take his body overseas in the service
of God. The conflict between the love of one's lady and the crusader's love
of God thus provides a different source of suffering and anguish in the
singer, even if the crusader's vows tend, perhaps inevitably, to win out
in the end. In the final stanza of Friedrich's song, the singer anticipates
the end of his relationship to his lady, whom he depicts as too limited
to understand the gravity of the spiritual commitment he has made.[15]

In another crusade song, "Ich var mit iuwern hulden" (I take leave with your blessings, 218, 5–28), Hartmann von Aue takes the inherent tension between *Frauendienst* and *Gottesdienst* in the direction of a more radical rejection of the former. Service to God in the crusades achieves, without fail, the ultimate reward, hence, this kind of *minne* is mutual in a way that love in the *hohe minne* model can never be: "ich wil mich rüemen, ich mac wol von minnen singen, / sît mich diu minne hât und ich si hân" (I will boast that I can sing well of love, since my love has me just as I have it, 218, 23–24). The singer's "higher" mutual love for God, marked by his resolve to participate in a crusade, is set off against the vainglorious and fruitless service of the minnesingers, whom he pointedly asks: "wâ sint diu werc? die rede hoere ich wol" (Where are the deeds? All I hear is words, 218, 14). It is important to bear in mind that, as far as we know, the crusader-role was another element of the poets' lyric repertoire, which enabled them to discuss love in a different way, and not (necessarily) an announcement of the singer's resolve or intention to participate in a crusade. It is quite possible that singers like Friedrich and Hartmann, after their performances of crusade songs such as the cited ones, returned to the standard model of *hohe minne* in subsequent performances.

Yet another departure from the standard song of *hohe minne* was the *tageliet*, or dawn song.[16] By presenting the lovers' awakening and imminent departure at the break of day, the dawn song depicts an illicit amorous relationship, but it does so in a situation and setting which, by its very nature, undercuts the singer's distance from and subordination to his lady that are the hallmarks of *hohe minne*. The dawn songs maintain a presence in the love lyrics from the earliest singers onward. Dietmar von Aist's "slâfest du vriedel ziere" is the earliest significant example of this song-type. In three stanzas structured as a *Wechsel* (see below), we experience the suffering of two lovers upon their departure. Interestingly, the words of the man are more formulaic; he seems almost stoically to accept love's association with suffering ("liep âne leit mac niht sîn," [there is no love without pain, 39, 24]), and then takes refuge in a service mentality that goes in the direction of *hohe minne*: "swaz dû gebiutest, daz leiste ich, vriundin mîn," (Whatever you command, I will carry it out, my beloved, 39, 25). The woman's voice, by contrast, seems more immediate and genuine. In the final stanza she begins to weep, and says — perhaps more to herself than to her companion, whose mind already appears to be in the world of day — "du rîtest hinnen und lâst mich eine. / wenne wilt du wider her zuo mir? / owê, du vüerest mîne vröide sant dir!" (You ride away and leave me alone. When will you return to me? Alas, you are taking all my joy away with you, 39, 27–29). The dawn song, with its depiction of consummated but endangered love, is taken up by later poets such as Heinrich von Morungen, who in his own characteristic way transforms the tender moments of awakening into an ethereal, almost ecstatic vision of the beloved,[17] and by Wolfram von Eschenbach, whose entire lyric production consisted of dawn songs.

The variations discussed above all have in common the tendency to undermine or disrupt, in one way or another, the distance from and subordination to the beloved lady that are inherent in *hohe minne*. The female voices articulating desire for their lovers in the *Frauenstrophen*, the vows of the knight departing on a crusade which supersede his obligations to his lady, the tearful parting embraces of lovers at dawn, all provide manners of depicting *minne* that are quite different from — if not at odds with — the painful, forlorn, and seemingly forever-fruitless love-service for an indifferent or hostile lady that is depicted in the majority of the songs. Another marked departure from the model of *hohe minne* seems to have been so radical in its implications that it was used only very sparingly, perhaps because it tended to undermine the courtly foundation for the performance of these lyrics (i.e. as a *Gesellschaftskunst* of nobility). If the love for a highborn lady is hopeless, painful, and ultimately fruitless, why not draw the consequences and seek the fulfillment of love with women of lower social standing? Walther von der Vogelweide, with his songs of *niedere minne* ("low love," in contrast to the *hohe minne* for highborn ladies) was the first to go somewhat persistently in this direction, though Hartmann von Aue before him had already considered this possibility in what has become known as his "Unmutston" (Song of Discontent). In this song, the singer tells us that he has learned to resist invitations from his knightly comrades to go and court noble ladies, because he did this once and was very contemptuously dismissed by the lady to whom he wished to dedicate himself. Based on this humbling experience, the singer has drawn the consequences: "ich mac baz vertrîben / die zît mit armen wîben" (I can spend my time better with women of modest background, 216, 39–40).

Formally, the majority of verses in *Minnesang* convey the perspective of the male singer, though we have seen that singers also frequently give voice to female perspectives. A form of song called the *Wechsel* (alternation), presents alternating female and male voices expressing their feelings about the situation in which they find themselves, without really speaking directly with each other (an example of this is a dawn song by Dietmar von Aist mentioned above; 39, 18–29). Another figure that occasionally appears in the lyrics is the *bote* (messenger), who acts as an intermediary between the singer and his lady. The relationship between the singer and his lady, however this may be structured in a given song, is frequently placed in some kind of relationship to the court, usually designated in the songs by the Middle High German word *werlt*. Though it can be called upon for support, the *werlt* tends to be depicted negatively as a danger or obstacle, which would be consistent with the idea that the love of the minnesingers is as illicit as it is fascinating.

The minnesingers employed a great variety of strophic and verse forms, one of the most important of which was the canzona-form adopted from the Romance lyrics. The canzona was a flexible type of stanza consisting of two initial groups of rhyming verses sung to the same melody, each one of which is called a *Stollen*, and a concluding group of verses with a different rhyme scheme and melody called the *Abgesang*. Given the attention paid by the singers to developing different forms of verses and stanzas, it is clear that the formal aspect of the singers' performances was a very significant one, and in the course of the thirteenth century the aspect of formal artistry became increasingly important.

It is likely that the music to which the lyrics were set in the original performances was just as important for the overall effect in this *Gesellschaftskunst* as the lyrics themselves. The Middle High German term *dôn* (modern German: *Ton*) referred to a melody, the related musical term *wîse* to the entire musical composition, the manner in which the poet set his lyrics to the music. Unfortunately, very little music from the original performances of the first few generations of minnesingers has survived, which suggests that there may have been little interest among medieval poets and audiences in preserving the music in written form, in contrast to the interest in preserving texts of the lyrics, which was achieved in manuscripts produced around 1300 such as the *Codex Manesse* (upon which the standard editions of the lyrics, such as *Des Minnesangs Frühling*, have been based). It is possible that the music was so popular and well-known among medieval audiences that it did not seem necessary to preserve it in written form.[18] Some of the melodies from these performances that survived the Middle Ages were preserved in the form of staffless neumes, mnemonic devices which reminded the singer where the melody went up and down in pitch and how the notes corresponded with the syllables of the lyrics. However, neumes provide no information about what pitches were involved, the intervals between notes, or what the rhythm would have been. A few songs with musical notes on musical staffs also survived in a number of manuscripts, notably the Jena Manuscript and the Münster Fragment. The latter manuscript contains the complete music for the *Palästinalied* of Walther von der Vogelweide, which, though not itself a love song, is thus "the best-attested melody by the best known of all minnesingers."[19]

The three major codices containing *Minnesang* are the above-mentioned *Codex Manesse*, also known as *Die große Heidelberger Liederhandschrift*, *Die kleine Heidelberger Liederhandschrift*, and the *Weingartner Liederhandschrift*. The standard edition of the seminal early period of the love lyrics is *Des Minnesangs Frühling* by Karl Lachmann and Moriz Haupt, which was originally published in 1857 and has since undergone dozens of revisions. In the thirty-seventh revised edition by Moser and Tervooren, the editors point to the possibility that the stanza, rather than the song, seems to have been the primary building block of the medieval performances, and that we have to reckon with the possibility that the organization of the individual stanzas into the larger units of songs was a very flexible and changeable process from the very beginning.[20] The search for the "original" version of a given song, once the guiding star of philology, has given way to an increased appreciation of the dynamic nature of medieval performances, which — not completely unlike live performances of contemporary popular music — might not play the same song in the same way on two different occasions.

Love literature in general and love lyrics (i.e. poetry set to music) in particular stand, and have probably always stood, in a very complex relationship to the individual experience of love. Recognition of this complex relationship is relevant to the ongoing scholarly debate about the biographical value of the medieval German love songs. In the nineteenth century, when the first critical editions of the love poetry were completed on the basis of the many extant manuscripts of the love lyrics, and when the scholarly occupation with these lyrics began in earnest, it was generally assumed that love as depicted in the songs of poets such as Friedrich von Hausen, Hartmann von Aue, and Walther von der Vogelweide was real love for real women. It is perhaps not surprising in the emerging discipline of *Germanistik* in the nineteenth century that the medieval poets were seen to be inspired by their feelings for their beloved ladies to give their love poetic expression, just as modern poets have done.

In the second half of the twentieth century, a new understanding of the lyrics gradually emerged that placed the biographical approach to them in doubt. The lyrics, it was argued, actually have little or nothing to do with any real experience of love for any real individuals on the part of the poets. Rather, they represent a kind of *Rollenspiel*, an elaborate, quasi-ritualized role-playing that would have taken place at the larger courts of powerful magnates during festive occasions. In his lyrics (according to the understanding of them as role-playing), the poet takes on the role of the pining lover, who talks about the beauty and accomplishments of the lady with whom he is in love, a lady who remains, seemingly by virtue of these very ideal qualities, remote from and thus inaccessible to the singer in all his imperfection; or, when the lady is actually depicted as present, she is unmoved by the singer's entreaties and occasionally even treats him with contempt. This basic situation, to which the poets themselves gave the name *hohe minne*, though it occurs in numerous different variations, and the language of *dienst* and *lôn* (service and reward) and more or less patient love-suffering, are so prevalent in the lyrics that it seems most difficult to see the highly conventional manner in which the singer talks about his love as anything other than role-playing. Correspondingly, even the divergences from this typical *hohe minne* model have been seen as role-playing rather than as the expressions of individual experience. Although the basic idea of role-playing has been articulated in a variety of different, and sometimes very complex ways in the critical literature, one of the basic underlying assumptions, however explicitly this may be articulated, is that no conclusions about the actual, biographical experience of love can be ventured on the basis of the poets' depiction of love in their lyrics. The two levels of experience that were so closely bound together in nineteenth century appraisals are thus strictly separated in this school of thought. If one heeds the main warning that is conveyed in the bulk of the critical literature on *Minnesang* in the last few decades, one will not confuse the singer's statements about love with any real, biographical expression of amorous feeling on his part. There are, though, some indications in the recent critical literature that the reaction against the biographical interpretation may have been an overreaction, and that a "biographical" consideration of them appropriate under certain conditions.[21] It is likely that the connections between a somewhat conventional lyrical language and an individual experience that is both poetic and emotional will continue to be a fascinating area of *Minnesang* research.

As *Rollenlyrik*, the love lyrics are approached as a formal art of creative variations on set themes. What would have been interesting to medieval audiences, it is assumed, would have been the new roles and perspectives that poets were able to introduce within the framework of a musical poetic performance — which was also a social event — in which the basic artistic parameters were quite stable and familiar to all participants. In contrast to modern love lyrics ("modern" here could mean the kind of love lyrics produced by poets from Goethe or Novalis onward), the medieval lyrics have been seen as a social art, or *Gesellschaftskunst*,[22] a term that endeavors to draw attention to the degree to which the medieval poets' art was bound not only by poetic conventions, but also by the wishes and expectations of their audiences, among whom we can assume were the patrons upon whom the poets depended for their livelihood. The poets' audiences can be imagined as consisting of knowledgeable and involved connoisseurs, in a position to appreciate the singers' subtle and occasionally not-so-subtle variations on set themes. Clearly, in the framework of a performance understood as *Gesellschaftskunst*, poets would have exploited the possibilities of formal variation with care, balancing in different ways the need for innovation with the reaffirmation of set paradigms. There would have been few artistic "revolutionaries," and it has been thought that *Minnesang* remains relatively stable in its basic generic characteristics — with the model of *hohe minne* (along with the various divergences from it) in the central position. Because of his introduction of the idea of "niedere minne," Walther has often been seen as a seminal figure in the history of *Minnesang*, but Walther nevertheless remained within the orbit of the *hohe minne*, and it was left to his younger contemporary Neidhart to make a more fundamental break with the *hohe minne* model, a break that might be considered revolutionary (even if it seems difficult to imagine without the previous expansion of the generic possibilities of *Minnesang* by poets such as Walther). Despite the innovations introduced by Neidhart (see below), love lyrics throughout the thirteenth century remained, for the most part, close to the model of *hohe minne*, at least with regard to thematic content, even if one observes an increasing tendency to transform the formal aspect of the love lyrics into an individual exercise in poetic virtuosity.

Besides the poet's own real amorous experiences, from which the lyrics of *Minnesang* are distinguished in different ways, there are other domains of socio-historical and political experience with which the love lyrics have been associated. The posture of extreme adoration on the part of the singer, whose love for his lady at times resembles veneration, if not worship, evinces similarities to the adoration of the mother of God in contemporary Marian poetry. This, along with the almost religious fervor of love-service in many of the songs, suggests parallels between the service of ladies (*Minnedienst*) and the service of God (*Gottesdienst*), with the logic of service and reward being common to both life domains, despite their very different primary points of orientation. However ethereal, sublime, even quasi-mystical the relationship to the lady may often be in the lyrics, the ultimate aim of the poets — to the extent that this can be made out — seems to be physical union with the beloved, which obviously diverges from the logic of religious service.

The manner in which the singers admonish their ladies to give them a reward for the love service they have rendered is also frequently evocative of the feudal relationship of service and reward between lord and vassal, which is likewise based on personal loyalty, or *triuwe*, a quality that many of the minnesingers underscore. In the feudal relationship, loyalty and military service to the lord in time of need, were central obligations of vassals. It has been thought by some that this posture of loyal service to a powerful lord has been transfigured in the framework of *Minnesang* to an amorous allegiance to the lady of the house. If there is any substance in the view of *Minnesang* as a sort of poetic "homage" to the most powerful female at court, then the love depicted in the lyrics would have to be regarded as adulterous. The idea that love as depicted in *Minnesang* is adulterous would be consistent not only with a poetic relationship with the lady of the house as described here, but also with the manner in which love is typically discussed in the High Middle Ages. During a time when marriage among nobles was usually a political arrangement in which emotional attachment between the partners was of little or no importance, the idea was entertained — at least in literature — that love has no place in marriage, and that it is thus by its very nature adulterous.[23] Unfortunately, the lyrics themselves provide almost no information about the marital status either of the poets or of their beloved ladies, and the idea that the ladies addressed in the lyrics were identical with the wives of the lords for whom the poets worked remains highly conjectural.

Another important domain of medieval experience with which the love lyrics have been associated concerns the social class of the singers, many of whom seem to have been *ministeriales* (ministerials), people who were of noble rank and often held important administrative and military positions, but who were nevertheless legally unfree and who could thus be sold, bartered, or traded by their masters. It has been argued that this discrepancy in the social and legal status of the ministerials — whose real political power was often at odds with their inferior legal status — led them to articulate their wishes for upward social mobility in lyric form.[24] According to this view, the desire for the high-standing lady is really the poetic representation of the ministerials desire for a higher social and legal status. This understanding of the love lyrics has been criticized on many grounds, one of the most important of which is the dearth of precise knowledge about the social status of most of the singers.[25] It is assumed that most of the minnesingers were ministerials, but this cannot be known for sure on the basis of the extant evidence. Furthermore, it is evident that the higher nobility — indeed as high as Emperor Heinrich VI, if the songs transmitted under his name were really composed and performed by this monarch — was also involved in composing love songs. Clearly, an understanding of the lyrics as articulating the desire for social mobility could not be valid in such cases.

It is not difficult to see broad similarities between the love lyrics and other domains of life in the High Middle Ages. Such similarities suggest a socio-political and literary milieu in which the love lyrics as a performative practice existed side by side with religious and feudal practices, with each of these life domains sharing certain basic structures (the relationship based on service and reward) and mutually embellishing and supporting the others. Such a view might help explain the continuing popularity of the love lyrics until the late Middle Ages. As long as the religious and feudal structures that accompanied its efflorescence in the late twelfth and thirteenth centuries remained in place, there appeared to be fertile cultural ground for the continuing cultivation of *Minnesang*. It will not be until the poetry of the Meistersinger in the fourteenth century, a poetry that we would associate with different classes of people in an entirely different socio-political milieu — burghers, tradespeople, and artisans in an urban setting — that the production of minne-songs will wane. Despite broad similarities between certain aspects of the love lyrics and other domains of medieval life, it is important to stress the need to see *Minnesang* as an cultural activity unto itself, analogous in some of its structures to religious and feudal practices, but ultimately with its own specific characteristics and concerns.

Minne remained a quite serious topic of discussion until Walther, in whose lyrics this discussion has been seen to achieve its culmination.[26] The same cannot be said of his immediate successor, Neidhart, who has been regarded along with Walther as one of the most original of the minnesingers, even if the corpus of songs he created seems more a parody than a continuation of *Minnesang* as it existed before him. In the two new types of songs he created, *Sommerlieder* and *Winterlieder* (summer songs and winter songs), Neidhart created a fictional world beyond the court populated with *dörper* (villagers), with whom, in the winter songs, the singer moves and with whom he has to contend for the love of his "lady" (who is also a *dörper*), in songs that move distinctly in the direction of epic narration. Neidhart's singer, who refers to himself in the songs as the one from *Riuwenthal* (the vale of regrets), is himself the object of desire in the summer songs, in which the *dörper*-woman, usually in a patently erotic way, expresses her resolve to have the love of the one from *Riuwental*. How seriously do we have to take *minne* in a song in which it is not even the maiden herself who is in love, but rather her old mother, who has to be restrained by her daughter from giving herself to "the one from Riuwental" (as in Sommerlied I)?[27] The construction of this non-courtly, transparently peasant world in the songs of Neidhart, and the implicit parody of the serious concern of *hohe minne* that went with it, though it clearly breaks from *Minnesang* as *Gesellschaftskunst*, was immensely popular with medieval audiences in the thirteenth century. The success of the manner in which Neidhart fictionalized himself as the adversary of the *dörper* is indicated by the lasting presence of Neidhart as a fictional character in Shrovetide plays until the time of Hans Sachs, as the chivalric adversary of the peasants pretending to be knights in Heinrich Wittenweiler's *Ring* (ca. 1400), and in the fictional biography *Neidhart Fuchs* composed at the end of the fifteenth century.

Minnesang thrived through the thirteenth century, particularly in the Swabian and Alemannic regions (what is today Switzerland and southwest Germany). Songs of *hohe minne* remained the dominant type, but singers disposed of a vast variety of different roles, perspectives, and ways of talking about love (ranging from idealizing to vulgar). A new tendency in songs by poets such as Burkhart von Hohenfels, Gottfried von Neifen, and Ulrich von Winterstetten, all three of whom were at least loosely connected with the Hohenstaufen court of Heinrich VII (the son of Friederich II), and which is also observable with Konrad von Würzburg, is a shift from the social-ethical implications of *Minnesang* to a preoccupation with its formal characteristics. Particularly Gottfried and Ulrich are known for their flowery, gallant, affected, even mannerist songs that generally follow the highly conventional thematic sequence of many early songs, beginning with a scene from nature, and followed by a suit for love's fulfillment and a complaint when the fulfillment remains outstanding.

As the thirteenth century proceeds, *Minnesang* as an art of courtly solidarity (*Gesellschaftskunst*) seems gradually to give way to *Minnesang* as a more strictly individual exercise in formal and musical virtuosity. In the *Frauendienst* of Ulrich von Liechtenstein, love songs have been built into a narrative that has been regarded by some as the first autobiographical text in the German vernacular. Here songs about *minne* have become the articulation of the story of Ulrich's love life. *Minne* as a medium for the expression of individual experience that goes in the direction of autobiography, or as a framework for the demonstration of one's musical and poetic virtuosity: we have clearly come a long way since the love songs that Heinrich von Melk viewed with such apprehension. A century after *Von des tôdes gehugede*, when *Minnesang* provides the framework for the expression of great variety of different artistic identities and perspectives that place people in different relationships to each other and the world, it is quite evident that authors and audiences in Germany did not heed Heinrich's warning about the dangers of love.

Notes

[1] *Der sogenannte Heinrich von Melk: Nach R. Heinzel's Ausgabe von 1867*, ed. Richard Kienast (Heidelberg: Winter, 1946).

[2] Despite the stark dualistic imagery of Heinrich's poem when it comes to love of God versus love of ladies in this context, things were not quite so black and white elsewhere in Heinrich's work; see Francis G. Gentry, "Heinrich von Melk," in *Dictionary of Literary Biography, vol. 148: German Writers and Works of the Early Middle Ages*, ed. James Hardin and Will Hasty (Detroit: Gale, 1995), 49–55.

[3] Even if, as we shall see, the position of lovers as depicted in *Minnesang*, however worldly, is often anything other than comfortable.

[4] See Helmut Brackert's afterword in *Minnesang: Mittelhochdeutsche Texte mit Übertragungen und Anmerkungen*, ed. with (modern German) translations by Helmut Brackert (Frankfurt am Main: Fischer Taschenbuchverlag, 1991), 261.

[5] See Brackert, *Minnesang*, 261–62.

[6] James V. McMahon, "The Music of Minnesang," in *Dictionary of Literary Biography, vol. 138: German Writers and Works of the High Middle Ages*, ed. James Hardin and Will Hasty (Detroit: Gale, 1994), 277–88. See especially 279.

[7] See Hubert Heinen, "Minnesang," in *Dictionary of Literary Biography, vol. 138: German Writers and Works of the High Middle Ages*, ed. James Hardin and Will Hasty (Detroit: Gale, 1994), 229–39, here 231.

[8] Following scholarly convention, the songs from *Minnesangs Frühling*, the standard edition of the early German love lyrics, will be identified according to Lachmann's numbering of the verses; the cited edition is *Des Minnesangs Frühling*, ed. Karl Lachmann, Moriz Haupt, Friedrich Vogt, and Carl von Kraus, 37th

rev. ed. Hugo Moser and Helmut Tervooren (Stuttgart: S. Hirzl, 1982). All English translations of the lyrics are by W. H.

[9] Brackert, *Minnesang*, 281.

[10] Of whom one, Heinrich VI, Barbarossa's son, is named in the manuscripts as the author of a couple of stanzas and a four-stanza song.

[11] See L. P. Johnson, "Down with 'hohe Minne'!," *Oxford German Studies* 13 (1982): 36–48, and Stephen Kaplowitt, *The Ennobling Power of Love in the Medieval German Lyric* (Chapel Hill: U of North Carolina P, 1986).

[12] Günther Schweikle, *Minnesang*, 2nd ed (Stuttgart: Metzler, 1995), 88.

[13] Der Burggraf von Regensburg, 16, 1–11 and Dietmar von Aist, 37, 4–17 and 38, 5–10.

[14] See Hartmann von Aue, 216, 1–28.

[15] But see Hartmann von Aue, 211, 20–26, for a lady who, apparently, bestows her blessings on her lover's participation in a crusade.

[16] See Arthur T. Hatto, *Eros: An Enquiry into the Theme of Lovers' Meetings and Partings at Dawn in Poetry* (The Hague: Mouton, 1965).

[17] 143, 22–144, 16.

[18] McMahon, "The Music of Minnesang," 277.

[19] McMahon, "The Music of Minnesang," 279.

[20] Moser and Tervooren, *Des Minnesangs Frühling*, 7–8.

[21] See Harald Haferland, *Hohe Minne: Zur Beschriebung der Minnekanzone* (Berlin: E. Schmidt, 2000).

[22] See Wolfgang Mohr, "Minnesang als Gesellschaftskunst," in *Der deutsche Minnesang*, ed. Hans Fromm (Darmstadt: Wissenschaftliche Buchgesellschaft, 1972), 197–228.

[23] The second book of Andreas Capellanus's treatise *De amore* makes quite clear that love is impossible between man and wife; see *The Art of Courtly Love by Andreas Capellanus;* with introduction, translation, and notes by John Jay Parry (New York: Columbia UP, 1990).

[24] Herbert Moller, "The Social Causation of the Courtly Love Complex," *Comparative Studies in Society and History 1*, 1958–59, 137–63 and Erich Köhler, "Vergleichende soziologische Betrachtungen zum romanischen und zum deutschen Minnesang," *Berliner Germanistentag* 1970, 63–76.

[25] See Ursula Peters, "Niederes Rittertum oder hoher Adel? Zu Erich Köhlers historisch-kritischer Deutung der altprovenzalischen und mittelhochdeutschen Minnelyrik, *Euphorion* 67 (1973): 244–60 and Ursula Liebertz-Grün, "Zur Soziologie das 'amour courtois,'" *Beihefte zum Euphorion*, 1977; for a discussion of this debate, see Brackert, *Minnesang*, 265–68.

[26] Schweikle, *Minnesang*, 90.

[27] *Die Lieder Neidharts*, ed. Edmund Wießner and Hanns Fischer, 4th revised edition by Paul Sappler (Tübingen: Niemeyer, 1984).

The German Heroic Narratives

Susann Samples

THE USE OF THE TERM "HEROIC NARRATIVES" in the title of this essay is a departure from earlier established tradition, but is in line with current scholarly consensus in medieval studies. The more traditional designation "heroic epic" is now usually employed to designate the *Nibelungenlied,* which is the prototypical German heroic epic and the model for all subsequent heroic literature. One of the dominant characteristics of this work is its apparent nihilism. But later heroic works view the world differently, with none coming close to the pessimism of the *Nibelungenlied.* Consequently, scholars are now arguing for a more flexible approach to the concept of genre regarding the heroic epic.[1] This essay will employ the term "heroic narrative" to refer to a diverse body of texts ranging from the *Alexanderlied* (ca. 1140–50), to the *Nibelungenlied* (ca. 1200), to *Biterolf und Dietleip* (ca. 1260). While court literature generally depicted the two recurring themes of courtly love (*minne*) and adventure (*âventiure*) within the framework of the courtly-chivalric value system, heroic narratives evoked a pre-courtly society in which loyalty and kingship were more important. In general, the heroic narratives dealt with figures or events derived from the historic past of the Germanic peoples. Each author reworked this old subject matter to fit his own agenda. Heroes typically demonstrated both physical and moral strength. One challenge of these authors was to transmit the hero's deeds in such a way that the audience would be able to recognize them as heroic. Many heroic narratives seem to have originated in the Bavarian-Austrian area, which had not been as heavily influenced by France as western Germany had been. This geographical origin of the heroic narratives may also help to explain their more conservative and traditional worldview.

The heroic narratives can be divided into four main groups. The two earliest, the *Alexanderlied* and the *Rolandslied,*[2] share three main characteristics: 1) they are based on historical figures and events, 2) each was patterned after a French text, and 3) the names of both authors are known. The *Nibelungenlied*[3] occupies a unique position in medieval German literature. Its unknown author boldly rejected the courtly-chivalric ethos by graphically depicting the tragic consequences of the clash between courtly and feudal-aristocratic worldviews. The *Klage*[4] and *Kudrun*[5] form the third group, since both appear to be contemporary responses to the nihilism of the *Nibelungenlied*. The fourth group consists of the heroic narratives about Dietrich, who is a popular medieval figure probably based on the historical Ostrogothic king Theoderic the Great (ca. 453–526). These stories or narratives, however, have little connection with this historical king. This group can be further divided into two categories: texts such as *Alpharts Tod, Das Buch von Bern* (*Dietrichs Flucht*), and the *Rabenschlacht*[6] are historically more transparent, reflecting the political realities of this period, while other texts, *Rosengarten zu Worms, Laurin, Eckenlied, Virginal, Sigenot, Goldemar*, and *Biterolf und Dietleip*[7] are much more oriented toward adventure.

The *Nibelungenlied, Kudrun*, and *Rosengarten zu Worms* have a similar strophic form (four long lines) to the rhymed couplet found in many of the post-*Nibelungen* heroic narratives:

> Ine kán iu niht bescheiden,   waz sider dâ geschach:
> wan ritter unde vrouwen   weinen man dâ sach,
> dar zuo die edeln knehte   ir lieben friunde tôt.
> hie hât daz maere ein ende: daz ist der Nibelunge nôt. (*NL*, 2379)

> [I cannot tell you what happened after this, except that knights and ladies, yes, and noble squires, too, were seen weeping there for the death of dear friends. This story ends here: such was the Nibelungs' Last Stand.]

> Ortwîn und Herwîc   die swuoren beide ensamt
> mit triuwen staete einander,   daz si ir fürsten amt
> nâch ir hôhen êren   vil lobelîche trüegen;
> swelhe in schaden wolten,   daz sie die beide viengen unde slüegen.
> (*K*, 1705)

> [Ortwin and Herwig swore a binding oath to each other that they would faithfully discharge their obligations as sovereigns with honor and that if anyone wished to do either of them harm they would join forces to capture and kill him.]

So ends the story of Kudrun.

> Sie sprâchen: 'lieber herre,   sît ir sît wider komen,
> sô hân wir *iuwer sünde*   gar ûf uns genomen,
> des vröuwet sich unser gemüete   und ist uns allen liep.'
> hiemite endet sich   daz Rôsengarten liet. (*R*, 390)

> [They spoke: "kind lord, since you are coming back again, we have thus taken your sin upon us; it is pleasing to our disposition and pleasant for us all." The story of the rose garden concludes here.]

The *Rabenschlacht* has a different rhyme pattern (a mixture of short and long lines). *Virginal, Eckenlied, Sigenot*, and *Goldemar* are written in a complex thirteen-line strophe, called the *Bernerton or Eckenstrophe*.

The *Alexanderlied* and the *Rolandslied*

The *Alexanderlied* and the *Rolandslied*, the two earliest heroic narratives, are also the most "historical" of the texts under discussion. In the *Alexanderlied* (ca. 1140–50), Pfaffe (Priest) Lamprecht depicted the heroic deeds of Alexander the Great who continued to be a popular figure during the Middle Ages. Three different versions exist. There is the Vorauer manuscript (which ends with the death of Darius); the Strassburg manuscript (it continues with adventures, a journey to India, and Alexander's death); and the Basel manuscript (it combines elements of the former two manuscripts). This poem is written in a rhymed couplet and is one of the earliest secular epics in German. For his *Rolandslied* (composed ca. 1170), Pfaffe (Priest) Konrad drew on the tragic Spanish campaign of 778 and the legendary fame of Karl (Charlemagne) as his subject matter. According to accounts, Charlemagne's rear guard, commanded by Roland, was trapped in the Roncevaux pass by the Basques, and all his men perished in the ensuing battle. The popularity of the story of Roland is evidenced by its numerous retellings in various languages, the most famous being the *Chanson de Roland* (ca. 1100). Both the *Alexanderlied* and *Rolandslied* share the distinction that the names of their respective authors are mentioned. Besides their names, however, no further information exists concerning either of these cleric-authors. As clerics, they were interested in depicting and affirming God's plan of salvation in their respective works.

The selection of a non-Christian to be the hero of his *Alexanderlied* no doubt presented a challenge to Lamprecht. From the onset this author places Alexander's heroism within a Christian, medieval context. His hero, Alexander, also exemplifies the ideal political leader. When Alexander speaks to his most trusted vassals, he is affirming a lord-vassal relationship based on loyalty and service, and it is clear that the obligations are mutual. Lamprecht is also careful to show that Alexander does indeed fit into the Christian view of the world and God's plan of salvation. The climax of the narrative is Alexander's combat with Darius, in which Alexander defeats the Persian king. The author thus intends to show this triumph of Alexander as the transfer of world dominion. The Persian Empire is replaced by Greece, which, in turn, will be replaced by Rome, followed by the Christian Middle Ages.

The author of the *Rolandslied* not only names himself: "ich haize der phaffe Chunrat" (I am called Priest Konrad, 9079), but his patron as well: "nû wunschen wir alle gelîche / dem herzogin Hainrîche, / daz im got lône" (We all wish for Duke Heinrich that God rewards him, 9017–19).[8] The extant manuscripts were written in different dialects. It is now commonly accepted that the original was in Bavarian. The language is simple and the poem is written in rhymed couplets. Konrad's *Rolandslied* possesses a fierce and ardent crusading religiosity and ideology that reflects the prevalent religious zeal of this century of crusades. Duke Heinrich der Löwe (the Lion), Konrad's patron, also engaged in his own crusade of sorts. For twenty years he waged an intermittent war against the pagan Slavs in the northeast. Historical evidence reveals that tension existed between Heinrich's secular and religious goals.[9] Perhaps with this portrayal of Karl, Lamprecht was offering an alternate model of Christian kingship for his patron.

In contrast to the *Chanson de Roland*, which glorified France, the *Rolandslied* recasts this story into an irreconcilable clash of Christian and non-Christian religions. The German version is the third version, following the French and Latin versions. Konrad appears to have had a limited knowledge of French. The *Rolandslied* is replete with Christian motifs, biblical allusions, and demonstrations of piety.[10] Indeed, the public speeches of Roland and Karl often resemble public prayer, and the twelve paladins of Karl symbolize the twelve apostles of Christ. Conversely, the Moorish adversaries are depicted as immoral, dishonorable, and cowardly, with no redeeming qualities. The hero Roland embodies the *miles Dei* (soldier of God), whose relations with his Christian God resemble that of a lord-vassal relationship. Unlike his kinsman, the traitorous Genelun,[11] Roland is willing to renounce the world and his own life in order to obtain eternal salvation as a martyr. Konrad devotes nearly five thousand lines to the battle in which Roland distinguishes himself repeatedly. At the end of the battle, Roland and his men die as martyrs and consequently achieve the greatest reward for their service, a place in heaven. The death of Roland and his men also acquires a practical significance, as their martyrdom inspires Karl and his army to victory over the infidels.

The other hero of the *Rolandslied* is Charlemagne, who exemplifies the ideal of Christian kingship.[12] Konrad idealizes and sublimates Karl's feudal relationship to God, calling him "gotes dînistman" (God's servant, 801) and "gotes degene" (God's warrior, 3412). Throughout this narrative Karl is continually shown to be a willing instrument of God with a twofold goal, to convert the Moors to Christianity and to enlarge and enrich the empire. With his participation in the final battle, Charlemagne affirms and enhances his kingship. He is the unifying force for his army, and for his service he expects protection from God. Konrad therefore has God demonstrate his loyalty to the king when God intercedes in Charlemagne's decisive battle with Paligan (the Moorish emperor), which ends with the triumph of Christianity.

The *Rolandslied* thus celebrates the *miles Dei*. Roland and his men conduct themselves according to Christian precepts, and their fighting for Christianity sublimates their status as warriors. In their desire to achieve the crown of eternal life, they renounce the world. Charlemagne, on the other hand, supersedes Roland as the *miles Dei* who achieves the actual goal of Christian supremacy. Thus, Konrad was the first vernacular author to make Christian chivalry the main theme of an epic work.[13] This portrait of the secular hero as *miles Dei* in the *Rolandslied* in turn influenced the literary concept of knighthood in Germany.

The *Nibelungenlied*

The *Nibelungenlied*, written around 1200 by an anonymous author, occupied a unique place in the contemporary literature because it questioned the very structure of the courtly-chivalric value system. The meter of the *Nibelungenlied* gives the poem flexibility in conveying different moods. The work is composed in strophes of four long lines that rhyme in pairs and are broken by a caesura; it is divided into thirty-nine parts or *âventiuren*, a configuration which is already found in the earlier manuscripts. These *âventiuren* are of varying lengths. The numerous surviving manuscripts of the *Nibelungenlied* (thirty-two manuscripts and fragments) affirm its popularity among medieval audiences. The three chief manuscripts are C (ca. 1220), B (ca. 1250), and A (somewhat later). It is now commonly accepted that A is a version of B, and most of the critical editions and translations are based on B. The C manuscript is noteworthy since it revises the narrative. This version juxtaposes blame by softening the vilification of Kriemhild and making Hagen more culpable. A is located in the State Library in Munich; B in the Stiftsbibliothek in St. Gall, and C in the Fürstenberg Collection. Given this discrepancy among the major manuscripts and her important role in all of them, Kriemhild especially has been the subject of much debate and discussion. She appears as a young maiden, a proud queen, a grieving widow, and an avenging queen. She thus functions as an important central character that holds together this narrative of two stories.[14] Understandably, different retellings of these two stories existed in the oral tradition. The story of Siegfried recounted his youth and his encounter with a dragon, his marriage to Kriemhild, his participation in the winning of Brünhild, Siegfried's transfer of Brünhild's girdle and ring to Kriemhild, the clash between Brünhild and Kriemhild, and his murder at Worms. The fall of the Burgundians related the marriage of Kriemhild to Etzel (based on the historical Attila the Hun), Etzel's invitation to Kriemhild's male relations to his court, and the tragic death of the warrior-class of both the Huns and the Burgundians. Family feuds and the strong lord-vassal bond integrated and enhanced these two popular tales in the *Nibelungenlied*.

The author of the *Nibelungenlied* rejected the courtly-chivalric literary vogue around 1200 in telling a magnificent tale of murder, treachery, and revenge, basing his work on popular early legends about Siegfried's murder and the fall of the Burgundians. The tragic mood is already established in the first few stanzas. Many warriors will die because of one woman,

Kriemhild. The impending tragedy — the death of Siegfried at the hands of Hagen and Gunther — is almost immediately reinforced by the young Kriemhild's troubling dream about a falcon, which is killed by two eagles. At the court of Worms Kriemhild resides with her mother Ute and her three brothers (the co-regents) Gunther, Gernot, and Giselher. The setting then shifts to Xanten, home of the valiant knight-prince Siegfried and his parents, Sigmund and Sigilind. Although Siegfried departs for Worms to court Kriemhild, he initially challenges Gunther's kingship. This matter, however, is peacefully resolved, and Siegfried becomes an important ally in the Saxon war against Liudeger and Liudegast. Siefgried is at the court in Worms for one year before he actually sees his beloved Kriemhild.

Before Siegfried may marry Kriemhild, he must help Gunther win the powerful and beautiful queen Brünhild. Both Siegfried and Gunther engage in deceit to accomplish this goal. Siegfried uses a magical *Tarnkappe* (a cloak that allows its wearer to become invisible and gives him the strength of twelve men) to overcome Brünhild. Later, Siegfried is once again forced to subdue Brünhild so that Gunther can consummate the marriage. With her virginity taken, Brünhild loses her extraordinary strength.

Siegfried and Kriemhild depart for Xanten, where Sigmund voluntarily renounces the throne in favor of his son. Years pass, and Brünhild convinces Gunther to invite his vassal Siegfried to Worms. At a tournament, the two queens argue over the importance and superiority of their respective husbands, which later leads to a confrontation outside the cathedral. Here Kriemhild tells Brünhild that Siegfried, not Gunther, took her virginity. Brünhild's public humiliation prompts Hagen, the chief vassal and advisor of the Burgundian kings, to seek revenge.

Hagen is able to trick Kriemhild into revealing Siegfried's one vulnerable spot. While out on a hunt Hagen slays Siegfried by hurling a spear at his back. There is great mourning over the loss of such a famous warrior. Kriemhild dissuades Sigmund and his men from avenging Siegfried's murder, and they depart. At the behest of her relatives, Kriemhild decides to stay in Worms. Eventually, reconciliation occurs with her three brothers, but she and Hagen remain enemies. Kriemhild's brothers convince her to bring Siegfried's treasure to Worms, but Hagen sees through her ulterior motives. This treasure would enable Kriemhild to attract and retain supporters, which, in turn, would destabilize Gunther's kingship and kingdom. Hagen thwarts her by taking the treasure away from her and sinking it in the Rhine.

Again, years pass. Helche, the wife of Etzel, dies, and his advisors urge him to marry Kriemhld. Etzel sends his trusted vassal, Rüdiger, to accomplish this task. Kriemhild is at first reluctant, but she is eventually persuaded to accept his proposal of marriage. Kriemhild then journeys with Rüdiger back to Etzel's court. Years later, Kriemhild convinces Etzel to invite her three brothers and Hagen to their court. The impending tragedy is foreshadowed by a series of warnings. Neither Ute's warning nor the sea nymphs' prophesy — both of which foretell the destruction of the Burgundians in the land of Etzel — deter them from their journey. Hagen now assumes a much more dominant role, single-handedly transporting the vast army across the Danube. Only after destroying the raft does he finally inform his lords of their impending doom. A fight ensues when the Bavarians attempt to avenge the ferryman whom Hagen has slain.

Their stay with Rüdiger is the last happy occasion for the Burgundians: Gieselher is betrothed to Rüdiger's daughter. After the Burgundians' arrival at Etzel's court, the tension becomes increasingly palpable until Kriemhild finally incites the Huns to fight. At a feast, warfare breaks out, and Hagen beheads the young son of Etzel and Kriemhild. Dietrich manages to rescue Kriemhild and Etzel, but all the other Huns in the hall perish. The fighting continues, and Rüdiger is drawn into the battle. He finds himself having to fight for his lord, Etzel, against his new kinsmen, the Burgundians. Hagen and Gieselher refuse to fight, but Gernot and Rüdiger slay one another.

Dietrich, too, is finally drawn into the melee and takes the only two surviving Burgundians, Hagen and Gunther, prisoner. These two warriors continue to demonstrate a steadfast and fierce loyalty to each other until their death. In the final scenes of the narrative Kriemhild reveals her desire to recover Siegfried's treasure. An enraged Kriemhild first kills her brother and then Hagen. Their deaths ensure that the whereabouts of this treasure will remain unknown. The killing of such a great warrior as Hagen by a woman demands immediate retribution: Hildebrand slays Kriemhild in front of Etzel and Dietrich. There is much mourning about the great loss of life.

Convincing evidence has been offered that the storyline dealing with the fall of the Burgundians was written prior to the first part relating the events leading up to Siegfried's murder.[15] While many elements of this narrative hark back to an earlier, pre-courtly era, the *Nibelungenlied* is actually a political narrative that sets out to document the systematic breakdown of social and political order. The *Nibelungenlied* author, conservative in his social views, attributes the unfolding dynastic tragedy to the irreconcilable clash between courtly-chivalric and feudal-aristocratic values.

One example of the manner in which the author reshaped his subject matter to depict this tragic clash involves the function of the bridal quests. Before the *Nibelungenlied*, bridal quests were essentially a recurring motif in the so-called minstrel epics (*Spielmannsepos*). The author of the *Nibelungenlied*, however, transformed bridal quests into a serious activity with profoundly tragic consequences. Bridal quests are shown to be extremely dangerous enterprises that place the king and hence his kingship at risk. In the *Nibelungenlied* the bridal quests of Siegfried, Gunther, and Etzel, though initially successful, have ultimately disastrous consequences.

The fame of Kriemhild and Brünhild causes their future husbands to seek them out. The word of their beauty, which is spread far and wide, is enough to motivate the heroes to seek them out and thus to set the plot in motion, as we see in the following verses that describe how Siegfried first hears of Kriemhild:

> Den herren muoten selten   deheiniu herzen leit.
> Er hôrte sagen maere,   wie ein scoeniu meit
> wáere in Búrgónden,   ze wunsche wolgetân,
> Von der er sît vil vreuden   und ouch árbéit gewan. (44)

[This prince was never troubled by heartfelt sorrow. But one day he heard a report that there was a maiden living in Burgundy who was of perfect beauty; and from her, as it fell out, he was to receive much joy, yet also great distress.]

Although Siegfried sets out to court Kriemhild, he is belligerent and threatening when he first arrives at Worms. Siegfried's continuing desire to possess Kriemhild as his wife causes him to become embroiled in activities that threaten his life and undermine his social status. While Siegfried's courage and valor are evident in his participation in the war against the Saxons, his most questionable conduct occurs when he helps Gunther win Brünhild as his bride by means of blatant deceit. When he introduces himself at Brünhild's court as Gunther's vassal, Siegfried himself is responsible for the blurring of his own social status: "er ist mîn herre" (he is my lord, 420, 4). Eventually, Siegfried will marry Kriemhild, but his actions in the service of Gunther have marked him as a destabilizing force in the Burgundian kingdom. By slaying Siegfried, Hagen proves his loyalty to Gunther as well as to Gunther's wife and queen, but he also sets into motion a series of events that will culminate years later in tragedy.

The events described prior to Gunther's decision to woo Brünhild reveal his unsuitability to be her husband. Initially, Gunther is passive. He depends on Hagen to identify Siegfried, and on his brother, Gernot, to prevent a fight with Siegfried when the latter first arrives in Worms. Further, Gunther remains in Worms during the war against the Saxons. As noted earlier, Gunther jeopardizes his own kingship to woo Brünhild and can only win her by deception. This bridal quest for Brünhild functions as a kind of adventure so that Siegfried can shine even more brightly. This bridal quest, however, alters the relationship between Gunther and Siegfried by distorting the political reality: it appears that Gunther is socially and physically superior to Siegfried. The result of this deceit and distortion will be the fate that befalls first Siegfried and then the Burgundians.[16]

The three kings depicted in the *Nibelungenlied* are weak and exhibit serious shortcomings. In the beginning, Siegfried's conduct at the Burgundian court is inexplicably bellicose when he openly threatens Gunther's kingship. Later on, Siegfried needlessly places his own life at risk on two occasions: when he participates in the war against the Saxons and when he returns to the land of the Nibelungen in disguise and fights against his own men (482–99). Little is said about his reign as king after his marriage to Kriemhild. Most telling is that Siegfried misjudges his wife and her ambitions when he confides in Kriemhild about his role in subduing Brünhild and gives Brünhild's girdle and ring to her. As a consequence of these actions, Siegfried is a destabilizing force in the feudal-aristocratic society of Worms. In the end, it would seem only his murder can maintain the integrity of the Burgundian kings' rule.

From the beginning of the narrative Gunther is an intriguing figure. He initially is portrayed as a weak king who shares his power with his two younger brothers. He relies on Hagen for advice about how to manipulate Siegfried for his political aims (the war against the Saxons) and personal ones (his bridal quest for Brünhild). Instead of confronting Siegfried after the two queens' quarrel, Gunther allows Hagen to carry out the murder of Siegfried and then later allows him to sink the *Hort* (Siegfried's treasure) in the Rhine. At Etzel's court, however, Gunther undergoes a transformation. He becomes a warrior-king, leading his men fiercely in battle. He proves his loyalty to Hagen by defying his sister, which results in his death at her hands.

Etzel's initial appearance is positive. He is shown to be a strong and courageous leader who rules over a diverse court of both Christians and non-Christians. After his marriage to Kriemhild, however, the characterization of Etzel darkens. He allows himself to be convinced by Kriemhild that she wishes to see her brothers and the Burgundians. Once the Burgundians arrive, Etzel appears to be unaware of the rising tensions between the Burgundians and the Huns at his court. Moreover, he passively witnesses the murder of his son and is forced to rely on Dietrich to escape from the hall. As the bloody battle unfolds, Etzel is again surprisingly passive as he watches the destruction of both warrior armies. In the *Nibelungenlied* Etzel thus ultimately appears as a very weak king.

Undeniably, Hagen most completely embodies the warrior ethos. In his relationship to the three Burgundian kings, Hagen is consistently portrayed as a loyal advisor. His actions, however questionable, stem from his fierce loyalty. Thus, he correctly identifies Siegfried as a threat to the Burgundian court. After Brünhild's public humiliation outside of the cathedral by Kriemhild, who (wrongly) suggests that her (Brünhild's) virginity was taken by Siegfried, Hagen's one overriding goal is to avenge her, and thus to restore the honor of his king and queen. His is a rigid, inflexible code of behavior. Much later, Hagen has no illusions about why Kriemhild has invited his lords to Etzel's court. Upon their arrival there, he quickly provokes a confrontation. He dies in the end, as he has apparently known he would since his discussion with the mermaids upon crossing the Danube (1535–40), but not before the warrior class of both the Burgundians and the Huns perishes, largely due to his ferocious fighting.

Despite its emphasis on the deeds of male warriors, the *Nibelungenlied* offers three female characters, Ute, Brünhild, and Kriemhild, who reveal three visions of womanhood. Ideal womanhood in the *Nibelungenlied* (as in the other heroic narratives) usually is predicated on passivity and self-abnegation. In other words, the female figures tend to acknowledge their subordinate role to the male figures and thus act accordingly. Of the three female figures under discussion, only Ute consistently conforms to this ideal. While she is often called the "queen-mother," she exerts no real power or influence. Ute's primary role is that of mother to her daughter and three sons, and she is most visible as that of chaperon-confidante to the young maiden Kriemhild. The opening lines of the *Nibelunglied* depict both the close bond between mother and daughter and also the latent tension between them. Troubled by her dream about the falcon that is killed by two eagles, Kriemhild seeks out her mother, but then rejects her advice. Ute appears here and elsewhere as a caring mother to her adult children, but she fails to exert any influence on them.[17]

Significantly, Ute resumes her role as chaperon after Siegfried's murder. She demonstrates her continuing loyalty to Kriemhild when she publicly mourns Siegfried (1051). As the senior female member of her *sippe* (clan), Ute offers her bereaved daughter solace and protection. Any bond between mother and daughter, however, is gone by the time the Burgundians travel to Etzel's court. The *Nibelungenlied* poet stresses the strong ties of these three kings to their mother and *sippe* by having Etzel call Gieselher, Gernot, and Gunther "der edelen Uoten kint" (Ute's noble children, 1406). This appellation resurfaces during the brothers' journey to Etzel's kingdom (1517, 1627, and 1723).

Brünhild's first appears as an independent female monarch. During this bride-winning episode the *Nibelungenlied* poet underscores her political power and independence. It is clear that her warriors and her ladies acknowledge Brünhild as their rightful sovereign. Brünhild is a mythic figure whose great strength stems from her virginity. She thus represents an unusual portrait of womanhood, engaging in typically masculine activities: she rules over her own kingdom, wears armor, and participates in physically demanding games. It is no coincidence that Hagen, the warrior's warrior, sees Brünhild as otherworldly and thus extremely dangerous to his understanding of the social and political order. Hagen calls Brünhild "des tiuveles wîp" (the devil's woman, 438) and "des übelen tiuvels brut" (the bride of the wicked devil, 450). In Brünhild the *Nibelungenlied* poet presents us with a person who paradoxically combines stunning feminine beauty and supernatural strength, and the poet stresses this dichotomy, employing it as a leitmotif during this contest scene. The defeat of Brünhild is based on deceit. It is clear that without Siegfried's assistance, Gunther would lose. Both men knowingly engage in deceit again when Siegfried must once again intervene on Gunther and Brünhild's wedding night to subdue the still powerful Brünhild so that Gunther can consummate the marriage. Brünhild's loss of independence and self-identity occurs in two stages. After her initial defeat in Iceland, she is forced to give up her kingdom and journey back to Worms. Later, her loss of virginity ensures her conformity to the more conventional female role: her identity and self-worth are now dependent on her role as Gunther's wife and queen. Not surprisingly, she recedes into the background until her quarrel with Kriemhild.

Initially, Kriemhild appears as an object of desire for Siegfried, whose ardent desire to possess her causes him to behave belligerently and dishonorably. Yet the passages describing Siegfried's attempt to win Kriemhild are replete with the motifs and language of courtly love. Like the beloved lady in *Minnesang*, Kriemhild is beautiful, noble, and inaccessible. This courtly love (*minne*) imagery actually functions to highlight the dependence of courtly-chivalric values on feudal-aristocratic ones. Gunther exploits Siegfried's desire for Kriemhild for his own political ends, and Kriemhild is the reward for Siegfried's subsequent service. As a daughter of a royal family, Kriemhild is a political object whose marriage is intended to solidify or establish political alliances. Kriemhild and Siegfried, however, are shown to be mutually attracted to each other, but their marriage nonetheless reflects the social-political reality of feudal-aristocratic society.

As the wife of the distinguished Siegfried, Kriemhild becomes so haughty and proud that she provokes a confrontation with Brünhild outside of the cathedral. Her inability to understand the serious repercussions of this quarrel is evidenced by her fatal mistake to trust Hagen, her brother's loyal advisor, with the secret of Siegfried's vulnerability. The murder of Siegfried transforms Kriemhild. She becomes obsessed with avenging Siegfried, despite the fact that in the heroic narrative revenge is a male prerogative. Not surprisingly, when Kriemhild slays Hagen, who embodies the warrior ethos, the *Nibelungenlied* poet has another laudable warrior, Hildebrand, slay her immediately. Tellingly, both Dietrich and Hagen, who embody the warrior ethos, call Kriemhild a "vâlandinne" (she-devil, 1748) which underscores her problematic role in the *Nibelungenlied*.

Brünhhild and Kriemhild share a number of common traits. Both women are the objects of a bridal quest, which ultimately has disastrous consequences. Brünhild and Kriemhild are also wronged women who succumb to the deception of the male figures. Gunther and Siegfried deliberately deceive Brünhild about Siegfried's social status as well as his role in the games. Hagen gains Kriemhild's trust in order to slay Siegfried. Brünhild changes from a powerful and self-aware female monarch into a passive and subordinate queen-wife, while Kriemhild first appears as a passive young maiden, but then becomes an "older" woman consumed by hatred and vengeance who wields immense power. The apparent nonconformity of these two women threatens the existing social-political order as depicted in the *Nibelungenlied*.

The influence of the Nibelungenlied on later medieval literature is evidenced by such works as the *Rosengarten zu Worms* (fifteenth century) and *Das Lied vom Hürnen Seyfrid* (transmitted in sixteenth-century manuscripts), which both draw on the Nibelung legend. During the nineteenth and twentieth centuries, the *Nibelungenlied* was viewed as *the* German national epic. As such, it came to serve various different national and nationalistic agendas, while a serious occupation with the narrative in its medieval context did not really occur.[18] Before German national unity could become a reality, it was imperative that a common cultural heritage be nurtured. The preoccupation with the Germans' shared linguistic and literary culture of the past, particularly of the Middle Ages, became a means to this end. The Romantics and their idealization of the Middle Ages were instrumental in popularizing the *Nibelungenlied*.[19] Karl Lachmann's critical edition (*Über die ursprüngliche Gestalt von der Nibelungen Noth*, 1816) offered a standardized Middle High German version that prompted increased academic interest. The original Middle High German of the *Nibelungenlied* prevented a wider popular reception until the Simrock translation into modern German appeared in 1827, which made the *Nibelungenlied* accessible to the general public.[20] The *Nibelungenlied* gradually acquired an important edifying role in German schools, where it was employed to teach German virtues, or "correct German behavior."[21]

During the First World War the *Nibelungenlied* again served propagandistic purposes. Germany expressed its commitment, and above all loyalty, to the Austro-Hungarian Empire by stressing *Nibelungentreue* (Nibelungen loyalty).[22] After the First World War, German soldiers were viewed by many as counterparts to the Burgundians, fighting against a terrible foe until their heroic downfall. During the Weimar Republic, the *Nibelungenlied* enjoyed a great resurgence of interest.[23] Without a doubt, the most egregious ideological subversion of the *Nibelungenlied* occurred during the Third Reich, which blatantly employed the narrative to celebrate Aryan superiority.[24] The *Nibelungenlied* has continued to fascinate readers and occupy scholars to the present day, perhaps because this narrative offers a unique opportunity to study the relationship between politics and literature. Modern scholarship affirms the continuing importance of the *Nibelungenlied* by stressing that the traditional tale of a dominant gender, class, and culture is simultaneously old and modern.[25]

As a political narrative, the *Nibelungenlied* provoked a significant contemporary reaction. Recent scholarship tends to view the two narratives *Diu Klage* (ca. 1220) and *Kudrun* (ca. 1230–40) as anti-*Nibelungenlied* responses.[26] The two authors of these heroic narratives offer a more optimistic and hopeful worldview than the stark pessimism of the *Nibelungenlied*.

Diu Klage

The *Klage* (ca. 1220) is appended to all but one of the extant *Nibelungenlied* manuscripts. It does not exist in an independent manuscript. In the final line the anonymous author actually names the narrative: "ditze liet heizt diu klage" (this song is called the lament, 4322). Since the author of *Diu Klage* was reacting against the pessimism of the *Nibelungenlied*, he deliberately recast the main figures of Kriemhild and Hagen in order to reassign the blame for the downfall of the Burgundians.

The *Klage* begins immediately after the fall of the Burgundians at Etzel's court. It is a time of great mourning. The ensuing burial preparations allow the author to express judgments about the various slain characters. Like the Burgundians, the Huns have suffered the loss of a generation of warriors. Once again, Etzel is not portrayed as a particularly strong king because he almost succumbs to his grief. By contrast, Dietrich von Bern is depicted as a stabilizing and moderating force. The *Klage*-author's chief goal is the rehabilitation of Kriemhild, whom he portrays sympathetically by emphasizing the importance of her loyalty to Siegfried and her limitations as a woman. Indeed, her strong fidelity to Siegfried earns her a place in heaven. Conversely, he vilifies Hagen, whose heroic stance is shown to be the result of hubris. Indeed, the *Klage's* author criticizes the Burgundian warriors for their *übermuot* (hubris) and shows that their destruction was a punishment. Starting at Etzel's court, the narrative follows the journey of the messengers as they inform relatives about the death of their loved ones. In stark contrast to the *Nibelungenlied,* which ends in senseless death and suffering, the *Klage* gradually changes from a dirge to tentative hope. At the conclusion, the crowning of the young Siegfried, the son of Brünhild and Gunther, and the wedding of Dietrich and Herrat signal the re-establishment of order and hope for the future. A more optimistic worldview prevails.

Kudrun

Kudrun was probably written between 1230 and 1240. This narrative has a number of sources, and its author is unknown. The dating of *Kudrun* is largely based on the reconstruction of the history of the *Kudrun* strophe, which is similar to and probably derived from the *Nibelungenlied* strophe. *Kudrun* is the story of three generations and has three parts. The first two parts deal with stories about Kudrun's maternal ancestors, focusing on her grandfather, Hagen, and then on her parents, Hilde (Hagen's daughter) and Hetel. The third and longest part alternates between Hilde and Kudrun. This inclusion of the family history of the hero (heroine) also occurs in other medieval German texts, for example, *Parzival* and *Tristan*.

Kudrun was probably a rebuttal to the fatalistic heroism so evident in the *Nibelungenlied*. This different worldview is apparent in the manner which the two authors treat alliances and revenge. In the *Nibelungenlied*, the strong lord-vassal relationship creates an exceedingly intricate and often conflicting network of loyalties. Kriemhild's desire for revenge eventually leads to the annihilation of the warrior-class of the Burgundians and the Huns. Conversely, alliances and revenge in *Kudrun* are more flexible, and significantly, Hagen and his two female descendents, Hilde and Kudrun, all demonstrate the ability for peacemaking.

As a youth, Hagen establishes the heroic standards that characterize and influence his descendants. Though exiled, Hagen remains loyal to his royal family, and his one overriding goal is to be reunited with them. Consequently, he exhibits a fierce determination to overcome the many challenges of this exile. He becomes the protector of the three princesses and finally kills the griffiths. After their rescue, his father's rival attempts to kill him upon learning of his true identity, but instead of seeking revenge, Hagen brings about reconciliation between these two foes, and a new alliance arises.

Hilde, Hagen's daughter, initially exhibits a more conflicted loyalty. She falls in love with Hetel, one of her numerous suitors, and participates in her own abduction. Here the narrative could have had tragic consequences since Hagen is intent on bringing his daughter back, even if he has to risk his own life. Like her father, Hilde is able to reconcile her father and her betrothed, Hetel. Peace is once again restored and a new alliance forged.

Kudrun, Hilde's daughter, must also endure a harsh exile in Normandy, but like her grandfather, Hagen, Kudrun does not succumb and remains loyal to her family, refusing to marry Hartmut, her abductor. Hilde's forces eventually defeat the Normans, and there is much bloodletting, but significantly, Kudrun acts as the peacemaker, reconciling the warring ruling families at the end of the narrative. This peaceful resolution may be attributed to a more Christian and courtly influence vis à vis revenge and loyalty. Nevertheless, this poem affirms the feudal order, which is restored at the end.

The invasion of the Norman kingdom by the Heglings is integral to the subsequent peacemaking process. The wrongs of the Norman abduction and the Heglings' defeat at Wülpensand are avenged. During this fierce and bloody battle, Wate embodies the more traditional feudal-aristocratic worldview. He is depicted as killing indiscriminately. As Hilde's physical representative, he personally kills Gerlint, the recognized instigator of all the suffering. Ludwig, Hartmut's father, also dies in this battle. The deaths of these two enemies signal the restoration of order. Ortwin and Hartmut, the adult children of Gerlint and Hartmut, conveniently are given an opportunity to distance themselves from their more notorious parents, and thus are permitted to participate in the subsequent reconciliation.

Understandably, the deaths of both Ludwig and Gerlint help to contain Hilde's need for further vengeance. This reconciliation, however, would not have been possible had it not been for the efforts of Hilde and Wate. In stark contrast to the *Nibelungenlied, Kudrun* concludes with a sign of hope: three marriages occur, uniting the adult children of the two opposing sides. Feuding families resolve their differences, and order is restored.

Heroic Narratives about Dietrich von Bern

The heroic narratives with Dietrich von Bern as their central figure, generally by anonymous authors, form the largest body of the heroic narratives. Although this literary Dietrich can be traced to Theoderic the Great (ca. 453–526), many of these narratives have no apparent connection to this historical figure. A number of the Nibelungen characters resurface in these Dietrich heroic narratives, which can be divided into two main groupings: 1) the political and 2) the adventure-oriented narratives.

The three politically oriented heroic narratives written about Dietrich are *Alpharts Tod, Das Buch von Bern* (*Dietrichs Flucht*), and the *Rabenschlacht*. The first two works are written in rhymed couplets, and the *Rabenschlacht* has a mixture of short and long lines. Their respective subject matters reflect the political realities of the *Stauferzeit* (that is, the period when the Hohenstaufen family provided princes and emperors for the Holy Roman Empire). The depiction of kingship in these texts differs from that in the *Nibelungenlied* and *Kudrun*. In spite of the political strife, the aristocratic-feudal order appears to be more stable, and the courtly-chivalric ethos is not portrayed as a threat. Dietrich, Emmerich, and Etzel all appear as kings, but these kingships lack the complexity of those in the *Nibelungenlied*.

Alpharts Tod was probably written around 1250. This poem has a strophic verse form similar to that of the *Nibelugenlied*. The story depicts a familial struggle for power and dominance, signaling the beginning of the animosity between Dietrich and his arch-foe and relative, Emmerich. The narrative has two distinguishable parts. The first part depicts the idealistic and brave young warrior-knight Alphart, who dies unfairly at the hands of Heime and Witege. Alphart's rigid adherence to the concept of knightly honor is shown to result in his death. His courtly worldview stands in contrast to the grim reality of feudal order. However, the politicizing of the death of this one individual becomes an inspiration for the collective, or the army of Dietrich. The second part relates how Dietrich procures assistance and eventually defeats Emmerich and his forces. Alphart's conduct, as well as that of Dietrich, demonstrates how heroes are supposed to comport themselves. Contrarily, Emmerich, Heime, and Witege are shown to be immoral opponents, appearing as cowards and traitors who flee the battlefield. Since Dietrich is not yet in exile, Etzel has no role in this narrative.

Das Buch von Bern (*Dietrichs Flucht*) was written around 1250. It is written in rhymed couplets and deals with two recurring themes of the Dietrich legends: 1) Dietrich's exile and 2) Dietrich's attempt to regain his lands with the assistance of Etzel. This heroic narrative portrays the conflict within ruling families (Dietrich and Emmerich) and its impact on kingdoms. The lord-vassal relationship and loyalty also play an important role in this narrative. Dietrich as king exhibits all the attendant kingly virtues. By his courage, generosity, and sincere grief, Dietrich demonstrates his strong and steadfast loyalty to his men. Indeed, Dietrich willingly gives up his hard-won land in order to free his captured warriors. Similarly, Dietrich's circle of warriors displays an unwavering loyalty to their lord. By contrast, Emmerich is disloyal, and the author calls him "ungetriuwe" (unfaithful, 2414). Emmerich's traditional role as villain is stressed here. He is portrayed as having no redeeming qualities whatsoever. Not surprisingly, his circle of warriors, Sibeche, Witege, and Heime, are all unsavory characters whose one outstanding common trait is their treachery. Etzel and his wife, Helche, are portrayed quite positively. As king, Etzel provides Dietrich with a refuge and assistance. Helche is much more visible and active than the typical female figures appearing in the heroic narratives. Like her husband, she, too, exhibits a strong loyalty to Dietrich. She not only provides Dietrich with material goods, but also with a wife. The narrative alternates between Dietrich's exile and his battles with Emmerich's forces. The battle scenes are numerous and graphic, and it would appear that the author takes delight in describing the carnage.

The dating of the *Rabenschlacht* is now commonly accepted to be in the last half of the thirteenth century. It appears to continue the narrative where the *Buch von Bern* ends, and depicts the conflict between the two ruling families of Dietrich and Emmerich. Here again, the characters tend to be painted as black and white. For example, when Witege unfairly kills the two young sons of Etzel and the younger brother of Dietrich, he fails to conduct himself honorably. While the *Buch von Bern* and the *Rabenschlacht* share some similarities, there are also some major differences. One scholar has argued that the author of the *Buch von Bern* had a better knowledge of geography and of military operations than did the author of the *Rabenschlacht*.[27] The narratives are composed in different verse forms: the *Buch von Bern* is in rhymed couplets, and the *Rabenschlacht* is in a strophic form that is distantly related to that of the *Nibelungenlied*. The *Rabenschlacht* depicts a Dietrich already in exile at Etzel's court. Etzel appears as a positive king who attempts to help Dietrich regain his kingdom. He exhibits his loyalty to Dietrich when he permits his two young sons to accompany Dietrich in this campaign. The slaying of Etzel's two sons by Witege leads to a crisis in which Etzel and

Helche's loyalty to Dietrich is greatly tested. In this narrative Rüdiger appears as a successful peacemaker, and he is able to bring about a reconciliation between Dietrich and Helche. In the *Nibelungenlied*, however, Rüdiger fails to bring about a reconciliation between the Burgundians and the Huns and is killed by Gernot.

The second group of Dietrich narratives centers on adventure rather than the moral or political qualities of their hero. The opponents thus are no longer moral adversaries, and their main function is to allow Dietrich to shine all the more brightly. Some of these narratives are also critical of the courtly-chivalric ethos. In these cases, the motif of the "happy ending" can be viewed as a parody of courtly literature. The narratives in this category are *Rosengarten zu Worms*, *Laurin*, *Eckenlied*, *Virginal*, *Sigenot*, *Goldemar*, and *Biterolf und Dietleip*.

The narrative *Rosengarten zu Worms* was written around 1250. It has a strophic form similar to that of the *Nibelungenlied*. The number of extant manuscripts (more than eighteen) shows the popularity of this heroic narrative in the Middle Ages. *Rosengarten* brings together the Burgundians and Dietrich and his warriors. In the Dietrich cycle, this text occurs before Dietrich's exile. Kriemhild is the owner of a rose garden and here Siegfried appears as her fiancé (which never happened in the *Nibelungenlied*). Kriemhild is shown to be the instigator of a battle involving the twelve warriors of Worms and the twelve of Bern. The cause of the conflict is revealed as the whim of a spoiled woman. In the scene with Kriemhild's messenger, Dietrich shows his disdain for fighting solely for adventure (an important component of the courtly-chivalric ethos) when he initially rejects her challenge. The author of *Rosengarten* continually exposes and criticizes the shortcomings of this value system. The twelve subsequent contests thus reveal a double standard concerning the conduct of these warrior-knights. The fights involving fellow warrior-knights do not end in death, but those with the giants do. The climax of these twelve battles, of course, is the fight between Siegfried and Dietrich. The recurring motif of Dietrich's reluctance to fight appears here. Dietrich, however, does eventually fight and overcome Siegfried. During this combat scene Kriemhild is further vilified; she is portrayed as taking delight in the bloodshed. Her conduct is both uncourtly and sadistic. She is indeed, as Hoffmann has stated, "die Verkörperung von übermuot und hochvart" (the embodiment of hubris and pride).[28] The *Rosengarten* author is highly critical of Kriemhild and her motives, at one point calling her a "vâlandinne" (she-devil, 116), a term also employed by the *Nibelunglied* author. At the end of the narrative, Kriemhild is punished; she must bestow fifty-two wreaths and kisses on the sharp-bearded monk Ilsan, which causes her cheeks to bleed.

The portrait of Ilsan and his fellow monks, offering some black humor, is actually contemporary social criticism. This narrative appears to be reacting to a perceived decline of morality in monastic life. Upon closer examination, Ilsan's fellow monks behave in a most unchristian manner when he departs. Their hypocrisy is quite evident when, instead of praying for his safe return, the monks curse him: "daz er niemer kaeme wider" (that he would never return again, 164,4). The tale of an arrogant Kriemhild as a courtly woman who instigates the senseless fighting between the two warrior groups offers an unflattering portrait of courtly love (*minne*) and adventure (*âventiure*) — the two integral components of the courtly-chivalric value system.

Laurin was written down around 1250 and probably harks back to a South Tyrolean tradition. It was composed in rhymed couplets, and shares with the *Rosengarten zu Worms* the motif of a rose garden. In *Laurin*, the rose garden is surrounded by a silk thread and is owned by the dwarf-king, Laurin. Here Dietrich is portrayed as seeking adventure by deliberately trespassing and destroying the rose garden. The narrative appears to borrow from the Siegfried legend, as the dwarf Laurin also possesses a *Tarnkappe* (a cloak that makes him invisible) and his armor has also been dipped in dragon's blood. These weapons and his possession of a magical belt make Laurin a most formidable opponent. Despite the trappings of a courtly-chivalric ethos, Dietrich exhibits a pre-courtly-chivalric attitude toward combat when he initially insists on killing the vanquished dwarf-king. Subsequently, Dietrich finds himself embroiled in a series of adventures.

This narrative combines the figure of Dietrich with two earlier, popular tales: the rose garden motif and the abduction of a lady by a dwarf.[29] The presence of Künhilt and her brother, Dietleip, two members of the royal family of Steiermark (Styria), lends this narrative a local flavor. The figure of Künhilt is noteworthy, for she shows herself to be courageous and resourceful when she helps her brother and the other warriors overcome their enemies. The conclusion of *Laurin* offers an optimistic worldview. Laurin and Dietrich eventually reconcile, but only when Laurin converts to Christianity.

The following four narratives, *Eckenlied*, *Virginal*, *Sigenot*, and *Goldemar* all share the verse form called the *Bernerton* or *Eckenstrophe*, which is composed of thirteen-line stanzas. Albrecht von Kemnaten was once believed to have been the author of all four heroic narratives, but it is now commonly accepted that he was the author of only one, *Goldemar*.

The *Eckenlied* was probably written around 1250. Through black humor and parody, the author of the *Eckenlied* criticizes the courtly-chivalric ethos. The shortcomings of this value system are embodied in the giant Ecke. Hearing of Dietrich's fame, Ecke desires to fight him. The involvement of the three queens is also a critique of *Frauendienst* (service to a courtly lady), since they allegedly encourage this adventure and equip him with armor. Because of his size, Ecke must forgo his horse, the ubiquitous symbol of knighthood. The recurring motif of Dietrich's initial reluctance to fight appears, but in this scene Dietrich functions as a spokesman, denouncing the knightly concept of adventure. The ensuing contest, which results in Ecke's death, is shown to be senseless. Betrayal and treachery characterize Dietrich's encounters with various opponents, whom he kills in self-defense. In the end, the three queens are shown to have been victims of Ecke, and by slaying the giant, Dietrich has freed them from his tyranny.

The narrative *Virginal* was written sometime after 1260. Twelve manuscripts exist, and though many are fragmentary, the number indicates the popularity of this narrative. *Virginal* has also appeared in some of the early editions under the title "Dietrichs erste Ausfahrt" (Dietrich's First Excursion), and some critical studies still retain this title. This narrative focuses on the strong lord-vassal relationship between Dietrich and Hildebrand. Indeed, here Hildebrand assumes a more fatherly and protective role for the presumably younger Dietrich. Accordingly, Hildebrand accompanies Dietrich when the latter seeks adventures. *Virginal's* structure has been the subject of much discussion. The narrative has three discernible stories. The first and probably the oldest story deals with Dietrich's first adventure. The second story portrays the Rentwin dragon episode. Finally, the Muter episode is reminiscent of the older tradition of Dietrich being imprisoned by giants and rescued by his men. The three stories are connected by the attempts of Virginal, the dwarf-queen (represented by her messenger, Bibung), to have Dietrich and his men visit her court. Dietrich's separation from Hildebrand is a recurring and unifying motif that occurs in all three stories. Adventures abound in this narrative in the form of giants, dwarfs, and dragons. The narrative also has numerous repetitions and discrepancies.

There are two versions of *Sigenot*: *Sigenot* and the *Jüngerer Sigenot*. About one hundred years separate these two versions (1250–1350). Whereas there is only one extant manuscript of the earlier *Sigenot*, numerous copies of the *Jüngerer Sigenot* (about twenty) exist, attesting to its continuing popularity. The opening and closing lines of *Sigenot* seem to suggest a connection with the *Eckenlied*: "dar nâch er Ecken stach" (after he slew Ecke, 1, 13) and "sus hebet sich Ecken liet" (so begins Eckenlied, 44, 13), but this is not the case. The one common trait of both narratives is the figure of a giant (Ecke and Sigenot) who appears as Dietrich's opponent. Whereas in *Eckenlied* Dietrich slays the giant, in *Sigenot*, the giant overcomes and imprisons Dietrich, who is saved by Hildebrand and Eggerich. The lord-vassal relationship between Dietrich and Hildebrand is stressed in this narrative. Hildebrand demonstrates his strong loyalty to Dietrich when he liberates his lord from the giant Sigenot. Dietrich's imprisonment by giants, a recurring motif, is also present. Eggerich, a dwarf, appears as Hildebrand's comrade-in-arms and rescuer of Dietrich. Eggerich's loyalty to Hildebrand is also praiseworthy, and his positive portrayal is reminiscent of Laurin, another dwarf-king.

The narrative *Goldemar* exists in one fragmentary manuscript and was probably written between 1230 and 1240. Its author identifies himself as "von Kemenâten Albreht /der tithe ditze maere" (by Albrecht von Kemenaten / who wrote this story, 2, 2–3). This narrative shares some similarities with *Laurin*. Both texts depict a kingdom of dwarfs in a mountain that is guarded by giants. Dietrich must fight giants who serve Goldemar. There is also a captive maiden who escapes ravishment. Goldemar's honorable conduct toward the maiden makes him a more laudable figure. Dietrich, the traditional critic of the courtly-chivalric ethos, appears in a different role here: he is the love-struck suitor. According to Werner Hoffmann, the author of *Goldemar* was reacting against this traditional image of Dietrich, whose relations with the ladies are polite, but distant.[30] The focus of this heroic narrative is therefore courtly love (*minne*), not adventure (*âventiure*).

Biterolf und Dietleip was written between 1260 and 1270 by an anonymous author. Some scholars question whether *Biterolf und Dietleip* should belong to the Dietrich narratives because of Dietrich's minor role. Unlike the other Dietrich narratives and the *Nibelungenlied, Biterolf und Dietleip* is not overtly critical of the courtly-chivalric ethos. Indeed, knighthood and adventure initially propel the narrative. Much like Arthur, Etzel enjoys a widespread fame, and his court becomes a magnet for warrior-knights. This ardent desire to experience *ritterschaft* (knighthood, 405) at Etzel's court prompts Biterolf to abandon his family and kingdom. Years later, Biterolf's son, Dietleip, also journeys to Etzel's court.

The narrative's emphasis on knighthood is apparent in the prominent role of Rüdiger. Here he appears again as a successful peacemaker, bringing about reconciliation between father and son. Later, as a messenger to Worms, Rüdiger exudes courtliness and is especially popular with the ladies at court. By contrast, Dietrich recedes into the background. No doubt, the author's apparent emphasis on knighthood would diminish the traditional role of a warrior such as Dietrich.

The climax of the narrative is the contest between the Burgundians and their allies (including Siegfried) and the Huns and their allies. Once again, a familiar motif occurs — Dietrich initially balks at fighting his opponent. The role of women at these contests is largely decorative. In *Biterolf and Dietleip*, they are not the objects of the fighting; instead, the warrior-knights appear to fight for the sake of fighting. Clearly, the emphasis is on manliness, not *minne*. It is worth noting that the two titular heroes of this narrative, Biterolf and Dietleip, vanish during this battle sequence: neither is singled out for praise. Their absence during the climax has prompted some critics to question whether Biterolf and Dietleip should be considered the actual heroes of this narrative. In this text, Emmerich appears as Dietrich's ally rather than his archenemy. *Biterolf und Dietleip* appears to evoke an earlier, happier time prior to the *Nibelungenlied* narrative.

Notes

[1] For more information, see the articles of Firestone, Haymes, and McConnell in *Genres in Medieval German Literature*, edited by Hubert Heinen and Ingeborg Henderson (Göppingen: Kümmerle Verlag, 1986).

[2] *Das Alexanderlied des Pfaffen Lamprecht. Das Rolandslied des Pfaffen Konrad*, edited by Friedrich Maurer, *Deutsche Literatur in Entwicklungsreihen: Geistliche Dichtung des Mittelalters*, vol. 5 (1940; rpt., Darmstadt: Wissenschaftliche Buchgesellschaft, 1964).

[3] *Das Nibelungenlied*, edited by Helmut de Boor, 22nd edition by Roswitha Wisniewski (Wiesbaden: Brockhaus, 1988) [based on the edition of Karl Bartsch] and *The Nibelungenlied*, edited by A. T. Hatto (London: Penguin, 1969). English translations of the *Nibelungenlied* are Hatto's.

[4] *Die Klage*, edited by Karl Bartsch (Darmstadt: Wissenschaftliche Buchgesellschaft, 1964); see also *The Lament of the Nibelungen (Diu Chlage)*, translated by Winder McConnell (Columbia, SC: Camden House, 1994).

[5] *Die Nibelungen Noth und die Klage*, edited by Karl Lachmann, 6th edition (Berlin: Walter De Gruyter & Co., 1960) and *Kudrun*, edited by Karl Stackmann, 5th edition (Wiesbaden: Brockhaus, 1965; rpt. 1980); see also *Kudrun*, translated by Winder McConnell (Columbia, SC: Camden House, 1992). English translations of *Kudrun* are McConnell's.

[6] *Alpharts Tod*, edited by Ernst Martin, *Deutsches Heldenbuch* (hereafter abbreviated as *DHB*), vol. 2 (Berlin: Weidmann, 1866; rpt. 1967 and 1975); *Dietrichs Flucht*, edited by Ernst Martin, *DHB* vol. 20 (Berlin: Weidmann, 1866; rpt. 1967 and 1975); and *Rabenschlacht*, edited by Ernst Martin, *DHB* vol. 2 (Berlin: Weidmann, 1866; rpt. 1967 and 1975).

[7] *Die Gedichte vom Rosengarten zu Worms*, edited by Georg Holz (Halle: Niemeyer, 1893); *Laurin*, edited by Georg Holz (Halle: Niemeyer, 1897); *Ecken Liet*, edited by Julius Zupitza, *DHB* vol. 5 (Berlin: Weidmann, 1870; rpt. 1968); *Virginal*, edited by Julius Zupitza, *DHB* vol. 5; *Sigenot*, edited by Julius Zupitza, *DHB* vol. 5; *Goldemar*, edited by Julius Zupitza, *DHB* vol. 5; and *Biterolf und Dietleip*, edited by Oskar Jänick, *DHB* vol. 1 (Berlin: Weidmann, 1866; rpt. 1963).

[8] *Priest Konrad's Song of Roland*, translated by J. W. Thomas (Columbia, SC: Camden House, 1994).

[9] See Jeffrey Ashcroft, "Konrads *Rolandslied*, Henry the Lion and the Northern Crusade," *Forum for Modern Language Studies* 22: 2 (1986): 184–208.

[10] See Susan E. Farrier, "*Das Rolandslied* and the *Song of Roland* as Moralizing Adaptations of the *Chanson de Roland*," *Olifant: A Publication of the Sociâetâe Rencesvals, American-Canadian Branch* 16: 1–2 (Spring-Summer 1991): 61–76.

[11] Genelun's role is shown to be that of Judas to the Christian empire of Karl. Significantly, Genelun is the only warrior who expresses reluctance to die for the cause of God, citing worldly matters — his family. The narrative relates how Genelun's actions stem from his hatred of his stepson, Roland. Later at his trial Genelun views his betrayal of Roland as a public feud. However, by plotting to bring about Roland's death, Genelun breaks his contract with his lord, Karl

(Charlemagne), and with his Christian God. Genelun is therefore guilty of both political and religious treason.

[12] See Maria Dobozy, "The Structure of the Crusade Epic and the Function of the King," *Neophilologus* 67: 1 (Jan. 1983): 90–108; Ulrich Ernst, "Kollektive Aggression in der *Chanson de Roland* und im *Rolandslied* des Pfaffen Konrad," *Euphorion* 82: 2 (1988): 211–25; and Jeffrey Ashcroft, "Konrad's *Rolandslied*, Henry the Lion, and the Northern Crusade," *Forum for Modern Language Studies* 22: 2 (1986): 184–208. Unless otherwise indicated, English translations are by S. S.

[13] Jeffrey Ashcroft, "Miles dei — Gotes Ritter: Konrad's *Rolandslied* and the Evolution of the Concept of Christian Chivalry," *Forum for Modern Language Studies* 17: 2 (1981): 155.

[14] Edward Haymes rejects the notion that the *Nibelungenlied* is a Kriemhild tragedy or a Kriemhild romance. See Edward R. Haymes, "A Rhetorical Reading of the 'Hortforderungszene' in the *Nibelungenlied*," in *American-German Studies on the Nibelungenlied Text and Reception*, edited by Werner Wunderlich and Ulrich Müller, *Göppinger Arbeiten zur Germanistik* Nr. 564 (Göppingen: Kümmerle Verlag, 1992): 81–82.

[15] Theodore M. Andersson, *A Preface to the Nibelungenlied* (Stanford: Stanford UP, 1987).

[16] Etzel's bridal quest also has tragic consequences. As in the case of Siegfried and Gunther, Etzel hears of Kriemhild's great beauty and nobility. However, unlike Siegfried and Gunther, Etzel does not expose himself to personal harm or humiliation. Instead, he sends Rüdiger to act as his marriage broker. Later with Etzel's warriors and wealth at her disposal, Kriemhild is able actively to plot the destruction of the Burgundians.

[17] Much later in the narrative Ute warns her sons of their impending doom if they journey to Etzel's court, but they ignore her warning.

[18] See Francis G. Gentry, "Die Rezeption des *Nibelungenliedes* in der Weimarer Republik," in *Das Weiterleben des Mittelalters in der deutschen Literatur,* edited by James F. Poag and Gerhild Scholz-Williams (Königstein/Ts: Athenäum, 1983): 143.

[19] See Josef Körner, *Nibelungenforschungen der deutschen Romantik* (Darmstadt: Wissenschaftliche Buchgesellschaft, 1968): 233–34.

[20] *Das Nibelungenlied,* translated into modern German by Karl Simrock (Stuttgart: Alfred Körner Verlag, 1954). While the Simrock translation has long since been discredited as inaccurate, it nevertheless has continued to be published. For an alternative modern German translation, see Günter Kramer, *Das Nibelungenlied: Mit 33 Zeichnungen von Ernst Barlach* (Berlin: Verlag der Nation, 1982.) The best English translation is that of A. T. Hatto: *The Nibelungenlied* (London: Penguin, 1969).

[21] See Otfrid Ehrismann, *Das Nibelungenlied in Deutschland,* edited by Werner Betz and Hermann Kunisch, *Münchener Germanische Beiträge* 14 (Munich: Wilhelm Fink Verlag, 1975): 217.

[22] Ehrismann, *Das Nibelungenlied in Deutschland,* 240.

[23] Gentry has argued that the conservative writers exploited the *Nibelungenlied* to undermine, or, at the very least, to demonstrate their opposition to the democratic Weimar Republic. Gentry, "Die Rezeption des *Nibelungenliedes* in der Weimarer Republik," 153.

[24] Once again, the Germans (soldiers, then later civilians) were given the role of the Burgundians as the war began to take a turn for the worse. Thus, in his *Wehrmachtsappell* (Army appeal) on 30 January 1943, Göring compared the plight of the German Army at Stalingrad with that of the Burgundians. Peter Krüger, "Etzels Halle und Stalingrad: Die Rede von Görings vom 30.1.1943," in *Die Nibelungen: Ein deutscher Wahn, ein deutscher Alptraum*, edited by Joachim Heinzle and Anneliese Waldschmidt (Frankfurt am Main: Suhrkamp Verlag, 1991): 162.

[25] See *The Nibelungen Tradition: An Encyclopedia*, ed. Francis G. Gentry, Winder McConnell, Ulrich Müller, and Werner Wunderlich (New York: Routledge, 2002).

[26] Werner Hoffmann, *Mittelhochdeutsche Heldendichtung* (Berlin: Erich Schmidt Verlag, 1974), 94.

[27] Hoffmann, *Mittelhochdeutsche Heldendichtung*, 95.

[28] Hoffmann, *Mittelhochdeutsche Heldendichtung*, 161–71.

[29] Manfred Zips, "König Laurin und sein Rosengarten: Ein Beitrag zur Quellenforschung," *Tiroler Heimat* 35 (1971): 5–50.

[30] Hoffmann, *Das Nibelungenlied in Deutschland*, 195–97.

Early Mystical Writings

Sara S. Poor

THE FLOWERING OF MEDIEVAL GERMAN LITERATURE that began in the decades around 1200 was not limited to the secular courts. Beginning in the early thirteenth century, changing currents in Christian religious thought and practice led to a notable increase in the production and consumption of religious writing in the vernacular. The rise of new religious orders advocating vernacular preaching facilitated the spread of religious enthusiasm for the pious life both within and outside of religious orders, especially among women. The religious and mystical literature of the German Middle Ages thus differs in one important respect from the secular tradition: it includes a number of significant texts written by women. Another important difference is that although the secular tradition bloomed in the southern German-speaking regions at aristocratic courts, which is reflected in the transmission of that literature in dialects considered to be Middle High German, the mystical tradition emerged initially in central and northern urban settings where Middle Low German and Middle Dutch were spoken. Hence, this essay considers not only the now canonical *Das fliessende Licht der Gottheit* (The Flowing Light of the Godhead) a 1345 translation (by Heinrich von Nördlingen) into Middle High German of Mechthild von Magdeburg's now lost Middle Low German original, which she wrote between 1250 and 1282, but also the writings of two of her predecessors who wrote in Middle Dutch: Beatrijs (Beatrice) van Nazareth's *Seven manieren van minne* (Seven Manners of Love, written around 1250), and Hadewijch's visions, letters, and poems (written around 1240).[1] These texts display not only similar Germanic dialects, but also similar tendencies in turning to the language of *minne* or courtly love in order to describe the indescribable, yet powerful and often erotic love between the soul and God. Extraordinary not only in their subject matter, but also in their poetics (imagery, rhyme, hybrid forms), they also mark the beginnings of a tradition of poetic German prose.

While it is significant that this new tradition finds its roots in the writings of women, religious women and men did not write in isolation from each other. It is more accurate, as Bernard McGinn has argued, to understand the relation between them according to a model of conversation.[2] Indeed, the texts themselves increasingly favor conversation in the form of dialogue, in particular, the dialogue between the soul and God. But as McGinn remarks, conversation operates on several levels: between divinely inspired women and the men providing them with spiritual care, between Latin and the emerging vernaculars, between spirituality and theology, and between ancient and biblical contemplative traditions and the impulse to revise them for expanding audiences. This essay explores the emergence of this dialogic, multi-voiced mysticism from the twelfth-century Latin writings of Bernard of Clairvaux, Hildegard von Bingen, and Elisabeth von Schönau. It will then examine the thirteenth-century vernacular mysticism of Beatrice, Hadewijch, and Mechthild to analyze how they both contribute to and are emblematic of this dialogic setting.[3]

An important consequence of this exploration is the reexamination of the concepts of authorship and literature. The dialogic situation from which mystical literature emerges often raises doubts about the identification of a single author. If a female author dictates to a scribe who writes down her work and revises it in consultation with her, who is the author of the text they produce? When only a translation of a book exists that itself survives only in copies made by friends of the translator, can we still speak of only one author? And yet the language of literary history has traditionally preferred single authors, a preference that has led to neglect of women's participation in literary history. Even in this volume, twelve chapters are identified by the names of single authors. But the mystical literature of medieval Germany (and Europe for that matter) offers persistent challenges to the assumptions about authorship that we bring to our reading. Moreover, it highlights intriguing affinities between the pre-modern modes of multiple or collaborative authoring and postmodern theorizations of the instability of author and text. Attention to the stories the texts reveal about their authoring and circulation leads not only to historically sensitive theories of authorship, but also enables us to become more aware of the significant contributions of women to literary production in this period.

Background and Context

The dialogic situation in thirteenth-century religious life and thought, as well as the increased participation in that life by women, grew out of a particular twelfth-century context of reform. The most prominent monastics before 1200 were the Benedictines whose order of monks and nuns advocated a life of devotion and prayer away from the world in a secluded monastery. The Benedictines came under criticism, however, for the contradiction between the opulent wealth of their monasteries and their contemplative mission. A new monastic order, the Cistercians led by Bernard of Clairvaux (1090–1153), hoped to reinvigorate the "lukewarm" religiosity of monasteries by creating physical and contemplative environments whose austerity and simplicity would not distract from, but rather foster such contemplation.[4] Moreover, Bernard in particular encouraged his monks to focus their contemplation on their own personal experience of God's presence.

Bernard's famous eighty-six sermons on the Bible's *Song of Songs* (hereafter referred to as "the Song"), directed religious individuals to take this dialogic and erotic poem about love as a model for their own relationship with the divine.[5] Although meant for monks, the sermons were widely transmitted in Latin and in the European vernaculars. Bernard's influence on the subsequent developments of religious practice and culture in the thirteenth century cannot be overestimated. By the turn of the thirteenth century, the Song and its personal and dialogic mode had become the dominant model for religious devotion.

Although Cistercian reform efforts were significant, they were not sufficient to address the needs of an increasingly urbanized and commercialized society. Their ideas were meant for male monastics living in rural, cloistered communities. The rise of towns, however, meant that cries for reform were coming not only from priests and monks, but from lay townspeople as well. Many of these lay reformers began to preach reform in the vernacular. Some of them were condemned as heretical for this reason.[6]

The principle behind the impulse to preach was the *vita apostolica* (the life of the apostles). Long held to be a religious ideal, this life of poverty, penance, and preaching took on increasing appeal in the late twelfth and early thirteenth centuries. To prevent such unauthorized and potentially heretical preaching, the Pope recognized two new religious orders in the early thirteenth century that gave people interested in the *vita apostolica* approved avenues for pursuing it: the Franciscans (founded in 1210), who emphasized poverty and penance, and the Dominicans (founded in 1216), known as the Preachers' Order, who sought to combat corruption and heresy through university training of its members. Both orders espoused preaching in the vernacular in the hope of reaching wider audiences and by so doing improving the spiritual life of all Christians.

Concurrent with these developments women were embracing the religious life in record numbers.[7] In addition to convents attached to the major orders, women began to form their own communities for religious devotion where they could live a religious life imitating Christ and the apostles. These women, known as Beguines, devoted themselves to poverty, chastity, penance, and contemplation, but unlike nuns, they did not take irrevocable vows.[8]

Inspired in large part by the divine conversation made accessible through the translation of the Song into the vernacular,[9] as well as the circulation of Bernard's sermons on it, these women could not live their lives of devotion talking to God alone. According to the rulings of the fourth

Lateran Council (1215), every Christian was to be confessed and to take communion at least once a year. Whereas monks and friars would have ordained priests within their communities to fulfill these spiritual needs, religious women required service from without, and much more often than once a year. Moreover, because they lacked formal theological training, they needed additional guidance and supervision to ensure that they would not fall into error. The dialogic mode of worship inspired by the Song came to be accompanied by official modes of dialogic exchange between women and their male spiritual advisors.

Women and Authorship

The twelfth-century reformist impulse was shared by two important contemporaries of Bernard — the Benedictine nuns, the abbess Hildegard von Bingen (1098–1179), and her contemporary, Elisabeth von Schönau (ca. 1129–64).

Hildegard's influence on thirteenth-century mystics is more difficult to establish with certainty than Bernard's. But with Hildegard's writings we begin to see emerging questions about authorship. Like Bernard, Hildegard was motivated by the apparent corruption of the clergy, as well as by heretical movements, against whom she wrote a tract in the 1160s.[10] She began writing the first of her six major books, *Scivias* (short for *Scito Vias Domini* or "Know the Ways of the Lord"), in 1141 and received papal approval for it in 1148.[11] Hildegard's critique, like Bernard's, is couched in the exegesis of divine words, but in her case these words come directly from God in visions instead of from the Bible. Hildegard frames the text as God's words and not hers. The fact that God chose her, a weak woman, to transmit them reflects the weakness and inadequacy of those people "who, though they see the inmost contents of Scriptures, do not wish to tell them or preach them, because they are lukewarm and sluggish in serving God's justice."[12] We are thus faced with a paradox in which a woman becomes an author without having to claim authorship, indeed, by indicating that she is not an author. The book's authority derives precisely from the fact that though Hildegard writes it, she is not its source.

The scene of Hildegard's writing raises further uncertainty about authorship. God sends her visions in which she not only sees a particular image, but also hears its exegesis. She dictates this exegesis in Latin to a scribe who writes it down on wax tablets and then edits the Latin for style in transferring it to parchment.[13] To a modern eye, Hildegard appears to have had co-authors, a fact which some have used to raise doubts about her literary and theological authority.[14] This type of scribal activity was quite common, however, and considering that even the pope believed Hildegard's words were coming from God, it is unlikely that the scribes would have exceeded basic copyediting. Nevertheless, the scene of writing here suggests a configuration of authorship that differs significantly from our own.

Few today would question Hildegard's status as author of her work or as an impressive thinker — she enjoys this status both in academic and popular circles. Yet it was Elisabeth von Schönau, Hildegard's younger contemporary, whose work enjoyed widespread circulation and popularity in the Middle Ages. As Barbara Newman has remarked, Elisabeth's works survive in over one hundred forty-five manuscripts, which is more than the manuscripts transmitting the works of Hildegard, Mechthild von Magdeburg, Hadewijch, and Julian of Norwich combined.[15] Moreover, they were translated from Latin into several other medieval vernaculars: Anglo-Norman, French, and Icelandic.[16] Like Hildegard, Elisabeth felt compelled to use her prophetic gift because the men currently in religious offices were woefully inadequate. But Elisabeth marks a transition to the women mystics of the thirteenth century in that her visions, in contrast to Hildegard's, are described in a first person voice and are autobiographical in content.[17] In further contrast to Hildegard, Elisabeth received her visions in trances that often occurred during or were even brought on by monastic and liturgical prayer. This practice of directing one's religious activity (prayer, fasting, vigils, attending mass, and the like) toward a contemplative state that lay open to divine visions became the ideal among both women and men in the thirteenth century and beyond.

Elisabeth's eight works, which she dictated in German, were written down and preserved in Latin, but not by her.[18] Initially her sisters in the convent, then her brother Ekbert, a monk in the adjoining monastery, recorded and published her revelations. Much more so than Hildegard's writings, then, Elisabeth's works were the result of complex sets of conversations that present problems for the attribution of authorship. In her trances, she "communicated" with an angel, saints, or the souls of recently deceased friends. These figures gave her messages to pass on, but Elisabeth also directed many questions to them. In a vision Elisabeth reported one Christmas Eve while praying, for example, she saw a virgin in the sun, crowned with gold and holding a gold cup. Elisabeth asked the angel who appears to her for an explanation (the virgin represents the "sacred humanity of Christ"). Three days after the vision, when John the Evangelist appeared to Elisabeth during mass, she asks him for a clarification, specifically at the prompting of her brother: "I questioned him, *as I had been advised*" (*Complete Works*, 124–25, my emphasis). Ekbert's intervention here demonstrates how his questions might have shaped the direction of the revelations and the lessons they were to convey. Ekbert's decision to revise and augment the books of visions and to incorporate some of Elisabeth's correspondence into these books is further evidence of a role as editor and author of these texts that exceeded that of Hildegard's scribes.

The relationship between the Elisabeth's writings as they have survived and the conversations to which they bear witness and from which they arise calls a monolithic understanding of Elisabeth's authorship into question. As Anne Clark notes, F. W. E. Roth, the nineteenth-century editor of Elisabeth's visions and Kurt Köster, who did much of the groundwork on the manuscript transmission, "assumed that the work they thought was the best — *The Book of the Ways of God* — must have been written by Ekbert."[19] Biases about the inherent abilities of a female versus a male writer were probably involved in this judgment. But the conversations between Elisabeth and Ekbert were two-way. The authority and skills that schooling provided Ekbert did not outweigh the very real authority granted Elisabeth because of her perceived contact with the divine. Despite the evidence of Ekbert's active revision of the writings, careful readings also reveal Elisabeth's resistance to Ekbert's influence as well as his own respect for the divine authority of her words. As Anne Clark has forcefully argued, Elisabeth was not merely the subject matter of the texts bearing her name, but also an agent in producing them.[20]

Bernard of Clairvaux's promotion of the idea that every soul should love God personally, coupled with a growing drive to re-energize the lethargic religious ranks, opened the door for devout women to claim authorship and authority. At the same time, this situation made authorship a much more confusing and yet culturally fascinating enterprise. Hildegard's shared authorship with her divine source and her scribes and Elisabeth's collaboration with her sisters and with Ekbert were but harbingers of things to come in the thirteenth century.

Vernacular Mysticism and Authorship

Both Hildegard and Elisabeth dictated their revelations in Latin, revealing a skill in that language thought to be miraculous. Although some revelations continued to be written and dictated in Latin in the thirteenth century, devout women and men wishing to record their visions increasingly chose the vernacular to do so. In addition, the focus of the revelations was more noticeably on *Gottesminne*, or divine love. These changes can be attributed to the affinity between religious poetry like the Song and the vernacular poetry of courtly love. In addition, vernacular preaching by the mendicant orders promoted the imitation of Christ, who himself represented a kind of vernacularization of the divine: he was God made common and local, he spoke to the downtrodden, and was disdained by the powerful.[21]

The three most notable mystics to write in Germanic vernaculars in the thirteenth century were Beatrice van Nazareth, Hadewijch, and Mechthild von Magdeburg. Beatrice was a Cistercian nun, whereas

Hadewijch and Mechthild were Beguines. The writings of each mystic raise different sets of issues surrounding authorship.

Beatrice and Hadewijch

Born in what is now Belgium in 1200, Beatrice brings together twelfth-century Cistercian modes of devotion and thirteenth-century mendicant attitudes, for she lived with a group of Beguines as part of her religious education before she entered the convent at the age of ten. Moreover, through contact with another former Beguine during her training Beatrice herself began to pursue a mystical path. These and the other details known about Beatrice's life come from a *vita* written about her shortly after her death.[22] Despite her convent education and knowledge of Latin, however, Beatrice chose to write her own religious works in Middle Dutch. As indicated above, the new uses of the vernacular were not exclusive of, but rather in dialogue with Latin and the world of Latinity. Beatrice's hagiographer acknowledges the use of the vernacular texts to write the *vita*, though all but one have been lost. Comparing the surviving treatise with the Latin reworking provides us not only with an example of the interaction between Latin and the vernacular, but also with another perspective from which to consider the questions about authorship and collaboration raised by Elisabeth's and Hildegard's texts. As opposed to the previous cases of collaboration between two living people, Beatrice's treatise becomes something else entirely when the hagiographer rewrites it after her death.

Beatrice's *Seven manieren van minne* is a descriptive tract about "heiliger minnen" or holy love. Each manner of love is more intense than the last and the depth and violence of feelings associated with holy love (ranging from sweet joy to tormenting pain) are reminiscent of the feelings of the lovers in the Song as well as those elicited by the powerful *vrowe minne* of Minnesang poetry. She writes of the seventh manner of love:

> Ay heilege begerte der minnen, wie staerc es uwe cracht in der minnen-der sielen! Het es ene salige passie ende .i. scarp torment ende ene uerlangen quale ende ene mordeleke doet ende steruende leuen.[23]

> [O holy desires of love, how strong your power is in the loving soul. It is a blessed passion, and a sharp torment, and a long-drawn-out suffering, and a murderous death, and a dying life.[24]]

While it is clear from this passage that the love Beatrice describes is deeply affective, the tendency of the *vita*, as Amy Hollywood has persuasively shown, is to translate these internal emotional states into tangible physical experiences that are evident externally. Indeed, the *vita* shows us first and foremost the ways in which the demands of hagiography, as a literary form adhering to a particular model for sanctity, come to bear on its "transla-tion" of the treatise. Because of these demands, the hagiographer trans-forms the interior spirituality advocated by Beatrice in the vernacular treatise into a spirituality made plain by exterior marks on Beatrice's body.[25]

In a passage from the fifth manner, Beatrice describes love and its increasingly violent effects on her person, both emotionally and physically. And yet, the language indicates that the physical aspects of the description are used to convey what something feels like, not what happened to Beatrice's body.[26] Love is so violently moving that it seems to wound the heart. Moreover:

> *Seven manieren*: . . . so dunct hare dat har adren ontpluken ende hare bloet verwalt ende hare march verswijnt ende hare been vercrencken ende hare borst verbernt ende hare kele verdroget, so dat hare anscijn ende al hare lede gevuelen der hitten van binnen ende des orwoeds van minnen. (64, lines 196–201)
>
> [. . . It *seems* to the soul that the veins are bursting, the blood spilling, the marrow withering, the bones weakening, the bosom burning, the throat parching, so that her visage and all her limbs feel this inward heat, and this is the fever of love.[27]]

Beatrice's choice of the word "seems" indicates that her veins are not bursting, but love makes her feel as if they were. The hagiographer, how-ever, gives the impression that Beatrice's love literally makes her bleed, per-haps hoping to suggest that she had experienced stigmata, an accepted physical sign of sanctity. Generally speaking, he makes the feelings she describes into perceptible physical symptoms:

> *Vita*: Indeed her heart, deprived of strength by this invasion, often gave off a sound like that of a shattering vessel, while she both felt the same and *heard it exteriorly*. Also the blood diffused through her bodily mem-bers *boiled over through her open veins*. Her *bones contracted* and the *mar-row disappeared*; the dryness of her chest produced *hoarseness of throat*. And to make a long story short, the very fervor of her holy longing and love blazed up as a fire in all her bodily members, *making her perceptibly (sensibiliter) hot* in a wondrous way.[28]

This example offers us an interesting counterpoint to Elisabeth von Schönau and her brother Ekbert. The hagiographer is trying to fit the new kind of holiness Beatrice represents into the older, more rigid mold of the saint's life, where holiness and sanctity are most frequently demonstrated through bodily torture and pain. Although Ekbert was interested in his audience's belief in Elisabeth's legitimacy, he chose not to write a saint's life, but to record what she told him of her visions and conversations with the divine. The difference between the text Beatrice authored, focused so completely on instructing its readers about how divine love and desire feels in the soul, and the text about her, focused on the evidence of the divine presence perceptible on her body, alerts us to the tension between Latin and the vernacular, between two differing concepts of what holiness means. Beatrice's hagiographer changed her writings not only because the genre in which he was writing required it, but also because the mysticism Beatrice was teaching marked a departure from the Latin traditions.

This dialogic mysticism takes on a particular vernacular character when Beatrice and others describe the qualities of divine love using the vocabulary, imagery, and even forms of vernacular courtly love literature.[29] In the passage quoted above from the seventh manner, the torment and longing associated with *minne* will seem familiar to anyone acquainted with classic French troubadour or German *Minnesang* lyrics. The *seruende leuen* or dying life brought on by the *cracht* (power) of minne also recalls the intensity of the passion between Tristan and Isolde, whose relationship is characterized by both *senegluot* (the pain of longing) and *herzewol* (heartfelt joy), inextricably bound together throughout the romance.[30] The "intertextual" conversation displayed in this integration of the divine love of the biblical Song and the secular love of the court has a curious result that also reflects on modes of medieval authoring. While in secular poetry, the voice of the suffering lover is usually male and the female object of desire often no more than a silent image, in divine courtly love the role of lover is played by the feminine soul, a subject position with which the women writers explicitly identify, though in strikingly different ways.

Hadewijch, for example, also writing in Middle Dutch in the mid-thirteenth century, wrote a series of poems in stanzas that explicitly adopt the forms of courtly lyric poetry to portray her understanding of the intensifying power of divine love. For Hadewijch, *minne* represents Christ or the Holy Ghost, but sometimes also God's love for humanity, the experience of loving, or humanity's love for God. Love is also associated with this set of meanings in Beatrice's and Mechthild's writings. Both Mechthild and Hadewijch write about *vrowe minne* (or Lady Love), but in Mechthild's *Das fließende Licht*, the feminine soul desires the masculine love object, Christ, the lover and bridegroom of the Song. In Hadewijch's stanzaic poems, however, Hadewijch's loving soul, rhetorically "dressed" as a knight, desires the female object — Lady *minne*.

Like many courtly lyrics, Hadewijch's poems begin with a reference to nature. In stanzaic poem 28, for example, it is winter while loving hearts reflect on the promise of spring and Lady Love's bounty:

> Die voghele sijn nu blide
> Die de winter dwanc
> So selen in corten tijde
> Dies hebbe die minne danc
> Die fiere herten die hare pine

> Ghedoghet hebben over lanc
> Op toeverlaet van minnen
> Sie hevet so rike ghewout
> Sie sal hen gheven sout
> Boven allen sinnen.

[The birds are glad now / That winter subdued. / Likewise will shortly be / — for which love be thanked — / The fierce hearts who have / Endured their pain overlong, / Trusting in love the while. / She has sovereignty so rich, / She will give them bounty / Beyond all senses.[31]]

In this elegant stanza, *minne*'s status as a noble and powerful lady is made clear with reference to her sovereignty and wealth. The lovers' position regarding *minne* also becomes evident — their "fierce hearts" indicate their willingness to do battle for Love, while their long-endured pain reveals their subordinate position to the sovereign lady.

The second stanza turns to the individual lover, who appears as definitively masculine. The one who desires love,

> Hi sal in allen sinnen
> Gherne daer na staen
> Dat hi die staercste doet . . .

[He shall, with all his faculties, / Gladly stand up / To brave the severest death . . .]

The tone of the poem is instructive. *He* who wishes to receive the bounty of the lady referred to in the first stanza must be willing to perform appropriate love service — to be constantly bold, to brave death, to embrace the lady's command, "whatever gentle love charges him with." It is generally assumed that Hadewijch wrote these poems for an audience of fellow Beguines whom she wished to inspire to greater devotion and holiness. She thus advises a group of women to act toward their God the way men (at least in courtly literature) act toward noble women. This reading can surely have a startling effect on the modern reader. Indeed, it is tempting to read these poems as Hadewijch's perhaps indirect resistance to oppressive gender relations in the devotional context. However, as Saskia Murk-Jansen has argued, this gender reversal is not as empowering as it seems; it was the Cistercians, particularly Bernard of Clairvaux, who employed images of gender reversal as a way for monks to understand their duties and devotions in a more precise way, that is, "to emphasize the fact that the soul's relationship to God was like nothing they had ever experienced."[32] Moreover, thinking of themselves in terms of women's subordinate roles or behavior helped them to understand more fully the humility before God that they were supposed to embrace as monks. Similarly, Hadewijch's use of gender reversal must be viewed from her point of view as a woman. In order to express the otherness of divine love, a love which requires intense suffering and abjection, but also an other-worldly reward of indescribable joy, Hadewijch adopts the role of the male lover and encourages her readers to do the same. The maleness of the subject position evokes for Hadewijch and her audience the total otherness of this divine love. Because of a social and historical situation in which women have only limited access to authority and power, this move seems bold indeed. But adopting the male subject position can also represent the renunciation of power and authority. For the position of the lover in courtly discourse is often one of powerlessness and abjection. For Hadewijch's courtly mysticism, becoming the male poet-lover in relation to the powerful noble lady represents the surrender of power, indeed, the surrender of self that is inherent in loving God.[33]

Hadewijch's poetry shows clearly not only how two traditions (courtly and biblical lyric) come into dialogue within this new vernacular culture of devotion, but also how gender becomes a rhetorical tool in the hands of a female author writing for women. Hadewijch's lyrical "cross-dressing," despite the implications of surrender discussed above, provides us with a striking sense of her poetic ability and authority. Indeed, Hadewijch's other writings, particularly her visions, set her up as an authority on a par with the Gospels.[34] Perhaps for this reason, Hadewijch's existence and authorship has never been doubted.

Mechthild of Magdeburg

In Mechthild von Magdeburg's *Das fließende Licht der Gottheit* (The Flowing Light of the Godhead), in contrast, it is the writer herself who doubts her authorship. Throughout the book we find expressions of anxiety about Mechthild's role as God's messenger. Such expressions of unworthiness are not uncommon — even Hildegard, who was authorized by the pope, called herself a weak woman chosen only because of a dearth of virtuous men. Mechthild's humility goes beyond the formulaic, however. Her union of the Song and courtly love appears to be related to her humility regarding authorship: the engagement of the dialogic qualities of these traditions serves to soften the claims on personal authority inherent in the project of writing, while at the same time advancing claims on the legitimacy of the product as God's word.[35]

Dialogue permeates this book. The soul speaks to God, *vrowe minne*, the senses; the narrator of visions speaks to those seen in the visions; Mechthild speaks to her readers and listeners in sermon-like commentaries; and she responds directly to her critics. Dialogues are even evident between some chapters. A series of short chapters in Book I, for example, documents an exchange between the soul and God. The first few words of each chapter follow:

> 11. O tube ane gallen, o maget ane sere, o ritter ane wunden . . . (O dove without gall, Oh maiden without sorrow, Oh knight without wounds)
>
> 12. O keyser aller eren, o crone aller fürsten, o wisheit aller meistern . . . (Oh emperor of all honor, oh crown of all princes, oh wisdom of all masters)
>
> 13. Ich kum zuo miner lieben als ein tovwe uf den bluomen. (I come to my love as dew on the blossoms.)
>
> 14. Eya vroeliche anschowunge! Eye liepliche gruos! . . . (Ah, joyful vision! Ah lovely greeting!)
>
> 15. Siest wilkomen, min liebú tube, du has so sere geflogen in dem ertriche, das dine vedern sint gewahsen in das himelriche. (Be welcome, my dear dove, you have flown so keenly over the earth that your feathers have grown up to heaven.)[36]

Amid allusions to knights, maidens, and love like dew on blossoms, we can also note an ambiguity as to who is speaking. In this series of chapters, we have in order the voice of Mechthild addressing those who battle for God, the first person voice of the soul praising God, God's voice describing his moment of arrival in the soul, the soul's reaction to this arrival, and God's welcome to the soul. The chapter titles, which I have not quoted here, serve to orient the reader in this dialogue, but without them, the voicing is far less clear.

This ambiguity of voice is a further defining characteristic of the text.[37] The intermingling of traditions and voices in combination with the dialogic form make a single authorial voice difficult to isolate. When an authoritative statement *is* made, its source (Mechthild, the literary and theological traditions in which she is writing, or God) is not always apparent. Although the narrative and instructive voice of Mechthild becomes more prominent in the latter parts of the book, the ambiguity is never fully resolved. This is one of the main reasons why the book is challenging to read. Not only does it defy generic expectations, but also it palpably resists the modern compulsion to identify a single author.

For most medieval writers, the source of authority for a text was rarely the writer himself or his originality of expression. Rather, authority came primarily from the source being copied or commented upon, or from God, the ultimate authority.[38] This understanding of authority is operating in the works of Hildegard, Elisabeth, Beatrice, and Hadewijch. Mechthild's text stands alone, however, in the way that it works through these issues of authority so explicitly. What is more, the result is a piece of writing that is strikingly original both in the eyes of its contemporary readers and in ours.

As an example, we can take another image from Mechthild's dialogue in Book I in which the soul praises God for his generosity towards loving souls: "Oh you lofty mountain, you are so bored through [*durgraben*] with little caves," the soul sings, "that in you only doves and nightingales can nest."[39] Mechthild responds in Book V to a comment that could have referred to this striking image:

> Meister Heinrich, úch wundert sumenlicher worten, die in diesem buoche gescriben sint. Mich wundert, wie úch des wundern mag. Mer: mich jamert des von herzen sere sid dem male, das ich súndig wip schriben muos, das ich die ware bekantnisse und die heligen erlichen anshowunge nieman mag geschriben sunder disú wort alleine; si dunken mich gegen der ewigen warheit alze kleine.[40]

> [Master Henry, you are surprised at some of the words written in this book. I am surprised how this can surprise you. Moreover, it has pained me deep in my heart since the time that I, sinful woman, was compelled to write, that I have never been able to describe the true revelation and the holy faithful visions except with these words alone; they seem to me all too insignificant next to the eternal truth.]

The voice of an author is unmistakeable here as we witness Mechthild's conversation with her confessor. And yet Mechthild simultaneously acknowledges and denigrates her authorship; in expressing her judgment that her words have been inadequate, she openly admits the author role. But by mentioning that she was *compelled* to write, she deflects some authorial responsibility for what she perceives as her literary failure. Asking God "was er har zuo spreche" (what he would say to this), she receives his unquestionable endorsement as his agent akin not only to the apostles, but also to Old Testament prophets like Moses and Daniel. What constitutes Mechthild's authority for us (her literary originality) was "surprising" and perhaps a problem for her peers, but her authority for them derived from her position as an author of *God*'s words.

The analysis of Mechthild's literary originality is further complicated by the fact that her book survives only in two translations (one into Latin from 1298 and one into Middle High German from 1345) — the Middle Low German has never been recovered. Ironically, the material transmission of a book in which the problem of mystical authorship and authority becomes a thematic and formal focus obscures the author Mechthild even further with its evidence of translators, scribes, and readers. In the religious culture characterized by the multiple dialogues surrounding the pursuit of divine love, however, the murky authorship of *Das fließende Licht* is thus appropriate.[41] More important, like the other texts discussed in this essay, it challenges us to confront our preconceptions about authorship, gender, religion, and identity, while also granting us a window onto the startling literary world of medieval mysticism.

Notes

[1] Beatrijs van Nazareth, *Seven manieren van minne: Middelnederlandse tekst met een inleiding en hertaling door Rob Faesen S. J.*, reproduction of 1926 critical edition (Kapellen: Uitgeverij Pelckmans, 1999); J. Van Mierlo, ed., *De Visioenen van Hadewych*, 2 vols. (Leuven: Vlaamische Boekenhalle, 1924–25); J. von Mierlo, ed., *Hadewijch Strophische Gedichten*, 2 vols. (Antwerp: Standaard Boekhandel, 1942). J. von Mierlo, ed., *Hadewijch Brieven*, 2 vols. (Antwerp: Standaard Boekhandel, 1947); Mechthild von Magdeburg, *Das fließende Licht der Gottheit: Nach der Einsiedler Handschrift in kritischem Vergleich mit der gesamten Überlieferung*, ed. Hans Neumann, prepared for printing by Gisela Vollmann Profe, 2 vols., MTU 100 and 101 (Munich: Artemis, 1990, 1993); Mechthild and Hadewijch are translated in the Paulist Press series Classics of Western Spirituality. Hadewijch, *The Complete Works of Hadewijch*, trans. Columba Hart (New York: Paulist Press, 1980) and Mechthild of Magdeburg, *The Flowing Light of the Godhead*, trans. Frank Tobin (New York: Paulist Press, 1998). See also Elizabeth A. Andersen, *Mechthild of Magdeburg: Selections* (Cambridge: D. S. Brewer, 2003). For Beatrice, see Fiona Bowie, ed., *Beguine Spirituality: Mystical Writings of Mechthild of Magdeburg, Beatrice of Nazareth, and Hadewijch of Brabant*, with Oliver Davies, trans. (New York: Crossroad, 1990).

[2] Bernard McGinn, *The Flowering of Mysticism: Men and Women in the New Mysticism (1200–1350)* (New York: Crossroad Publishing Company, 1998), xiii.

[3] It should be noted that vernacular mysticism is not an exclusively female phenomenon. In their vernacular writings, Meister Eckhart (1260–1328) and his student Heinrich Seuse (1295–1366) (among others) build on the mysticism that emerges in the women's texts, though in different directions: Eckhart's mysticism develops the apophatic or negative qualities of mystical experience; Seuse embraces the lyrical, affective, and dialogic mode of his predecessors. Both bring their own institutional authority to the mix.

[4] On Cistercian architecture, see, for example, Terryl Nancy Kinder, *Cistercian Europe: Architecture of Contemplation* (Grand Rapids, MI: W. B. Eerdmans Pub. Co., 2002).

[5] Bernard of Clairvaux, *Bernard of Clairvaux Selected Works*, trans. G. R. Evans (New York: Paulist Press, 1987), Sermon 2 ("On the Kiss"), 215.

[6] Regarding the Waldensian and Cathar heresies of the twelfth century, see Edward Peters, ed., *Heresy and Authority in Medieval Europe: Documents in Translation* (Philadelphia: U of Pennsylvania P, 1980).

[7] Herbert Grundmann, *Religious Movements in the Middle Ages: The Historical Links between Heresy, the Mendicant Orders, and the Women's Religious Movement in the Twelfth and Thirteenth Century, with the Historical Foundations of German Mysticism* (originally published in German in 1935) trans. Steven Rowan with an introduction by Robert E. Lerner (Notre Dame: U of Notre Dame P, 1995).

[8] The standard history of the Beguines in English is still Ernest W. McDonnell, *The Beguines and Beghards in Medieval Culture* (New York: Octagon Books, 1969). See also Walter Simons, *Cities of Ladies: Beguine Communities in the Medieval Low Countries, 1200–1565* (Philadelphia: U of Pennsylvania P, 2001).

[9] See for example, the *St. Trudperter Hohelied:* Friedrich Ohly, ed., *Das St. Trudperter Hohelied: Eine Lehre der liebenden Gotteserkenntnis,* Bibliothek des Mittelalters 10 (Frankfurt am Main: Deutsche Klassiker Verlag, 1998).

[10] Barbara Newman, *Sister of Wisdom: St Hildegard's Theology of the Feminine* (Berkeley: U of California P, 1987), 12.

[11] For a comprehensive list of Hildegard's works in editions and translations, see Sabina Flanagan, *Hildegard of Bingen, 1098–1179: A Visionary Life,* 2nd ed. (New York: Routledge, 1998), 217–19.

[12] Hildegard of Bingen, *Scivias,* trans. Mother Columba Hart and Jane Bishop (New York: Paulist Press, 1990), 67.

[13] Hildegard describes her visionary writing in a letter to Guibert of Gembloux, which is quoted extensively in Newman, *Sister of Wisdom,* 6–7 and 23.

[14] See the literature quoted in Joan Ferrante, "*Scribe quae vides et audis:* Hildegard, Her Language, and Her Secretaries," in *The Tongue of the Fathers: Gender and Ideology in Twelfth-Century Latin,* ed. David Townsend and Andrew Taylor (Philadelphia: U of Pennsylvania P, 1998), 102–35, at 103 and 130 n. 5.

[15] Barbara Newman, "Preface," Elisabeth of Schönau, *The Complete Works,* trans. Anne L. Clark (New York: Paulist Press, 2000), xi. All quotations from Elisabeth's writings refer to this edition.

[16] Anne L. Clark, "Introduction," in Elisabeth of Schönau, *The Complete Works,* 33–34.

[17] Clark, "Introduction," 34.

[18] For Elisabeth's works, see F. W. E. Roth, ed., *Die Visionen der hl. Elisabeth und die Schriften der Aebte Ekbert und Emecho von Schönau* (Brünn: Verlag der Studien aus dem Benedictiner- und Cistercienser Orden, 1884) and Elisabeth of Schönau, *The Complete Works.*

[19] Clark, "Introduction," 29.

[20] "Holy Woman or Unworthy Vessel? The Representations of Elisabeth of Schönau," in *Gendered Voices: Medieval Saints and Their Interpreters,* ed. Catherine M. Mooney (Philadelphia: U of Pennsylvania P, 1999), 35–51 and 202–7.

[21] On this reversal and its relation to vernacular theology, see Nicholas Watson, "Conceptions of the Word: The Mother Tongue and the Incarnation of God," *New Medieval Literatures,* 1 (1997): 85–124.

[22] Roger De Ganck, ed., *The Life of Beatrice of Nazareth 1200–1268,* Cistercian Fathers Series 50 (Kalamazoo, MI: Cistercian Publications, 1991).

[23] Beatrijs van Nazareth, *Seven manieren van minne* (see n. 1), 80 (lines 372–75).

[24] My translation.

[25] Amy Hollywood, "Inside Out: Beatrice of Nazareth and Her Hagiographer," in *Gendered Voices: Medieval Saints and Their Interpreters,* 78–98 and 220–29.

[26] For Hollywood's full reading of these passages, see her "Inside Out," 87–91.

[27] My emphasis. Translation (slightly modified) is from Hollywood, "Inside Out," 88.

[28] My emphasis. Roger De Ganck, ed., *The Life of Beatrice,* 308–11. Translation from Hollywood, "Inside Out," 88–89.

[29] Barbara Newman, "*La mystique courtoise*: Thirteenth-Century Beguines and the Art of Love," in her *From Virile Woman to WomanChrist: Studies in Medieval Religion and Literature* (Philadelphia: U of Pennsylvania P, 1995), 137–67.

[30] Gottfried von Strassburg, *Tristan*, ed. Rüdiger Krohn (Stuttgart: Reclam, 1984) lines 112 and 116.

[31] Marieke J. E. H. T. van Baest, ed., *Poetry of Hadewijch*, Studies in Spirituality Supplement 3 (Leuven: Peeters, 1998), here 196–97.

[32] See Saskia M. Murk-Jansen, "The Use of Gender and Gender-Related Imagery in Hadewijch," in *Gender and Text in the Later Middle Ages*, ed. Jane Chance (Gainesville: UP of Florida, 1996), 52–68; here 53.

[33] Murk-Jansen, "The Use of Gender," 54–55 and also 59.

[34] Bernard McGinn, "The Four Female Evangelists of the Thirteenth Century. The Invention of Authority," in *Deutsche Mystik im abendländischen Zusammenhang: Neu erschlossene Texte, neue methodische Ansätze, neue theoretische Konzepte*, ed. Walter Haug and Wolfram Schneider-Lastin (Tübingen: Niemeyer, 2000), 175–94, especially 178–80.

[35] Sara S. Poor, "Cloaking the Body in Text: Mechthild von Magdeburg and the Question of Female Authorship," *Exemplaria* 12.2 (2000): 417–53.

[36] Mechthild von Magdeburg, *Das fließende Licht*, 14 (Book I, chapters 11–14). The translations are my own.

[37] The phrase "ambiguity of voice" is coined by Sarah Beckwith in her essay "Problems of Authority in Late Medieval English Mysticism: Language, Agency, and Authority in the Book of Margery Kempe," *Exemplaria* 4.1 (1992): 171–89.

[38] A. J. Minnis, *Medieval Theory of Authorship* (London: Scolar Press, 1985).

[39] "O du hoher stein, du bist so wol durgraben, in dir mag nieman nisten denne tuben und nahtegalen!" Mechthild von Magdeburg, *Das fließende Licht*, 14.

[40] Mechthild von Magdeburg, *Das fließende Licht*, 166 (Book V, chapter 12).

[41] Mechthild's male successors, the Dominican preachers Meister Eckhart, Heinrich Seuse, and Johannes Tauler for example, have an institutional authority that makes the extreme humility found in Mechthild's book unnecessary. But their texts, too, use dialogic structures in their transmission that raise doubts about authorship and authenticity. I mention here, for example, the many texts in vernacular compilation manuscripts attributed to Eckhart which cannot be confirmed as his, or Seuse's warning to readers in his *Büchlein der ewigen Weisheit* (Little Book of Wisdom) to transmit his book in its complete form and not in fragments for fear of the resulting misinterpretation and error for which he would be responsible.

Part III

Continuity, Transformation, and Innovation in the Thirteenth Century

Wirnt von Gravenberg's *Wigalois* and Heinrich von dem Türlin's *Diu Crône*

Neil Thomas

Wirnt's *Wigalois*

*W*IGALOIS IS A COURTLY ROMANCE of some twelve thousand lines (following the three and four stress metrical pattern typical of this genre) composed by Wirnt von Gravenberg. Little is known of the author of *Wigalois* beyond his given name and his connection with Gravenberg (the modern Gräfenberg northeast of Nuremberg and Bayreuth).[1] Dating is also uncertain with competent scholars having issued conjectures ranging from 1205 to 1235. While it was once supposed that Wirnt knew only the first six books of Wolfram's *Parzival* (which probably came into circulation ca. 1204–10), his lofty praise of Wolfram, of whom Wirnt says "leien munt nie baz gesprach" (No layman ever spoke better, 6343–46), has more recently been taken to imply an acquaintance with *the whole* of *Parzival*.[2] Although the exact chronology remains unclear, it appears that *Wigalois* was enriched by a broader acquaintance with Wolfram's work(s) than was once supposed by an earlier generation of scholars.

Preceded by an account of Gawein's marriage to Florie in a wondrous kingdom where the goddess Fortuna resides as the tutelary deity, the story of Wigalois, son of Gawein, begins after his father has forsaken his wife and infant son, Wigalois, by riding back to Camelot. In early manhood the son is prompted to seek out his unknown father at the Arthurian Court where Gawein (whom, we are told, the son does not recognize) is appointed as his chivalric mentor. In an initial series of skirmishes with sundry adversaries under the censorious gaze of a female emissary (Nereja), he persuades his skeptical guide that he is the equal of his father (whose services she had explicitly requested in preference to those of the youth). He thereby wins the qualification to proceed to the major challenge of releasing the unquiet soul of King Lar from its tribulations, a task he carries out with the aid of an abundance of holy objects which enable him to defeat the Mohammedan necromancer, Roaz of Glois, Lar's murderer. The work of salvation completed, he marries the old king's daughter, Larie, and becomes the new king of the now restored waste land of Korntin. In the extensive sequel he is joined by his father (whose identity has in the interim been formally revealed to him) and other Arthurian knights in his campaign against a second malefactor, Lion of Namur. The siege of Namur successfully accomplished, Wigalois pays a "state visit" to Arthur at Nantes before resuming kingship in the land of Korntin where his rule maintains standards of statesmanship and Christian compassion inaugurated by the late King Lar.

Wirnt's romance is commonly accounted a "hybrid" work lying athwart a number of genres, and how he came across his diverse material is not certain.[3] According to the narrator himself, he received his story by word of mouth from a young *knappe* (squire). Possibly because the adduced source is so unpretentious (the narrator makes no claim to have had a prestigious, *written* source), many critics have taken these words at face value. There may however have been a self-exculpatory motive in the narrator's introduction of an unverifiable oral source, namely, the desire to establish a scapegoat for any breaches with received tradition perceptible to his first audiences. A comparison of *Wigalois* with similar works of the time shows that Wirnt must have been composing his narrative eclectically from a variety of written sources, many of them now unrecoverable.

Many later thirteenth-century romance writers implicitly follow the literary example of Hartmann by limiting themselves to an exploration of the traditions of the fictional chivalric value-system, ignoring the opportunity to explore the spiritual dimension of knightly existence initiated by Wolfram's treatment of the grail motif in *Parzival*. *Wigalois*, by contrast, although it does not contain the grail *motif*, is a romance whose underlying religious *theme* was borrowed by Heinrich von dem Türlin to carry the metaphysical logic of his grail sequence in *Diu Crône*. When Heinrich's Gawein succeeds in redeeming the old grail King from a limbo girt with "wonders" of hellish or purgatorial fire (the terms were not yet differentiated in vernacular literature),[4] the author portrays a similar mode of messianic salvation as that described by Wirnt von Gravenberg when his eponymous hero releases Lar's wraith from its purgatorial abode in the castle full of unearthly flames and lamentations.

Wigalois's challenge bears Christological features in that he must brave the realm of death. That this phrase is meant literally rather than in the purely metaphorical sense is revealed in the typological link supplied by Lar's surviving subjects in their equation of Wigalois's impending liberation with Christ's Harrowing of Hell (3990–4002). Common to *Wigalois*, *Diu Crône* and other romances of the grail cycle (*Perceval*, *Parzival*, *Peredur*, *Sir Percyvell of Galles* and Manessier's Continuation of Chrétien's *Perceval*) is a disquiet concerning a gratuitous death in chivalric combat, a homicidal "dolorous stroke" (to use Malory's term). This usurpation of God's traditional prerogative as the sole arbiter of life and death was regarded as a sacrilege great enough to bring divine wrath upon the bereaved people and a blight over the victim's land. These curses must be overcome by a savior knight either by the exercise of spiritual power or by exacting vengeance on the original malefactor, or both. The duty to lift the curse is linked to a further moral obligation awaiting the redeemer who, having avenged his late predecessor, must restore order and dominion within his blighted realm. These narrative patterns are evident in *Wigalois* where the hero triumphs over Roaz and his pagan deities with God's aid, avenges the murdered king, and then assures a proper continuation of the rule usurped by Roaz.

Advancing a similar range of themes as *Parzival, Wigalois* can as well be understood as a variant of the grail tradition as a story of the Fair Unknown, the story of an unknown knight who overcomes his initial obscurity by proving himself fully equal to more lauded peers (as in *Wigalois, Le Bel Inconnu* by Renaut de Beauje, the Middle English *Libiaus Desconus*, and in the fourteenth-century Italian *Carduino*).[5] *Wigalois* is in that sense a creative confrontation with Wolfram written in a frequently homiletic style by an author who appears to view his role as that of a practical moralist with a duty to provide ethical glosses and correctives to material found in his predecessor's work. The combination of a straightforward moralistic position with a relatively unadorned and uncomplicated style is already made evident in the prologue:

> Swer nâch êren sinne,
> triuwe und êre minne,
> der volge guoter lêre —
> daz vürdert in vil sêre —
> unde vlîze sich dar zuo
> wie er nâch den getuo
> den diu werlt des besten giht,
> und die man doch dar under siht
> nâch gotes lône dienen hie;
> den volge wir, wan daz sint die
> den got hie sælde hât gegeben
> und dort ein êweclîchez leben;
> dar nâch wir alle sulen streben. (20–33)

[He who thinks about bettering himself and loves loyalty and honor should follow good teaching, as this will promote his endeavor. Let him think about how he can follow the model of those to whom the court gives the highest praise and those who continue to serve for God's reward in this life. Let us follow these, for they are the ones whom God has blessed with good fortune here and eternal life in the beyond. We should all strive for this.[6]]

The stylistic differences from the notoriously difficult and obscure prologue of Wolfram are more than evident, and these differences extend from style to literary conception. Although Wolfram's creative commitment to the "fair unknown" dimension of the Parzival story is apparent in his unsparing treatment of Parzival's numerous errors and in the fact that the only knowledge he has of his father is gained indirectly through the tug of heredity (we are told that his father's *art* [nature] stirs within him),[7] the moral force of the "unknown" theme is considerably blunted in *Wigalois.* Here we are told that the hero knows his father's identity *before* he goes out in search of him; when officially informed at a later stage that his father is the same Gawein he had encountered when the latter was assigned to him as his tutor, he implausibly denies that he had known that this *particular* Gawein had been his father. In any case, regardless of whether an audience might have "believed" Wigalois knew that his mentor at the Arthurian Court was his father, it is expressly stated that he enjoyed the educational advantages, even if not the emotional support, of a father-son relationship. Although Wigalois in his probationary period with Nereja commits certain acts that may be reprehensible — he overreacts to one opponent by killing him when it was necessary only to overpower him, and he kills another opponent in order to ingratiate himself with Nereja[8] — these actions at least have the smack of a proto-Machiavellian cunning and are not totally witless like the follies of the young Parzival. Lest the two characters should be confused by any listeners, Wirnt assures them that Wigalois chivalrously tied the horse of one of his victims to a tree and attempted no despoliation of his corpse, thus dissociating Wigalois from Parzival's action against Ither when he committed the grievous offence of *rêroup* — robbing the corpse of another knight.

The Wolframian conception of a young man both ignorant and noble with the ability to discover stores of hidden potential clearly held little appeal for Wirnt. His narrative persona of the conservative moralist repeatedly moved him to defend a socially exclusive definition of the chivalrous estate, expressing vivid premonitions of social chaos should any social opportunist succeed in making his way up through the ranks (2339–48). According to his frequent moral and political commentaries, chivalry should be passed down in dynastic succession; any breach of this procedure would lead to social anarchy as surely as neglect of God's law would produce moral chaos (2137–48, 10245–305). These political views will inevitably have put Wirnt out of sympathy with the potentially leveling tendencies inherent in the Fair Unknown tradition where a boorish unknown proves himself the equal of aristocratic peers. Whereas Wolfram's partiality to his erring hero caused him to change the traditional premises on which the grail could be achieved (from an initial requirement that the Question be posed unprompted to the later revision that tuition was permissible to remedy past cognitive lapses), for Wirnt the great act of redemption is to be performed not by a holy fool but by a scion of the Arthurian nobility acting with knowledge, albeit obscure, of his father's example.

A signal difference between *Wigalois* and the other works within the Fair Unknown tradition (*Le Bel Inconnu, Libiaus Desconus,* and *Carduino*) is that, through his early identification as a knight keen to emulate (as opposed to merely find) a famous father, Wirnt's hero is little calculated to endorse the cause of the obscure and untutored, much less those to whom the stigma of bastardy had become attached (as was the case with the earliest known version of the Gawein/Florie story in the Old French *Livre d'Artus* where Gauvain's son is the illegitimate issue of a fleeting sexual encounter). The narrator's ideological position tends rather to the dynastic principle encountered at various points in Arthurian tradition,[9] which views birth and worth as synonymous. The hero's initial exploits are more concerned with a validation of his father's teachings through deeds performed "nâch sînes vater lêre" (according to his father's precepts, 3019) than they are with unprompted discoveries of hidden talents. It is perhaps not merely coincidental that the sequence involving Wigalois's attempts to impress Nereja corresponds so closely in temper with Gawan's attempts to win the graces of the haughty Orgeluse in *Parzival*,[10] for the early adventures may be better understood as the story of how Gawein's son fulfils his paternal legacy than as a bona fide contribution to the Fair Unknown tradition.

With a largely inerrant knight as protagonist, Wirnt clearly could not tackle the major issues of God and world in the same way as Wolfram. Instead, Wigalois's career proceeds in a carefully graduated movement in a manner better suited to Wirnt's didactic purposes. To delineate these discrete stages of his hero's career Wirnt uses an indirect mode of characterization by means of objects familiar from the genre of the fairytale. When Wigalois, initially called the Knight of Fortuna's Wheel ("der rîter mit dem rade," 5132) loses the belt which is a token of that goddess's favor (in *Diu Cróne* we are told how Fortuna fashioned it as a protective talisman), Wirnt problematizes the issue by revealing that God's help is henceforth required to save the knight from future reverses. The loss of Fortune's trophy bears a programmatic significance, announcing a new phase in the hero's career where he leaves behind the championship of purely knightly ideals under the tutelage of Fortuna. Instead, *Wigalois* espouses the Christian mission of redeeming the soul of the murdered king. The implication is that lucky talismans have their place in the hero's early life but that he now requires a new arsenal of Christian apotropaic objects, that is, objects having the power to ward off bad luck, such as the sacred letter containing an abundance of prayers and Christian formulae wrapped round his sword by a priest,[11] and a sacred Host given him by Larie (not a conventional lady's gift: in the secular atmosphere of the analogous passage in the fifteenth century *Chevalier du Papegau* the lady gives her champion the more conventional token of a piece of silk).[12]

If Wigalois's exorcism of the purgatorial flames and lamentations engulfing Korntin have points of contact with the theme of messianic salvation otherwise linked to the grail tradition, the final depiction of his rule as a particularly assimilative Christian theocracy in which Asiatic nobles are welcomed as equals may also have been influenced by Parzival's ecumenical form of grail kingship where the pagan half-brother, Feirefiz, is permitted to marry the grail bearer, Repanse de Schoye. The reconsecrated castle of Korntin becomes a place where sectarian boundaries are erased, and there is little of dogmatic zeal in what we are told of the ethics of practical Christianity undergirding the protagonist's mission to renew Lar's charitable works on behalf of the poor. Furthermore, the campaign against Lion, which has been likened to an internal crusade, and even claimed to represent a literary stimulus to crusading activity,[13] is in fact not a crusade at all since it unites figures from both sides of the sectarian divide in what is a bipartisan civil action. The *casus belli* is in fact the Western European Lion's murder of the innocent Amire of Libya in order to procure Amire's wife; there is no diabolic conspiracy between the heathen Roaz and Lion who, although he makes one approving reference to that devil's disciple, does so in the context of opportunistic insults hurled at Wigalois. The implication of these verbal attacks is that he, Lion, will not be defeated so easily as Roaz was, this being all part of a conventional oath of scorn for his opponent (10168–73). Lion's reference to the previous enemy in this context constitutes a piece of psychological warfare.

The charge has been leveled at Wolfram that it was his hero's *way* to grail kingship that engaged him rather than the discharge of obligations attendant on his tenure of that office, and that the evocations of an ecumenical utopia are therefore tenuous.[14] It is possible that Wolfram later perceived this as a moral aporia in his earlier work and that there may have been an element of self-criticism implicit in Wolfram's second work, *Willehalm*, where the author rejects fabulous subject matter in favor of the all-too-real theme of the Cross/Crescent divide in the epoch of the Crusades.[15] In *Willehalm* the Oriental utopia associated with the figure of "Prester John" (supposed to have ruled over a populace of mixed-faith subjects in a location never properly identified within the vastnesses of India) yields to a more serious engagement with the sectarian dilemma that prompts Wolfram to an even-handed treatment of both warring camps and to an unsparing deconstruction of "Crusading" warfare as *mort* (carnage).

Wirnt was probably working on his romance at approximately the same time as or even shortly after Wolfram was composing *Willehalm*. Regardless of whether he knew or did not know Wolfram's piece of literary self-criticism, *Wigalois* may be viewed as a critique of Wolfram's ahistorical utopia in *Parzival*, authored by a moralist eager to draw practicable lessons from his predecessor's work. Rejecting Wolfram's purely ideal realm of the grail, Wirnt develops a considerably more naturalistic presentation of his new king's rule in which romance conventions are largely discarded. The Lion engagement is not depicted as an adventure performed by a solitary knight, but as a military siege in which responsibility is more credibly delegated to numerous combatants in massed combat with a realistic time frame of six weeks.[16] Furthermore, the person whom Wigalois summons by letter to conduct the day-to-day military practice of his regime is his father, Gawein. The integrative function performed by Gawein's presence at the new king's court possibly supplies a further corrective to Wolfram's work, for when Wolfram depicts his ecumenical vision of the pagan half-brother Feirefiz returning to accompany Parzival to the grail, he makes no mention of Parzival's *chivalric* confrère, Gawan, and the impression arises of an incompatibility of "Arthurian" and "grail" realms. Wirnt by contrast gives an encore to Wolfram's neglected deuteragonist (as well as to the accompanying Erec, Iwein, and Lanzelet), giving concrete shape to a harmonization of Arthurian and theocratic elements to which Wolfram appears to allude in a narrator's aside,[17] (*Parzival*, 827, 19–24), but which he does not realize in *concrete* terms at the conclusion of his work.

Heinrich's *Diu Crône*

The author of *Diu Crône* gives his name in the form of an extended acrostic on the initial letters of a sequence of verses: HEINRIKH VON DEM TVRLIN HAT MIKH GETIHTET (Heinrich von dem Türlin wrote me, 182–216).[18] He also names himself less cryptically in the body of the text (246–49, 8774, 10,443–44) but gives no information about his domicile or the name of any possible patron.[19] Heinrich's romance, composed ca. 1220–25 and consisting of 30,041 verses that absorb motifs from a host of other, mainly French, romances,[20] represents a re-imagining of the story of the Arthurian order as an institution (the title can ultimately be understood metonymically as meaning *Arthur*'s crown). The work proceeds from a description of somewhat tremulous beginnings to chart the Court's ascent to the "grail" (here depicted largely as a *chivalric* challenge under Gawein's stewardship) as the zenith of its narrative teleology. Rather like the French romance *Perlesvaus* (ca. 1240), *Diu Crône* opens with a dismal account of the humiliations, defections, and schisms scarring the Arthurian Court, then a moral wasteland whose tarnished honor Gawein eventually sets out to remedy on behalf of his king. The grail action comes only toward the end of as the work as the crowning achievement of a series of chivalric interventions in which Gawein, himself an erstwhile defector, returns to sustain the honor of his liege lord by negotiating numberless crises. One of the more notable of these is his peaceful resolution of a sexual challenge to Arthur made by a stranger knight (Gasozein) who claims that Guinevere had been his betrothed before Arthur had met her. After preventing what would have been the worst possible defection (for Guinevere shows some covert signs of attachment to the pretender), Gawein's quest for the grail is initiated in a sequence based on the Gawan adventures of Wolfram's

Parzival. Here he is sworn to quest for the grail as a penance laid upon him for the accidental killing of the brother of Angaras of Karamphi. In this endeavor he is helped by the magician, Gansguoter (a benign version of Wolfram's Clinschor whose "magic" often consists in expertise in castle construction and siege tactics) who helps Gawein to gain entry to the grail kingdom, and he is given further advice by Manbur, Gansguoter's sister and *châtelaine* of the grail castle. At that castle, the old grail king explains the origins of the grail curse and its associated "wonders" as being due to the sin of Cain having been committed by one of Parzival's kinsmen. The curse had spread its fatal influence far and wide, and the king himself is a walking corpse. After Gawein has asked the requisite question of the specter (as to the meaning of the strange sights he witnesses), he receives a special sword from the king as acknowledgment that he is the long-awaited deliverer, after which he and his retinue of "undead" retainers are by miraculous means granted release from the terminal sufferings of their present limbo. The grieving Angaras, who originally imposed the quest upon Gawein as a penitential office for the loss of his brother, is conciliated by the successful grail quest, even to the extent of agreeing to enter the Arthurian ranks. This is the last we hear of the "grail" since, after Gawein's successful quest, he does not assume kingship in the grail lands but simply returns to the Arthurian ranks.

Some modern readers have speculated that Chrétien de Troyes might have brought Gauvain and Perceval together before the grail had it been given to him to complete his *Conte du Graal,* and so have given symbolic expression to a rapprochement between Arthurian and grail realms. This approach was not adopted by Wolfram for, despite the presence of a number of intratextual references to Parzival and Gawan serving to link the careers of both knights, Wolfram treated Chrétien's Gauvain sequence as a semi-independent narrative in which Gawan, his vow to seek the grail left as a blind motif, becomes instead the savior of the emotionally damaged Orgeluse and of the segregated male and female denizens of *schastel marveile.*[21] This deflection from the grail quest might have left contemporaries unsatisfied, who might have hoped that the best Arthurian knights would have experienced greater success where Parzival had failed.[22] This expectation was responded to by Heinrich von dem Türlin, but not in a conciliatory spirit. Rather, he showed a partiality to Gawein at the expense of Parzival, which led him to a radical revision of Wolfram's ethics.[23]

While Heinrich may have followed the example of the First Continuation of Chrétien's unfinished grail romance[24] in choosing Gawein as his protagonist, his attitude to that hero is more positive than that of the continuator whose Gauvain fails to mend the symbolic fissure in the grail sword (Heinrich's Gawein is granted an intact sword as a sign of his unqualified success in his grail mission). This unequivocal endorsement of Gawein (a figure not known elsewhere in legendary tradition as a knight of special spiritual distinction) implies an ambition to make the quester a more worldly knight than Wolfram's Parzival or the Galahad of the influential French prose tradition. Heinrich seems to have been more influenced by the spirit of some of the post-Chrétien *verse* romances that represent behavior patterns more adapted to the practical exigencies of medieval knighthood.[25]

Heinrich von dem Türlin appears to have shaped his own romance in part as a literary counterblast to the French Lancelot Grail cycle.[26] References to the character of Parzival in *Diu Crône* are relentlessly negative. His failure to ask the question at the grail castle in Wolfram's version is adduced as the cause of his failure in the first of the tests of honor in *Diu Crône* (2210–15) and his failing is thereafter dwelt on persistently. The narrator Heinrich says that Parzival's failure to ask the question at the grail castle is the cause of the disrepute into which Arthur's court has fallen:

> Daz er in ungevrâget liez,
> Noch alsô sêre riuwet mich;
> Daz künec Artûs velschet sich
> Und die tugentrîche ritterschaft
> An dirre traegen gsellschaft,
> Ez entouc niht ir magenkraft. (14,003–8)

[That Parzival left the question unanswered still causes me great sorrow; King Arthur and his great knights are shamed by virtue of their association with him, which is beneath their dignity.]

Parzival would have done better to keep to his rustic retreat, opines Heinrich in an allusion to Parzival's youth in rural Wales in Wolfram's version. He does not possess the heroic stature of Gawein, whom he would have viewed as a god, continues Heinrich in a reference to Wolfram's passage where the unenlightened Parzival erroneously takes three knights in shining armor to be gods and abases himself in front of them in an attitude of worship (*Crône*, 6372–93; *Parzival*, 120, 27–121, 2).

Despite some formal genuflections in the direction of Christianity and the honorable number of mentions which the goddess Fortuna and her hypostatizations receive throughout *Diu Crône*, the narrator places little faith in metaphysical notions of Providence or of "good fortune." When in some striking scenes Gawein arrests the motion of Fortuna's wheel and receives her assurance of future prosperity for the Arthurian court, we might suppose that a signal benediction were taking place; yet the encounter would seem to point more to her powerlessness than her omnipotence, for shortly afterward Gawein falls victim to strange volcanic eruptions raining hot marl on him — all this before he has even left the perimeter of Fortune's own kingdom — thus conveying the impression that her writ does not run even within her own territory. Hence, although Christian and pre-Christian mythological conceptions are frequently syncretized in locutions expressing faith in the joint sovereignty of Fortuna and the Christian God, Heinrich's commitment is ultimately neither to Fortuna's boons nor Christian soteriology but to the strength of the chivalric order embodied in a knight who finally triumphs not by means of magic, but rather valor.

Prowess together with that skill in *Realpolitik* which prompts Gawein to borrow what might nowadays be termed "technical support" from the magician cum military tactician, Gansguoter (The appellative means "completely good"), are the real determinative factors. The seemingly omnipresent and omnipotent figure of Gansguoter is, in the absence of any strong sense of a controlling God, the *de facto* "director" of the romance. The name of this "completely good" figure might even represent an ironic Germanicization of one of the favorite medieval periphrases for God: the *summum bonum*. It is Gawein's compact with him that turns out to represent the best way of achieving Heinrich's "grail" (in the profane sense of the acme of the chivalric estate). In comparison with Wirnt von Gravenberg, Heinrich emerges as a philosophical materialist for whom the metaphysical realms are little more than a poet's fancy (as is evidenced in his modern sounding references to *Natura*).[27] The way to Heinrich's lower-case grail comes not so much from progressive spiritual revelation or from divine aid as from the ability to manipulate the correct military/mechano-magical levers.

While Wirnt shows how the Arthurian ideal can be safeguarded only if it allies itself with the spiritual forces of the Christian religion, the piety of *Diu Crône* is so nominal that even the status of the work as a grail romance (in the sense of a spiritual quest) has been queried on the grounds that Heinrich's grail is simply "un objet de conte, dépourvu de tout symbolisme mystique et religieux" (a story-tale device innocent of any mystic or religious symbolism).[28] For after Heinrich's nebulously described "grail" has disappeared from human ken, there is no attempt to describe a distinct grail *realm*. The narrator's concluding remarks about not spoiling his "wol gesmite(r) krône" (well-wrought crown, 29917) with gratuitous additions provide indications of a desire to place a "copyright" over his chosen form of closure, effectively preventing a continuator from adding an account of any exotic form of kingship detrimental to Heinrich's *Arthurian* Crown. Jillings's contention that *Diu Crône* "is intended to undermine chivalry from within by its satirical treatment of courtly figures and values"[29] is opposed by Heinrich's uncritical apologias for the standards of the Court. *Diu Crône* is, rather, an unequivocal endorsement of a secular, Arthurian ideal which clearly maintained its appeal in Germany well beyond the "classical" period of the first decade of the thirteenth century.

Notes

[1] *Wigalois. Der Ritter mit dem Rade*, ed. J. M. N. Kapteyn (Bonn: Klopp, 1926); the text is translated with an introduction by J. W. Thomas, *Wigalois: The Knight*

of Fortune's Wheel (Lincoln: U of Nebraska P, 1977). For a fuller discussion of many points below see Neil Thomas, *Wirnt von Gravenberg's "Wigalois": Intertextuality and Interpretation* (Cambridge: D. S. Brewer, 2005).

[2] Friedrich Neumann, "Wann verfasste Wirnt den Wigalois?" *Zeitschrift für deutsches Altertum* 93 (1964): 31–62.

[3] Stefan Fuchs, *Hybride Helden: Gwigalois und Willehalm: Beiträge zum Heldenbild und zur Poetik des Romans im frühen 13. Jahrhundert* (Heidelberg: Winter, 1997).

[4] See Jacques Le Goff, *The Birth of Purgatory*, trans. Arthur Goldhammer (Chicago: U of Chicago P, 1984), especially 39–43.

[5] For a fuller discussion of this tradition, see Neil Thomas, *Wirnt von Gravenberg's "Wigalois,"* 21–43.

[6] English translations are by N.T.

[7] See Anthony van der Lee, *Zum Literarischen Motiv der Vatersuche*, Verhandelingen der Koninklijke Nederlandse Akademie van Wetenschappen, afd. Letterkunde, n.s. vol. 62, no. 3 (Amsterdam: North Holland, 1957), esp. 145–54.

[8] See Jutta Eming, "Aktion und Reflexion. Zum Problem der Konfliktbewältigung im Wigalois am Beispiel der Namurs-Episode," in *Spannungen und Konflikte menschlichen Zusammenlebens in der deutschen Literatur des Mittelalters*. Bristoler Colloquium 1993, ed. Kurt Gärtner, Ingrid Kasten, Frank Shaw (Tübingen; Niemeyer, 1996), 91–101.

[9] On this point see Alfred Ebenbauer, "*Wigamur* und die Familie," in *Artusrittertum im späten Mittelalter*, ed. Friedrich Wolfzettel (Giessen: Wilhelm Schmitz, 1984), note 40, and Ann G. Martin, "The Concept of *reht* in *Wigamur*," *Colloquia Germanica* 20 (1987): 1–14.

[10] The similarity was pointed out by Jessie L. Weston, *The Legend of Sir Gawain* (London: Nutt, 1897), 56, n. 2.

[11] These were called *Schwertbriefe* or *Himmelsbriefe* in Germany. See W. R. Jones, "The Heavenly Letter in Medieval England," *Medievalia et Humanistica*, n.s. 6 (1975): 163–78.

[12] Ed. Ferdinand Heuckenkamp (Halle: Niemeyer, 1896); for the analogous section see 57–75.

[13] See Claudia Brinker, "*Hie ist diu âventiure geholt!*. Die Jenseitsreise im *Wigalois* des Wirnt von Gravenberg: Kreuzzugspropaganda und unterhaltsame Glaubenslehre?" in *Contemplata aliis tradere. Studien zum Verhältnis von Literatur und Spiritualität*, ed. Brinker (Bern: Lang, 1995), 87–110.

[14] See the introduction of A. T. Hatto's translation of Wolfram's *Parzival* (Harmondsworth: Penguin, 1980), 8.

[15] Horst Brunner, "*Artus der wise höfsche man*: Zur immanenten Historizität der Ritterwelt im *Parzival* Wolframs von Eschenbach," in *Germanistik in Erlangen: Hundert Jahre nach der Gründung des deutschen Seminars*, ed. Dieter Peschel (Erlangen: Universitätsbund Erlangen-Nürnberg 1983), 61–74, here 72.

[16] Wolfgang Mitgau, "Nachahmung und Selbständigkeit Wirnts von Gravenberc in seinem *Wigalois*," *Zeitschrift für deutsche Philologie* 82 (1963): 321–37.

[17] Wolfram von Eschenbach, *Parzival*, ed. Karl Lachmann, 6th ed. (Berlin: de Gruyter, 1926), 827, 19–24.

[18] G. H. F. Scholl, *Diu Crône von Heinrich von dem Türlin* (Stuttgart: Bibliothek des Litterarischen Vereins no. 27, 1852; reprint Amsterdam: Rodopi, 1966); *Die Krone (Verse 1–12281) nach der Handschrift 2779 der Österreichischen Nationalbibliothek*, ed. Fritz Peter Knapp and Manuela Niesner (Tübingen: Niemeyer, 2000). See also *The Crown: A Tale of King Arthur's Court*, trans. with an introduction by J. W. Thomas (Lincoln: U of Nebraska P, 1989); for a more detailed analysis see Neil Thomas, *"Diu Crône" and the Medieval Arthurian Cycle* (Cambridge: D. S. Brewer, 2002).

[19] See Bernd Kratz, "Zur Biographie Heinrichs von dem Türlin," *ABÄG* 11 (1977): 123–67.

[20] Christine Zach, *Die Erzählmotive der "Crône" Heinrichs von dem Türlin und ihre altfranzösischen Quellen: Ein kommentiertes Register* (Passau: Richard Rothe, 1990).

[21] See Neil Thomas, "Sense and Structure in the Gawan adventures of Wolfram's *Parzival*," *MLR* 76 (1981): 848–56.

[22] Bonnie Büttner, "Gawan in Wolfram's *Parzival*," Dissertation, Cornell University, 1984, 108.

[23] *Diu Crône* presents "the most favourable portrayal of Gawein in German literature" (Bart Besamusca's article on "Gawain" in *A Dictionary of Literary Heroes: Characters in Medieval Narrative Traditions and Their Afterlife in Literature, Theatre and the Visual Arts*, trans. Tanis Guest (Woodbridge: Boydell Press, 1998), 113–20, note 117); on Heinrich's prejudice against Wolfram's *Parzival* see the special study of Ralph Read, "Heinrich von dem Türlin's *Diu Krône* and Wolfram's *Parzival*," *Modern Language Quarterly* 35 (1974): 129–39.

[24] See the translations of Chrétien's *Perceval* and of its continuations in *Perceval, The Story of the Grail*, by Nigel Bryant (Cambridge: D. S. Brewer, 1982).

[25] On the more pragmatic spirit of the verse romances see Keith Busby, *Gauvain in Old French Literature* (Amsterdam: Rodopi, 1980) and Beate Schmolke-Hasselmann, *The Evolution of Arthurian Romance: The Verse Tradition from Chrétien to Froissart*, trans. Roger and Margaret Middleton with an introduction by Keith Busby (Cambridge: Cambridge UP, 1998).

[26] See Elizabeth Andersen, "Heinrich von dem Türlin's *Diu Crône* and the Prose *Lancelot*; an Intertextual Study," *Arthurian Studies* 7 (1987): 23–49.

[27] Nature (rather than the non-exercise of free will) is made responsible for moral lapses in women (4345–47; 446–55); and perversely (it is implied) gives Lord Laniure daughters rather than a desired son (7911–13). On this figure see G. D. Economou, *The Goddess Natura in Medieval Literature* (Cambridge, MA: Harvard UP, 1972).

[28] Danielle Buschinger, "Un roman arthurien post-classique: *La Couronne* de Heinrich von dem Türlin," *Le Moyen Âge* 89 (1983): 381–95, here 393.

[29] Lewis Jillings, *"Diu Crône" of Heinrich von dem Türlein: The Attempted Emancipation of Secular Narrative* (Göppingen: Kümmerle, 1980), 12.

Der Stricker

Michael Resler

D ER STRICKER (THE WEAVER, ca. 1190–1250), who flourished in the first half of the thirteenth century, is known chiefly for his short verse narratives and fables, of which approximately 170 have survived. In addition, he wrote two longer works: the Arthurian romance *Daniel von dem Blühenden Tal*[1] (translated as *Daniel of the Blossoming Valley by der Stricker*) around the period 1210 to 1225, and, apparently somewhat later,[2] the heroic epic *Karl der Große (Charlemagne)*.[3] It is generally accepted that these two major poems were written first, and that the shorter stories — which form the foundation of der Stricker's literary repute — are the product of his later years.

Der Stricker was among the earliest of the so-called "post-classical" German writers. Unlike many of the German poets of the High Middle Ages, Der Stricker appears not to have been a member of the chivalric order; he was in all likelihood a professional itinerant poet. While he spent a major portion of his life in present-day Austria, he appears to have been born somewhere in central Germany.

Like most of his contemporaries, little information is preserved about the life of Der Stricker. Even his name appears to be an assumed one. Despite some competing theories, a consensus exists among scholars that this probable pseudonym was meant to indicate a "weaver" or a "knitter." If one accepts this explanation, then the poet, by calling himself "the weaver," quite possibly meant to allude to his literary role as a weaver of stories.

As already mentioned, it is virtually certain that Der Stricker, unlike many of his contemporary poets in Germany, was not a knight. It is Der Stricker's own attempt at that most "knightly" of literary genres — his Arthurian romance, *Daniel* — that supplies the most compelling evidence. For unlike Hartmann von Aue and Wolfram von Eschenbach — whose romances brim with real-life minutiae of knighthood — Der Stricker, in his *Daniel*, betrays little intimate knowledge of the practices and traditions of chivalry. The writer must have been largely dependent, like most medieval writers, on wealthy patrons for material support of his poetry. His longer works, in particular, almost certainly could not have been undertaken without such backing. Yet somewhat oddly and in contrast to many contemporary poets, he never directly names any such patrons. To be sure, scholars have attempted to identify Der Stricker with various courts and with specific patrons — both ecclesiastical and secular — yet to date all such hypotheses remain inconclusive.[4] Still, there is compelling evidence (chiefly, the large number of manuscripts in which certain of his works are transmitted) to suggest that our poet was a popular and recognized bard during his day. Thus, he must have been welcome at prominent courts in Germany during the first half of the thirteenth century. That he apparently never saw fit to document his stays at these courts — not even indirectly, by naming patrons — constitutes but another of the gaps that cloud his blurry and speculative biography.

By contrast, a great deal more can be reliably affirmed concerning Der Stricker's poetic output. As mentioned, his surviving works number approximately 170 — a sizable corpus given the whole set of problems surrounding the transmission of tales composed eight hundred years ago. And not only was he quite prolific; his works also display considerable literary diversity, for he authored stories across a broad range of genres. Early in his career he wrote his two longest works — *Daniel* and *Karl* — and with the exception of *Pfaffe Amîs* (*Priest Amîs*) and "Die Frauenehre" (Ladies' Honor), he seems to have concentrated in his later years on shorter poems. From a historical standpoint, he is a major transitional figure from the lofty courtly realm of the cultural blossoming of the high medieval period to the more ordinary, commonplace milieu characteristic of German post-classical literature. In fact, within his own works Der Stricker spans this very gap: his two elaborate early works — *Daniel* and *Karl* — yield in his later years to simpler and less sublime verse narratives and fables.

Der Stricker's sole Arthurian romance, *Daniel* (ca. 1210–25), is thought to have been the first such freely invented tale in the German tradition. Up until this point German Arthurian poets had been following the example of Hartmann — whose *Erec* (ca. 1185) harks back directly to the Old French *Erec et Enide* of Chrétien de Troyes — by basing their stories on pre-existing French sources. In fabricating the 8,483-line story of Daniel, Der Stricker made a remarkable break with this convention. What is every bit as interesting as Der Stricker's innovativeness is the fact that he seemingly felt obliged to disavow his own creativity by making a bogus assertion of a French source whom he names as Albrich von Bisenze (of Besançon) and whose name may have been Aubry. In his prologue he claims that he is taking on the task of translating, for his German listeners, a French tale of Daniel by this Albrich:

> Von Bisenze meister Albrich,
> der brâhte ein rede an mich
> ûz wälscher zungen.
> die hân ich des betwungen,
> daz man sie in tiutschen vernimet,
> swenne kurzwîle gezimet

[Master Alberich of Besançon has brought to me a story from the French which I have translated that it might be heard in German whenever entertainment suits the occasion, 7–12.]

Nonetheless, scholars are unanimous in dismissing this claim as a formulaic nod to the French poets, who had long set the standards for Arthurian romance.

In his *Daniel*, the eponymous hero, a hitherto unknown knight, proves himself in combat and is received into King Arthur's company. An unnamed giant, acting as emissary for King Matur of Cluse, brashly challenges Arthur to travel to Cluse and to surrender there to Matur. While Arthur prepares for this journey, Daniel sets out in secret for Cluse. Along the way, he is diverted from his goal, first by a maiden whose land is under siege by a wicked dwarf, then by a countess under attack by another demon. Daniel prevails in both contests, and, arriving at the entrance to Cluse, defeats the messenger giant's brother. Meanwhile, King Arthur and his men arrive and initiate battle with the first of the seven armies of Cluse. Arthur slays King Matur, whose first army is defeated by Arthur's men. During a nighttime truce Daniel leaves the encampment to search for an abducted comrade, but is sidetracked by yet another petitioner, whose land is afflicted by an evil foe. Daniel prevails, locates his lost comrade, and returns in time to help Arthur vanquish, over a period of several days, the remaining armies of Cluse. Arthur rewards Daniel by offering him both the land of Cluse and Matur's widow in marriage. The ensuing wedding celebration is interrupted by the abduction of King Arthur and Parzival, but Daniel steps in to set them free.

Daniel abounds with the usual conventions of Arthurian romance. For one thing, the title hero engages in a series of adventures through which he establishes his standing as a member of King Arthur's court. In the course of his various conquests, Daniel takes on not only fellow knights, but giants, dwarves and assorted magical creatures. Moreover, the story is replete with beautiful ladies, a splendid festival at Whitsuntide, bizarre animals, fantastic realms, and supernatural weapons. And fully in keeping with Arthurian convention, the author invests his tale with the requisite happy ending.

Yet much is also different here. Four major points of divergence set *Daniel* off from traditional Arthurian romance, as established by Chrétien and adhered to by the German poets up until Der Stricker. First, King Arthur himself engages in battle in *Daniel*; Der Stricker reports,

> Dô ersprancte der künic Artûs,
> daz man hôrte den sûs
> als ein weter dâhin gevarn.
> einen gekrœnten arn
> fuorte er an sînem schilte.
> sîn herze vor fröuden spilte
> daz er in versuochen solde

[King Arthur (. . .) vaulted forth with the rush of a storm. He bore a crowned eagle upon his shield, and his heart pounded with joy that he was about to do battle, 3007–13.]

This stands quite in contrast to Arthur's conventional role as the older, "retired" monarch, whose court serves the finest knights as a base from which to pursue their own adventures. Secondly, in his various conquests Daniel abundantly supplements his physical fighting prowess (traditionally the ultimate virtue of Arthurian heroes) with cunning — at times even trickery; Daniel himself asserts, "dem man ist dicke diu wîsheit / ze man-gen dingen harte guot, / daz er mit sterke niht entuot" (A man can often accomplish with wisdom full many a thing which he could not achieve by relying upon strength alone, 1504–6). (Interestingly, in the poet's later, non-chivalric works, guile takes precedence repeatedly over brute strength — further resonance perhaps of Der Stricker's own status outside of the chivalric order.) In a third break from established Arthurian convention, Der Stricker infuses his tale with extended mass battle scenes, in which Arthur's knights engage in warfare against an army of opposing knights. This fighting mode stands quite at odds with classical Arthurian romance, where combat typically consists of one-on-one dueling. And finally, Der Stricker deviates from the established path in the utter absence here of *minne* (courtly love). In the classical romances, by contrast, the knight's love for a lady typically serves as a chief catalyst for that protagonist's adventures. Even the brief episode near the end, in which Daniel sues for the hand of his dead opponent's wife, is devoid of the amorous sentiment that traditionally suffuses such a scene; we are told, with a virtually dynas-tic detachment, that the priests who perform the wedding ceremony have thereby granted the hero, "ouch darzuo mê: / daz künicrîch und die krône" (even more than a wife: they bestowed upon Daniel the kingdom and the crown as well, 6336–37). In a broader sense, this is vintage Stricker, for nowhere in his works does this poet convincingly portray the salutary power of love upon his characters.

Though Der Stricker apparently wrote his tale of Daniel from scratch, this is not to say that he was unaware of — or uninfluenced by — other works of literature. Quite to the contrary, even at first glance *Daniel* betrays numerous strains of literary influence. Of all the German works of the day, Hartmann's *Iwein* appears to have had the most sweeping impact on *Daniel*. In addition, a broad array of other contemporary works (Pfaffe Konrad's *Rolandslied*, Hartmann's *Erec*, Heinrich von Veldeke's *Eneide*, Wirnt von Gravenberg's *Wigalois*, Ulrich von Zatzikhoven's *Lanzelet*) as well as literary and legendary reminiscences from antiquity (among others, the head of Medusa, the Sirens, the sorceress Circe) likewise left their mark on Der Stricker's tale.[5] Thus, while the bard took a bold step toward orig-inality by fabricating the basic plot for his *Daniel*, nonetheless the work is — on the micro-level of specific themes and images — brimming with recollections from a wide assortment of other literary strains.

In striking contrast to *Daniel*, Der Stricker's originality is far less apparent in *Karl*. For this long epic of 12,206 lines is essentially a stylistically updated retelling of the twelfth-century *Rolandslied* of Priest Konrad — a work which in turn was a German-language adaptation of the Old French *Chanson de Roland*. The title hero of Der Stricker's epic is none other than Charlemagne, known in German as "Karl der Große." And the story that Der Stricker retells here is the real-life battle waged by Charlemagne — or Karl — against the Spanish Moors in the year 778. In light of the crusading fervor that was sweeping over large parts of Europe during Der Stricker's lifetime, it is no accident that ancient tales such as this would have enjoyed renewed popularity, even four hundred years after Charlemagne's time.

The hero of Der Stricker's *Karl der Große* journeys to Spain to convert the Moors to Christianity through battle. Together with his nephew Roland and others, Karl and his immense army initially defeat the infidels following a hard-fought battle, only to fall prey six years later to a plot by the Moor king Marsilies and Genelun, a turncoat commander under Karl, that isolates Roland and his forces in Spain, leading to Roland's death in battle. The main torso of Der Stricker's story consists of extended deliberations prior to the fighting and of descriptions of the battles themselves. As regards the actual plot, *Karl* does not differ substantially from the earlier *Rolandslied*. Even in those few passages where Der Stricker endeavors to set out on his own, poetic cohesion is not always the result. It seems that the author had little aptitude for transforming or expanding the narrative as he had received it from Priest Konrad. Instead, he took it as his principal task to refine the story — on the level of rhyme, meter, and vocabulary — so as to conform more aptly to the literary expectations of his courtly listeners.

Early on, Der Stricker tells of Karl's youth and of his later ardor for converting the infidels. God's angel appears to Karl, saying: "Sone soltuz langer niht sparn, / du solt ouch hin ze Spanje varn: / got wil dich dâ mit êren. / du solt daz liut bekêren" (You shall delay no longer, but journey to Spain, for God wishes to bestow honor on you with this charge. Once there, you shall convert the people [to Christianity], 355–58). The angel prophesies that Karl's valiant nephew Roland will play a key role in the approaching clash. At this juncture Der Stricker introduces the leaders of the Christians, among them Genelun, who later will turn traitor to the Christian cause. In the first skirmish, Karl's vast army defeats the infidels, imposing Christianity on the survivors. Then, after six years, Karl encounters an immense militia led by the Moor king Marsilies. As a result of treachery by Genelun, whom the Moors manage to bribe, Karl is tricked into returning to Aachen and leaving behind only a modest force in Spain. Once Karl has departed, Marsilies attacks. During the so-called Battle of Runceval, the Christian forces are defeated, in part because Roland fails to call for help from the departing Karl by sounding his horn Olivant. By the time Roland does finally give the signal, it is already too late. From a poetic standpoint, Roland's death scene on the battlefield is both potent and memorable, for the hero's demise is heralded by a flash of light from the heavens, "als der himel über al / ein klâriu sunne wære" (as though all the sky were filled by a dazzling sun, 8256–57) and by an earthquake so violent "daz diu hiuser kûme stênde bliben / [. . .] in Spanje lant" (that the houses in [. . .] the land of Spain were barely left standing, 8262–63). However, as with so many aspects of the work, Der Stricker inherited much of his imagery here from the earlier *Rolandslied*.

After protracted fighting and despite being outnumbered two hundred to one, the Christians eventually prevail in the Spanish campaign, and Roland's death is avenged. In a long and poignant passage — again drawn in large part from the *Rolandslied* — Karl laments over the body of Roland: "wê mir [. . .] dirre nôt, / Ruolant lieber neve mîn, / daz ich nu muoz enbern dîn" (Woe is me for this torment, o Roland, my dear nephew! Ah, that I must now be dispossessed of you! 8344–46). After much debate over Genelun's fate, the traitor's arms and legs are tied to each of four savage horses, which proceed to tear him asunder. Only Judas himself, the poet declares, was a more wicked traitor than Genelun. In a short epilogue Der Stricker urges his listeners to follow the example of "sante Karle" (Saint Karl, 12, 206), while appealing to God for everlasting salvation.

As noted, Der Stricker's achievement is primarily of a formal nature, as he adds little of literary substance to the Charlemagne or Roland legends. Nonetheless, the fact that *Karl* is preserved in over forty manuscripts speaks convincingly for the popularity of Der Stricker's epic. Indeed, it was this account of the struggle against the Spanish infidels — and not the acclaimed *Rolandslied* — with which audiences of the later Middle Ages were most familiar.

Of Der Stricker's presumably later poems, only a handful are of sufficient expanse to be regarded as freestanding works. The most memorable is *Pfaffe Amîs*, a compilation of twelve *Schwänke* (farcical tales) held together by the persona of the protagonist, a knavish priest named Amîs. By practicing mental adroitness to perpetrate irreverent escapades and various comic wiles, Amîs exploits, over the course of 2,510 verses, the naiveté of his fellow human beings. For example, his bishop in England becomes jealous of Amîs's grandiose lifestyle, and plots to defrock the scoundrel by exposing him as a fraud. To that end, the invidious bishop interrogates Amîs with a string of unanswerable questions. The bishop asks how many days have passed since the creation; only seven, replies Amîs, but these same seven have recurred repeatedly. Foiled by this and other evasions, the bishop directs Amîs to teach a donkey to read. The roguish priest utterly thwarts his nemesis by sprinkling oats between the pages of a book; the hungry donkey is quick to grasp that he can uncover one savory treat after another by successively turning the pages with his nose. Unable to prove that the donkey is in fact *not* reading the words in the book, Amîs's bishop must finally acknowledge defeat. During a long series of travels throughout Europe, Amîs practices his duplicity on unsuspecting victims from every conceivable social class. Only near the end does Amîs finally undergo a conversion, which prompts him to renounce his life of secular mischief, find a true belief in God, and enter a monastery. By the time of his death, Amîs has demonstrated deep contrition for his long-standing chicanery and is granted his heavenly reward.

Pfaffe Amîs is not solely the product of Der Stricker's own poetic creativity. Instead, many of the individual scenes and motifs are rooted in older narrative material from various literary traditions. Scholars have even attempted to show that Der Stricker may have worked from a French source. While no such connection has ever been convincingly established, the spirit of *Pfaffe Amîs* has much in common with that of the *fabliaux* that were at that time enjoying great popularity in France. In any event, Der Stricker displays his poetic dexterity here by adeptly splicing together and captivatingly retelling the individual anecdotes that make up *Pfaffe Amîs*.

Critics are in nearly unanimous agreement that Der Stricker's enduring legacy lies in the shorter poems that constitute the later portion of his corpus. These poems are quite diverse: from eight to 1,902 lines in length, and composed in a range of different genres, including prayers, fables, *Schwänke*, didactic poems, and *exempla*. These short poems are often grouped together under the comprehensive rubric of *Kleindichtung* (short poetry).[6] With few exceptions, these poems resist any attempt at dating, either with an absolute year of composition or in terms of their chronology relative to one another. The characters who populate Der Stricker's *Kleindichtung* run the gamut of medieval life: innkeepers and dukes, priests and laypersons, husbands and wives, peasants and monarchs, farmers and knights. Similarly, the topics that Der Stricker addresses in his short poems range widely, though many are marked by Der Stricker's characteristically comic depiction of human flaws and vulnerabilities.

In general it is difficult to classify Der Stricker's *Kleindichtung* into tidy genre groups, simply because there is so much overlap among his favorite forms. Whereas one of his *mæren* (stories), for example, may be largely comic in tone, the next *mære* might center on a moral issue. Likewise, one *bispel* (example; cf. Latin *exemplum*) might impart a spiritual point, while another may address a more secular theme. However, most of Der Stricker's *Kleindichtungen* betray, to a greater or lesser degree, two distinct components: a narrative segment (the story proper) and a didactic segment (the poet's moral explication of that story). Depending on which facet is more prominently featured, a poem will lean towards one or the other pole along a scale between narrative and didactic. However, seldom is either of the two segments — narrative or didactic — entirely lacking in a given poem.

The single most distinct genre among Der Stricker's short didactic poems is the *bîspel*. Indeed, Der Stricker is celebrated within German literary history as both the inventor and the consummate master of this type of story, which harks back to both Biblical parables and the Aesopian tradition, and which was also a fundamental feature of medieval sermon-writing. A notable subgenre of Der Stricker's *bîspel* are the so-called *tierbîspel* (beast fables), in which common animals typically embody human vices and virtues. Among Der Stricker's favorite beasts in his *tierbîspel* is the wolf, whose recurrent setbacks in life epitomize the inexorable folly of mankind.

Der Stricker's *Kleindichtungen* regularly serve as a pulpit from which a variety of lessons can be preached. In "Das wilde Ross" (The Wild Horse), for instance, he associates his tale of a willful horse with the virtue of constancy. In addition, a number of his *mæren* touch on the theme of marital discord. In lieu of the knight and his lady, whose relationship is so pivotal to much of high courtly literature, the poet often portrays an ordinary peasant and his wife. Typically, their bickerings revolve around the mundane conflicts of married life — not around the sublime predicaments posed by *minne*.

The recurring topos of the shrewish wife in many of these poems has subjected Der Stricker to the suspicion of misogyny.[7] In fact, however, he pokes his poetic barbs at virtually all sectors of medieval society. Moreover, in his "Frauenehre," the longest of the *Kleindichtungen*, he offers a sweeping encomium to women, in a style reminiscent of the courtly tradition of *minne*. In this regard, it is an interesting footnote that, despite his contemporaneity with *Minnesang* and despite his own multifaceted literary output, Der Stricker wrote not a single *Minnelied*. In fact, in "Die Minnesänger" he actually derides the poets of *Minnesang* with acerbic irony.

Whatever his stance toward women, love, and marriage, Der Stricker consistently denounces adulterous love by depicting extramarital liaisons in a dark light — for instance in "Der kluge Knecht" (The Shrewd Servant), where a woman takes a priest as her lover. Indeed, clerical transgressions are the topic of a considerable number of poems. Frequently the wrongdoing involves the inability of a priest to uphold his vow of chastity. Der Stricker harbors similarly adamant reproach for homosexuality, whose practitioners he doggedly reprehends — in "Die gepfefferte Speise" (The Peppered Meal) as well as in "Gegen Gleichgeschlechtlichkeit" ("Against Homosexuality") — as "sodomites." Among the assorted vices that Der Stricker addresses in his *Kleindichtungen*, a favorite is drunkenness — for instance, in "Die Martinsnacht" (St. Martin's Night), where a peasant becomes so inebriated that he falls victim to the deceptions of a swindler. And yet, as so often in Der Stricker's poems on insobriety, the author's censure is mitigated here by his bemusedly detached mode of narration, which invites his listeners to smile benignly at yet another such human foible.

One last thematic category stands out among der Stricker's *Kleindichtungen*: those with a religious focus. Many of these poems are simple prayers, while others deal with liturgical and theological issues. The pivotal role of sin and atonement within Der Stricker's religious opus has given rise to speculation that our poet may have been acquainted — perhaps under the aegis of some unnamed, but ecclesiastically connected patron — with the transactions of the Fourth Lateran Council of 1215, a conclave which devoted a great deal of attention to penitential theology.[8]

In the final accounting, Der Stricker is remembered for the versatility of his works and for his transitional role as an early herald of the more mundane, less elegant literature of the later Middle Ages. Above all, however, Der Stricker stands out as the first significant poet to endow German didactic literature with a spirited and witty narrative tone.

Notes

[1] *Der Stricker: Daniel von dem Blühenden Tal*, 2nd rev ed., ed. Michael Resler, Altdeutsche Textbibliothek 92 (Tübingen: Niemeyer, 1995). Translated as *Daniel of the Blossoming Valley by der Stricker. Translation with Introduction and Notes* by Michael Resler. Garland Library of Medieval Literature, Vol. 58. New York and London: Garland, 1990. Also available in a dual-language edition *German Romances, 1: Daniel von dem Blühenden Tal by der Stricker*. Trans. and ed. Michael Resler. Arthurian Archives, 9. Woodbridge, UK, and Rochester, NY: D. S. Brewer, 2003.

[2] Michael Resler, "Zur Datierung von Strickers *Daniel von dem Blühenden Tal*," *Euphorion* 78 (1984): 17–30.

[3] Der Stricker, *Karl der Große*, ed. Karl Bartsch (Quedlinburg & Leipzig: Basse, 1857; reprinted, Berlin: De Gruyter, 1965).

[4] See for example Stephen Wailes, "Stricker and the Virtue *Prudentia*. A Critical Review," *Seminar* 13 (1977): 136–53.

[5] See Gustav Rosenhagen, *Untersuchungen über Daniel vom Blühenden Tal vom Stricker*, Diss., U. of Kiel (Kiel: C. Schaidt, 1890); Peter Kern, "Rezeption und Genese des Artusromans: Überlegungen zu Strickers 'Daniel vom blühenden Tal,' " in special issue of *Zeitschrift für deutsche Philologie* 93 (1974): 18–42; and Karl Bartsch, ed., *Karl der Große* (Quedlinburg and Leipzig: Gottfried Basse, 1857).

[6] *Die Kleindichtung des Strickers*, vol. 1, ed. Wolfgang Wilfried Moelleken, Göppinger Arbeiten zur Germanistik, 107 (Göppingen: Kümmerle, 1973). This five-volume work is the most comprehensive critical edition of the *Kleindichtung*. A selection of these tales is available in English translation in J. W. Thomas's *Fables, Sermonettes, and Parables by der Stricker* (Lewiston, NY: Mellen, 1999). Unless otherwise noted, all English renderings in the present essay are by M. R.

[7] Albrecht Classen, "Misogyny and the Battle of Genders in the Stricker's Maeren," *Neuphilologische Mitteilungen* 92 (1991): 105–22.

[8] Ute Schwab, "Beobachtungen bei der Ausgabe der bisher unveröffentlichten Gedichte des Strickers," in *Beiträge zur Geschichte der deutschen Literatur* 81 (1959): 61–98.

Rudolf von Ems

Elizabeth A. Andersen

R UDOLF VON EMS (ca. 1200–ca. 1255) is one of the most significant and prolific authors in the development of thirteenth-century "post-classical" German narrative literature (ca. 1220–90). His five extant works are thought to have been written in the following order: *Der guote Gêrhart* (Good Gerhard, ca. 1220–25), *Barlaam und Josaphat* (ca. 1225–30), *Alexander* (begun ca. 1230 and continued in the 1240s after the composition of *Willehalm von Orlens*), *Willehalm von Orlens* (ca. 1235–40) and the *Weltchronik* (Chronicle of the World, ca. 1250).[1] These texts are cast in the dominant narrative verse form of the "classical" period (ca. 1170–1220) in their uniform composition in rhyming four beat couplets, but the scope of their subject matter is far greater and more diverse than that encompassed by classical courtly literature.

Although Rudolf is not attested in any historical documents, we nonetheless have a keen sense of his historical presence through the expression of a pronounced authorial identity in his works.[2] The name "Ruodolf" occurs in all his narratives, both as an explicit self-reference or as an acrostic embedded in the text.[3] In an intertextual nod to Hartmann von Aue,[4] Rudolf declares himself in *Willehalm von Orlens* to be a "dienest man ze Muntfort" (15629), a knight in the service of the counts of Montfort who held lands south east of Lake Constance. Furthermore, the anonymous continuator of the incomplete *Weltchronik* informs us that Rudolf was "von Ense" (33496),[5] that is from a family of imperial *ministeriales* whose ancestral castle was situated above present-day Hohenems near Dornbirn in Vorarlberg and whose political significance was in the ascendant during the rule of the Hohenstaufen emperors.[6]

Our knowledge of the social and political contexts in which Rudolf was engaged is extended by his delineation of himself as a professional poet, for Rudolf is unusual in the amount of information he provides about the source of his material, how he came by it and who commissioned it. The earlier texts were fostered in clerical circles. The epilogue of *Der guote Gêrhart* suggests that a namesake of Rudolf, Rudolf von Steinach, a *ministerialis* in the service of the Bishop of Constance, sponsored the work. This text is perhaps most accurately described as an "Exempelroman" (a narrative with an exemplary moral function).[7] In it the story of the good merchant Gêrhart is framed by the story of the emperor Otte. After seeking to know his reward in Heaven for having founded the archbishopric of Magdeburg, Otte is sent by an angel from God to learn from Gêrhart, his social inferior, the true nature of Christian humility through an account of the personal sacrifices Gêrhart made in order firstly to rescue the beautiful Norwegian princess Êrêne and her escort from heathen captivity in Morocco, then to reunite Êrêne with Willehalm, her betrothed, and finally to restore Willehalm to the kingship of England. Otte, deeply humbled by Gêrhart's tale, recognizes the error of his own presumptuousness.

The commission to cast the hagiographical legend of Barlaam and Joasaph into German came from clerical circles too, this time from the Cistercian Wido, who was abbot of the monastery at Kappel in Canton Zurich. This legend, a Christianized version of the Buddha story, was one of the most popular in medieval Europe. It is the story of the conversion of the young prince Josaphat to Christianity, against his father's wishes, but in fulfilment of a prophecy made at his birth. The hermit Barlaam, sent by God, wins Josaphat over in a series of dialogues in which he gives a lengthy (8092 of the total 16164 verses) and comprehensive presentation of Christian history and doctrine through a narrative punctuated by biblical stories, parables and exemplary fables.[8] Josaphat's newly found faith is tested by his father Avenier who himself eventually converts, convinced by Josaphat's exemplary and effective rule as a monarch. Josaphat concludes his life by abdicating his rule and withdrawing from society to live as a pious hermit.

Alexander is exceptional among Rudolf's works in not naming a patron, but this omission is probably more by default than design, as this text is incomplete and it could be that a patron was to have been identified in the epilogue. Rudolf's ambitious account of the life of Alexander the Great breaks off in the midst of the sixth of, probably, ten planned books. After an account of Alexander's unorthodox conception, his education by Aristotle and his succession to the throne of Macedonia on the death of his nominal father Philip, the main plot is concerned with the military clashes between Alexander and the great Persian king Darius, the death of Darius, the defeat of Darius's supporters and the story of Bessus, Darius's treacherous kinsman.

For the composition of his later works Rudolf enjoyed the patronage of the royal Hohenstaufen court in Swabia which had once more become a center for literary production, hosting not only Rudolf but also Ulrich von Türheim and having close links with the Swabian *Minnesänger* Ulrich von Winterstetten and Gottfried von Neiffen. *Willehalm von Orlens* was commissioned (15662–66) by Konrad von Winterstetten (d. 1243), the imperial cup-bearer and governor of the duchy of Swabia, who had the French source text from a fellow *ministerialis*, the Swabian Johannes von Ravensburg (15601–24). In his role as tutor and then advisor to the sons of the emperor Friedrich II, the young German kings Heinrich VII and Konrad IV, Konrad was one of the most influential men in the Hohenstaufen imperial administration. *Willehalm von Orlens* is a courtly romance in which the eponymous hero Willehalm is orphaned and then adopted by Jofrit von Brabant, who raises him in an exemplary courtly manner. When Willehalm is sent to the English court he falls in love with Amelîe, King Reinher's daughter. The course of their love conforms to a paradigm (the awakening of love, love sickness, the separation of the lovers, their constancy and final reunion) whose origins can be traced back to Hellenistic prose romance. When Willehalm and Amelîe are eventually reunited, Willehalm succeeds to the throne not only of his adoptive father but also of his father-in-law.

The *Weltchronik* has the distinction of being the first work since the *Heliand*, as far as we know, to be commissioned by a king.[9] Konrad IV himself charged Rudolf with the monumental task of composing this universal history, promising him a substantial reward for his efforts (21656–67; 21686–90). The *Weltchronik* is an account of salvation history organized according to the established paradigm in Christian historiography, derived from the concept of the six days of creation, of six *aetates mundi* (world ages). These were identified as the ages of Adam, Noah, Abraham, Moses, David and Christ. The text breaks off in the fifth age with the death of Solomon. The *Weltchronik* follows the course of Old Testament history. However, from his account of the Tower of Babel onwards, Rudolf introduces incidentally an account of secular history conceived as a succession of world empires.

The interests of Rudolf's patrons may be presumed to be reflected in their choice of subject matter. *Der guote Gêrhart* is an exemplary moral tale about humility, charity, loyalty and compassion. This work shares in that tradition of religious exemplary tales that, since the twelfth century, were increasingly used in the preaching of sermons. *Barlaam und Josaphat* is a story of religious instruction and conversion to the Christian faith. Rudolf's patrons for these two works, Rudolf von Steinach and Abbot Wido, did not, however, seek out a man of the cloth to render their source material into German, but rather a professional poet, whose brief was to reach a wider lay audience. Rudolf reports that Konrad von Winterstetten and Johannes von Ravensburg wanted the French source of *Willehalm von Orlens* cast into German to please and entertain their ladies (15615; 15655). However, the love story of Willehalm and Amelîe is couched in a narrative that is preoccupied with the normative conduct of the nobility. The detail with which Rudolf describes the education of Willehalm, his investiture as a knight and his conduct as a prince may easily be construed as instructional reading for Konrad von Winterstetten's young charge, Konrad IV.[10] A comparison with Priest Lamprecht's *Alexanderlied* (ca. 1150) reveals the extent to which Rudolf has shaped his Alexander into a model chivalric king of the thirteenth century, who is not only an accomplished fighting knight and courageous war leader but also a wise ruler. Here too, within the context of the patronage of the Hohenstaufen court, aspects of the text may be read as a repository of instruction on the proper conduct of princes for Heinrich VII and Konrad IV. The tendentious nature of patronage emerges most sharply in the *Weltchronik* which is conceived as "ein ewiclih memorial" (a [literary] memorial for all time) to Konrad IV (21697). In the encomium of Konrad (21572–707), inserted between the fourth and fifth ages, the previously parallel narrative strands of salvation and secular history converge. The fusing of the offices of David, the prototype of the divinely ordained ruler, and of Caesar in the person of Konrad legitimizes the Hohenstaufen claim to world rule.[11]

There is a striking difference in the nature of Rudolf's source material compared with that of the authors of the classical period of courtly literature. Where Heinrich von Veldeke, Hartmann von Aue, Gottfried von Strassburg and Wolfram von Eschenbach had all been engaged in the cultural and linguistic appropriation of vernacular French texts, Rudolf's sources, with the exception of that for *Willehalm von Orlens*, were in Latin. He returned to that subject material of the nascent vernacular tradition in the twelfth century that was drawn from the clerical Latin tradition and that had been largely displaced by the vogue for the Arthurian romance.[12]

For both *Der guote Gêrhart* and *Barlaam und Josaphat* Rudolf traces a complex path of textual transmission back to, in keeping with hagiographical convention, an eye witness account.[13] Gêrhart's story, we learn, was written down by clergy, presumably in Latin, at the behest of the Emperor Otte who had heard the tale from Gêrhart himself and wished that it might be "ein bezzerunge [. . .] der kristenheit" (for the edification of Christendom, 6802–3). Rudolf reports how a man from Austria had given it to Rudolf von Steinach, who in turn had asked Rudolf von Ems to cast it into German verse. In *Barlaam und Josaphat* we learn that King Barachias, Josaphat's friend and successor, has an account of Josaphat's life written down as an example to others. This account was translated from Greek into Latin by John of Damascus. Abbot Wido brought it into "tiuschiu lant" (German lands, 144) where Rudolf was commissioned to render it into German (149). Although, as in the case of *Der guote Gêrhart*, the source text for *Willehalm von Orlens* is no longer extant, it has been demonstrated that it was the same as that used by Philippe de Remi for his French romance *Jehan et Blonde*.[14]

Whereas in *Der guote Gêrhart*, *Barlaam und Josaphat* and *Willehalm von Orlens* Rudolf refers to a single source text, in *Alexander* and the *Weltchronik* he is pluralist in his approach. Rudolf's principal source for the *Weltchronik* was the Vulgate Bible, together with Peter Comestor's *Historia scholastica* (ca. 1165), the standard work on Biblical history in the

Middle Ages. Among other sources, Rudolf also drew on Godfrey of Viterbo's *Pantheon* (ca. 1185), an influential history of the world in the medieval period; the *Imago mundi* (ca. 1120) of Honorius of Autun, a treatise on cosmography, astronomy, meteorology, and chronology; Isidore of Seville's encyclopaedic *Etymologiae* (ca. 600), the textbook most in use throughout the greater part of the Middle Ages; and Jerome's translation (ca. 379) from Greek into Latin of the *Chronicle* (ca. 315), a summary of universal history, by Eusebius, commonly known as "the Father of Church History." In composing his account of Alexander's life Rudolf is at pains to assure his readers of the comprehensive nature of his research (12965–70). For the first phase of this text (up to line 5014) Rudolf followed the *Historia de preliis Alexandri Magni* (ca. 950), the most important recension of Archpresbyter Leo of Naples' *Nativitas et victoria Alexandri Magni regis*, but then took the *Historiae Alexandri Magni* (ca. 45 A.D.) of the Roman historian Quintus Curtius Rufus, in whose work there had been a revival of interest since the mid-twelfth century, as his principal source, working with the original text. This must be accounted a distinctive feature of Rudolf's literary production, for all other Middle High German texts that deal with literature from antiquity, with the exception of Albrecht von Halberstadt's adaptation of Ovid's *Metamorphoses* (ca. 1190), draw on medieval sources, be they in Latin or in a vernacular rendering of the classical original. Rudolf also drew on the Bible, the account of Alexander's reign in the *Antiquities of the Jews* (ca. 60 A.D.) by the Jewish historian Flavius Josephus, the Latin translation (late third century A.D.) by Julius Valerius of the Greek romance of Alexander, the prophecies attributed to St. Methodius of Patara (a martyred bishop of the fourth century) which are now generally regarded as the work of a pseudonymous author writing in about 680 A.D., and the *Alexandreis, sive gesta Alexandri Magni,* a long epic in Latin hexameters by the twelfth-century French writer and theologian Walter of Châtillon. Furthermore, Rudolf cites three earlier versions of the Alexander legend in German, Priest Lamprecht's *Alexanderlied* (15783–88) and two works, no longer extant, by Berthold von Herbolzheim (15772–82) and one Biterolf (15789–803). The range of sources in Latin is an intimation of Rudolf's erudition, based on an extensive education received perhaps at either the monastery of St. Gallen, which lived under the rule of St. Benedict, or the monastery of St. Luzius in Chur, which belonged to the order founded in 1120 by St. Norbert at Prémontré, near Laon in France. At the same time the German sources indicate Rudolf's inclusion of a distinct vernacular tradition in his particular rendering of the history of Alexander the Great.

The emergence of a coherent corpus of texts in the classical period of courtly literature generated lively contemporary debate.[15] This is expressed nowhere more clearly than in Gottfried von Strassburg's literary excursus in *Tristan* (4619–818).[16] Rudolf similarly inserts literary excurses in *Willehalm von Orlens* (2172–300) and *Alexander* (3063–294). However, where Gottfried is polemical and critical in his review of contemporary poets, Rudolf's listing of poets is presented as a canon of vernacular literature, reminiscent of the canon of Latin authors prescribed for study in the schools. The formative influence of the scholarly study of Latin literature on Rudolf's conception of vernacular composition is evident in his formal identification of *auctores* (canonical authors) whose writings serve as a model. Drawing on the conventional modesty *topos*, Rudolf positions himself amongst the literary successors to the illustrious Heinrich von Veldeke, Hartmann von Aue, Wolfram von Eschenbach and Gottfried von Strassburg. In Rudolf's narratives there are constant echoes of Hartmann's expression and, particularly in passages of heightened rhetoric, of Gottfried's. In the courtly romance of *Willehalm von Orlens* there are passages that read almost as a collage of expressions culled from Rudolf's reading of the poets listed in his excursus. However, this close calquing of a stylistic model is not so much to be understood as a lack of originality as an attempt to establish a vernacular literary tradition that might claim a rightful place alongside the Latin literary tradition.[17] Rudolf's distinctive synthesis of Latinate and vernacular literary conventions is also evident in the organization of his material in his later works. Here he divides the continuous narrative into book-like sections that are prefaced by prologues.[18] In these prologues he employs the prominent narratorial voice that is such a characteristic and fundamental feature of the composition of the classical courtly romance as shaped by Hartmann, Wolfram and Gottfried.[19]

Rudolf does not just set up Hartmann, Wolfram and Gottfried as *auctores* to be emulated, he also engages with issues that emerge from their narratives. This is most evident in *Willehalm von Orlens* which may be read as a corrective to Gottfried's *Tristan*.[20] In his prologue to Book 1 Rudolf immediately establishes a link between the two texts in his citing of Gottfried's concept of the "edele herze" (noble hearts). Many parallels may be drawn between the two pairs of lovers, but the social context of the love shared by Willehalm and Amelîe stands in marked contrast to the illicit, adulterous context of Tristan and Isolde's love. Although society places obstacles in the paths of Willehalm and Amelîe, these are overcome and the couple lives in social harmony, assuming the responsibilities that accompany their social rank. Whereas Gottfried is exclusive in his address to the "edele herze," Rudolf is inclusive in his presentation of a model of love accessible to all.

The world of the classical Arthurian romance is characterized by its lack of historical reference and the vagueness of its geography. The action of the courtly romance of *Willehalm von Orlens*, however, unfolds in familiar geographical locations — in Brabant and Hainaut, in Flanders and Normandy, in France and England, and more remotely, in Norway and Spain, and at the end of the romance Willehalm's son, Jofrit, is identified as the historical figure of Godfrey of Bouillon, the first prince of the Christian kingdom of Jerusalem, founded in 1099. In his earlier works too Rudolf incorporated a historical perspective. The framing story of the emperor Otte in *Der guote Gêrhart* is drawn from that popular historical tradition surrounding the figure of Emperor Otto that also provides a historical context in *Herzog Ernst* B (ca. 1200–1210) and in Konrad von Würzburg's *Heinrich von Kempten* (ca. 1265–70). In *Barlaam und Josaphat* Barlaam gives an account of Christian history. However, it is in *Alexander* and the *Weltchronik* that Rudolf's shift of interest from the *fabula* to the *historia* becomes most sharply defined.[21]

Rudolf reveals the influence of his clerical education in his interpretation of the life of Alexander. History was to be studied for its instructional value and so Rudolf declares that it is his intention to infuse his narrative with "guoter lêre" (good instruction, 12693). The premise that literature was to be interpreted for its moral-philosophical value underlies Rudolf's delineation of Alexander. He eliminated those negative aspects of Alexander's character he found in his sources in favor of the enhancement of his positive traits. Rudolf does not seek so much to present Alexander's individuality as his exemplarity. Rudolf's protagonists generally do not undergo the maturation process that is so typical of the Arthurian romance hero, but rather they demonstrate their exemplary nature in the face of adversity.

Rudolf's engagement with history and historiography culminated in his monumental *Weltchronik*. The writing of this universal history was a far cry from the production of those poets he included in his literary excurses. The vernacular *Kaiserchronik* ("Chronicle of Emperors," ca. 1126–47) may, in some measure, be regarded as a precursor of this work with its account of emperors from the foundation of the Roman Empire, through the translation of the Empire to Germany by Charlemagne, to the contemporary Holy Roman Empire and the reign of Konrad IV. However, in the thirteenth century the writing of history continued to be largely the domain of the monastery and the clergy, who wrote in Latin and in prose. Rudolf's *Weltchronik*, together with the *Sächsische Weltchronik* (ca. 1230–50) and the Thuringian *Christ-herre-Chronik* (ca. 1250–88), stands at the beginning of a tradition of chronicle writing that was to extend through to the fifteenth century.[22] Although incomplete, the *Weltchronik* became a very influential text, serving both as a rich repository and as a model for later chronicle writers such as Heinrich von München (ca. 1300–1350).

The numerous portraits of Rudolf as an author at his desk included in extant manuscripts from the later thirteenth to the fifteenth centuries of those works written under the patronage of the Hohenstaufen court are evidence of the continued regard in which this scholarly poet was held in the later Middle Ages.[23] Rudolf's reception in modern times was, until the late 1960s, less favorable. Ironically, the self-deprecation expressed in his literary excurses was given new meaning in the ubiquitous labeling of him as an "epigone." However, in the last thirty years or so Rudolf has emerged once more as the learned poet who had a very particular contribution to make to the evolution of German narrative literature both with regard to his adaptation of Latin literary traditions and in his response to the work of his predecessors in that vernacular tradition with which he identified.

Notes

[1] *Der guote Gêrhart*, ed. John A. Asher, 3rd. rev. ed. (Tübingen: Niemeyer, 1989); *Barlaam und Josaphat*, ed. Franz Pfeiffer (Leipzig: Göschen, 1843); *Alexander*, ed. Victor Junk, 2 vols. (Leipzig: Hiersemann, 1928 and 1929); *Willehalm von Orlens*, ed. Victor Junk (Berlin: Weidmann, 1905); *Weltchronik*, ed. Gustav Ehrismann (Berlin: Weidmann, 1915). Rudolf also makes mention of other works that are no longer extant. In the prologue to *Barlaam und Josaphat* he refers in a general manner to earlier works (verse 153) and in *Alexander* (verse 3289) he refers to a retelling he made of the legend of St. Eustace.

[2] See Sebastian Coxon, *The Presentation of Authorship in Medieval German Narrative Literature*, 1220–90 (Oxford: Clarendon Press, 2001), 37–94.

[3] Explicit self-reference: *Der guote Gêrhart* (verse 6827), *Barlaam und Josaphat* (11756), *Willehalm von Orlens* (2164). Acrostic embedded in the text: *Barlaam und Josaphat* (16151–57), *Alexander* (1–25), *Willehalm von Orlens* (1–7), *Weltchronik* (1–7).

[4] Hartmann von Aue, *Der arme Heinrich*, ed. Hermann Paul, rev. Kurt Gärtner (Tübingen: Niemeyer, 2001), v. 5.

[5] This continuator was responsible for approximately the final 3000 verses.

[6] Xenja v. Ertzdorff, *Rudolf von Ems: Untersuchungen zum höfischen Roman im 13. Jahrhundert* (Munich: Fink, 1967), 52. *Ministerialis* is the Latin legal term used to distinguish the "serving knight" from the free-born nobility.

[7] Klaus Speckenbach, "Die Ausbildung des Exempelromans bei Rudolf von Ems und Konrad von Würzburg," *Texttyp und Textproduktion in der Literatur des Mittelalters.* Tagungsband des 17. Anglo-deutschen Colloquiums, ed. by Elizabeth Andersen, Manfred Eikelmann and Anne Simon (Berlin: de Gruyter, 2005).

[8] On the expansion of the compass of the saint's legend see Ulrich Wyss, "Rudolfs von Ems 'Barlaam und Josaphat' zwischen Legende und Roman," *Probleme mittelhochdeutscher Erzählformen*, ed. Peter Ganz and Werner Schröder (Berlin: Erich Schmidt, 1972), 214–38.

[9] Joachim Bumke, *Geschichte der deutschen Literatur im hohen Mittelalter*, 4th ed. (Munich: DTV, 2000) 106.

[10] On the significance of Konrad von Winterstetten as Rudolf's patron see Helmut Brackert, *Rudolf von Ems: Dichtung und Geschichte* (Heidelberg: Winter, 1968), 244 and von Ertzdorff, 99.

[11] See von Ertzdorff, 150, 378; Brackert, 199; and 83–91.

[12] Rudolf evinces no interest in native Germanic heroic literature, as represented by the *Nibelungenlied*, although he does make a passing reference to Dietrich von Bern in his literary excursus in *Alexander* (20668).

[13] See Coxon, 38, 40, 46.

[14] See von Ertzdroff, 150, 378, and Brackert, 199.

[15] See *Dichter über Dichter in mittelhochdeutscher Literatur*, ed. Günther Schweikle (Tübingen: Niemeyer, 1970).

[16] Gottfried von Straßburg, *Tristan*, ed. Peter Ganz, Deutsche Klassiker des Mittelalters 4, 2 vols. (Wiesbaden: Brockhaus, 1978).

[17] Joachim Heinzle, *Geschichte der deutschen Literatur von den Anfängen bis zum Beginn der Neuzeit*, II/2 Wandlungen und Neuansätze im 13. Jahrhundert (Tübingen: Niemeyer, 1984), 26–27.

[18] Nigel F. Palmer, "Kapitel und Buch: Zu den Gliederungsprinzipien mittelalterlicher Bücher," *Frühmittelalterliche Studien* 23 (1989), 43–88; here 70–71.

[19] Coxon, 58, 59

[20] Walter Haug, *Literaturtheorie im deutschen Mittelalter. Von den Anfängen bis zum Ende des 13. Jahrhunderts* (Darmstadt: Wissenschaftliche Buchgesellschaft, 1985), 320–34. Haug also looks at *Der guote Gêrhart* (279–89) as a response to those premises on which success and good fortune rest in the Arthurian romance.

[21] Brackert, 234.

[22] The *Sächsische Weltchronik* is in Low German and, by way of exception, in prose.

[23] See Coxon, *The Presentation of Authorship in Medieval German Narrative Literature*, 59–62; 91–94.

Ulrich von Liechtenstein. A miniature from the Codex Manesse.

Ulrich von Liechtenstein

Ulrich Müller and Franz Viktor Spechtler

T HE STYRIAN NOBLEMAN Ulrich von Liechtenstein (ca. 1200/ 1210–January 26, 1275)[1] played an important role in the politics of his country, and at the same time he composed love songs, an autobiographical romance, and a treatise about love.[2] The words of his love songs, but unfortunately not the melodies, have been transmitted in the most prestigious collection of Middle High German Lyrics, the Codex Manesse.[3] Included is a painting (*Miniatur*) depicting Ulrich in the ambiguous role of the goddess Venus, a female "Knight of Love."[4] The songs are also transmitted in his romance *Frauendienst* (Service of the Ladies), which is preserved in a single manuscript.[5] The *Frauenbuch* (Book about Ladies), a treatise about love, is known only by means of a late, but important manuscript of the early sixteenth century, the *Ambraser Heldenbuch*, which was commissioned by King Maximilian I and written by Hans Ried, secretary at Bozen in South Tyrol from 1504 to 1516.

Ulrich was not only a famous German-speaking poet of the thirteenth century, but also one of the most important politicians of his time in the dukedom of Styria, which maintained contacts with medieval Austria and Carinthia. The sovereigns of Styria were the Babenberger Duke Leopold VI (1195–1230) and subsequently Friedrich II (1230–46), the last duke of the Babenberg dynasty, whose death in the battle on the Leitha River against Hungary is described by Ulrich at the end of his *Frauendienst*. The decades between the death of the last Hohenstaufen emperor Friedrich II in 1250 and the election of Rudolf von Habsburg in 1273 were difficult. In 1254 King Bela of Hungary became sovereign of Styria, succeeded in 1260 by Przemysl Ottokar II of Bohemia. At this time, the prominent noble families of the Orts, Pettaus, Stubenbergs, Wildons, and Liechtensteins grew ever stronger as they defended their traditional privileges. The energetic self-confidence of Ulrich may have its roots in the dynasty of the Traisen-Faistritz (who formed a medieval dukedom in what is today Lower Austria), an old free dynasty that was the ancestor of the Liechtensteins. Ulrich I himself was the son of Dietmar of Liechtenstein (documented 1164–1218) who lived at his castle Liechtenstein near Judenburg (Styria). His wife was Perchta von Weissenstein, and the couple had four children: Ulrich II, Otto II, Diemut, and Perchta (the wife of the poet Herrand von Wildon).

Ulrich's important political activities are clearly shown in ninety-four documents dated from November 17, 1227 to July 27, 1274. He is an issuer as well as a party to a contract, a guarantor, witness, sealer, arbitrator, and mediator by order of Friedrich II, duke of Styria, Austria, Carinthia, and Krain. He also held the important ceremonial positions of high steward and marshall at the court of this duke. In 1272 he is mentioned in documents as *Landrichter* (judge of the dukedom of Styria) under Przemysl Ottokar, and also as the duke's representative in the court of justice of Styria. Although Ulrich von Liechtenstein was an eminent politician of his time, the political activities documented for him play no role in his *Frauendienst*, and the tournaments and adventurous voyages of the romance cannot be proven by any historical documents to have actually taken place.

Besides being an important Styrian nobleman, Ulrich was the center of a literary circle in Styria that included the poets Herrand von Wildon (Ulrich's son-in-law), Rudolf von Stadeck, Heinrich von der Muore, and three poets now known only as von Obernburg, von Scharpfenberg, and von Suonegge. Also, the voluminous *Österreichische Reimchronik* (Austrian Rhyme Chronicle, ca. 1300) was written by a feudal servant of Otto II von Liechtenstein, son of Ulrich, Ottokar aus der Gaal. The colorful "*Heldenroman*" (heroic romance) *Biterolf und Dietleib* was conceived by an unknown author in the mid-thirteenth century, when Ulrich created his *Frauendienst*, which has come to be regarded as the first "Ich-Roman" (romance narrated from the first-person perspective) in the German language.

We do not know if Ulrich's poetry was widely heard or read, but his songs were popular enough to be included in the Codex Manesse, and his treatise about love was still read at the beginning of the sixteenth century. We learn from his texts that he was familiar with the tradition of Middle High German love poetry and romances, and perhaps even with literature in northern and southern France and northern Italy. He says several times in his *Frauendienst* that he performed his songs himself, but he also mentions that he sent them to his lady, and that other singers presented them to an audience.

Ulrich stresses that he could not read and had to wait for his secretary to recite a letter he had received from his lady (*Frauendienst*, stanzas 169–71), but this might be a poetic way of saying that as a noble layman he had no need of reading and writing on his own. Members of the Styrian and Austrian upper class were probably his audience, presumably ladies, but also some of his knightly colleagues. As with all poetry of that epoch, Ulrich's songs and texts were originally composed to be performed, but as time passed they increasingly served as literature for private reading. In the 1960s, academic interest in Ulrich's life and poetry intensified, and since then he has become one of the best-documented singers and writers of the German Middle Ages.[6]

Ulrich's *Frauendienst* was probably conceived in the forties and early fifties of the thirteenth century. It consists of 1850 stanzas, each consisting of four-stress rhymed couplets. Fifty-eight songs and poems about love, three rhyming discourses, and two letters in prose and five in verse, all dealing with the problems of love, have been inserted into the romance. This structure puts the *Frauendienst* in the tradition of a "prosimetrum," a combination of different verse and prose forms. The verses of Ulrich's tale are structured as stanzas, thus combining two patterns of medieval narrative works, that is, the stanzas of the heroic poetry and the four-stress verses of the courtly romances.

The story is told by a narrator called "Uolrich von Liechtenstein," the author himself, and treats noble ladies and the service of ladies, love and courtly adventures. In the first part (stanzas 8–1389; stanzas 1–7: prologue) Ulrich tells of his youthful first love for a noble lady. To prove his sincere love, the young Ulrich drinks the water in which the lady has washed her hands, endures a crucial surgery, takes part in a tournament in the city of Friesach, and cuts his wounded finger with a knife. He goes on an *áventiure* in the role of Venus, fights duels with many noble knights (whose names are painstakingly listed), and twice meets the "queen of his heart," but without experiencing success. The first time he meets her, as a young man, he is unable to speak a single word; the second time she treats him in a very unfriendly, even hostile way, and humiliates him. This lady eventually commits some unspecified transgression, and Ulrich renounces his service to her. In the second part the author speaks about his service to another noble lady: He composes many songs for her, and departs on a second *áventiure* (now disguised as King Arthur). Yet Ulrich's "vreude" (joy of love) is interrupted by the death of the Austrian duke Friedrich II of Babenberg, who is killed in one of his numerous battles and wars in 1246 (stanzas 1659–1677). From this point on, love and politics are in conflict. Ulrich — according to his romance — is imprisoned for more than a full year (1696–1731), but he nevertheless remains a loving servant of his lady. He conceives a discourse for noble knights and ladies, and at last his lady asks him to write a book which he dedicates to her and to all noble ladies (see stanza 1850, the final one of the work).

The *Frauendienst* is a courtly romance about love and knightly *áventiure* with the crucial difference that the protagonist is not a noble knight, perhaps of King Arthur's Round Table, but rather the author himself. It is Ulrich von Liechtenstein who tells the story of his career as a knight-errant serving noble ladies and enduring numerous tribulations on their behalf for the duration of his life. It is not known if any of these adventures actually occurred. Many if not all of them of them seem to be fictional rather than autobiographical, though the author Ulrich gives the impression to his audience that he is telling of his own life. A great many interpretations of the work have been put forward, but Ulrich's *Frauendienst* remains one of the most puzzling romances of the German Middle Ages. To the present day there is no scholarly consensus on how to understand Ulrich's *Frauendienst*, the first "Ich-Roman" in German.

It is clear that Ulrich does not tell about his everyday life, but rather presents the staged life of a courtly knight and servant of noble ladies. It is unclear to what end. Is the intention serious or comical? Should the audience be astonished, impressed, or amused? Different interpretations of the songs, and the romance of which they form an integral part, are possible: is this work a courtly romance, a lascivious novel, an erotic folly, a critique of courtly love, a political parable, a courtly clown's tale to make the audience laugh, a fictitious autobiography, or an autobiographical romance? Despite the elements that would appear to make it conventional or contrived, we would suggest that Ulrich's *Frauendienst* can and should be read as a sincere autobiographical romance (*"Ich"-Roman*), which reveals much of the author's unconscious or only semi-conscious fears, anxieties, and even obsessions.[7] The *Frauendienst* tells the story of a nobleman called Ulrich von Liechtenstein, who is uncertain about his identity as a man and aristocrat, and in which his very individual, largely hidden anxieties and wishes can often be recognized.

There is only one other work of medieval poetry that can be compared with Ulrich's *Frauendienst*: *La Vita Nuova* (ca. 1293) of Dante, which is likewise a prosimetrum. In both works the narrators (Ulrich, and presumably Dante) tell their love stories in a highly stylized manner, combining narration, poems and — especially in the case of Dante — explications and interpretations of these texts. Both authors are supposed to have been influenced by the Languedoc genres of troubadour *vidas* and *razos*, that is, biographies (lat. *vita*) and explications (lat. *ratio*) of troubadours that have been transmitted in several manuscripts that may go back to the troubadours themselves, but on the other hand may be interpretations of other, later singers.

Ulrich's love songs for his ladies are incorporated into the *Frauendienst*, and all of them have a special position in his career. Most of these songs are dedicated to the ladies of his first and second service.[8] Ulrich also encloses seven love letters and three poetical essays about the problems of love and love-sickness. The fifty-eight songs clearly show how well Ulrich was informed about the love lyrics of the late twelfth and early thirteenth century in German-speaking areas, and he even quotes a well-known song of Walther von der Vogelweide.[9] It should be underscored that Ulrich's love poems are of high quality, and their topics correspond broadly with the tradition of *Minnesangs Frühling*, Walther von der Vogelweide, and the love poets of the early thirteenth century.[10]

Two stanzas from a longer song of five stanzas illustrate the style and quality of Ulrich's poetry:

Ditz ist ein rei

I Sumervar ist nur gar
heide, velt, anger, walt
hie und da, wiz, rot, bla,
gel, brun, grüene, wol gestalt.
wunneclich, vreuden rich
ist gar, swaz die erde treit.
saelic man, swer so chan
dienen, daz sin arbeit
in liebe geit. . . .
V Minne solt wirt geholt
volleclich, da ein man
und ein wip umb ir lip
lazent vier arme gan.
decke bloz, freude groz
wirt da beidenthalben chunt —
ob da niht mer geschiht?
chleinvelhitzeroter munt
wirt minnen wunt —
dar nach gesunt.

[This is a round-dance.

The signs of spring can be found / in meadows, fields, plains and woods, / here and there: they are white, red, blue, yellow, brown, and green. / Everything on earth / is full of lust and joy. He is a blessed one / who is able receive love / by serving . . .

The rewards of love are earned, / when a man and a woman / embrace with four hands. / Blankets away — great joy for both of them. Might there happen something more? / Frivolous and soft and burning and red lips are first wounded by love, / afterwards comforted.[11]]

Ulrich's final work was his *Frauenbuch*, a dialogue between a lady and a knight, which he wrote thirty-five years after he was made a knight, which would have been around 1257. The content and significance of this lesser-known book is much less controversial than that of the *Frauendienst*: a lady and a knight discuss the problems of relations between men and women, and each holds the other responsible for deteriorating values in matters of love. In the end, the narrator, "von Liechtenstein her Uolrich," concludes the discussion in favor of the lady. The significance of this work rests in the author's call for a conservative solution to social problems in order to stem the decline of courtly ethics.

Ulrich's story and songs have enjoyed a modest artistic reception in the modern period. Gerhart Hauptmann wrote a comedy entitled *Ulrich von Lichtenstein*, which was published in 1939 but never became a success on the stage. Hugo von Hofmannsthal used one of Ulrich's poems in his play *Jedermann* (Everyman, 1911), which has continued to be produced in German-speaking countries to the present time, particularly at the Salzburg Festival since 1920. Everyman's friend, the "Lustige Gesell" (The humorous companion) sings this song at the last banquet of the protagonist, shortly before Death appears. In 1981 Ulrich had a very special revival which might have pleased the medieval author: the *Frauendienst* appeared as a comic book (1981), designed by the young Viennese Martin Neubaur. A successful new melody for Ulrich's song mentioned above was composed by the Ensemble "Dulamans Vröudenton" (CD 1990), who also recorded the reconstructed melody (CD 1997). The first complete modern German translation of the *Frauendienst* by Spechtler in 2000 now makes this interesting romance accessible to German-speaking readers; an English translation by J. W. Thomas had been published in 1969.[12] Lately, Ulrich's name, if not his works, have reached a popular audience as the incognito identity of the hero of the Hollywood film *A Knight's Tale* (2001).

Notes

[1] The New High German spelling of the name is Liechtenstein, or sometimes Lichtenstein.

[2] Standard editions of the discussed works are *Ulrich von Liechtenstein, Frauendienst,* ed. Reinhold Bechstein, 2 vols. (Leipzig: Brockhaus, 1888); *Ulrich von Liechtenstein,* ed. Karl Lachmann, mit Anmerkungen von Theodor von Karajan. (Berlin: G. E. Reimer, 1841; reprint Hildesheim-New York: Olms, 1974); *Ulrich von Liechtenstein, Frauendienst,* ed. Franz Viktor Spechtler (Göppingen: Kümmerle, 1987; 2nd ed. 2003); *Ulrich von Liechtenstein, Frauenbuch,* ed. Franz Viktor Spechtler (Göppingen: Kümmerle, 1989; 2nd ed. 1993).

[3] *The Große Heidelberger Liederhandschrift: University Library, Heidelberg, cpg 848.*

[4] See *Ulrich von Liechtenstein, "Frauendienst" ("Jugendgeschichte"): Abbildungen aus dem Münchner Cod. germ. 44 und der Großen Heidelberger Liederhandschrift,* ed. Ursula Peters (Göppingen: Kümmerle, 1973).

[5] Bayerische Staatsbibliothek Munich, cgm 44: fourteenth century.

[6] There are new editions of the *Frauendienst* (Göppingen: Kümmerle, 1987; 2nd ed. 2003) and *Frauenbuch* (Göppingen: Kümmerle, 1989; 2nd ed. 1993) by Franz Viktor Spechtler, and a facsimile of the *Frauendienst* by Ursula Peters (Göppingen: Kümmerle, 1973). A comprehensive glossary for Ulrich's works is provided by Klaus M. Schmidt (Munich: Kraus, 1980), and a complete bibliography covering scholarship until the late 1990s by Schmidt and Barbara Meier (in Franz Viktor Spechtler and Barbara Maier, eds., *Ich — Ulrich von Liechtenstein: Literatur und Politik im Mittelalter* [Klagenfurt: Wieser, 1999]: 495–509; the latter volume

contains recent interpretation from the proceedings of a Liechtenstein conference at Friesach (an important Austrian town for Ulrich). To analyze Ulrich's texts see the University of Salzburg's online database MHDBDB (Mittelhochdeutsche Begriffsdatenbank; http://mhdbdb.sbg.ac.at), which was conceived by Klaus M. Schmidt of Bowling Green State University, Ohio.

[7] See Ulrich Müller, "Männerphantasien eines mittelalterlichen Herren: Ulrich von Lichtenstein und sein *Frauendienst,*" in *Variationen der Liebe: Historische Psychologie der Geschlechterbeziehung,* ed. Thomas Kornbichler, Wolfgang Maaz. Tübingen: edition diskord, 1995, 27–50; and Ulrich Müller, "Ulrich von Liechtenstein und seine Männerphantasien: Mittelalterliche Literatur und moderne Psychologie," in Spechtler and Maier, ed., *Ich — Ulrich von Liechtenstein: Literatur und Politik im Mittelalter,* 297–317.

[8] It might be possible to reconstruct the melody of one song (Anthonius H. Touber, "Ulrichs von Liechtenstein unbekannte Melodie," *Amsterdamer Beiträge zur Älteren Germanistik* 26 (1987): 107–18; CD by Dulamans Vröudenton, *Minnesänger in Österreich,* 1997).

[9] Walther von der Vogelweide, song 56, 14, "Ir sült sprechen willechomen": stanza 776/777.

[10] Many of Ulrich's songs have titles, for example "tanzwise," "reie," "frouwentanz," "tagewise" See Jürgen Kühnel, "Zu den Tageliedern Ulrichs von Liechtenstein," *Jahrbuch der Oswald von Wolkenstein-Gesellschaft* 1 (1980/81): 99–138; see also Hubert Heinen, "Ulrich's von Liechtenstein Sense of Genres," in *Genres in Medieval German Literature,* ed. Hubert Heinen and Ingeborg Henderson (Göppingen: Kümmerle, 1986), 16–29.

[11] Song 29; recorded by Dulamans Vröudenton 1990, with a new modern melody. Translation is that of the authors.

[12] See Franz Viktor Spechtler, *Ulrich von Liechtenstein, Frauendienst: Aus dem Mittelhochdeutschen ins Neuhochdeutsche übertragen* (Klagenfurt/Celovec: Wieser, 2000) and J. Wesley Thomas, *Ulrich von Liechtenstein's Service of Ladies* (Chapel Hill: U of North Carolina P, 1969); there is also a recent modern German translation of the *Frauenbuch* by Christopher Young: *Ulrich von Liechtenstein: Das Frauenbuch* (Stuttgart: Reclam, 2003).

Konrad von Würzburg. A miniature from the Codex Manesse (383r).

Konrad von Würzburg

Rüdiger Brandt

UNTIL THE FIFTEENTH CENTURY, Konrad was not only the most productive medieval German author, but he also represented the broadest spectrum of genres.[1] Though this is quite unusual for his time, Konrad worked in all three of the major vernacular lyric genres simultaneously, composing a secular and a religious *Leich* (lay; a long lyrical form not divided into strophes), twenty-three love songs, and more than fifty moral-didactic poems (*Sangsprüche*). Beyond this, he wrote three courtly romances, *Partonopier und Meliur* (based on a French source), *Der Trojanerkrieg* (The Trojan War, based on French and Latin sources[2]), and *Engelhard* with its lengthy strophic prologue (with no known source, but based on the Latin story of friendship between Amicus and Amelius). The latter work, because of its brevity (only 6504 verses), can perhaps be regarded as an experiment with the usually longer epic form. The courtly *legenda* is represented by *Silvester*, *Alexius*, and *Pantaleon*, each of which manifests a different type of saint. Shorter secular verse narratives are *Der Schwanritter* (The Swan Knight, from the Lohengrin material), *Das Turnier von Nantes* (The Tournament of Nantes; perhaps based on the *Clipearius Teutonicorum* of Konrad von Mure [d. 1281]), *Das Herzmäre* (Tale of the Heart), *Heinrich von Kempten*, and *Der Welt Lohn* (Reward of the World). The most richly transmitted work of Konrad, *Die Goldene Schmiede* (The Golden Smithy, in about 2000 rhymed couplets), in which his poetic art is most elaborately and ornately developed, was especially important in shaping the perception of Konrad in the Middle Ages. Both secular and religious genres are strongly represented in Konrad's work, and patrons for the works in these two domains overlap to some degree: *Der Trojanerkrieg* was composed for a member of the Basel cathedral chapter; the *legenda Alexius* and *Pantaleon* for a patrician in Basel. The order in which many of the works were composed cannot be known. References in the works to patrons suggest the order *Partonopier*, *Silvester*, *Heinrich von Kempten*, *Alexius*, *Pantaleon*, and *Trojanerkrieg*. Nothing beyond this can be dated with any certainty.[3]

This very large and varied collection of works indicates Konrad's success with his audiences, and he remained a famous and esteemed poet long after his own lifetime. Many of his texts were transmitted widely and over a long period of time,[4] and with the exception of *Heinrich von Kempten*, and the *Silvester* and the *Pantaleon legenda*, scholars have plausibly shown that all of his works influenced later authors. To be sure, there was no single image of Konrad in the Middle Ages, but rather different conceptions of him that were shaped above all by these different genres in which he worked, and also sometimes by chance. In two manuscripts, the *Herzmäre* is attributed to Gottfried von Strassburg, because Konrad's praise of Gottfried in the prologue was misunderstood. The plagiarism of Konrad's name and the attribution to him of the verse story *Die halbe Birne* (The Half Pear; a story from the fourteenth and fifteenth century about a knight who plays a fool in order to come in contact with a princess) are indicative of familiarity with Konrad's short epic form as represented by *Heinrich von Kempten* and *Herzmäre*. Melodies of his *Sangsprüche* were transmitted under his name by the meistersingers until the end of the seventeenth century. Beyond this, there seems to have been a local tradition in Würzburg involving Konrad: Michael de Leone (d. 1355), chancellor of the Neumünster seminary, collected religious, worldly, and technical literature (*Fachliteratur*) in a manuscript produced between 1348 and 1353. The manuscript contains three works of Konrad, of which *Die Klage der Kunst* and *Das Turnier von Nantes* are transmitted only here, and in which *Die Goldene Schmiede* manifests a scribal addition at the end that states Konrad's name and that he was buried in Freiburg im Breisgau. Besides this, there are words of praise for Konrad by various later medieval authors, which however reveal more about the situations of those authors themselves than about Konrad. Lupold von Hornburg (mid-fourteenth century), for example, praises Konrad as the best among a group of poets that also includes Neidhart and Walther von der Vogelweide, with regard to *kunst* — which in this specific case is best translated as "craftsmanship."

The almost exclusively positive, and sometime even enthusiastic view of Konrad in the Middle Ages — the north German poet Hermann Damen (d. after 1310) praised him as one of the best German poets! — was not shared by modern scholars until quite recently. Schooled in the authors of the so-called "classical" period of Hartmann von Aue, Wolfram von Eschenbach, and Gottfried von Strassburg, many generations of Germanists wanted to see in Konrad only an imitator, a very able craftsman to be sure, but a poet who seemed to lack originality and individual style. Only since the 1970s have scholars begun to appreciate the unique characteristics of Konrad's works, first with a view to their sociological aspects,[5] and to become fascinated with their singular juxtaposition of traditional and innovative elements.[6] In the meantime Konrad has become one of the most intensively researched medieval German authors. Between 1987 and 1996, more was published about him than from 1847 to 1966. Next to more traditional scholarly topics such as transmission, textual criticism, and investigations of verifiable and suspected patrons are studies of peculiarities in the characterization of persons,[7] sensualistic and psychological tendencies in the depiction of extreme situations (the juvenile love of *Partonopier;* the lady who is forced by her husband to eat the heart of her lover in *Herzmaere*), realistic tendencies (the depiction of leprosy in *Engelhard* compared with that of Hartmann von Aue in *Der arme Heinrich*), specific aesthetic aspects, the competition between affected and rational modes of depiction,[8] attempts to establish a new position of the artist in society,[9] and much more. Correspondingly, the spectrum of methodological approaches has broadened. In Konrad research, existential philosophy,[10] structuralism,[11] deconstruction,[12] ritual theory,[13] and media history and theory[14] have all been represented.

Konrad's sponsors and patrons belonged to the clerical and secular elites. Whether his primary office was that of poet is contested, but his literary output clearly brought him affluence and high regard in a way that suggests he was an author who was able to make a living from his works.[15] Support for this view of Konrad as a career poet can be found in the Dominican chronicle mentioned below; in the connection between references to sponsors and the large scope of Konrad's collected works, which suggests long-term working relationships; in the corresponding emphasis of the theme of *milte* (largesse) in the *Sangsprüche* and in the *Klage der Kunst*; and in a justification of panegyrics in *Spruch* 32,241. Commissions meant dependence, but success creates flexibility, which Konrad used to develop himself more as an artist than was generally possible for medieval poets dependent on patronage.

A medieval author bases his poetry on authoritative sources, for the branch of rhetoric that concerns finding a story or topic — *inventio* — does not allow an author to be original. The author also subordinates himself to the rules of a métier: art, science, and craftsmanship all fall together in the term *ars*, and the Middle High German word *kunst* has a similarly broad spectrum of meaning. Consequently, art — like a craft or science — is learnable, something that makes the idea of "artistic genius" difficult if not impossible in the Middle Ages. However, in both epic and lyric poetry, Konrad clearly tests the artistic limits of his time. In the *Trojanerkrieg*, he stresses in a traditional way that he has used sources, but then at the same time he defies every *humilitas* topos by claiming, "ich will ein maere tihten, / das allen maeren ist ein her" (I will tell a story that bests them all). In the love songs he works with conventions, which must have made their composition easier and draws attention to the importance of craftsmanship, but he also demonstrated within the conventions a great richness of variation.[16] Konrad parts ways with traditional *Minnesang* in the way in which he almost always drops the role of the singer singing of his own feelings, and instead adopts the role of the more or less coolly critical observer.[17] Konrad here shows himself to be an especially capable artist of *language* and *form*. The songs have almost manneristic tendencies. Mannerism is generally not considered a stylistic tendency as such in medieval theories of art. The general rule is the correspondence of form and content, and an author who can break this rule manifests a high degree of self-consciousness. With good reason Konrad has been considered an "author between commission and autonomy."[18]

Considering that he is a thirteenth-century author, there are a relatively large number of historical references to Konrad, though some are contradictory.[19] A Dominican chronicle in Alsace mentions his year of death as 1287 and calls Konrad a *vagus* (a wandering poet for hire); the names of patrons of a number of his works offer the possibility of establishing a relative chronology. However, there is also a group of texts that contain no reference at all to a patron: the lyrics (with the exception of the two *Sangsprüche* mentioned below), and also *Das Herzmäre, Der Welt Lohn, Die Klage der Kunst, Die Goldene Schmiede, Das Turnier von Nantes, Der Schwanritter* and *Engelhard*. Konrad's origin in Würzburg is based only on self-references in his works and references to him by other medieval poets, and dialect features are consistent with such an origin. However, the extant evidence — the place of origin of most of his patrons and the deed of his house — place Konrad only in Basel. The sponsor of *Heinrich von Kempten*, Bertold von Tiersburg, possibly lived in Strasbourg. Whether Konrad also lived there, or worked for Bertold while living in Basel, is not known. Based on genealogical evidence gleaned from *Engelhard, Schwanritter*, and *Turnier von Nantes*, plausible arguments have been made that Konrad composed these works in the lower Rhein region before his time in Basel began.[20]

It is clear that Konrad was highly educated. He mastered Latin and (although perhaps somewhat later) French. He knew the vernacular literature of his time and possessed knowledge in the areas of theology, law,[21] and heraldry (which is especially evident in the *Turnier von Nantes*, a short narrative about a chivalric tournament, in which the heraldic descriptions possibly have political implications). Little is known about his social status. He says of himself in *Spruch* 32, 189 that he was not noble. Because he was married, he could not have been a cleric, though it is possible he retired to a monastery after the death of his wife and daughter.[22] Even if he spent a first phase of activity on the lower Rhine, he would have been active in Basel from 1258 at the latest. Since his house was in the episcopal district,[23] his education has been associated with some kind of activity at the episcopal court, which stands at odds with the posture, manifested in the *Sangsprüche*, of a man who must request *Lohn*, or a reward for his artistic production (assuming this posture is not merely a playful pose). Since the *Sprüche*, at least in large part, were composed in Basel, it seems both legitimate and sensible to dwell briefly on Basel as the socio-historical setting of Konrad's works.

Thirteenth-century Basel, a city with approximately 8,000 inhabitants, was characterized both by a rich literary life and intense political infighting. Urban existence in the thirteenth century did not yet have much to do with modern notions of a middle class. The different social groups besides nobility and clergy were concerned above all with demarcating themselves from each other. In Konrad's time, Basel was dominated by traditional elites, though power relations were tenuous. Nobles in the city were opposed to nobles in the countryside and to the bishop as lord of the city. The advocates of a greater role in city government for craftsmen also had their opponents. In the cultural domain these oppositions seem to some degree to have been suspended. Konrad received literary patronage from both the pro-episcopal leader Peter Schaler (for *Partonopier*) and also from Johannes Arguel (for the *Pantaleon legenda*), although the two were political opponents.[24] In the second half of the thirteenth century, the urban nobility still quite obviously shared the literary interests of the courtly nobility (*Partonopier* counts as the earliest example of a courtly epic composed for an urban audience), though the function of commissioned poetry was not exhausted in noble or clerical representation. In some of Konrad's works, more specific, special interests suggest themselves: *Partonopier* — with its story of love, separation, and reunion between a young nobleman and a fairy-like daughter of an emperor, similar to the romances of love and adventure — possibly suggests, with its occasional criticism of non-noble social climbers, the interests of Peter Schaler.[25] *Heinrich von Kempten*, composed for a patron in Strasbourg, dwells on the positive results of solidarity among nobility vis-à-vis other city-dwellers, which has led to the thesis that this work refers to actual events in Strasbourg.[26] In this story, a *ministerialis* becomes involved in a conflict with an emperor and frees himself by forcing an act of imperial clemency: at the end he comes across the emperor again during a military campaign and saves him from a trap set by the inhabitants of an Italian city. On the surface, *Der Welt Lohn* propagates a generic religious dualism: while reading stories about *minne* (love), a knight beholds a beautiful woman, who reveals herself as the one whom he has always served — Dame World. Then she turns around and reveals her maggot-infested back, after which the knight, deeply shaken, leaves his family for the Holy Land as a crusader. Yet this text might also be associated with propagandistic literature distributed on the upper-Rhine for the crusade of 1267.[27] Even the panegyric of Mary in *Die Goldene Schmiede*, by mentioning the *siticus* (parakeet) among its many Marian symbols, possibly reveals a political position: the *siticus* was the emblem of the pro-episcopal party, the "Psitticher," the leader of which was Peter Schaler. Externally Basel was involved in numerous conflicts in the thirteenth century, and reflections of these can also perhaps be found in Konrad's works. Against the backdrop of a feud between the bishop of

Basel and Rudolf von Habsburg, the *Silvester* presents the example of a functioning collaboration of spiritual and worldly power, and verses 40, 208ff. of the *Trojanerkrieg* warn explicitly of the danger of discord. Of course these passages cannot be construed as specific references to the feud, but contemporaries might have made such an association.

Above all, Konrad's works are, like all works of poetry, not only documents of the time and place in which they were produced, but also artistic creations that stand in literary-historical traditions. These traditions are repositories of genres, forms, materials, and techniques with which authors engage themselves in productive and receptive ways. In the thirteenth century, there was not, to be sure, a single literature encompassing all German-speaking regions, but rather only regional and local literary centers. Knowledge of the literary products of these centers was spread, in the case of religious literature, by means of the church, in the case of worldly literature by means of social contacts among nobles. The reception of worldly literature was still largely dependent on oral performance, but the capacity of written texts to store and interconnect a greater amount of content was being increasingly used. Konrad's *Trojanerkrieg* (the first 40,000 verses of which constitute only the prelude!), mainly based on Benoît de Sainte-Maure's *Roman de Troie* (ca. 1160), is a prominent example. Konrad himself speaks of his romance as a "sea," that has been nourished from innumerable sources. Written literature had nearly replaced the older oral literature among the nobility: in *Spruch* 32,286, Konrad speaks condescendingly of the oral presentation of heroic poetry. Obtaining literacy was still attached to clerical institutions of education, which had linguistic and aesthetic consequences: knowledge of Latin was acquired in a clerical education, and every author was given a store of exemplary, rhetorical adornments. German authors vary in the degree of their use of these, and Konrad belongs to those who are more strongly rhetorical. He is among the first "Blümern" (flowerers) in German literature and his flowery style is later praised by Heinrich von Meißen (known as "Frauenlob," d. after 1313). Hugo von Trimberg also praises Konrad in the *Renner* (1300), but suggests at the same time that such well-polished texts are really too much for a non-cleric. Nevertheless, Konrad does not limit himself in the application of his knowledge, and he makes it clear to his audiences in his works that that he is a learned poet. This is typical of the late Middle Ages, as is the greater emphasis on the aspect of craftsmanship in poetry and the greater interest in history (as expressed above all in *Trojanerkrieg*), or in the self-stylization of authors as "specialists for ethics" (see the prologue of *Engelhard* or the *Sprüche* 32, 136, 181, 196). The great model for his artistry in language (including the highly artificial structure of his verse couplets and also the learned and didactic impetus) is Gottfried von Strassburg, whom Konrad invokes in the prologue of his *Herzmære* when he says that stories about true love have a didactic effect:

> diu rede ist âne lougen:
> er minnet iemer deste baz
> swer von minnen etewaz
> hœret singen oder lesen.
> dar umbe wil ich flîzec wesen
> daz ich diz schœne mære
> mit rede alsô bewære
> daz man dar ane kiesen müge
> ein bilde daz der minne tüge,
> diu lûter unde reine
> sol sîn vor allem meine. (18–28)

[It is completely true that everybody understands *minne* better when they have heard something about it in a song or a book. For this reason I will exert myself to tell this beautiful story so truthfully that one will be able to regard it as an exemplary model in the service of love, which should be free of any defect.][28]

There is as yet little research on the degree to which Konrad was influenced by Middle Latin literature. It could be that his education not only made Latin sources available to him, but also brought him to experiment with genres or at least to translate Latin genre traditions into German literature. Particularly the genre of *legenda* in the German vernacular finds in him one of its first noteworthy representatives. Konrad's *Silvester* depicts the life of the first pope of the Roman Empire, his *Alexius* the life of an ascetic, and his *Pantaleon* the life of a holy martyr, and all three of these *legenda* draw on Latin sources. *Der Welt Lohn* is both traditional *contemptus mundi* literature and also allegory; the *Klage der Kunst* — which depicts a trial involving the Twelve Virtues in which Largesse is being accused by Art of rewarding poets who are not deserving — connects standard themes of the *Sangsprüche* (e.g. the praise of generous lords and the stinging criticism of stingy ones) with allegory, Konrad stands in the formal tradition of Middle Latin literature with his religious lay, which is structured like a sequence. *Die Goldene Schmiede* — an extended series of images and religious concepts praising the Virgin and her role in salvation history — represents both linguistically and with regard to its length (about two-thousand rhymed couplets) a quite singular example of Marian panegyric. The Latin source of *Engelhard* has clearly influenced not only its content, but also its form. This work about the exemplary Engelhard, whose loyalty is tested when he has to sacrifice his two children in order to effect the blood cure of his friend Dietrich, who has been stricken by leprosy, is designed to underscore the value of friendship in the manner of the Latin genre of the exemplum, and its relative brevity, which led to the early scholarly verdict that this work was a failed hybrid between a romance and a short story, actually goes back to the source. The familiarity with Middle Latin narrative literature might also have been the reason why Konrad, with his *Heinrich von Kempten* and *Herzmäre* (the tale of an absolute love in which a lady expires after consuming the heart of her dead lover that is served to her by her jealous husband), numbers among the earliest representatives of the so-called *Märe* (a short epic sub-genre recognized by scholars in the late 1970s).[29] Before Konrad, this genre was already prevalent in Middle Latin literature, but in German literature it was represented only by a few anonymous works and some texts by Der Stricker, who possessed theological learning and was therefore also certainly familiar with Middle Latin literature.[30] Konrad's learnedness is not merely pretense, and that it was recognized nearly as much as his art seems to be indicated by the fact that references to him nearly always call him *meister*. This title seems to have amounted to a license to diverge from traditions. In the prologues of *Trojanerkrieg* and *Partonopier*, he leaves behind the obligatory imbedding of his art in its social usefulness. If no one listens to him, he says, he will do as the nightingale — and sing only for himself (see also *Spruch* 32, 30). This is a surprisingly modern anticipation of the idea of *l'art pour l'art*. It is important to remember that Konrad, in view of his great success with his audiences, was never forced to make good on this threat. But it is nevertheless decisive that he was capable of articulating such an idea in the thirteenth century.

— Translated by Will Hasty

Notes

[1] Editions of Konrad's works include: *Der trojanische Krieg von Konrad von Würzburg*, ed. Adelbert von Keller (Amsterdam: Rodopi, 1965); *Kleinere Dichtungen I. Der Welt Lohn. Herzmære. Heinrich von Kempten*, ed. Edward Schröder, 10th ed. (Zurich: Weidmann, 1970); *Heinrich von Kempten, Der Welt Lohn, Das Herzmaere*, trans. Heinz Rölleke (Stuttgart: Reclam, 1968), which is based on Schröder's edition; Michael Bernhard Hinner, "Konrad von Würzburg's "maere": A Translation and Analysis" (Diss. State Univ. of New York at Stony Brook, 1985), which includes the three texts from Schröder's edition and also English translations of the prologues of *Partonopier* and *Trojanerkrieg*, the *Klage der Kunst*, the *Schwanritter*, the *Turnier von Nantes*, and *Die halbe Birne*; *Kleinere Dichtungen II: Der Schwanritter. Das Turnier von Nantes*, ed. Edward Schröder, 5th ed. (Zurich: Weidmann, 1974); *Kleinere Dichtungen III: Die Klage der Kunst. Leiche, Lieder, Sprüche*, ed. Edward Schröder, 4th ed. (Zurich: Weidmann, 1970); *Die Legenden, I: Silvester*, ed. Paul Gereke (Halle: Niemeyer, 1925); *Die Legenden, II: Alexius*, ed. Paul Gereke (Halle: Niemeyer, 1926); *Die Legenden, III: Pantaleon*, ed. Winfried Woesler, 2nd ed. (Tübingen: Niemeyer, 1974); *Engelhard*, ed. Ingo Reiffenstein, 3rd rev. ed. (Tübingen: Niemeyer, 1982); Jutta Breckling, "'Engelhard' by Konrad von Würzburg. A Translation and Evaluation" (Diss.

State Univ. of New York at Stony Brook, 1988); *Konrads von Würzburg Partonopier und Meliur*, ed. Karl Bartsch (Berlin: de Gruyter, 1970); *Die Goldene Schmiede des Konrad von Würzburg*, ed. Edward Schröder, 2nd ed. (Göttingen: Vandenhoeck & Ruprecht, 1969). English translations of Konrad's verses are the editor's.

[2] Seminal are the studies of Elisabeth Lienert, *Geschichte und Erzählen: Studien zu Konrads von Würzburg "Trojanerkrieg"* (Wiesbaden: Reichert, 1996), 325.

[3] Peter Schaler for *Partonopier* (1258), Liutold von Roeteln for *Silvester* (1260), Berthold von Tiersberg for *Heinrich von Kempten* (1261), Heinrich Isenlin and Johannes von Bermeswil for *Alexius* (1265/1273), Johannes von Arguel for *Pantaleon* (1277), Dietrich an dem Orte for *Trojanerkrieg* (1281), Konrad or Ludwig von Lichtenberg for *Spruch* 32, 261 (1269). Each year in parenthesis is a terminus *ad* or *post quem* for dating the respective work. Besides this, there is *Spruch* 32, 216 for King Ottokar of Bohemia, the content of which indicates it was composed either in 1276 or 1278.

[4] A tabular overview is offered by Rüdiger Brandt, *Konrad von Würzburg. Kleinere epische Werke* (Berlin: Schmidt, 2000), 65.

[5] Inge Leipold, *Die Auftraggeber und Gönner Konrads von Würzburg: Versuch einer Theorie der "Literatur als soziales Handeln"* (Göppingen: Kümmerle, 1976).

[6] See, for example, Peter Oettli, *Tradition and Creativity: The Engelhard of Konrad von Würzburg. Its Structure and Sources* (Frankfurt am Main: Lang, 1986).

[7] Cyril W. Edwards, "Aims and Methods of Characterization in the Secular Epics of Konrad von Würzburg. With Special Reference to 'Engelhard' and 'Partonopier und Meliur'" (Diss. Oxford University, 1975).

[8] Susanne Rikl, *Erzählen im Kontext von Affekt und Ratio: Studien zu Konrads von Würzburg "Partonopier und Meliur"* (Frankfurt am Main: Lang, 1996).

[9] Trude Ehlert, "Zu Konrads von Würzburg Auffassung vom Wert der Kunst und von der Rolle des Künstlers," in *Jahrbuch der Oswald von Wolkenstein-Gesellschaft* 5 (1988/89): 79–94; Werner Schröder, "Zur Kunstanschauung Gottfrieds von Straßburg und Konrads von Würzburg nach dem Zeugnis ihrer Prologe," in Schröder, *Über Gottfried von Straßburg, Kleinere Schriften*, vol. 4. (Stuttgart: Hirzel, 1994): 104–77.

[10] Timothy R. Jackson, "Abraham and Engelhard: Immoral Means and Moral Ends," in *Connections: Essays in Honour of Eda Sagarra on the Occasion of Her 60th Birthday*, ed. Peter Skrine, Rosemary E. Wallbank-Turner, and Jonathan West (Stuttgart: Akademischer Verlag Heinz, 1993), 117–26.

[11] On *Partonopier* see Ralf Simon, *Einführung in die strukturalistische Poetik des mittelalterlichen Romans: Analysen zu deutschen Romanen der matière de Bretagne* (Würzburg: Königshausen & Neumann, 1990).

[12] Helmut Brall, "Geraufter Bart und nackter Retter. Verletzungen und Heilungen des Autoritätsprinzips in Konrads von Würzburg *Heinrich von Kempten*," in *Festschrift für Herbert Kolb*, ed. Klaus Matzel and Hans-Gert Roloff (Frankfurt am Main: Lang, 1989): 31–52; Dagmar Dahnke-Holtmann, "Die dunkle Seite des Spiegels. Das Verneinen in der *Goldenen Schmiede* Konrads von Würzburg," in *Jahrbuch der Oswald von Wolkenstein-Gesellschaft* 5 (1988/89): 157–68.

[13] Maria Dobozy, "Der Alte und der Neue Bund in Konrads von Würzburg *Heinrich von Kempen*," in *Zeitschrift für deutsche Philologie* 107 (1988): 386–400.

[14] Peter Strohschneider, "Ursprünge. Körper, Gewalt und Schrift im *Schwanritter* Konrads von Würzburg," in *Gespräche — Boten — Briefe. Körpergedächtnis und Schriftgedächtnis im Mittelalter*, ed. Horst Wenzel (Berlin: Schmidt 1997): 127–53.

[15] Konrad possessed a house in a prominent neighborhood, and according to an anniversary book he was interred together with his wife Berchta and his daughters Gerina and Agnesa in a chapel of the Basel minster; see Rüdiger Brandt, *Konrad von Würzburg* (Darmstadt: Wissenschaftliche Buchgesellschaft, 1987), 63–65.

[16] Erika Essen, *Die Lyrik Konrads von Würzburg* (Marburg: Bauer, 1938); Manfred Brauneck, "Die Lieder Konrads von Würzburg" (Diss. University of Munich, 1965).

[17] Thomas Cramer, "Minnesang in der Stadt. Überlegungen zur Lyrik Konrads von Würzburg," in *Literatur, Publikum, historischer Kontext*, ed. Gert Kaiser (Frankfurt am Main: Lang, 1977), 91–108; here 93.

[18] The phrase is taken from the subtitle of Hartmut Kokott's monograph, *Konrad von Würzburg: Ein Autor zwischen Auftrag und Autonomie* (Stuttgart: Hirzel, 1989).

[19] For details see Rüdiger Brandt, *Konrad* (1987), 63–80 and Brandt, "Literatur zu Konrad von Würzburg 1987–1996," in *Archiv für das Studium der neueren Sprachen und Literaturen* 236 (1999): 347–49.

[20] Horst Brunner, "Genealogische Phantasien. Zu Konrads von Würzburg *Schwanritter* und *Engelhard*," *Zeitschrift für deutsches Altertum und deutsche Literatur* 110 (1981): 274–99; Horst Brunner, "*Das Turnier von Nantes*. Konrad von Würzburg, Richard von Cornwall und die deutschen Fürsten," in *De poeticis medii aevi quaestiones: Festschrift Käthe Hamburger* (Göppingen: Kümmerle, 1981): 105–27. This thesis is rejected by some scholars; for a discussion of the arguments in this discussion, see Brandt, *Konrad* (2000), 27–31.

[21] On the *Schwanritter* see Stefanie Cain van D'Elden, "Does Might Make Right? The *Schwanritter* by Konrad von Würzburg," in *Courtly Literature, Culture and Context*, ed. Keith Busby and Erik Kooper (Amsterdam: Benjamins, 1990), 549–59. On *Engelhard* see Peter Kesting, "*Diu rehte wârheit*. Zu Konrads von Würzburg *Engelhard*," *Zeitschrift für deutsches Altertum und deutsche Literatur* 99 (1970): 246–59; Rüdiger Schnell, "Die *Wahrheit* eines manipulierten Gottesurteils. Eine rechtsgeschichtliche Interpretation von Konrads von Würzburg *Engelhard*," *Poetica* 16 (1984): 24–60.

[22] See Dietz-Rüdiger Moser, "Nachtrag," in *Literatur in Bayern* 10 (1987): 55.

[23] In the High Middle Ages bishops were frequently powerful political leaders with their own palaces and districts in many cities, as was the case in Basel.

[24] Peter Schaler represented the interests of the patrician nobility to which he belonged, while Johannes von Arguel, though himself also of noble birth, advocated the interests of the guilds, which put these two men at cross-purposes; for details, see Rüdiger Brandt, *Konrad* (1987), 74–77.

[25] Trude Ehlert, "*In hominem novem oratio?* Der Aufsteiger aus bürgerlicher und aus feudaler Sicht. Zu Konrads von Würzburg *Partonopier und Meliur* und zum altfranzösischen *Partonopeus*," *Zeitschrift für deutsche Philologie* 99 (1980): 36–72.

[26] Hubertus Fischer and Paul Gerhard Völker, "Konrad von Würzburg: Heinrich von Kempten. Individuum und feudale Anarchie," in *Literaturwissenschaft und Sozialwissenschaften*, vol. 5, *Literatur im Feudalismus*, ed. Dieter Richter (Stuttgart: Metzler, 1975), 83–130; on the promotion of solidarity among nobles, see also the *Spruch* 32, 121.

[27] Reinhard Bleck, *Überlegungen zur Entstehungssituation der Werke Konrads von Würzburg, in denen kein Auftraggeber genannt wird* (Vienna: Halosar, 1987).

[28] Citing the Reclam publication of Schröder's edition.

[29] See Hanns Fischer, *Studien zur deutschen Märendichtung* (Tübingen: Niemeyer 1968; 2nd ed. expanded and revised by Johannes Janota, 1983).

[30] As the sources for a number of Stricker's *Mären* and other shorter epic texts, scholars have similarly posited Latin sermon *exempla* and collections of *Schwänke* (farces).

Wernher der Gärtner

Ruth Weichselbaumer

HISTORICAL SOURCES REVEAL NOTHING ABOUT Wernher der Gärtner, author of the short verse narrative *Helmbrecht*. It is therefore difficult to know exactly when and where he lived and what his social status may have been. Some biographical information can be reconstructed on the basis of his work. We know the name of the poet from the final lines of *Helmbrecht*, in which he asks his audience to include him in their prayers:

> Swer iu ditze mære lese,
> bitet daz im got genædec wese
> und dem tihtære,
> Wernher dem Gartenære. (1931–34)

> [Whoever might read this tale to you, pray that God will bestow His grace upon him and upon the poet Wernher der Gärtner.]

There are several unsuccessful attempts to understand what the name Gartenære may say about the poet. The possibilities extend from the derivation of a place name, to a family name and, finally, to a metaphoric expression of Wernher's profession (that is, one who toils in the "garden" of poetry).[1] It is unlikely that Wernher was a cleric,[2] because of a passage in *Helmbrecht* that suggests his life involved wandering:

> swie vil ich var enwadele,
> sô bin ich an deheiner stete,
> dâ man mir tuo, als man im [Helmbrecht] tete. (848–50)[3]

> [However much I travel here and there, I never find myself in a place where I am treated as well as he was.]

A further reason for this assumption is that his work is characterized by a starkly legalistic lay morality lacking "kirchliche Färbung" (ecclesiastical coloring).[4] The consensus today is that Wernher was a wandering poet like Der Stricker.[5] It is not possible to know if he received an education, but numerous passages suggest knowledge of religious (biblical) moral teaching, nature allegory, vernacular literature (*Minnesang*, classical epics, heroic epics) and regional law (*Landrecht*).[6] Evidence for dating *Helmbrecht* is provided by a reference to the lyric poet Neidhart as already deceased (217). Further evidence is provided by poem XV of *Seifried*

Helbling, a collection of didactic poems that contains a reference to *Helmbrecht.* Neidhart is assumed to have died between 1237 and ca. 1246, while *Seifried Helbling* was produced in the last decade of the thirteenth century. It is consequently assumed that *Helmbrecht* was composed in the 1270s or 1280s.

The story of Meier Helmbrecht is the only work that has been preserved under the name Wernher der Gärtner.[7] The verse narrative counts as one of the most significant examples of the verse novella genre in Middle High German literature. Older research focused primarily on establishing the exact place of origin of the text and on localizing the depicted events. This interest was based on the once prevalent assumption that the story was probably based on historical events.[8] This assumption found support in a formulation in the prologue of *Helmbrecht* (9), which claims that the story is an eyewitness account. In the meantime it has been recognized that this statement, along with other claims to veracity in this story, are commonplaces in Middle High German literature, part of an old literary convention.[9] Recent research has concentrated on the investigation and comparison of motifs and themes, on sociological questions, and on the reception of the text in the late Middle Ages.

Wernher der Gärtner tells the story of Helmbrecht in about 1900 verses. Helmbrecht is the son of a *Meier,* or tenant farmer who has taken on administrative responsibilities from his landlord. Helmbrecht is unhappy with his life. Instead of doing farm work and leading an appropriately modest life, he would prefer to live as a knight in a castle. The father, also named Helmbrecht, sternly warns his son not to leave his ancestral surroundings and his prescribed course of life as a yeoman farmer. When his warnings fall on deaf ears, the father reluctantly provides his son with the necessary chivalric equipment. Helmbrecht is taken in by the lord of a castle whose men are robber-knights who terrorize peasants in the vicinity. After a year of living among these men, Helmbrecht returns to visit his family. He is warmly received, richly hosted, and has occasion to tell of his new, ostensibly courtly manner of living. The father attempts again in vain to persuade his son to return to the life of a farmer, but, far from following this advice, Helmbrecht talks his sister Gotelint into coming with him and marrying one of his companions. The wedding, which takes place a short time later, is interrupted by constables of the territorial lord. The robber-knights are caught and condemned to death by hanging. Helmbrecht is the only one who is spared, but he is blinded and mutilated. When Helmbrecht now seeks help and lodging from his father, the latter mocks him and sends him away. For a year Helmbrecht wanders through the land, until he is taken prisoner and hanged by peasants whom he had once robbed and mistreated.

With his *Helmbrecht,* Wernher der Gärtenære demonstrates by means of parable the consequences of morally wrong behavior. Helmbrecht and

his downfall serve as a negative example and warning for "selpherrischiu
kint" (self-aggrandizing youths, 1913). The main emphasis in the story
falls on the dialogues between father and son,[10] which make up more than
half of the text. Disputations and didactic discussions in father-son con-
stellations are a feature of earlier court literature — one thinks for example of the discussion between the abbot and Gregorius in Hartmann von
Aue's *Gregorius*, or of Gurnemanz's instruction of Parzival in Wolfram von
Eschenbach's *Parzival* — and they are also characteristic of moral-didactic
literature (*Der Winsbecke* and *Der deutsche Cato,* both anonymous,
thirteenth century). In *Helmbrecht* the dialogues function to inform about
past events and illustrate the present condition of the hero, but also to
relay the didactic message. Helmbrecht behaves wrongly, because he puts
himself beyond the basic, divinely established principles of social order in
the Middle Ages: family[11] and social position.[12] The instigator of
Helmbrecht's socially destructive behavior is his *superbia*, his presumption
and arrogance. By ignoring the warnings of his father, he disregards the
patriarchal hierarchy that is valid within the family. Here also we witness a
generation conflict: the son leaves the prescribed path and follows "niuwen
siten" (new customs, 1039). The father represents tradition, the old customs (981), and warns the son against leaving his proper place in society:
"wan selten im gelinget, / der wider sînen orden ringet. / dîn ordenunge
ist der phluoc" (No one is ever successful who struggles against his proper
station in life. Your station is at the plough, 289–91). All other ambitions
will only bring him the scorn of "der rehten hoveliute" (real courtiers,
296). The admonitions are reinforced by means of forebodings and
dreams, which show themselves in the end to be a prophetic anticipation
of the fate of the son. The consequences of Helmbrecht's wish to be a
knight are thus more than just a family argument: the whole familial hierarchy is disrupted by the son's disobedience and desire for social mobility.

The elder Helmbrecht is proud of being a farmer. He is happy with his
life and therefore sees no reason why his son would want to change his.
This does not mean that the social status of farmers is being placed above
the others. When the father criticizes prevailing social injustices in a
laudatio temporis acti, praise of things past (964–83), he nevertheless
remains of the opinion that knighthood and courtly life are honorable. The
message is, rather, that the social position into which one is born cannot
be changed by whim and that the responsibility associated with one's place
in society has to be borne as well as possible. The elder Helmbrecht formulates the thought of a nobility of virtue (*Tugendadel*), the idea that the
worth of a person is not established by social position, high birth, and
inherited possessions, but that it is the person's good deeds and nobility of
mind that distinguish and thus confer some "nobility." These statements
on the part of the father cause no change in the son, whose desire to climb
to the position of knighthood is not motivated by an inner need or calling,

but by extraneous considerations. He is of the opinion that his cap, hair and clothing are so beautiful, "daz si baz zaemen einem tanz / dan der eiden oder dem phluoc" (that they're more appropriate to a dance than to a harrow or a plough, 514–15). As a consequence, Helmbrecht does not act "edellîche" (nobly, 505) in accordance with his new social status. The proper duty of a lord and knight would be to protect weaker people,[13] but as a robber-knight he harms them. The punishment he receives for his transgressions against divine and worldly order consists not only of blinding and mutilation, but also of the rejection by his father. The parallels to the biblical parable of the prodigal son are evident,[14] but in *Helmbrecht* there is no reconciliation, the father does not pardon his son — even if "sîn herze krachte" (his heart was breaking, 1776) — but instead dooms him to death.

Two things are especially noteworthy about Helmbrecht: his blond hair, which he wears long and curly like a nobleman, and his finely embroidered cap. Neither corresponds to the expected appearance of a young farmer.[15] Cap and hair, which are frequently mentioned in the story, symbolize Helmbrecht's presumption, the false path that he takes. The description of the cap is extensive, taking up some seventy-eight verses. Besides numerous birds, there are scenes from antique mythology, scenes of courtly dance, and moral exempla — much more than would actually fit on a cap. Helmbrecht's dress is also entirely inappropriate for his social position. His appearance in the precious articles of clothing, furs, and weapons with which his family fits him out shows him to be a vain and ridiculous figure. The medieval reader/listener would probably have been reminded of the *dörper* (peasant figure) Hildemar of whom the lyric poet Neidhart sings in his *Winterlieder* (winter songs).[16] In Neidhart's winter song 29,[17] Hildemar wears a cap with birds like that of Helmbrecht, beneath which he has long curly hair, and he yearns to be equal to the people at court. Strange language, which Helmbrecht uses to try to make a courtly impression during his visit back to the familial home, corresponds to the language used by another *dörper* in Neidhart's winter song 27. Conversely, Helmbrecht's father manifests no such behavior, but is an exemplary model of the worthy farmer. As a consequence of these parallels, Helmbrecht has been interpreted as a transposition of the plot structure of the courtly-chivalric romances into the surroundings, of a farm in a manner that is analogous to the way Neidhart transposed the love lyric to a village setting.[18] Despite numerous correspondences such as these, no direct source for Wernher's *Helmbrecht* has yet been identified.[19]

The reception of the Helmbrecht story was largely confined to Bavaria and eastern Austria. Already in the late Middle Ages there are indications that Helmbrecht was regarded as a historical person,[20] but later poets make references to Wernher's work and to Helmbrecht without implying his historicity. There are references and parallels to Helmbrecht in the *Seifried*

Helbling, in Ottokar von Steiermark's *Österreichische Reimchronik* (Austrian Rhyme Chronicle, fourteenth century), and in the thirteenth-century tale *Schlegel* of Rüdiger von Hinkhofen, and in the drama *Streit zwischen Herbst und Mai* (Conflict between Fall and May, fourteenth century).[21]

The Helmbrecht story was rediscovered in the nineteenth century and understood as a historical legend along the lines of a "village history," or *Dorfgeschichte*. Since then there have been numerous translations and re-workings, plays and novels, which present the story in very different ways.[22] For the last seventy years, Helmbrecht festival plays have been performed in the Bavarian city Burghausen, which is treated as the historical setting of the story.

— Translated by Will Hasty

Notes

[1] See Fritz Peter Knapp, "Wernher der Gärtner," in *Die deutsche Literatur des Mittelalters: Verfasserlexikon*, vol. 10, ed. Burghart Wachinger (Berlin: de Gruyter, 1999), 927–36; here 927.

[2] See Friedrich Keinz, *Helmbrecht und seine Heimat* (Leipzig: Hirzel, 1887), 10–11.

[3] References to Helmbrecht are based on *Wernher der Gartenære: Helmbrecht*, ed. Friedrich Panzer, 9th rev. ed. by Kurt Ruh (Tübingen: Niemeyer 1974). English translations are the editor's.

[4] Kurt Ruh's introduction to the cited edition of *Helmbrecht*, xviii.

[5] Knapp, "Wernher der Gärtner," 927.

[6] Knapp, "Wernher der Gärtner," 927.

[7] On the transmission of Helmbrecht see Ruh's introduction to *Helmbrecht*, ix–xi and Knapp, "Wernher der Gärtner," 928, the facsimile edition of Franz Hundsnurscher (Göppingen: Kümmerle, 1972), and Ulrich Seelbach's study of the transmission and late medieval reception, *Späthöfische Literatur und ihre Rezeption im späten Mittelalter: Studien zum Publikum des "Helmbrecht" von Wernher dem Gartnaere* (Berlin: Schmidt, 1987).

[8] Gustav Ehrismann, *Geschichte der deutschen Literatur bis zum Ausgang des Mittelalters. Zweiter Teil: Die mittelhochdeutsche Literatur. Schlußband* (Munich: Beck, 1969), 104.

[9] See Hanns Fischer, "Gestaltungsschichten im *Meier Helmbrecht*," *Beiträge zur Geschichte der deutschen Sprache und Literatur* (PBB) 79 (1957): 85–109; here 89–90.

[10] See Erika Langbroek, "Warnung und Tarnung im *Helmbrecht*: Das Gespräch zwischen Vater und Sohn Helmbrecht und die Haube des Helmbrecht," *Amsterdamer Beiträge zur älteren Germanistik* 36 (1992): 141–68.

[11] See Peter von Matt, *Verkommene Söhne, missratene Töchter: Familiendesaster in der Literatur* (Munich: C. Hanser, 1995), 51–79, and Dagmar Hüpper, "Familie Helmbrecht in der Krise: Rechtsnormen und ihre Kontrafaktur in den Sprachhandlungen des Maere," in *Symbole des Alltags, Alltag der Symbole: Festschrift für Harry Kühnel*, ed. Gertraud Blaschitz et al. (Graz: Akademische Druck- und Verlagsanstalt, 1992), 641–59.

[12] See Petra Menke, *Recht und Ordo-gedanke im Helmbrecht* (Frankfurt am Main: Lang, 1993.

[13] See Fritz Peter Knapp, "Standesväter und Heimatverächter in der bayrisch-östterreichischen Literatur des Spätmittelalters," *Wernher der Gärtner "Helmbrecht." Die Beiträge des Helmbrecht-Symposions in Burghausen 2001*, ed. Theodor Nolte and Tobias Schneider (Stuttgart: Hirzel, 2001), 2–24; here 11.

[14] Lucas 15, 11–32; Fischer lists the parallels in tabular form ("Gestaltungsschichten im *Meier Helmbrecht*," 92).

[15] See Menke, *Recht und Ordo-gedanke im Helmbrecht*, 10.

[16] See Ulrich Seelbach, "Hildemar und Helmbrecht: Intertextuelle Bezüge des *Helmbrecht* zu den Liedern Neidharts," in *Wernher der Gärtner*, ed. Nolte and Schneider, 45–69.

[17] *Die Lieder Neidharts*, ed. Edmund Wiessner, continued by Hanns Fischer, 4th rev. ed. by Paul Sappler (Tübingen: Niemeyer, 1984).

[18] See Ruh, introduction to *Helmbrecht*, xxii–xxiii. A study of similarities of motifs between Wolfram's *Parzival* and *Helmbrecht* is Bernhard Sowinski, "Parzival und Helmbrecht. Höfische Kalokagathie und bäurische Usurpation," in *Von Wyssheit würt der Mensch geert: Festschrift für Manfred Lemmer zum 65. Geburtstag*, ed. Ingrid Kühn and Gotthart Lerchner (Frankfurt am Main: Lang, 1993), 117–27.

[19] The source may have been an *exemplum* in a Latin sermon, according to Joachim Bumke, *Geschichte der deutschen Literatur im hohen Mittelalter* (Munich: DTV, 1990), 284.

[20] In the Austrian Innviertel there is a farmyard named after Helmbrecht; see Keinz, *Helmbrecht und seine Heimat*, 7ff. Keinz also mentions "Helml" as a derogatory name for a careless young person (5). Seelbach points to the use of "Helmbrecht" to denote a bon-vivant or man about town in fourteenth-century Prague (19).

[21] On the Helmbrecht reception see Seelbach, 118–68.

[22] Seelbach lists the modern works in *Bibliographie zu Wernher der Gartenaere* (Berlin: Schmidt, 1981).

Part IV

Historical Perspectives

Court Literature and Violence in the High Middle Ages

William H. Jackson

VIOLENCE, ESPECIALLY IN ITS politically most prominent form as military force, is an essential and complex feature of the German literary landscape in the High Middle Ages. In order to understand the role of violence in this literature it is necessary to reflect on the use of force as a cultural and historical variable so as to avoid projecting onto medieval German literature concepts of violence and its relation to ethical, political and social values that belong to other historical contexts.

In modern societies the licit use of armed force is generally seen as a prerogative of the state, not the individual. The position was different in Germany during the Middle Ages, when some individuals still had the right to settle their disputes by military means, in trial by combat or in the process of feud. The carrying of knightly arms was seen as the hereditary right of a particular sector of society, the aristocracy. Moreover, the socially demarcating function of arms was becoming increasingly prominent during the literary upsurge of the twelfth and thirteenth centuries as even the lesser knighthood sought to close itself off from other sectors on the criterion of a hereditary right of arms. As a result of these factors there was considerable interpenetration of the military and everyday life at this time, as social status was largely defined, for the secular audiences of aristocratic poetry, by a right of arms that was never forgotten, even in peacetime, while the conduct of military action was seen as primarily a matter for the aristocracy. In this constellation the use of armed force was central to the self-understanding and to the cultural manifestations of the secular aristocracy. There was no standing army and no police force in medieval Germany; rather training in arms was part of the education of every noble. The mounted war games of *buhurt*,[1] tourney and jousting were, besides hunting, major aristocratic exercises.

But the absence of a state monopoly on armed violence does not mean that conditions of unchecked, anarchic strife were the norm in the Middle Ages. What might look like a high degree of individual autonomy — when viewed from the political standpoint of the modern nation state — was in fact subject to a whole range of ideological, pragmatic, social, and institutional constraints that bore on the individual's exercise of violence.

Repeatedly in the history of war, particularly great violence and cruelty have been shown in wars involving religious differences.[2] In the Middle Ages the full weight of mortal warfare — which permitted indiscriminate slaughter — was brought to bear in warfare against non-Christians.[3] However, there was no adherence to a concept of total war between warring Christians, which was by far the most common type of conflict, and war to the death was uncommon inside medieval Christendom.[4] One of the leading principles of medieval military strategy was the avoidance, where possible, of pitched battle in the open country, because of the unpredictable outcome and the possibility of sudden death in such encounters, while the main features of warfare were the more controllable actions of devastation of lands, pillaging, raids, and sieges.[5] Duby points out that surprisingly few knights were killed in warfare in the twelfth century, while Asmus observes that the means of conducting feuds in north Germany were not killing or wounding but spoiling the opponent's property, and there were few fatalities even in pitched battles.[6] The relative effectiveness of the knights' defensive armor, and, more important, the tactical and material usefulness of taking prisoners for ransom and as a way of exercising pressure in negotiation, as well as the desire to avoid the risk of a blood feud all worked together to limit deaths in warfare. However, these material and social factors afforded greater protection to the aristocracy than to commoners, and the view gained ground in the High Middle Ages that, while a knight ought not to kill another knight in battle if he could instead take him prisoner, armed peasants and townsmen could be killed more freely.[7]

Warfare was also closely linked to the idea of justice, and this too could act as a stimulus to arms and as a restraining factor. Family and feudal ties were a source of much conflict, since members of the group could be called upon to defend an injury done to another member, but the need to consult with family, friends and allies about the advisability or legitimacy of undertaking military action was also a form of constraint that limited the bellicosity of the individual. On this point, as often, the structure of medieval social relations was paradoxically both conducive to warfare and a restraining factor, as the "Selbstherrlichkeit," or self-aggrandizement of the military aristocrat was limited by his need for social support.[8]

Whereas modern societies regard peace as the normal state of affairs, war was endemic in medieval Europe.[9] However, what has been less widely recognized is that endemic warfare, especially in the form of innumerable feuds, was also accompanied throughout the Middle Ages by equally ubiquitous processes of mediation, arbitration, and compromise which can be observed before, during, and after armed conflicts as those involved sought to bring disputes to an amicable settlement.[10] These processes have recently been studied by Hermann Kamp, whose book *Friedensstifter und Vermittler im Mittelalter*[11] (Peacemakers and Mediators in the Middle Ages) sheds light on the conduct of conflict settlement that was a matter of immediate interest to the audiences of court literature. Kamp shows how mediation had its origins in the early Middle Ages in the context of family conflicts. From the end of the eleventh century mediators (*mediatores pacis*) appear with increased frequency, and their activities gain in profile. Kings, queens, bishops and princes (*Fürsten*) appear as mediators. Royal arbitration gained in strength from the twelfth century onward. Bishops were particularly important as mediators because their religious office gave them the aura of peacemakers in succession to Christ. The secular magnates, with their self-understanding as men of the sword, appear less often as mediators than the bishops, but they too played a part, and sometimes appeared side by side with bishops in mediation that backed the pursuit of peace with the threat of military force.

The history of mediation in the Middle Ages shows a "creeping institutionalization" of negotiations aiming to control armed violence.[12] A more overt complex of institutionalized aggression controls emanated from church initiatives with the Peace of God and the Truce of God, and from German secular authorities in the enactments known as *Landfrieden* (territorial peaces).

The duty of keeping peace and protecting the weak was, together with the defense of justice, pre-eminently a duty of the king or other secular ruler in the Middle Ages. However, with the decline of royal power in France in the tenth century, bishops sought to protect the populace against the depredations of feuding by calling on support from the leading secular magnates and declaring in France first a Peace of God during the last quarter of the tenth century, and a few decades later a Truce of God.[13] The Peace of God sought to limit the scope of violence by proclaiming immunity for certain categories of person, places and things, especially churchmen, peasants, merchants and women, churches, and peasants' cattle. The Truce of God was an attempt to stop all violence at certain times, especially on holy days. The ecclesiastical peace movement had only a late and limited impact in the German empire, where royal institutions had remained stronger than in France. However peaces were proclaimed by bishops at Liège (1082), Cologne (1083), and Mainz (1085). Reflexes of the church's Truce of God are rare in German literature, but appear in *Parzival*,[14] where Wolfram draws on his French source to have Parzival reproved for carrying arms on Good Friday (*Parzival*, 447, 13–18), and in Gottfried Hagen's rhymed chronicle of the city of Cologne (1270)[15] with an appeal for a cessation of hostilities during the forty days of Lent (806–11).[16] In both cases Christ's suffering is evoked as a reason for the putting aside of arms.

The spread of armed conflict in the empire led the secular authorities to take up the promulgation of peace in Germany. Emperor Heinrich IV declared a peace for the whole empire at Mainz in 1103, and from then until the end of the fifteenth century a series of *Landfrieden* emanated from the German kings and territorial rulers, with the coexistence of general and regional peaces reflecting the interplay of political und judicial authority between the king and the territorial rulers, who were growing in authority from the thirteenth century on.[17]

The *Landfrieden* form the main type of royal and princely legislation in medieval Germany and are of importance for an understanding of the socio-political framework of aristocratic literature because they provide criteria for judging acts of violence. The peaces of the late twelfth and early thirteenth centuries are of special interest because they form the most intensive phase in the legislative concern with the conduct of feuds, and they show a developing engagement with the problem of restraining violence. In his first imperial peace of 1152 Friedrich Barbarossa tried to subject all forms of killing, save in self-defense, to capital punishment, a step which, had it been successful, would have meant the end of feuding and the emergence of something akin to the modern state's monopoly on the licit use of force. But the German crown lacked the jurisdictional and political means of holding this extreme position, and later peaces recognize the right of feud while trying to limit its conduct.

Typical constraints that the peaces tried to place on knightly violence are well illustrated in the Rhenish Franconian *Landfriede* of 1179. Here immunity from attack was granted to villages and their inhabitants, clerics, monks, women, merchants, mills, Jews, and huntsmen. Pursuit of an enemy is permitted only in the open field (*in campo*), without damage to the enemy's property, or the enemy may be captured and immediately delivered to the competent judge. If the enemy takes refuge in a mill or a village he enjoys immunity. Pursuit of an enemy is allowed only on Mondays, Tuesdays, and Wednesdays; on the other four days he shall have full immunity from attack. The constitution against arsonists of 1186 tried to limit the practice of burning. This peace also introduced the requirement that anyone wishing to attack an enemy shall give at least three days' notice, thus drawing a line between a just feud and disordered aggression — and anticipating the declaration of war in modern international law. The Mainz *Reichslandfriede* of 1235 tried to insist that complainants should first seek redress by judicial means before taking arms, but it still recognized the right of feud, which was not banned completely until the *Ewiger Landfriede* of 1495. Only with the formal criminalizing of the aristocracy's right of feud did the monopoly of the legitimate use of armed force pass to the state, and it is a mark of different political developments in western Europe that this monopoly was exercised in France by the king but in the German empire by the territorial rulers to whom the power of jurisdiction had passed by the early modern period.[18]

Feuding remained widespread in Germany throughout the Middle Ages, and it is unclear just how much impact the *Landfrieden* had on the actual conduct of feuds. Asmus sees the formal declaration as the most strictly observed procedure of feud, and concludes that clerics, women,

Jews, churches and monasteries enjoyed considerable immunity. He finds little reference to immunity for merchants and peasants, and in his sources from southern Hanover, as elsewhere in Germany, pillage and arson were familiar actions of feuding.[19] However, the peace enactments of the German rulers did provide an important normative legal thread in the discourse of violence and order that runs through German culture in the High Middle Ages.[20] The literature produced with a view to secular, aristocratic audiences in the twelfth and thirteenth centuries plays an important part in this discourse, and the remainder of this chapter will sketch the interplay of violence and constraint in works from various genres, drawing on heroic poetry, Arthurian romances, the *Alexander* of Rudolf von Ems, and Ottokar von Steiermark's *Österreichische Reimchronik*.

The willingness to inflict or suffer death in combat as a means of securing honor is a key source of conflict in warrior societies and a recurrent theme of heroic poetry. In the German Middle Ages, this ethos is most violently expressed in the *Nibelungenlied*.[21] But even this work, a warrior epic with a strong sense of political realities, presents constraints on the use of force. For instance, when Siegfried challenges the Burgundian kings to defend their lands in combat, the seneschal Ortwin angrily calls for arms, but Gernot asserts a ruler's authority and insists on settling the matter in an amicable fashion (strophes 107–27). The presentation of armed combat and diplomatic conciliation ("suone," strophe 116, 3) here as alternative ways of settling conflict is characteristic of a strand that runs through the literature of the twelfth and thirteenth centuries. On a broader stage, the good treatment of captives taken in the Saxon war (248–51), and Siegfried's counsel that the Burgundians should not seek punitive reparations from the defeated Saxons (311–16), show a restrained practice of warfare. It is typical of a broader current that these gestures of restraint arise largely from the authority of rulers or military leaders. However, in the later stages of the epic, all attempts to avert or restrain violent conflict following the murder of Siegfried prove fruitless: royal authority, ties of kinship, attempts at negotiation, even Dietrich's final noble gesture of taking Hagen and Gunther alive fail to halt the mass slaughter.

The *Nibelungenlied* can thus be seen as the epic of failed violence controls; it was evidently a problematical feature of the work already for medieval audiences that the unremitting bloodshed of the later parts of the work is presented ambivalently as both the destruction of courtly order and a chain of great heroic deeds.[22] In its extreme presentation of destructive violence, the *Nibelungenlied* remains exceptional even in heroic poetry of the Middle Ages, and it is accompanied in most of the complete manuscripts by the *Klage*,[23] which attempts to accommodate the unsettling violence of the *Nibelungenlied* within a moral and dynastic framework by condemning Hagen, praising Kriemhild as a model of fidelity, and providing a dynastic future for the Burgundian house. The epic *Kudrun*[24] is also something of a response to the challenge of the *Nibelungenlied*. The *Kudrun* narrator shows much interest in constraints on violence in warfare. For instance, when the Heglings are attacked by Hartmut's army, Hilde wisely orders them to close the city gates and assume defensive positions, but her men, in their foolish overconfidence, disregard this sound tactical command and insist on taking the battle into the open outside the gates, with disastrous consequences. The contrast struck here between foolish heroics and wise restraint is a recurrent motif in accounts of military action in the Middle Ages. On a broader thematic front the *Kudrun* poet treats, in the figure of *Kudrun*, a situation that is comparable to that of the *Nibelungenlied*, with the difference that whereas the pursuit of vengeance leads to mutual destruction in the *Nibelungenlied*, *Kudrun* ends in reconciliation and a series of marriage alliances that bring together former enemies.

If we turn to Hartmann's *Erec* and *Iwein*[25] and Wolfram's *Parzival*, works that exercised a formative influence on the future development of narrative literature, especially the Arthurian verse romance, bloodshed and killing play a far less dominant part than they did in the *Nibelungenlied*. There are few collective battles in these works. The spotlight is on individual combat, and the dialectic of order and violence is played out largely in the new realm of knightly *âventiure*. Recurrently in Arthurian verse romance, from its beginning with Hartmann's *Erec* to its fading around a century later, combats are a focus for discussion of the legitimacy and the limits of the use of force. The exchange of words that Hartmann adds to Chrétien's version in his account of the first encounter between Erec and the chivalric king Guivreiz (4326–77) expresses a difference of view about the appropriateness of Guivreiz's challenge and shows "das kämpferische Draufgängertum" (combative daredevilry) in a problematical light.[26] The exchange has a paradigmatic function in signaling that in Arthurian romance the use of armed force is not necessarily to be taken for granted, but calls for deliberation. The first encounter with Guivreiz ends with another gesture of violence-limitation that becomes a norm in Arthurian romance, when Erec accepts his defeated opponent's surrender and spares his life (4460–67).

In the opening stages of *Iwein*, Kalogrenant famously defines *âventiure* solely in terms of the pursuit of personal glory at the risk of life in combat with another knight (527–37), and Iwein kills his opponent, Askalon, who has fled, fatally wounded, from the combat (1051–1107). These two passages have provoked widely differing interpretations of the ethics of combat in Hartmann's romance.[27] What is important for the topic of constraints on violence is that Arthur's court seems to find nothing objectionable in Kalogrenant's definition of *âventiure*, and bestows praise on Iwein for his victory. Evidently, in the code of Arthurian chivalry, the norm of sparing an opponent's life is closely connected with the opponent's willingness to surrender. Wolfram, in his *Parzival*, shows considerable unease on the topic of chivalric killing, referring to deaths in battle only briefly, and actually describing only one act of killing: Parzival's killing of Ither.[28] Wolfram also goes a step further than Hartmann by explicitly questioning the value of chivalric combats undertaken without any reason other than the pursuit of personal renown.[29] The terms used in *Parzival* to describe combats without good reason, "âne schulde" (without cause, 538, 2) and "ân nôt" (without necessity, 538, 6), express a recurrent motif in the critical strand of comment on such combats in the twelfth and thirteenth centuries. Wolfram presents military force as a means of conflict resolution in collective battles and in single combats, but he is also attentive to the importance of reconciliation, and in Book 14 he presents Arthur as a king who achieves a peaceful resolution of the conflict between Gawan and Gramoflanz.[30]

The tendency to tone down the brutality of warfare that surfaces as an aesthetic constraint on violence in Arthurian romance also spreads into heroic poetry in the later thirteenth century. In the prologue to Albrecht von Kemenaten's *Goldemar*[31] the narrator distances himself from the warrior mentality of Dietrich's times, when a man's reputation was based on the number of opponents he had killed in needless combat: the phrase "âne schulde" (*Goldemar* 1, 11) echoes the wording of Wolfram's reflection. Kurt Ruh has discussed the questioning of military recklessness in heroic poetry in the late Middle Ages, showing how the portrayal of Dietrich as a cautious warrior who at times expresses distaste for unnecessary adventure emphasizes a more pragmatic heroism than that of the *Nibelungenlied*.[32] With this attitude, Dietrich has affinities with Gawan in Wolfram's *Parzival*.

The advocacy of restraint in martial violence in Arthurian romance and in heroic poetry stops well short of a fundamental questioning of the aristocracy's right to carry arms and goes hand in hand with a continuing affirmation of violent conflict. Dietrich gives voice to an important view of conflict in this literature when he says that a true hero should be "bold, not too bold" ("wis küene und niht ze küene"), should show restraint in responding to verbal provocation, but should then show his mettle in case of need (*Laurin*, 322–32).[33] In other words the warrior who practices restraint is not, for that, less tough when the fight is on. Hartmann's and Wolfram's knightly heroes show awesome strength and prowess in actual combat, and the action of the romances attaches a positive social value to the knightly use of force.[34] The norm of sparing a defeated opponent's life also has limits in these two seminal chivalric authors. With Hartmann the custom applies only to fellow knights, not to giants from outside the chivalric world, and indeed not to robber knights and morally degenerate nobles.[35] In *Parzival* the mentor figure Gurnemanz urges Parzival to accept a defeated opponent's submission and allow him to live, but Wolfram adds to Chrétien's text the qualification that this injunction does not apply if the defeated opponent has done the victor mortal wrong (171, 28–29). Gurnemanz advocates not absolute Christian mercy but a limited, aristocratic generosity that retains for the victor the crucial right of retribution for a wrong done.

Indeed, the constraints on violence in Arthurian romance do not point toward a utopian vision of a pacified society, they appear rather to give moral legitimacy to the aristocracy's use of force. In his study of peace in German literature down to the fourteenth century, Albrecht Hagenlocher follows legal historians to distinguish, for the German Middle Ages, between an ideal concept of peace as the harmonious arrangement of society, and peace in a more technical, functional sense as a legal instrument that takes specific forms and is usually limited to specific persons, social groups, times or places.[36] Significantly, in courtly narrative poetry it is the limited, instrumental sense that dominates. Hagenlocher shows that the term *vride* remains closely bound up with territorial rule, as an expression of the ruler's authority, for instance when Erec establishes peace in his homeland at the end of Hartmann's romance. Moreover, the opening episode of *Iwein* shows a certain tension between the Arthurian concept of *âventiure* and the political tendency of the German *Landfrieden*, as the territorial ruler Askalon accuses the adventuring knight Kalogrenant of breach of the peace.[37] The term *vride* remains tied to the exercise of rule and to real legal forms throughout the history of Arthurian romance in the twelfth and thirteenth centuries, with no transcendence toward a higher, ideal concept of universal peace and harmony (Hagenlocher, 50–52). There seems, then, to be some ambivalence in the relationship of Arthurian romance to the notion of peace and social order, with one strand tending to an affirmation of order, while the very existence of the wandering knight seeking adventure also risks disturbing this order.[38] The adventure of the fountain in *Iwein* is a symbolic expression of this ambivalence, as the custom of the fountain at once disturbs the peace of the realm and demonstrates in the victor the military power that is needed for the maintenance of peace and justice.

The securing of peace and justice was a central task of the ruler in medieval society, and this complex raises the question of the role of kingship in the literary processing of constraints on violence. In Arthurian literature King Arthur is head of a great court, and he exercises a restraining authority over his knights, for example when he insists that, on the expedition in search of the Red Knight (Parzival), the knights of the Round Table should not undertake any combat without his express permission (*Parzival*, 280, 18–281, 8). However, German Arthurian romance focuses more strongly on the individual knightly hero than on the political role of Arthur as king. The *Alexander* of Rudolf von Ems[39] brings, in contrast, a more centralist perspective, is dominated by the portrayal of Alexander the Great as exemplary king and general, and throws much light on norms of political and military conduct amongst the German aristocracy in the context of the Staufen court towards the middle of the thirteenth century.[40]

Central tenets in the advice given by the philosopher Aristotle to the young Alexander (1402–1830) are that the ideal ruler should conduct his military affairs with intelligence and good sense, should beware irrational anger and should pursue vengeance only after careful deliberation and in due measure. Alexander puts these precepts into practice in the wars he fights. He shows further ethical restraint in his form of engagement with the enemy in that he refuses to attack in a treacherous fashion under cover of darkness (11852–78) and he orders his men to respect the law of sanctuary for those who have taken refuge in temples (9400–9406). Interestingly Rudolf draws on his Latin source, the *History of Alexander* by the Roman historian Quintus Curtius Rufus (probably first-century A.D.), in these two passages, which thus show a link between the ancient and the medieval world in the conventions of warfare. Rudolf, however, often departs from his source to portray exemplary restraint in Alexander and his armies, strikingly when Alexander's men plunder and rape after their victory in the battle of Issus in Curtius Rufus, while Rudolf transforms them into disciplined knights who treat the captive women with utmost tact and sympathy (7547–72).

On the other hand, even Rudolf's Alexander at times exacts stern vengeance by ordering capital punishment. For instance when the citizens of Tyre violate Alexander's honor by killing the emissaries he has sent to negotiate terms with them, he responds by having 2,000 Tyreans put to death after his victory (9407–20). Rudolf's Alexander appears as a great historical precedent for the Staufen rulers, provisions of whose *Landfrieden* appear in the Macedonian king's settlement of conquered lands.[41] His disciplined army is a model for the contemporary German princes and knighthood in their relation to the ruling dynasty. This political ideology also informs the treatment of captives in Rudolf's text, for the mercy shown by Alexander seems to be not an ethical absolute, since it stops short of condoning offenses against royal honor.

Ottokar von Steiermark's *Österreichische Reimchronik*[42] (composed in the first two decades of the fourteenth century) is a wide-ranging account of events in the empire after the death of Friedrich II in 1250, with a special focus on Austrian affairs. Ottokar stemmed from a family of the lesser nobility in Styria. He held a conservative and aristocratic position in political and social matters. Ottokar tells of King Heinrich VII of Germany (crowned 1309) attempting to stem feuds by declaring a *lantfride* (95937) and calling on even the great magnates to settle their quarrels by peaceful means (95906–69). The promulgation of *Landfrieden* and advocacy of negotiated settlements to conflicts were related expressions of a strengthening of central authority which sought to control military activity, and which in the German empire ultimately concentrated the right to use force in the hands of the territorial rulers. However, the *Österreichische Reimchronik* also documents the prevalence of war in Germany and beyond. Ottokar ascribes a socially hierarchical value to the practice of arms when he criticizes the granting of the rights and functions of knighthood to sons of peasants, townsmen and artisans, and refers approvingly to the advice of Helmbrecht's father (26417).[43] His account of conflict between the forces of King Albrecht and Bishop Gerhard of Mainz throws light on the regional and ideological complexity of warfare in the transition to the later Middle Ages. In this conflict the Styrian captain, Ulrich von Walsee, wins a victory by using a tactic learned from warfare against the Hungarians, as he has his men take off their heavy armor so as to gain speed of movement, keep a distance from the enemy, and attack with bows and arrows (77293–310). In an argument about these tactics after the battle, Bishop Gerhard's Swabian knights and those from the Netherlands accuse Ulrich of dishonorable conduct because he avoided the close encounter of "classic" chivalric combat, to which Ulrich replies illuminatingly that he is willing to serve ladies by close combat in tournament or joust, but it would be foolish to follow this style against superior numbers in serious warfare (77528–53).

The gap that opens in Ulrich's words between tactics of the tournament and tactics of serious warfare is symptomatic of a historic stage in the development of military affairs. The mass tournament and individual jousting were the most prominent manifestations of the ideal of controlled violence as a demonstration of the social and cultural supremacy of the aristocracy in the Middle Ages.[44] In the late Middle Ages tournaments became ever more regulated in their style of combat and, especially in Germany, ever more socially restricted, to the exclusion of those not of noble birth, so that the ideal of a ritually constrained exercise of military force was realized in the limited space of the tournament field. At the same time, from the late thirteenth century onward, non-noble troops became increasingly important in warfare, and the constraint on killing which was a pragmatic feature of warfare between nobles became increasingly eroded in warfare involving commoner infantry. Ottokar himself reports on a key stage in this development when he tells how the Flemish infantry showed no quarter to the French knighthood at the Battle of Courtrai (11 July 1302). Interestingly Ottokar presents this terrible bloodshed not as a sign of brutality on the part of the Flemings but as God's punishment on the king of France (64611–810). Here, as often in medieval sources, unconstrained violence is justified by reference to the will of God.

As a work that combines historiographical and courtly literary traditions, presents a dispute between knights on the proper, honorable conduct of warfare, and advocates non-military settlement of conflicts as well as interpreting mass killing as a judgment of God, Ottokar's *Reimchronik* draws together some of the main threads in the thirteenth century discourse on violence and forms an apt note on which to close this chapter.

What is at stake in the debate between Ulrich von Walsee and the knights from Swabia and the Netherlands is not whether war is a legitimate or appropriate way of settling a conflict, but how warfare is to be conducted and to what constraints it might be subject. In this sense the debate addresses a central concern of German literature in the High Middle Ages.

As late as the end of the thirteenth century the use of armed force was seen as a legal right of the German aristocracy. The aristocratic audiences of the thirteenth century were still far from being a pacified gentry, and recent scholars have rightly drawn attention to the importance of violence, aggression, dominance and self-assertion in the aristocracy's self-understanding and in the court literature of the period.[45] At the same time historical sources in the narrow sense and court literature also show a wide range of forces that acted as constraints on violence. Some of these forces arose, as it were, outside the military aristocracy, in the form of religious injunctions and, more important, enhanced control mechanisms connected with the strengthening of territorial rule. Other restraints were a product of internal social interaction, as the survival of aristocratic society also called for some limitation of the warrior function on which this society was predicated. The court literature of the High Middle Ages in Germany draws much of its energy from this paradoxically symbiotic relation of violence and constraint that shaped the culture of the aristocracy before the nation state asserted its monopoly over the licit use of force.

Notes

[1] On the practice of the *buhurt* see Joachim Bumke, *Courtly Culture: Literature and Society in the High Middle Ages*, translated by Thomas Dunlap (Berkeley, Los Angeles, Oxford: U of California P, 1991), 258–60.

[2] *War, Peace and World Orders in European History*, edited by Anja V. Hartmann and Beatrice Heuser (London and New York: Routledge, 2001), 247–48.

[3] Robert C. Stacey, "The Age of Chivalry," in *The Laws of War: Constraints on Warfare in the Western World*, edited by Michael Howard et al. (New Haven and London: Yale UP, 1994), 27–39 (here 28).

[4] M[aurice] H. Keen, *The Laws of War in the Late Middle Ages* (London: Routledge and Paul Keen, 1965), 104–5, 189.

[5] Philippe Contamine, *War in the Middle Ages*, translated by Michael Jones (Oxford: Blackwell, 1984), 219.

[6] Georges Duby, *Le dimanche de Bouvines: 12 juillet 1214* (Paris: Gallimard, 1985), 183–86; Herbert Asmus, *Rechtsprobleme des mittelalterlichen Fehdewesens: Dargestellt an Hand südhannoverscher Quellen vornehmlich der Stadt Göttingen* (Phil. Diss. Göttingen, 1951), 45–48.

[7] See Stacey, 30.

[8] On war, justice and consultation see Jan Willem Honig, "Warfare in the Middle Ages," in *War, Peace and World Orders*, 113–26 (here 118–21).

[9] See Keen, 104.

[10] Gerd Althoff, "Genugtuung (satisfactio). Zur Eigenart gütlicher Konfliktbeilegung im Mittelalter," in *Modernes Mittelalter: Neue Bilder einer populären Epoche*, edited by Joachim Heinzle (Frankfurt am Main: Insel, 1994), 247–65.

[11] Hermann Kamp, *Friedensstifter und Vermittler im Mittelalter* (Darmstadt: Wissenschaftliche Buchgesellschaft, 2001).

[12] Kamp, 260.

[13] H. E. J. Cowdrey, "The Peace and the Truce of God in the Eleventh Century," *Past and Present* 46 (1970), 42–67; Reinhold Kaiser, "Gottesfrieden," in *Lexikon des Mittelalters*, edited by Robert-Henri Bautier et al., vol. 4 (Munich and Zurich: Artemis, 1989), cols 1587–92.

[14] Wolfram von Eschenbach, *Parzival*, in *Wolfram von Eschenbach*, edited by Karl Lachmann, 6th edition (Berlin: de Gruyter, 1926), 13–388.

[15] *Des Meisters Godefrit Hagen Reimchronik der Stadt Cöln*, edited by E. von Groote (Cologne: DüMont-Schauberg, 1834; reprint Walluf: Sändig, 1972).

[16] See also Albrecht Hagenlocher, *Der* guote vride*: Idealer Friede in deutscher Literatur bis ins frühe 14. Jahrhundert* (Berlin, New York: de Gruyter, 1992), 52–53, 276.

[17] On the *Landfrieden* see Asmus, 58–67; Joachim Gernhuber, *Die Landfriedensbewegung in Deutschland bis zum Mainzer Reichslandfrieden von 1235* (Bonn: Röhrscheid, 1952); W. H. Jackson, *Chivalry in Twelfth-Century Germany: The Works of Hartmann von Aue* (Cambridge: Brewer, 1994), 88–92 and passim; Benjamin Arnold, *Medieval Germany 500–1300: A Political Interpretation* (Houndsmill: MacMillan, 1997), 151–57. Texts of the *Landfrieden* in *Monumenta Germaniae Historica: Constitutiones et acta publica imperatorum et regum*, especially vols. 1–2, edited by Ludwig Weiland (Hanover: Hahn, 1893–1896); and (with German translations of Latin texts) in *Quellen zur deutschen Verfassungs-, Wirtschafts- und Sozialgeschichte bis 1250*, selected and translated by Lorenz Weinrich (Darmstadt: Wissenschaftliche Buchgesellschaft, 1977), and *Quellen zur Verfassungsgeschichte des römisch-deutschen Reiches im Spätmittelalter (1250–1500)*, selected and translated by Lorenz Weinrich (Darmstadt: Wissenschaftliche Buchgesellschaft, 1983).

[18] Reinhold Kaiser, "Selbsthilfe und Gewaltmonopol. Königliche Friedenswahrung in Deutschland und Frankreich im Mittelalter," *Frühmittelalterliche Studien* 17 (1983), 55–72.

[19] Asmus 45–52; on the conduct of feuds see also Otto Brunner, *Land und Herrschaft: Grundfragen der territorialen Verfassungsgeschichte Österreichs im Mittelalter*, 6th edition (Darmstadt: Wissenschaftliche Buchgesellschaft, 1970), 77–101.

[20] For a discussion of violence and order in terms of discourse analysis see Udo Friedrich, "Die Zähmung des Heros: Der Diskurs der Gewalt und der Gewaltregulierung im 12. Jahrhundert," in *Mittelalter: Neue Wege durch einen alten Kontinent*, edited by Jan-Dirk Müller and Horst Wenzel (Stuttgart and Leipzig: Hirzel, 1999), 149–79.

[21] *Das Nibelungenlied,* edited by Karl Bartsch, revised by Helmut de Boor, 21st edition (Wiesbaden: Brockhaus, 1979).

[22] See Jan-Dirk Müller, *Spielregeln für den Untergang: Die Welt des Nibelungenliedes* (Tübingen: Niemeyer, 1998), 440–43.

[23] *Die Klage,* in *Die Nibelungen,* edited by Paul Piper. Part One: *Einleitung und die Klage* (Berlin and Stuttgart: W. Spemann, 1889); *The Lament of the Nibelungen (Diu Chlage),* translated by Winder McConnell, with transcription of Manuscript B (Columbia SC: Camden House, 1994).

[24] *Kudrun,* edited by Karl Bartsch, 5th edition revised by Karl Stackmann (Tübingen: Niemeyer, 2000).

[25] Hartmann von Aue, *Erec,* edited by Albert Leitzmann, 6th edition revised by Christoph Cormeau and Kurt Gärtner (Tübingen: Niemeyer, 1985); *Iwein,* edited by G. F. Benecke and K. Lachmann, 7th edition, revised by Ludwig Wolff (Berlin: de Gruyter, 1968).

[26] Christoph Huber, "Ritterideologie und Gegnertötung: Überlegungen zu den *Erec*-Romanen Chrétiens und Hartmanns und zum *Prosa-Lancelot,*" in *Spannungen und Konflikte menschlichen Zusammenlebens in der deutschen Literatur des Mittelalters. Bristoler Colloquium 1993* (Tübingen: Niemeyer, 1996), 59–73 (quotation 63).

[27] See Jackson, *Chivalry,* 237–42, 262.

[28] See Dennis Howard Green, "Homicide and *Parzival,*" in *Approaches to Wolfram von Eschenbach,* edited by Denis Howard Green and Leslie Peter Johnson (Bern, Frankfurt am Main, Las Vegas: Lang, 1978), 11–82.

[29] Green, 62.

[30] See Monika Unzeitig-Herzog, "*Artus mediator.* Zur Konfliktlösung in Wolframs *Parzival* Buch XIV," *Frühmittelalterliche Studien* 32 (1998): 196–217.

[31] Albrecht von Kemenaten, *Goldemar,* in *Deutsches Heldenbuch,* vol. 5, edited by Julius Zupitza (Berlin: Weidmann, 1870; reprint Dublin and Zurich: Weidmann, 1968), 203–4.

[32] Kurt Ruh, "Verständnisperspektiven von Heldendichtung im Spätmittelalter und heute," in *Deutsche Heldenepik in Tirol: König Laurin und Dietrich von Bern in der Dichtung des Mittelalters. Beiträge der Neustifter Tagung 1977 des Südtiroler Kulturinstituts* (Bozen: Athesia, 1979), 15–31 (22–24).

[33] *Laurin,* in *Deutsches Heldenbuch,* vol. 1, edited by Oskar Jänicke (Berlin: Weidmann, 1866; reprint Berlin and Zurich: Weidmann, 1963), 201–37; see also Ruh, 24.

[34] See Will Hasty, *Art of Arms: Studies of Aggression and Dominance in Medieval German Court Poetry* (Heidelberg: Winter, 2002) 31–46.

[35] See Green, 19–21.

[36] Hagenlocher, 6–7.

[37] Hagenlocher, 49; see also Jackson, *Chivalry,* 238, 262.

[38] For a wider study of chivalry in terms of a tension between violence and public order see Richard W. Kaeuper, *Chivalry and Violence in Medieval Europe* (Oxford: Oxford UP, 1999); see also the same author's "Chivalry and the 'Civilizing

Process'," in *Violence in Medieval Society*, edited by Richard W. Kaeuper (Woodbridge: Boydell, 2000), 21–35.

[39] Rudolf von Ems, *Alexander* edited by Victor Junk (Leipzig: Hiersemann, 1928–29; reprint Darmstadt: Wissenschaftliche Buchgesellschaft, 1970). Rudolf worked on the *Alexander* before ca. 1235 and between ca. 1240 and 1254. The work was left unfinished.

[40] For what follows see W. H. Jackson, "Warfare in the Works of Rudolf von Ems," in *Writing War: Medieval Literary Responses*, edited by Corinne Saunders, Françoise Le Saux, and Neil Thomas (Cambridge: D. S. Brewer, 2004), 49–75.

[41] See Helmut Brackert, *Rudolf von Ems: Dichtung und Geschichte* (Heidelberg: Winter, 1968), 67–71.

[42] *Ottokars Österreichische Reimchronik*, edited by Joseph Seemüller, 2 vols. (Hanover: Hahn, 1890, 1893).

[43] See Horst Wenzel, *Höfische Geschichte: Literarische Traditon und Gegenwartsdeutung in den volkssprachigen Chroniken des hohen und späten Mittelalters* (Bern, Frankfurt am Main, Las Vegas: Lang, 1980), 146–47; I am indebted to Wenzel's study (140–75) for much of what follows on the *Österreichische Reimchronik*.

[44] On the interplay of violence and control in the tournament see Juliet Vale, "Violence and the Tournament," in Kaeuper (ed.), *Violence in Medieval Society*, 143–58.

[45] Kaeuper, *Chivalry and Violence*; Hasty, *Art of Arms*.

Mobility, Politics, and Society in Medieval Germany

Charles R. Bowlus

THE LITERATURE OF MEDIEVAL GERMANY portrays a society in motion. In the Latin poem, *Ruodlieb*, which was written in the last third of the eleventh century in the Bavarian monastery of Tegernsee, the hero flees the arbitrary demands of lords in his homeland to wander about looking for the honorable service that he finally finds at the court of a good, but distant king. In one of medieval literature's great satires, the bard Ulrich von Liechtenstein travels from the Adriatic to Bohemia. Clad as a woman, Ulrich participates in a tournament in Friesach. Poor Heinrich (*Der arme Heinrich*) journeys from Germany to Sicily to seek medical aid in hope of curing a young peasant woman of leprosy. In describing the adventures of Parzival, Wolfram von Eschenbach leads his audience over a huge geographic expanse. Even the youthful Helmbrecht, son of a prosperous yeoman farmer, leaves home to seek fortune in the following of a robber baron. Further examples could easily be found.

The mobility depicted in this literature should not surprise us. Despite its reputation as a relatively static society, the civilization that produced medieval German literature was one with broadening geographic horizons.[1] It is no wonder, then, that horizontal mobility left an imprint on the literature of this epoch. Although there certainly were peasants who lived out their years in ancestral villages and monks who never left the cloister, it is no exaggeration to state that German society during the twelfth and thirteenth centuries was a machine of perpetual motion powered by energies inherent in the political and social structures of that era.

Some of that energy emanated from the highest levels of the polity. Modern scholars have coined the term "itinerant kingship" (*Reisekönigtum*) to describe one of the most essential characteristics of German governance during the Middle Ages.[2] Rulers were continually on the move and, in the process, they stimulated mobility throughout the entire society. German kings did not govern their diverse realms (*regna*) from a capital city. Accompanied by an entourage that numbered in the thousands, members of the upper aristocracy, high-ranking clerics, court chaplains, scribes, servile military-administrative retainers (*ministeriales*), specialized craftsmen, mule drivers, baggage handlers, entertainers, kings, and emperors moved incessantly about.

Royal perambulations, however, were neither arbitrary nor capricious. Indeed, quite the opposite was the case. The movements of the ruler were carefully calculated tools of governance. German kings, who generally also held the title of Roman emperor (since the German realms were a part of the Holy Roman Empire), legitimized their authority through festive rituals that purported to establish their right to rule by the grace of God.[3] As a practical matter, however, they were very different from absolute rulers. To work his will the ruler had to establish relationships that could only be cultivated through frequent personal contacts with magnates residing at some distance from royal centers. For this reason among many others he spent a great portion of his reign on the back of a horse.

Although the German realm had no official capital, a king presided over a core region or regions, where he could support his entourage from his own means and where he spent much of his time.[4] The power of the ruler was greatest within the core regions because it was there that the bulk of his resources was situated. The core varied, however, from dynasty to dynasty. The line of Heinrich I (ca. 876–936) and Otto I (912–73) (the Ottonians) was anchored in Saxony. Nonetheless, the last ruler from this dynasty, Heinrich II (973–1024), was duke of Bavaria before becoming king.[5] On the other hand, the Salians, who succeeded the Ottonians, ruled for a century from the middle Rhine. Members of this house emphasized their heritage from the Salian Franks, which explains their dynastic name.[6] On the banks of the Rhine, the Salians raised the great cathedral of Speyer that served as a massive symbol of their wealth in the region that undergirded their political power. At the beginning of Konrad II's reign in 1024, Speyer was a backwater town, a status to which it largely returned when the dynasty died out a century later. During the Salians' days of glory, however, Speyer could pretend, at least, to be the capital of Europe, despite the fact that the Salian kings apparently spent relatively little time there. The Hohenstaufens, on the other hand, were based in Swabia, but shifted toward the Mediterranean, where the dynasty met its end in southern Italy at the latter half of the thirteenth century.[7]

The assets providing a steady stream of revenue that enabled kings to govern credibly consisted of allodial possessions and fiscal lands that had not been given out as fiefs, as well as jurisdictions, advocacies, tolls, minting privileges, and rights that the ruler's ancestors had managed to accumulate. Although most of these resources were concentrated in core region(s), many royal assets were scattered throughout the realms where rulers claimed to assert authority. These assets were frequently distributed along communication routes, for, in order to exercise their prerogatives beyond the core, the ruler had to demonstrate his royal presence by journeying periodically to distant regions, where his personal wealth and powers were more circumscribed. In such distant regions a king had to negotiate, cajole, and sometimes bribe princely magnates who, more often than not, considered themselves to be his equal. Princes who presided over and resided in remote regions of the realm reveled in the luster of royal visits and in the opportunities that they provided to court royal largess. However, princes resented royal meddling in their affairs, and they only grudgingly provided hospitality for prolonged stays, lest the heavy demands of the king's entourage exhaust finite princely resources. But royal assets outside the core region could paradoxically also create problems that not uncommonly led to rebellions. Despite the fact that the Salian heartland was in the middle Rhine region, this dynasty controlled great wealth in Saxony, sometimes called "the king's kitchen." Especially important were royal assets on the fringes of the Harz Mountains where large quantities of silver were being extracted. Heinrich IV (1050–1106) administered fiscal lands in Saxony with "foreign" Swabian *ministeriales*, who grated on native Saxons, resulting in a major uprising that had long-term consequences for medieval German kingship during and after the Investiture Controversy.

When rulers journeyed from the core to distant regions, they passed through transit zones (*Durchzugsgebiete*) where fiscal properties supported their perambulations. In these regions, palaces, courts, royal monasteries, episcopal sees, and, at the end of this period, imperial cities provided support for the king's entourage. During the Carolingian and early Ottonian eras, palaces, presided over by special counts palatine, were common stopping points for rulers on the move through transit zones. For example, rulers marching from the middle Rhine to Bavaria frequented the palace of Forchheim in Franconia.[8] In the reign of Heinrich II, however, bishoprics assumed an increasingly important role in supporting royal peregrinations, not only while the king was in an episcopal city, but also when he was at a considerable distance from it. Heinrich and other rulers donated to bishops fiscal lands scattered over large areas that gave them the wherewithal to support the court (and armies) on the move. For example, when Heinrich founded the see of Bamberg, he provided it with *Streubesitz* (strewn-out possessions) stretching from Main-Franconia through the Bavarian and Carinthian Alps to Italy.[9] The role of bishops in providing transportation infrastructures for the ruler was a major factor leading to the evolution of the so-called imperial church system (*Reichskirchensystem*) that the reformed papacy vigorously challenged during the Investiture Conflict.[10] When Heinrich IV made his humiliating journey to Canossa during the winter of 1076–77, he was forced to take a circuitous route to Italy over the treacherous 6,834-foot high Mt. Cenis pass because more direct and comfortable routes from Germany to Italy were in the hands of ecclesiastical reformers.[11]

The rulers of Germany in the High Middle Ages held multiple titles. They were not only kings in Germany, but frequently in Italy and Burgundy (*Burgund*, a kingdom that encompassed the Rhone-Saône watershed) as well.

Although kings spent less time in Burgundy than in Germany or Italy, the example of Konrad II shows that rulers could intervene decisively in Burgundy when they felt that their interests were threatened there. In the winter of 1032–33, one of the coldest on record, Konrad broke off a Polish campaign to march his forces into Burgundy, which was coveted by Count Odo II of Champagne.[12]

Most important, however, German kings had the possibility of becoming Roman emperors. The concept of a Western Roman Empire was revived in 800, when Pope Leo III crowned Charlemagne emperor of the Romans in St. Peter's in Rome. The circumstances and motives behind Charlemagne's coronation are a matter of dispute. Some historians contend that this king of the Franks never intended to be crowned in Rome by the pope. Nevertheless, in the ninth century it became a matter of accepted practice that a king aspiring to become emperor must go to Rome for a formal coronation ceremony presided over by a reigning pontiff. Following Otto I's imperial coronation in 962, the king of Germany (then still called the East Frankish kingdom) automatically became a candidate for the title of Roman emperor. Yet he still had to cross the Alps and Apennines to receive the dignity officially in Rome. During the course of the twelfth century, a German king who had not yet participated in an imperial coronation was known as the "king" of Rome until the ceremony in Rome had taken place. It was also during this century that Friedrich I "Barbarossa" (ca. 1123–90) officially proclaimed that he ruled the "Holy" Roman Empire (*Sacrum imperium Romanum*).

The amount of time that rulers spent in Italy varied greatly. Heinrich II crossed the passes to Italy on just three occasions and remained there only briefly. Friedrich II (1194–1250), in contrast, spent most of his reign there.[13] All of them, however, were very much aware of Rome's symbolic importance and understood the economic significance of Italy. Rulers obviously knew that it was essential to cultivate supporters in key positions in Italy, and they went to great lengths to maintain transportation infrastructures in the Alps ensuring them entrance to and egress from Italy.[14]

Kings, emperors, and their followings, however, were not the only persons incessantly on the move. Great lay and ecclesiastical princes were quite mobile as well. Leading members of wealthy and powerful families reveled in gaining proximity to the king (*Königsnähe*). Thus, they frequently did not wait for the ruler to come to them. A royal visit strained princely resources and could lead to unwanted inquiries into the management of crown lands. Consequently, princes often traveled over great distances to meet with the king either in the royal heartland or in a transit zone. There were numerous occasions for powerful persons to gather with rulers. Solemn ceremonies on holy feast days, coronations, and crown wearing events provided opportunities for princes to meet with the emperor in person, to petition for favors or to plea for the redress of grievances.

Since rulers made much of their responsibility to keep the peace, conclaves of notables with the king to establish regional order (*Landfrieden*) were often accompanied by agreements that affected the realm as a whole.[15]

Moreover, the powerful of medieval Germany traveled for reasons other than to meet with the king. Archbishops, for example, went to Rome to receive the pallium, a fleece signifying their high office. They also called their suffragan bishops together for diocesan synods. Lay princes too met in the absence of the ruler. Obviously, when aristocrats plotted the rebellions that punctuated the history of medieval Germany, they hatched their conspiracies at clandestine conclaves in the king's absence. There were also pacific occasions that witnessed the gathering of important persons. Weddings, for example, were opportunities for individuals from distant parts to come together. Since marriage involved complicated exchanges of property, marital contracts frequently resulted in the acquisition of scattered possessions, the administration of which necessitated the movement of the notable or his underlings. Aristocratic wealth and privileges were not neatly concentrated territorially. Powerful dynasties such as the Hohenstaufens, Welfs, Andechs, Babenbergs, Zähringer, and others possessed widely dispersed allods, fiefs, castles, and advocacies, all of which had to be administered and visited, at least occasionally. In the process of managing assets, magnates were frequently in motion. The power of the house of Andechs, for example, was first established in western Bavaria near a lake called the Ammersee. But by the mid-thirteenth century, when the male line died out, the dynasty's possessions were scattered over a huge region from Thuringia to the Adriatic.

When the great princes of medieval Germany moved about, they set hundreds, if not thousands of others in motion as well. The power of a magnate was measured by the size of his entourage. Like kings, lay and ecclesiastical princes maintained scores of retainers (*ministeriales*) who were trained warriors and who, despite their unfree status, could become quite wealthy depending on whom they served.[16] Some imperial *ministeriales* rose to positions of high administrative and military competence in the empire. John B. Freed, however, has illuminated the frustrations of the servile retainers of lesser princes.[17] These men chafed under restrictions which limited their marital opportunities and the possibility of upward social advancement that could come with it. On the other hand, it is important to note that while fetters on vertical social mobility disgruntled some *ministeriales*, others experienced through their service a high degree of horizontal and sometimes even vertical mobility, which conferred on them broader views of the world and their place in it. Despite laws that emphasized their servile status, ministerials did not really constitute a homogeneous social class.

The horizontal mobility of medieval German rulers, princes, and their retinues extended well beyond Germany and Italy. During the twelfth century the emperors Konrad III (1093–1152) and Friedrich I launched major crusades that sent thousands of German warriors eastward. To be sure, these two crusades ended in fiascos. Nevertheless, they cannot simply be dismissed as romantic, meaningless adventures that were undertaken without proper preparation. Rudolf Hiestand has shown that Barbarossa's expedition, despite its ultimate failure, exhibits evidence of detailed planning with special attention given to logistics.[18] In addition to armed expeditions that were called for specific purposes, individuals took the cross and went to the Holy Land on their own. These were hardly "unscheduled" ventures because they booked passage on ships that made regularly scheduled voyages to the East.[19] During the course of the Middle Ages transportation infrastructures developed that conveyed scores of thousands on a regular basis from Europe to the Levant. The crusades to which historians have assigned numbers were major expeditions led by kings or princes. However, the crusades were much more than that; they constituted a continual pilgrimage of thousands of lesser status. From the foundation of the Kingdom of Jerusalem in 1099 to the fall of Acre in 1291, there was a stream of "pilgrims" to the East to defend Latin principalities, to worship at holy places, and even to settle there. To convey these pilgrims, transportation networks were established and maintained.

It is important to remember that the crusades were a part of a general European expansionist movement in the centuries following the turn of the first millennium.[20] Pilgrims journeyed not only to the Holy Land, but also crossed the Pyrenees to participate in the conquest of the Islamic emirates of Spain and to worship at the shrine of St. James in Compostella at the extreme northwestern corner of the Iberian Peninsula. Many Germans became deeply involved in yet another expansionist movement along the shores of the Baltic that can, I believe, properly be understood under the rubric of crusade. Certainly, military-religious orders similar to those in the Levant and in Spain became prominent in Eastern Europe during the course of the thirteenth century for the purpose of converting pagan peoples residing there.

The movement of people, thousands of them, whether it was from the Rhineland to Jerusalem, from Hamburg to Rome, or just from Bamberg to Mainz, necessitated transportation infrastructures that had an enduring impact on millions of medieval Europeans. This perpetual motion affected the lives of many who never strayed far from their ancestral homelands, but who became, nonetheless, cogs in the wheels of transportation networks. Just as the movements of kings and princes was far from arbitrary or capricious, the movements of less important individuals followed well defined routes, along which there were shipwrights, baggage handlers, farriers, mule drivers, innkeepers, toll collectors, money changers, river pilots, and many others.[21]

Natural transportation arteries facilitated movement in medieval Germany. Foremost among these are fluvial systems whose origins lie deep in the interior of the continent. Because annual rainfall in Germany is evenly distributed, the flow of most rivers is relatively constant even in summer. The most important river network was that of the Rhine River and its major tributaries, the Ruhr, Mosel, and Main. The latter river was extremely important because a very easy portage from a tributary of the Main, the Rednitz, to the Altmühl, a tributary of the Danube, linked the Rhine with the only major fluvial system that flows eastward to reach the Black Sea. Charlemagne tried (and failed) to construct a canal on the narrow divide between these great watersheds.[22] Nevertheless, the portage connecting the river systems permitted easy passage through Franconia, which explains its importance as a transit zone. In the Middle Ages it was much easier to move north or south via river systems than east or west.[23] Not only the Rhine, but also the Elbe, Oder, and Vistula rivers are oriented primarily in a south-north direction. The colonization and Christianization of the Baltic littoral made it possible to use the Oder and the Vistula to tap the wealth of the interior of east-central Europe, moving men, ideas, and material goods first northward toward the sea, then westward to the booming port of Lübeck. In the thirteenth century, the growing urban communities of northeastern Europe formed an association called the Hanseatic League (*Hansa*) that linked the Rhineland and the ports of the North Sea with the Baltic.[24]

Of course, there were also overland routes along which infrastructures existed that supported the movement of men, animals, and goods in an east-west direction. The most famous of these was the so-called *Hellweg* (a term indicating a *via regia*, a royal highway) that, in Carolingian times, ran from Cologne through Westphalia to the Weser. It was later extended to Halle and Magdeburg and points further east.[25] Although the towns along this west-east corridor also joined the Hanseatic League, they operated according to a different legal system than did the Baltic towns, whose constitutional framework was based on the law of Lübeck, a maritime town. The towns along the *Hellweg* adopted constitutions derived from Magdeburg law, which was better suited for overland commerce. By the end of the thirteenth century the towns of medieval Germany had become well-defined juridical entities according to the specifications of their charters. The highest-ranking urban centers were the imperial free cities that were self-governing, which meant that they possessed *Reichsunmittelbarkeit*: there was no intermediate authority between them and the emperor. The origins of cities varied greatly. Some, such as Cologne, Augsburg, and Regensburg, had been sizable settlements in Roman times and witnessed a major spurt of growth in the early years of the second millennium. Others, such as Magdeburg and Lübeck, only became prominent during the Middle Ages. Still others, such as Strasbourg and Augsburg, were episcopal centers that managed to gain autonomy from their bishops, while sites that had originally been royal palaces evolved into urban centers because of their importance to the king's itinerary. An example of the latter is Ulm, a royal facility situated on an easy Danube crossing on a major route from the middle Rhine to Italy, which led Hohenstaufen rulers to stop there on a regular basis during the twelfth century.[26] Sometimes the existence of a palace with its garrison was viewed as a menace to the autonomy of towns. In 1262, the citizens of Zurich demolished the imperial palace on the Lindenhof as a means of gaining chartered privileges.[27]

There are many examples of towns that sprang into existence during the High Middle Ages without formal authorization of king or bishop. Members of the high aristocracy founded towns with increasing frequency in the twelfth and thirteenth centuries. The founding of Munich reveals some of the motives that were directly related to the development of transportation infrastructures.[28] The bishop of Freising controlled the lucrative commerce on the important Augsburg-Salzburg highway because the bridge over the Isar at Föhring was situated on the property belonging to his see. In 1154 the duke of Bavaria, Heinrich (der Löwe), with the intention of establishing his authority over traffic on this road, built a bridge where a number of villages were clustered on the banks of the river, and then destroyed the structure belonging to the bishop. Thus, the duke forged an amalgam of villages into a town that outlasted the authority of his dynasty in Bavaria. Members of the high aristocracy also established towns in regions that had been by-passed earlier and were just beginning to develop in the twelfth century. In the southwestern corner of German-speaking Europe, the dukes of Zähringen established towns by the score as they created new lordships out of the wilderness regions such as the Black Forest and parts of western Switzerland.[29] As the success of such new towns as Freiburg im Breisgau and Bern became known, a rash of urban foundations ensued.[30] However, many of these establishments failed to meet the expectations of their founders. Although they possessed charters and were called towns, they became picturesque "dwarf towns," which they remain today. Nevertheless, they contributed to the maintenance of transportation infrastructures, for, by the end of the thirteenth century settlements, no matter how small, existed within a day's march from one another.

Not only did kings, bishops, members of the nobility, their followings, and merchants move around, but some peasants and specialized laborers did as well. Despite legal restrictions on their mobility (*Freizügigkeit*), the unfree sometimes moved, frequently over great distances, to settle in remote regions. Farmers from the lowlands of Western Europe were encouraged by landlords in the marshes of Eastern Europe to migrate, drain swamps, and create productive lands.[31] In the interior of Europe, the dukes of Zähringen, mentioned above, were among the leaders of colonization efforts into medieval Europe's vast internal frontier. In the high Alps of Vorarlberg, eastern and central Switzerland, German-speaking colonizers called Walser penetrated into rugged valleys that had previously been left unpopulated.[32]

Peasants were not the only ones to face difficult circumstances on the frontiers of medieval Europe. Miners plied their dangerous trade in such forbidding regions as the Harz Mountains, the Bohemian Forest, the eastern Alps, and the Carpathians.[33] Fur traders and trappers sought precious wares in the frigid forests of northeastern Europe. Less dangerous, but extremely demanding occupations associated with the arts also set thousands in motion taking them far from the so-called core regions, the watersheds of the Rhine, the Thames, the Seine, and the Loire. The great churches of medieval Europe were not all raised in the proximity of the Isle de France. The craftsmanship of high Gothic sculpture had obviously reached such eastern parts of Germany as Bamberg and Naumburg by the thirteenth century. Hence, it should not be surprising that an eastern German prince such as Hermann, the landgrave (*Landgraf*) of Thuringia, became a major patron of a cosmopolitan movement in literature at approximately the same time.[34] Even the colonizers, the Zähringer, were patrons of literature.[35]

The perpetual motion that was so characteristic of Germany (and Europe) in the twelfth and thirteenth centuries slowed considerably in the fourteenth and fifteenth centuries. Rulers, for example, rarely went to Rome to receive the imperial title. Rudolf of Habsburg, who rose to fill the vacuum created by the demise of the Hohenstaufen dynasty in 1268, started a trend. He did not become Roman emperor. Although there were earlier rulers who had won the title of "German king," but who then failed to be crowned in a formal ceremony in Rome, such cases were rare during the more than three centuries between Otto I's imperial coronation in 962 and Rudolf's election to the kingship in 1273. Benjamin Arnold has called attention to an animal fable of the fourteenth century, representing Rudolf as a wily fox who was shrewd enough to avoid the temptations of the Lion's den (Italy).[36] In fact, however, Rudolf did have imperial ambitions, and, during his reign, he came to control all of the major Alpine routes to the south, which gave him the means to reach for the imperial crown.[37] Moreover, on three occasions dates for his coronation were established, each of which he failed to honor. He remained in Germany to be buried (as a king, not as an emperor) with the Salians in the cathedral of Speyer, which by then had once again become a middling town with no claim to be the capital of Europe.

The decreasing mobility of people in the late Middle Ages is not only reflected in the activities of the men who held the title of king, but also in the structure of the German aristocracy. During the High Middle Ages Germany was ruled by an elite consisting of a small number of extended families whose lineages were well known throughout that society. The boundaries between this elite and the remainder of the population were so clear that they needed no formal legal definition. By the late thirteenth century, however, most of the great princely families had died out in the male line. Hohenstaufens, Welfs, Andechs, Babenbergs, and Zähringer, whose lordships and privileges were scattered over much of central Europe, Italy, and beyond, had ceased to exist, and they were replaced by families whose territorial bases were smaller and more concentrated.[38] Although the pedigree of such families as the Habsburgs and Wittelsbachs was not without distinction, their lineage and their wealth cannot not be compared to that of the great dynasties of the early thirteenth century. By the end of the thirteenth century, a *Who's Who* of the German aristocracy became necessary. Thus, the *Heerschildordnung*, a legally defined feudal pyramid ranking members of the upper social orders, was formulated.[39] In the two centuries following 1273, no princely family succeeded in establishing a dominant position in the empire. The result was fierce competition for German kingship, a less prestigious prize than the imperial title. Moreover, the principal of election triumphed over the ability of a reigning king to select his son as co-ruler and successor.[40] As the fourteenth century dawned, horizontal mobility lessened and the political and social order became more clearly defined.

Notes

[1] See Hagen Keller, *Zwischen regionaler Begrenzung und universalem Horizont: Deutschland im Imperium der Salier und Staufer 1024 bis 1250* (Berlin: Propyläen, 1986). Some recent histories have been translated into English. The best translation is that of Horst Fuhrmann's *Deutsche Geschichte im hohen Mittelalter von der Mitte des 11. bis zum Ende des 12. Jahrhunderts*, 2nd ed. (Göttingen: Vandenhoeck & Ruprecht, 1983), published in English as *Germany in the High Middle Ages c. 1050–1200*, trans. Timothy Reuter (Cambridge: Cambridge UP, 1986), but I prefer Alfred Haverkamp's *Aufbruch und Gestaltung, Deutschland, 1056–1273* (Munich: C. H. Beck, 1984), published in English as *Medieval Germany, 1056–1273*, trans. H. Braun and R. Mortimer (Oxford: Oxford UP, 1984), because Haverkamp, like Keller, interprets medieval German history in a larger geographic framework and continues his narrative to 1273 and the election of Rudolf of Habsburg. An excellent short history covering the entire Middle Ages is that of Benjamin Arnold, *Medieval Germany, 500–1300: A Political Interpretation* (Toronto: U of Toronto P, 1997). Note should also be taken of a short but significant article by M. Toch, "Welfs, Hohenstaufen and Habsburgs," in *The New Cambridge Medieval History*, vol. 5 (ca. 1198–ca. 1300), ed. D. Abulafia (Cambridge UP, 1999), 375–404.

[2] See Hans C. Peyer, "Das Reisekönigtum des Mittelalters," *Vierteljahrschrift für Sozial- und Wirtschaftsgeschichte* 51 (1964): 1–21. An excellent explanation of this type of rule is available in English: J. W. Bernhardt, *Itinerant Kingship and Royal Monasteries in Early Medieval Germany* (Cambridge: Cambridge UP, 1993), 60–68. Also see Arnold, *Medieval Germany*, 170–74.

[3] For a summary of trends in medieval German political history, see C. R. Bowlus, "The Early Kaiserreich in Recent German Historiography," *Central European History* 21 (1990): 349–67.

[4] Andreas C. Schlunk, *Königsmacht und Krongut: Die Machtgrundlage des deutschen Königtums im 13. Jahrhundert* (Stuttgart: F. Steiner Verlag, 1988).

5 Stefan Weinfurter, "Kaiser Heinrich II. (1002–1024) — ein Herrscher aus Bayern," *Oberbayerisches Archiv* 122 (1998): 31–53. Weinfurter has produced a comprehensive study of Heinrich II's reign, *Heinrich II. (1002–1024): Herrscher am Ende der Zeiten* (Regensburg: Pustet, 1999).

6 Weinfurter's *Herrschaft und Reich der Salier: Grundlinien einer Umbruchzeit* (Sigmaringen: Thorbecke, 1991) now available in English translation under the title, *The Salian Century: Main Currents in an Age of Transition*, trans. Barbara Bowlus (Philadelphia: U of Pennsylvania P, 1999), with a historiographical introduction by C. R. Bowlus and German and English bibliographies. Hereafter, I shall cite the English translation. For a comprehensive view of the Salian era, see the essays in *Die Salier und das Reich*, 3 vols. ed. Weinfurter (Sigmaringen: Thorbecke, 1991).

7 On the shift of the Hohenstaufen *imperium* toward the Mediterranean, see the essays in *Friedrich Barbarossa: Handlungsspielräume und Wirkungsweisen des Staufischen Kaisers*, ed. Alfred Haverkamp (Sigmaringen: Thorbecke, 1992). For the movements of Friedrich I, see T. Kölzer, "Der Hof Friedrich Barbarossas und die Reichsfürsten," in *Stauferreich im Wandel: Ordnungsvorstellungen und Politik in der Zeit Friedrich Barbarossas*, ed. Stefan Weinfurter (Stuttgart: Thorbecke, 2002), 220–36. For the great changes in the structure of the empire that occurred during the reign of Barbarossa, see also the other essays in this volume.

8 Wilhelm Störmer, "Karolingische Pfalzen in Franken," in *Regensburg, Bayern und Europa: Festschrift für Kurt Reindel zum 70. Geburtstag*, ed. L. Kolmer and P. Segl (Regensburg: Universitätsverlag, 1995), 161–73.

9 Weinfurter, *Heinrich II.*, 250–68.

10 T. Reuter, "The 'Imperial Church System' of the Ottonian and Salian Rulers: A Reconsideration," in *Journal of Ecclesiastical History*, 347–74, raised doubts about the utility of the concept "imperial church system." His objections notwithstanding, the concept can still be used with caution, as in Ute-Renate Blumenthal, *The Investiture Controversy: Church Monarchy from the Ninth to the Twelfth Century* (Philadelphia: U of Pennsylvania P, 1988).

11 Weinfurter, *The Salian Century*, 149.

12 Weinfurter, *The Salian Century*, 47–50.

13 See Weinfurter, *Heinrich II.* and D. Abulafia, *Frederick II: A Medieval Emperor* (London: Penguin, 1988).

14 The literature on transportation infrastructure during the middle ages is very large and growing. Wilhelm Störmer has been writing about such structures between Germany and Italy for more than thirty years. His most recent publication is "Alpenübergänge von Bayern nach Italien. Transitprobleme zwischen Spätantike und Hochmittelalter," in *Bayern und Italien: Politik, Kultur, Kommunikation (8–15. Jahrhundert). Festschrift für Kurt Reindel zum 75. Geburtstag*, eds. H. Dopsch, S. Freund, and A. Schmid (Munich: C. H. Beck, 2001), 37–54. See also a recent article by Stephan Freund, "Kommunikation in der Herrschaft Heinrichs II," *Zeitschrift für bayerische Landesgeschichte* 66 (2003), 1–32. Major methodological breakthroughs in understanding how transportation infrastructures were established and maintained and how they functioned have recently been made by Michael McCormick in *The Origins of the European Economy: Communications and*

Commerce, A.D. 300–900 (Cambridge: Cambridge UP, 2001). Although McCormick deals primarily with the early middle ages (especially the eighth and ninth centuries), his methodology can be applied to later periods.

[15] See the collected studies on the *Landfrieden* and its importance to the relationship between the king and local notables by E. Wadle, *Landfrieden, Strafe, Recht: Zwölf Studien zum Mittelalter* (Duncker & Humblot: Berlin, 2001). An excellent collection by a variety of historians is *Landfrieden: Anspruch und Wirklichkeit*, ed. A. Buschmann and E. Wadle (Paderborn, Munich, Vienna, Zurich: Ferdinand Schöningh, 2002).

[16] The classic study of the *ministerialität* is that by Karl Bosl, *Die Reichsministerialität der Salier und Staufer: Ein Beitrag zur Geschichte des hochmittelalterlichen deutschen Volkes, Staates und Reiches* (Stuttgart: Hiersemann, 1950–51). For more recent reading on ministerials, see John B. Freed, *Noble Bondsmen: Ministerial Marriages in the Archdiocese of Salzburg, 1100–1343* (Ithaca: Cornell UP, 1995) and Benjamin Arnold, *German Knighthood 1050–1300* (Oxford: Clarendon Press, 1985).

[17] Freed, *Noble Bondsmen.*

[18] See, especially, R. Hiestand, *"precipua tocius christianismi columpna:* Barbarossa und der Kreuzzug," in *Friedrich Barbarossa,* ed. Haverkamp.

[19] Giles Constable, "Medieval Charters as a Source for the History of the Crusades," in *Crusade and Settlement: Papers Read at the First Conference of the Society for the Study of the Crusades and the Latin East and Presented to R. C. Smail,* ed. Peter Edbury (Cardiff, U of Cardiff P, 1985), 64–88, and by the same author, "The Financing of the Crusades in the Twelfth Century," in *Outremer — Studies in the History of the Crusading Kingdom of Jerusalem Presented to Joshua Prawer,* ed. B. Z. Kedar, H. E. Mayer, and R. C. Smail (Jerusalem: Yad Izhak Ben-Zvi Institute, 1982), 64–88. Both articles have been republished in Giles Constable, *Monks, Hermits and Crusaders in Medieval Europe* (London: Variorum Reprints, 1988), articles viii and ix.

[20] Robert Bartlett, *The Making of the Middle Ages: Conquest, Colonization and Cultural Change 950–1350* (Princeton: Princeton UP, 1993).

[21] For the social complexities of travel networks, see the essays in *Gastfreundschaft, Taverne und Gasthaus im Mittelalter,* ed. H. C. Peyer, Schriften des Historischen Kollegs 3 (Munich: Oldenbourg, 1983).

[22] H. Hoffmann, "Fossa Carolina," *Karl der Große,* ed. H. Beumann (Düsseldorf: Schwann, 1965), 437–53.

[23] K. Schünemann, "Deutsche Kriegführung im Osten während des Mittelalters," *Deutsches Archiv* 2 (1938): 54–84, in an article that can still be read with much profit, called attention to the military difficulties involved in moving from west to east.

[24] Philippe Dollinger, *La Hanse: 12e–17e siecles* (Paris: Aubier, 1964).

[25] See the essays by Albert K. Hömberg, *Zwischen Rhein und Weser: Aufsätze und Vorträge zur Geschichte Westfalens* (Münster: Aschendorff, 1967).

[26] Fuhrmann, *Germany,* 197.

[27] Anton Largiader, *Geschichte von Stadt und Landschaft Zürich* (Zurich: Eugen Rentsch Verlag, 1945), 85. The Zürcher revolted against the Hohenstaufens,

whom they had, until then, supported. Consequently, they won from Richard of Cornwall the coveted *Reichsunmittelbarkeit*.

[28] See the studies of Louis Carlen, "Les communautés rurales des pasteurs en Allemagne, Autriche et en Suisse," *Recueils de la Societé Jean Bodin* 44 (1987), 113–26, and by the same author, *Kultur des Wallis im Mittelalter* (Brig, Switzerland: Rotten Verlag, 1981).

[29] The important role of the Zähringen family in creating lordships through colonization of sparsely settled regions was first pointed out in a classic article published in 1935 by Theodor Mayer, "Der *Staat* der Herzöge von Zähringen," reprinted in his *Mittelalterliche Studien* (Lindau: Thorbecke, 1959), 404–24. Geoffrey Barraclough has translated Mayer's essay in a companion volume to his *The Origins of Modern Germany* (Oxford: Blackwell, 1946). For recent studies of the Zähringens, see the essays in K. Schmid, ed., *Die Zähringer*, 3 vols. (Sigmaringen: Thorbecke, 1986–90).

[30] Hans Planitz, *Die deutsche Stadt im Mittelalter: Von der Römerzeit bis zu den Zunftkämpfen* (Graz, Cologne: Böhlau, 1954), especially 132–48 and 173–79.

[31] Charles Higounet, *Die deutsche Ostsiedlung im Mittelalter* (Berlin: Siedler, 1986).

[32] On inner Alpine colonization, see Toch's article and references, "Welfs," 399, as in note 1. On the concept of the "internal frontier" during the Middle Ages, see A. R. Lewis, "The Closing of the Medieval Frontier: 1250–1350," *Speculum* 33 (1958): 475–83.

[33] J. Nef, "Mining and Metallurgy in Medieval Civilisation," *Cambridge Economic History* 2 (1952): 432–87.

[34] Joachim Bumke, *Mäzene im Mittelalter: Die Gönner und Auftraggeber der Höfischen Literatur in Deutschland 1150–1300* (Munich: Beck, 1979), 159–68.

[35] Volker Mertens, "Das literarische Mäzenatentum der Zähringer," in Schmid, *Die Zähringer*, vol. 2, 116–33.

[36] Arnold, *Medieval Germany*, 123.

[37] See the essays in *Rudolf von Habsburg 1273–1291: Eine Königsherrschaft zwischen Tradition und Wandel*, ed. E. Boshof and F.-R. Erkens (Cologne: Böhlau, 1993).

[38] See T. Martin, "Die Pfalzen im dreizehnten Jahrhundert," in J. Fleckenstein, ed., *Herrschaft und Stand: Untersuchungen zur Sozialgeschichte im 13. Jahrhundert*, Veröffentlichungen des Max-Plank-Instituts für Geschichte, vol. 51, 277–301; Martin argues that the loss of fiscal lands by the Hohenstaufens restricted the movement of later rulers outside of their core regions.

[39] K.-F. Krieger, *Die Lehnshoheit der deutschen Könige im Spätmittelalter (ca. 1200–1437)* (Aalen: Scientia, 1979), 117–55, and "Fürstliche Standesvorrechte im Spätmittelalter," *Blätter für deutsche Landesgeschichte* 122 (1986): 91–117.

[40] For the most recent historical research on the establishment of a system of imperial electors, see F.-R. Erkens, *Kurfürsten und Königswahl: Zu neuen Theorien über den Königswahlparagraphen im Sachsenspiegel und die Entstehung des Kurfürstenkollegiums*, Monumenta Germaniae Historica. Texte und Studien 30 (Hannover: Hahnsche Buchhandlung, 2002).

Primary Literature

German Anthologies

An Anthology of German Literature, 800–1750. Ed. Peter Demetz and W. T. H. Jackson. Englewood Cliffs, NJ: Prentice Hall, 1968.

Anthology of Medieval German Literature. Ed. Albert K. Wimmer. 3rd rev. ed. <http://www.nd.edu/~gantho/>; 2nd ed. Berrien Springs: Vande Vere Publishing, 1991.

Deutsche Dichtung des Mittelalters. Ed. Michael Curschmann and Ingeborg Glier. Vol. 2. Munich: Hanser, 1980–81.

Deutsche Liederdichter im 13. Jahrhundert. Ed. Carl von Kraus. Revised ed. Gisela Kornrumpf. 2 vols. Tübingen: Niemeyer, 1978.

Die deutsche Literatur: Texte und Zeugnisse. Ed. Helmut de Boor, et al. Vols. I/1 & I/2. Munich: Beck, 1965.

Frauen in der deutschen Literaturgeschichte. Die ersten 800 Jahre. Ein Lesebuch. Ed. Albrecht Classen. Frankfurt am Main: Peter Lang, 2000.

Mittelhochdeutsches Lesebuch: Mit Grammatik und Wörterbuch. Ed. Albert Bachmann. Zurich: S. Höhr, 1982. 16th ed. Zurich: Beer & Cie, 1960.

Politische Lyrik des deutschen Mittelalters. Ed. Ulrich Müller. 2 vols. Göppingen: Kümmerle, 1972.

Works

Das Alexanderlied (ca. 1150)

Das Alexanderlied des Pfaffen Lamprecht. Das Rolandslied des Pfaffen Konrad. Ed. Friedrich Maurer. Deutsche Literatur in Entwicklungsreihen: Geistliche Dichtung des Mittelalters, 5. 1940. Reprint: Darmstadt: Wissenschaftliche Buchgesellschaft, 1964. English trans.: *The Strassburg Alexander and the Munich Oswald: Pre-Courtly Adventure of the German Middle Ages*. Trans. J. W. Thomas. Columbia, SC: Camden House, 1989.

Alpharts Tod (ca. 1250)

Alpharts Tod. Ed. Ernst Martin, in *Deutsches Heldenbuch*, 5 vols. Vol. 2: 3–54. Berlin: Weidmann, 1866.

Beatrijs van Nazareth (1200–1268)

Seven manieren van minne. Middelnederlandse tekst met een inleiding en hertaling door Rob Faesen S. J., reproduction of 1926 critical edition. Kapellen:

Uitgeverij Pelckmans, 1999. English trans: *Beguine Spirituality: Mystical Writings of Mechthild von Magdeburg, Beatrice of Nazareth, and Hadewijch of Brabant.* Ed. and introduced by Fiona Bowie. Trans. Oliver Davies. New York: Crossroad, 1990.

Biterolf und Dietleip (mid-13th century)

Biterolf und Dietleip. Ed. Oskar Jänick, in *Deutsches Heldenbuch*, 5 vols. Vol. 1: 1–197. Berlin: Weidmann, 1866.

Dietrichs Flucht (ca. 1250)

Dietrichs Flucht. Ed. Ernst Martin, in *Deutsches Heldenbuch*, 5 vols. Vol. 2: 57–215. Berlin: Weidmann, 1866.

Ecken Liet (ca. 1250)

Ecken Liet. Ed. Julius Zupitza, in *Deutsches Heldenbuch*, 5 vols. Vol. 5: 219–64. Berlin: Weidmann, 1870.

Eilhart von Oberg (before 1189–after 1209)

Tristrant. Ed. Franz Lichtenstein. Hildesheim: Olms, 1973. English trans.: *Eilhart von Oberge's "Tristrant."* Trans. J. W. Thomas. Lincoln: U of Nebraska P, 1978.

Elizabeth von Schönau (ca. 1129–65)

St. Elizabeth. *Die Visionen der hl. Elisabeth und die Schriften der Aebte Ekbert und Emecho von Schönau.* Ed. F. W. E. Roth. Brünn: Verlag der Studien aus dem Benedictiner- und Cistercienser Orden, 1884. Modern English translation: Elisabeth of Schönau, *The Complete Works.* Trans. Anne L. Clark. With a Preface by Barbara Newman. New York: Paulist Press, 2000.

Freidank (fl. 1220–30)

Bescheidenheit. Ed. Heinrich Ernst Bezzenberger. Halle: Waisenhaus, 1872. Modern German translation: *Freidanks Bescheidenheit: Auswahl, Mittelhochdeutsch-Neuhochdeutsch.* Trans. and ed. with an introduction by Wolfgang Spiewok. Leipzig: Reclam, 1985.

Albrecht von Kemenaten (late 13th century)

Goldemar. In *Deutsches Heldenbuch*, vol. 5., ed. Julius Zupitza. Berlin: Weidmann, 1870. Reprint Dublin and Zurich: Weidmann, 1968.

Gottfried von Strassburg (died before 1230)

Tristan. Ed. Friedrich Ranke. Munich: Bruckmann, 1925. Modern German trans.: *Gottfried von Straßburg, Tristan.* Ed. and trans. Rüdiger Krohn, vol. 1. Stuttgart: Reclam, 1984. English trans.: *Gottfried von Straßburg, "Tristan."* With the surviving fragments of the *Tristran* of Thomas. Trans. A. T. Hatto. London: Penguin, 1960, 1967, 1974.

Hadewych (ca. 1150–ca. 1200)

De Visioenen van Hadewych. Ed. J. Van Mierlo, 2 vols. Leuven: Vlaamische Boekenhalle, 1924/25.

Hadewijch Brieven. Ed. J. Van Mierlo, 2 vols. Antwerp: Standaard Boekhandel, 1947.

Hadewijch Strophische Gedichten. Ed. J. Van Mierlo, 2 vols. Antwerp: Standaard Boekhandel, 1942.

Poetry of Hadewijch. Ed. Marieke J. E. H. T. van Baest. Leuven: Peeters, 1998. English translation: *Beguine Spirituality. Mystical Writings of Mechthild von Magdeburg, Beatrice of Nazareth, and Hadewijch of Brabant.* Ed. and introduced by Fiona Bowie. Trans. Oliver Davies. New York: Crossroad, 1990.

Hartmann von Aue (ca. 1160–ca. 1210)

Der arme Heinrich. Ed. Hermann Paul, rev. Kurt Gärtner. Tübingen: Niemeyer, 2001. English trans.: *Hartmann von Aue. Arthurian Romances, Tales, and Lyric Poetry: The Complete Works of Hartmann von Aue.* Trans. with a commentary by Frank Tobin, Kim Vivian, and Richard H. Lawson. University Park: Pennsylvania State UP, 2001 and *The Narrative Works of Hartmann von Aue.* Trans. R. W. Fisher. Göppingen: Kümmerle, 1983.

Erec. Ed. Albert Leitzmann. 6th rev. ed. by Christoph Cormeau and Kurt Gärtner. Tübingen: Niemeyer, 1985. English trans.: *Hartmann von Aue. Arthurian Romances, Tales, and Lyric Poetry: The Complete Works of Hartmann von Aue.* Trans. with a commentary by Frank Tobin, Kim Vivian, and Richard H. Lawson. University Park: Pennsylvania State UP, 2001; *The Narrative Works of Hartmann von Aue.* Trans. R. W. Fisher. Göppingen: Kümmerle, 1983; and *Erec.* Trans. with an introduction and commentary by Michael Resler. Philadelphia: U of Pennsylvania P, 1987.

Gregorius. Ed. Friedrich Neumann. Stuttgart: Reclam, 1963. English trans.: *Hartmann von Aue. Arthurian Romances, Tales, and Lyric Poetry: The Complete Works of Hartmann von Aue.* Trans. with a commentary by Frank Tobin, Kim Vivian, and Richard H. Lawson. University Park: Pennsylvania State UP, 2001 and *The Narrative Works of Hartmann von Aue.* Trans. R. W. Fisher. Göppingen: Kümmerle, 1983.

Iwein. Ed. G. F. Benecke and Karl Lachmann. 7th rev. ed. by Ludwig Wolff. Berlin: de Gruyter, 1968. English trans.: *Hartmann von Aue. Arthurian Romances, Tales, and Lyric Poetry: The Complete Works of Hartmann von Aue.* Trans. with a commentary by Frank Tobin, Kim Vivian, and Richard H. Lawson. University Park: Pennsylvania State UP, 2001 and *The Narrative Works of Hartmann von Aue.* Trans. R. W. Fisher. Göppingen: Kümmerle, 1983.

Die Klage — Das (zweite) Büchlein. Ed. Herta Zutt. Berlin: de Gruyter, 1968. English trans.: Hartmann von Aue. *Klagebüchlein.* Ed. and trans. by Thomas L. Keller. With an introduction by Keller. Göppingen: Kümmerle, 1986. *Hartmann von Aue. Arthurian Romances, Tales, and Lyric Poetry: The Complete Works of Hartmann von Aue.* Trans. with a commentary by Frank Tobin, Kim Vivian, and Richard H. Lawson. University Park: Pennsylvania State UP, 2001.

Lieder. Ed. and trans. (Modern German) Ernst von Reusner. Stuttgart: Reclam, 1985. English translation of the lyrics: *Hartmann von Aue. Arthurian Romances, Tales, and Lyric Poetry: The Complete Works of Hartmann von Aue.* Trans. with a commentary by Frank Tobin, Kim Vivian, and Richard H. Lawson. University Park: Pennsylvania State UP, 2001.

Heinrich von dem Türlin (fl. ca. 1230)

Diu Crône von Heinrich von dem Türlin. Ed. G. H. F. Scholl. Stuttgart: Bibliothek des Litterarischen Vereins, no. 27, 1852. Reprint Amsterdam: Rodopi, 1966; *Die Krone (Verse 1–12281) nach der Handschrift 2779 der Österreichischen Nationalbibliothek.* Ed. Fritz Peter Knapp and Manuela Niesner. Tübingen: Niemeyer, 2000. Translation in English: J. W. Thomas, *Heinrich von dem Türlîn. The Crown: A Tale of King Arthur's Court.* Lincoln: U of Nebraska P, 1989.

Heinrich von Freiberg (wrote ca. 1300)

Tristan und Isolde (Fortsetzung des Tristanromans Gottfrieds von Straßburg). Ed. Danielle Buschinger, trans. (modern German) Wolfgang Spiewok. Greifswald: Reineke, 1993.

Heinrich von Veldeke (ca. 1145–ca. 1190)

Eneasroman: Die Berliner Bilderhandschrift mit Übersetzung und Kommentar. Ed. Hans Fromm. With the miniatures of the manuscript and an essay by Dorothea and Peter Diemer. Frankfurt am Main: Deutscher Klassiker Verlag, 1992. English trans.: *Eneit.* Trans. J. W. Thomas. New York: Garland, 1985.

Jüngerer Titurel (ca. 1270–75)

Albrechts von Scharfenberg Jüngerer Titurel. Ed. Werner Wolf. Continued by Kurt Nyholm. 6 vols. to date. Berlin: Akademie Verlag, 1955–.

Diu Klage (ca. 1220)

Die Klage. Ed. Karl Bartsch. Darmstadt: Wissenschaftliche Buchgesellschaft, 1964. English trans.: Winder McConnell, *The Lament of the Nibelungen (Diu Chlage).* Columbia, SC: Camden House, 1994.

Konrad von Würzburg (fl. ca. 1257–87)

Engelhard. 3rd rev. ed. Ingo Reiffenstein. Tübingen: Niemeyer 1982. German translation: *Engelhard.* Trans. Klaus Jörg Schmitz. Göppingen: Kümmerle. English trans.: *"Engelhard" by Konrad von Würzburg: A Translation and Evaluation.* Trans. Jutta Breckling. Diss. State Univ. of New York at Stony Brook, 1988.

Die Goldene Schmiede des Konrad von Würzburg. Ed. Edward Schröder. 2nd ed. Göttingen: Vandenhoeck & Ruprecht, 1969.

Kleinere Dichtungen I. Der Welt Lohn. Herzmære. Heinrich von Kempten. Ed. Edward Schröder, 10th ed. Zurich: Weidmann, 1970. German translation: *Heinrich von Kempten: Der Welt Lohn. Das Herzmaere.* Translated with an afterword by Heinz Rölleke. Following the edition of Edward Schröder. Stuttgart: Reclam, 1968.

Kleinere Dichtungen II: Der Schwanritter. Das Turnier von Nantes. Ed. Edward Schröder, 5th ed. Zurich: Weidmann, 1974.

Kleinere Dichtungen III: Die Klage der Kunst. Leiche, Lieder, Sprüche. Ed. Edward Schröder, 4th ed. Zurich: Weidmann, 1970.

Konrads von Würzburg Partonopier und Meliur. Ed. Karl Bartsch. Berlin: de Gruyter, 1970.

Die Legenden, I: Silvester. Ed. Paul Gereke. Halle: Niemeyer, 1925.

Die Legenden, II: Alexius. Ed. Paul Gereke. Halle: Niemeyer, 1926.

Die Legenden, III: Pantaleon. Ed. Winfried Woesler. 2nd ed. Tübingen: Niemeyer, 1974.

Der trojanische Krieg von Konrad von Würzburg. Ed. Adelbert von Keller. Amsterdam: Rodopi, 1965.

Kudrun (ca. 1230–40)

Kudrun. Ed. Karl Bartsch. 5th rev. ed. by Karl Stackmann. Tübingen: Niemeyer, 2000. Modern English translation: Winder McConnell, *Kudrun.* Columbia, SC: Camden House, 1992.

Laurin (ca. 1250)

Laurin. Ed. Oscar Jänicke. In *Deutsches Heldenbuch*, vol. 1. Berlin: Weidmann, 1866. Reprint Berlin and Zurich: Weidmann, 1963. 201–37; *Laurin.* Ed. Georg Holz. Halle: Niemeyer, 1897.

Lohengrin (ca. 1280s)

Lohengrin. Ed. Thomas Cramer. Munich: W. Fink, 1971.

Der Marner (fl. 1250)

Der Marner. Ed. Philipp Strauch. Strasbourg: Trübner, 1876.

Mechthild von Magdeburg (ca. 1207–ca. 1282)

Das fließende Licht der Gottheit: Nach der Einsiedler Handschrift in kritischem Vergleich mit der gesamten Überlieferung. Ed. Hanns Neumann. 2 vols. Munich: Artemis, 1990 and 1993. English trans.: *The Revelations of Mechthild von Magdeburg (1210–1297); or, The Flowing Light of the Godhead.* Trans. and ed. Lucy Menzies. London: Longmans, Gree, 1953; and *Beguine Spirituality: Mystical Writings of Mechthild von Magdeburg, Beatrice of Nazareth, and Hadewijch of Brabant.* Ed. and introduced by Fiona Bowie. Trans. Oliver Davies. New York: Crossroad, 1990.

Minnesang (12th and 13th centuries)

Des Minnesangs Frühling. Ed. Karl Lachmann, Moriz Haupt, Friedrich Vogt, and Carl von Kraus, 37th rev. ed. by Hugo Moser and Helmut Tervooren. Stuttgart: S. Hirzl, 1982. Translations in modern German: Helmut

Brackert, *Minnesang: Mittelhochdeutsche Texte mit Übertragungen und Anmerkungen*. Frankfurt am Main: Taschenbuchverlag, 1991. English trans.: *The Minnesingers*. Trans. Jethro Bithell. 2 vols. New York: Longmans, 1909; *German and Italian Lyrics of the Middle Ages*. Trans. Frederick Goldin. New York: Norton, 1973; and *Medieval German Lyric Verse in English Translation*. Trans. J. W. Thomas. Studies in Germanic Languages and Literatures. Chapel Hill: U of North Carolina P, 1968.

Neidhart (ca. 1185–ca. 1240)

Die Lieder Neidharts. Ed. Edmund Wießner, continued by Hanns Fischer. 4th rev. ed. Paul Sappler. Tübingen: Niemeyer, 1984. German translation: *Die Lieder Neidharts*. Trans. and ed. Siegfried Beyschlag. Darmstadt: Wissenschaftliche Buchgesellschaft, 1975; English translations of some of Neidhart's lyrics are in: *The Minnesingers*. Trans. Jethro Bithell. 2 vols. New York: Longmans, 1909; *German and Italian Lyrics of the Middle Ages*. Trans. Frederick Goldin. New York: Norton, 1973; and *Medieval German Lyric Verse in English Translation*. Trans. J. W. Thomas. Studies in Germanic Languages and Literatures. Chapel Hill: U of North Carolina P, 1968.

Das Nibelungenlied (ca. 1200)

Das Nibelungenlied. Ed. Helmut de Boor. 22nd ed. by Roswitha Wisniewski. Wiesbaden: Brockhaus, 1988. Modern German translation: Karl Simrock, *Das Nibelungenlied*. Stuttgart: Alfred Körner Verlag, 1954. English trans.: *The Nibelungenlied*. Ed. and trans. A. T. Hatto. Harmondsworth: Penguin, 1965.

Rabenschlacht (latter half of the 13th century)

Rabenschlacht. Ed. Ernst Martin, in *Deutsches Heldenbuch*, 5 vols. Vol. 2: 219–326. Berlin: Weidmann, 1866.

Reinmar von Zweter (fl. ca. 1257–87)

Reinmar von Zweter. *Die Gedichte Reinmars von Zweter*. Ed. Gustav Roethe. Leipzig: Hirzel, 1887.

Das Rolandslied (ca. 1170)

Das Rolandslied des Pfaffen Konrad. Ed. Friedrich Maurer. In *Deutsche Literatur in Entwicklungsreihen: Geistliche Dichtung des Mittelalters* 5. 1940; reprint: Darmstadt: Wissenschaftliche Buchgesellschaft, 1964. English trans.: J. W. Thomas, *Priest Konrad's Song of Roland*. Columbia, SC: Camden House, 1994.

Rudolf von Ems (ca. 1200–ca. 1255)

Alexander. Ed. Victor Junk. 2 vols. Leipzig: Hiersemann, 1928 and 1929. Reprint Darmstadt: Wissenschaftliche Buchgesellschaft, 1970.

Barlaam und Josaphat. Ed. Franz Pfeiffer. Leipzig: Göschen, 1843.

Der guote Gêrhart. Ed. John A. Asher. 3rd rev. ed. Tübingen: Niemeyer, 1989. Modern German translation: *Der gute Gerhart*. Trans. Karl Tober, ed. Engen Thurner. Bregenz: Russ, 1959.

Weltchronik. Ed. Gustav Ehrismann. Berlin: Weidmann, 1915.

Willehalm von Orlens. Ed. Victor Junk. Berlin: Weidmann, 1905.

Sangsprüche and *Meisterlieder* (12th and 13th centuries)
Repertorium der Sangsprüche und Meisterlieder des 12. bis 18. Jahrhunderts. Ed. Horst Brunner and Burghart Wachinger. Tübingen: Niemeyer, 1986–2001.

Sangspruchdichtung. 2nd rev. ed. by Helmut Tervooren. Stuttgart: Metzler, 2001.

Wernher von Elmendorf. Ed. Joachim Bumke. Tübingen: Niemeyer, 1974.

Winsbeckische Gedichte nebst Tirol und Fridebran. Ed. Albert Leitzmann. Rev. ed. Ingo Reiffenstein. Tübingen: Niemeyer, 1962.

Sigenot (ca. 1250)
Sigenot. Ed. Julius Zupitza, in *Deutsches Heldenbuch*, 5 vols. Vol. 5: 207–15. Berlin: Weidmann, 1866.

Der Stricker (ca. 1190–1250)
Die bisher unveröffentlichten geistlichen Bispelreden des Strickers. Ed. Ute Schwab. Göttingen: Vandenhoeck & Ruprecht, 1959.

Karl der Große. Ed. Karl Bartsch. Quedlinburg: Basse, 1857. Reprint Berlin: De Gruyter, 1965.

Die Kleindichtung des Strickers. Vol. 1. Ed. Wolfgang Wilfried Moelleken. Göppingen: Kümmerle, 1973.

Der Stricker: Daniel von dem Blühenden Tal. 2nd rev. ed. by Michael Resler. Tübingen: Niemeyer, 1995. English trans.: *German Romance, vol. 1: Daniel von dem blühenden Tal.* Ed. and trans. Michael Resler. Woodbridge, UK: D. S. Brewer, 2003.

Thomasin von Zerclaere (fl. 1215)
Thomasin von Zerclaere, *Der welsche Gast.* Ed. F. W. von Kries. Göppingen: Kümmerle, 1984.

Ulrich von Liechtenstein (ca. 1200–January 26, 1275)
Ulrich von Liechtenstein, Frauenbuch. Ed. Franz Viktor Spechtler. 2nd ed. Göppingen: Kümmerle, 1993.

Ulrich von Liechtenstein, Frauendienst. Ed. Franz Viktor Spechtler. 2nd ed. Göppingen: Kümmerle, 2003. Modern German translation: Franz Viktor Spechtler, *Ulrich von Liechtenstein, Frauendienst. Aus dem Mittelhochdeutschen ins Neuhochdeutsche übertragen.* Klagenfurt/Celovec: Wieser, 2000. English trans.: *Ulrich von Liechtenstein's Service of Ladies.* Trans. J. W. Thomas. Studies in Germanic Languages and Literatures. Chapel Hill: U of North Carolina P, 1969.

Ulrich von Türheim (ca. 1195–ca. 1250)

Ulrich von Türheim: Rennewart, aus der Berliner und Heidelberger Handschrift. Ed. Alfred Hübner. Berlin: Weidmann, 1938. Reprint: Berlin: Weidmann, 1964.

Ulrich von Türheim, Tristan und Isolde (Fortsetzung des Tristan-Romans Gottfrieds von Straßburg), Originaltext (nach der Heidelberger Handschrift Pal. Germ. 360), Versübersetzung und Einleitung von Wolfgang Spiewok in Zusammenarbeit mit Danielle Buschinger. Trans. (modern German) Danielle Buschinger and Wolfgang Spiewok. Greifswald: Reineke-Verlag, 1992.

Ulrich von Zatzikhoven (fl. ca. 1200)

Lanzelet. Ed. K. A. Hahn. Frankfurt: Brönner, 1845. Reprint Berlin: de Gruyter, 1965. Modern German translation: Wolfgang Spiewok, *Ulrich von Zatzikhoven. Lanzelet mittelhochdeutsch/neuhochdeutsch.* Greifswald: Reineke-Verlag, 1997. English trans.: K. G. T. Webster, *Lanzelet: A Romance of Lancelot,* rev. ed. Roger Sherman Loomis. New York: Columbia UP, 1951.

Virginal (after 1260)

Virginal. Ed. Julius Zupitza. In *Deutsches Heldenbuch.* Vol. 5: 1–200. Berlin: Weidmann, 1866.

Walther von der Vogelweide (ca. 1170–ca. 1230)

Die Lieder Walthers von der Vogelweide, vol. 1: *Die religiösen und politischen Lieder,* 4th ed. and vol. 2: *Die Liebeslieder,* 3rd ed. Ed. Friedrich Maurer. Tübingen: Niemeyer, 1967–69.

Werke, Gesamtausgabe. I: Spruchlyrik. Ed. and trans. (modern German) Günther Schweikle. Stuttgart: Reclam, 1994.

English translations of some of Walther's lyrics are in: *The Minnesingers.* Trans. Jethro Bithell. 2 vols. New York: Longmans, 1909; *German and Italian Lyrics of the Middle Ages.* Trans. Frederick Goldin. New York: Norton, 1973; and *Medieval German Lyric Verse in English Translation.* Trans. J. W. Thomas. Studies in Germanic Languages and Literatures. Chapel Hill: U of North Carolina P, 1968.

Werner der Gärtner (fl. ca. 1265–80)

Wernher der Gartenære, Helmbrecht. Ed. Friedrich Panzer. 9th rev. ed. Kurt Ruh. Tübingen: Niemeyer, 1974. English trans.: Linda Parshall, *Werner der Gartenaere: Helmbrecht.* New York: Garland, 1987.

Wirnt von Grafenberg (ca. 1170–ca. 1235)

Wigalois: Der Ritter mit dem Rade. Ed. J. M. N. Kapteyn. Bonn: Klopp, 1926; English trans.: J. W. Thomas. *Wigalois: The Knight of Fortune's Wheel.* Lincoln: U of Nebraska P, 1977.

Wolfram von Eschenbach (ca. 1170–after 1220)

Parzival. In *Wolfram von Eschenbach*. Ed. Albert Leitzmann. Rev. ed. Wilhelm Deinert. Vol. 1: Buch I–VI; Vol. 2: Buch VII bis XI; Vol. 3: Buch XII bis XVI. Tübingen: Niemeyer, 1961–. Modern German translation: *Parzival*. Trans. Wolfgang Mohr. Göppingen: Kümmerle, 1977. English translation: *Wolfram von Eschenbach: Parzival*. Trans. A. T. Hatto. New York: Penguin, 1980.

Songs. In *Wolfram von Eschenbach*. Ed. Albert Leitzmann. Vol. 5: *Willehalm*, Buch VI bis IX; *Titurel; Lieder*. Tübingen: Niemeyer, 1961–. Modern German translation: *Wolfram von Eschenbach: "Titurel," Lieder, Mhd. Text und Übersetzung*. Ed. and translated into modern German by Wolfgang Mohr. Göppingen: Kümmerle, 1978.

Titurel. In *Wolfram von Eschenbach*. Ed. Albert Leitzmann. Vol. 5: *Willehalm*, Buch VI bis IX; *Titurel; Lieder*. Tübingen: Niemeyer, 1961–. Modern German translation: *Wolfram von Eschenbach. "Titurel," Lieder, Mhd. Text und Übersetzung*. Ed. and translated into modern German by Wolfgang Mohr. Göppingen: Kümmerle, 1978; English trans.: *Wolfram von Eschenbach: "Titurel" and the "Songs."* Ed. and trans. Marion E. Gibbs and Sidney M. Johnson. New York & London: Garland Publishing, 1988.

Willehalm. In *Wolfram von Eschenbach*. Ed. Albert Leitzmann. Vol. 4: *Willehalm*, Buch I bis V and Vol. 5: *Willehalm*, Buch VI bis IX; *Titurel; Lieder*. Modern German translation: *Willehalm*. Ed. Werner Schröder. Trans. Dieter Kartschoke. Berlin: de Gruyter, 1989; English trans.: *Willehalm*. Trans. Marion E. Gibbs and Sidney M. Johnson. Harmondsworth: Penguin, 1984. Reprint 1992.

Select Secondary Literature

General

Abulafia, David. *Frederick II: A Medieval Emvperor*. London: Penguin, 1988.

Arnold, Benjamin. *German Knighthood 1050–1300*. Oxford: Clarendon Press, 1985.

————. *Medieval Germany 500–1300: A Political Interpretation*. Houndsmill: Macmillan, 1997.

Bartlett, Robert. *The Making of the Middle Ages: Conquest, Colonization and Cultural Change 950–1350*. Princeton: Princeton UP, 1993.

Bernhardt, John W. *Itinerant Kingship and Royal Monasteries in Early Medieval Germany*. Cambridge: Cambridge UP, 1993.

Bertau, Karl. *Deutsche Literatur im europäischen Mittelalter*. 2 vols. Munich: Beck, 1972–73.

de Boor, Helmut. *Die höfische Literatur: Vorbereitung, Blüte, Ausklang*. 5th ed. Munich: Beck, 1962.

Boshof, Egon, and Franz-Rainer Erkens, eds. *Rudolf von Habsburg 1273–1291: Eine Königsherrschaft zwischen Tradition und Wandel*. Cologne: Böhlau, 1993.

Bosl, Karl. *Die Reichsministerialität der Salier und Staufer: Ein Beitrag zur Geschichte des hochmittelalterlichen deutschen Volkes, Staates und Reiches*. Stuttgart: Hiersemann, 1950–51.

Bowlus, Charles R. "The Early Kaiserreich in Recent German Historiography." *Central European History* 21 (1990): 349–67.

Bumke, Joachim. *Geschichte der deutschen Literatur im hohen Mittelalter*. 4th ed. Munich: Deutscher Taschenbuch Verlag, 2000.

————. *Mäzene im Mittelalter: Die Gönner und Auftraggeber der höfischen Literatur in Deutschland 1150–1300*. Munich: Beck, 1979.

Buschinger, Danielle. "L'image du marchand dans les romans de Tristan en France et en Allemagne." *Tristania: A Journal devoted to Tristan Studies* 10 (1984–85): 43–51.

Contamine, Philippe. *War in the Middle Ages*. Trans. Michael Jones. Oxford: Blackwell, 1984.

Cowdrey, H. E. J. "The Peace and the Truce of God in the Eleventh Century." *Past and Present* 46 (1970): 42–67.

Coxon, Sebastian. *The Presentation of Authorship in Medieval German Narrative Literature, 1220–90*. Oxford: Clarendon Press, 2001.

Czerwinski, Peter. *Der Glanz der Abstraktion: Frühe Formen von Reflexivität im Mittelalter.* Frankfurt am Main: Campus Verlag, 1989.

Economou, G. D. *The Goddess Natura in Medieval Literature.* Cambridge, MA: Harvard UP, 1972.

Ehrismann, Gustav. *Geschichte der deutschen Literatur bis zum Ausgang des Mittelalters.* Vols. 2.1–2.2.1. Munich: Beck, 1927.

Fuhrmann, Horst. *Germany in the High Middle Ages c. 1050–1200.* Trans. Timothy Reuter. Cambridge: Cambridge UP, 1986.

Friedrich, Udo. "Die Zähmung des Heros: Der Diskurs der Gewalt und der Gewaltregulierung im 12. Jahrhundert." In *Mittelalter: Neue Wege durch einen alten Kontinent.* ed. Jan-Dirk Müller and Horst Wenzel. Stuttgart: Hirzel, 1999, 149–79.

Gentry, Francis G., ed. *A Companion to Middle High German Literature to the 14th Century.* Leiden: Brill, 2002.

Gibbs, Marion E., and Sidney M. Johnson. *Medieval German Literature: A Companion.* New York: Garland, 1997.

Hasty, Will. *Adventure as Social Performance: A Study of the German Court Epic.* Tübingen: Niemeyer, 1990.

———. *Art of Arms: Studies of Aggression and Dominance in Medieval German Court Poetry.* Heidelberg: Winter, 2002.

Hasty, Will, and James Hardin, eds. *German Writers and Works of the High Middle Ages: 1170–1280. Dictionary of Literary Biography.* Vol. 138. Detroit: Bruccolli, 1994.

Haug, Walter. *Literaturtheorie im deutschen Mittelalter: Von den Anfängen bis zum Ende des 13. Jahrhunderts.* Darmstadt: Wissenschaftliche Buchgesellschaft, 1985.

Haverkamp, Alfred, ed. *Friedrich Barbarossa: Handlungsspielräume und Wirkungsweisen des Staufischen Kaisers.* Sigmaringen: Thorbecke, 1992.

———. *Medieval Germany, 1056–1273.* Trans. H. Braun and R. Mortimer. Oxford: Oxford UP, 1984.

Heinzle, Joachim. *Geschichte der deutschen Literatur von den Anfängen bis zum Beginn der Neuzeit.* Vol. 2/2: *Wandlungen und Neuansätze im 13. Jahrhundert.* Königstein/Taunus: Athenäum, 1984.

Jackson, W. H., and S. A. Ranawake. *The Arthurian Legend in Medieval German and Dutch Literature.* Cardiff: U of Wales P, 2000.

Johnson, L. Peter. *Geschichte der deutschen Literatur bis zum Beginn der Neuzeit.* Vol. 2/1: *Vom hohen zum späten Mittelalter: Die höfische Literatur der Blütezeit.* Tübingen: Niemeyer, 1999.

Jones, Martin, and Roy Wisbey, eds. *Chrétien de Troyes and the German Middle Ages,* ed. Martin Jones and Roy Wisbey. Cambridge: Brewer, 1993.

Kaeuper, Richard W. *Chivalry and Violence in Medieval Europe.* Oxford: Oxford UP, 1999.

Keen, Maurice H. *The Laws of War in the Late Middle Ages.* London: Routledge and K. Paul, 1965.

Köhler, Erich. *Ideal und Wirklichkeit in der höfischen Epik: Studien zur Form der frühen Artus- und Graldichtung.* Tübingen: Niemeyer, 1970.

Le Goff, Jacques. *The Birth of Purgatory.* Trans. Arthur Goldhammer. Chicago: U of Chicago P, 1984.

Lejeune, Rita. "Rôle littéraire d'Aliénor d'Aquitaine et de sa famille." *Cultura Neolatina* 14 (1954): 31–36.

Lewis, A. R. "The Closing of the Medieval Frontier: 1250–1350." *Speculum* 33 (1958): 475–83.

Lienert, Elizabeth. *Deutsche Antikenromane des Mittelalters.* Berlin: E. Schmidt, 2001.

McDonnell, Ernest W. *The Beguines and Beghards in Medieval Culture.* New York: Octagon Books, 1969.

Minnis, A. J. *Medieval Theory of Authorship: Scholastic Literary Attitudes in the Later Middle Ages.* London: Scolar Press, 1985.

Ó Riain-Raedel, Dagmar. *Untersuchungen zur mythischen Struktur der mittelhochdeutschen Artusepen.* Berlin: E. Schmidt, 1978.

Patterson, Lee. *Negotiating the Past: The Historical Understanding of Medieval Literature.* Madison: U of Wisconsin P, 1987.

Peters, Edward, ed. *Heresy and Authority in Medieval Europe: Documents in Translation.* Philadelphia: U of Pennsylvania P, 1980.

Peyer, H. C. "Das Reisekönigtum des Mittelalters." *Vierteljahrschrift für Sozial- und Wirtschaftsgeschichte* 51 (1964): 1–21.

Rasmussen, Ann Marie. *Mothers and Daughters in Medieval German Literature.* Syracuse: Syracuse UP, 1997.

Reuter, Timothy. "The 'Imperial Church System' of the Ottonian and Salian Rulers: A Reconsideration." *Journal of Ecclesiastical History* 33 (1982): 347–74.

de Rougemont, Denis. *L'Amour et L'Occident.* Paris: Plon, 1939.

Ruh, Kurt, et al., ed. *Die deutsche Literatur des Mittelalters: Verfasserlexikon.* 2nd ed. Berlin: de Gruyter, 1978–present.

Schlunk, Andreas C. *Königsmacht und Krongut: Die Machtgrundlage des deutschen Königtums im 13 Jahrhundert.* Stuttgart: F. Steiner Verlag, 1988.

Schmid, Karl, ed. *Die Zähringer.* 3 vols. Sigmaringen: Thorbecke, 1986–90.

Schröder, Werner. "Zur Chronologie der drei großen mittelhochdeutschen Epiker." *Deutsche Vierteljahrschrift für Literaturwissenschaft und Geistesgeschichte* 31 (1957): 274–83.

Schweikle, Günther, ed. *Dichter über Dichter in mittelhochdeutscher Literatur.* Tübingen: Niemeyer, 1970.

Stacey, Robert C. "The Age of Chivalry." In *The Laws of War: Constraints on Warfare in the Western World.* ed. Michael Howard et al. New Haven: Yale UP, 1994, 27–39.

Stevens, Adrian. "Heteroglossia and Clerical Narrative." In *Chrétien de Troyes and the German Middle Ages*, ed. Martin Jones and Roy Wisbey. Cambridge: D. S. Brewer, 1993, 241–55.

Vale, Juliet. "Violence and the Tournament." In *Violence in Medieval Society*, ed. Richard Kaeuper. Woodbridge, UK: Boydell, 2000, 143–58.

Watson, Nicholas. "Conceptions of the Word: The Mother Tongue and the Incarnation of God." *New Medieval Literatures* 1 (1997): 85–124.

Weir, Alison. *Eleanor of Aquitaine: By the Wrath of God Queen of England*. London: Jonathan Cape, 1999.

Genres

Heinen, Hubert, and Ingeborg Henderson, eds. *Genres in Medieval German Literature*. Göppingen: Kümmerle, 1986.

Heroic Poetry

Gottzmann, Carola L. *Heldendichung des 13. Jahrhunderts: Siegfried — Dietrich — Ortnit*. Frankfurt am Main: Lang, 1987.

Hoffmann, Werner. *Mittelhochdeutsche Heldendichtung*. Berlin: E. Schmidt, 1974.

Wolf, Alois. *Heldensage und Epos*. Tübingen: Narr, 1995.

Minnesang

Bäuml, Franz H. *From Symbol to Mimesis: The Generation of Walther von der Vogelweide*. Göppingen: Kümmerle, 1984.

Dronke, Peter. *Medieval Latin and the Rise of the European Love Lyric*. Oxford: Clarendon, 1966.

Eikelmann, Manfred. *Denkformen im Minnesang*. Tübingen: Niemeyer, 1988.

Fromm, Hans, ed. *Der deutsche Minnesang*. 2 vols. Darmstadt: Wissenschaftliche Buchgesellschaft, 1961, 1985.

Haferland, Harald. *Hohe Minne: Zur Beschreibung der Minnekanzone*. Berlin: E. Schmidt, 2000.

Heinen, Hubert. "Minnesang." In *Dictionary of Literary Biography*, vol. 138: *German Writers and Works of the High Middle Ages*, ed. James Hardin and Will Hasty. Detroit: Gale, 1994, 229–39.

Johnson, L. P. "Down with 'hohe Minne'!" *Oxford German Studies* 13 (1982): 36–48.

Kaplowitt, Stephen. *The Ennobling Power of Love in the Medieval German Lyric*. Chapel Hill: U of North Carolina P, 1986.

Kasten, Ingrid. *Frauendienst bei Trobadors und Minnesängern im 12. Jahrhundert*. Heidelberg: Winter, 1986.

Krohn, Rüdiger, ed. *Liebe als Literatur*. Munich: Beck, 1983.

McMahon, James V. "The Music of Minnesang," In *Dictionary of Literary Biography*, vol. 138: *German Writers and Works of the High Middle Ages*, ed. James Hardin and Will Hasty. Detroit: Gale, 1994, 277–88.

Mohr, Wolfgang. "Minnesang als Gesellschaftskunst." In *Der deutsche Minnesang*, ed. Hans Fromm. Darmstadt: Wissenschaftliche Buchgesellschaft, 1972, 197–228.

Moller, Herbert. "The Social Causation of the Courtly Love Complex." *Comparative Studies in Society and History* 1 (1958–59): 137–63.

Müller, Ulrich, ed. *Minne ist ein swaerez spil: Neue Untersuchungen zum Minnesang und zur Geschichte der Liebe im Mittelalter*. Göppingen: Kümmerle, 1986.

Räkel, Hans-Herbert. *Der deutsche Minnesang*. Munich: Beck, 1986.

Richey, M. F. *Essays on Mediaeval German Poetry*. Oxford: Blackwell, 1969.

Sayce, Olive. *The Medieval German Lyric 1150–1230: The Development of its Themes and Forms in their European Context*. Oxford: Clarendon, 1982.

Schweikle, Günther. *Minnesang*. 2nd ed. Stuttgart: Metzler, 1995.

Taylor, Ronald J. *The Art of the Minnesinger*. 2 vols. Cardiff: U of Wales P, 1968.

Tubach, Friedrich. *Struktur im Widerspruch: Studien zum Minnesang*. Tübingen: Niemeyer, 1977.

Wapnewski, Peter. *"Waz ist Minne": Studien zur mittelhochdeutschen Lyrik*. Munich: Beck, 1975.

Mystical Writing

Bowie, Fiona, ed. *Beguine Spirituality: Mystical Writings of Mechthild of Magdeburg, Beatrice of Nazareth, and Hadewijch of Brabant*. New York: Crossroad, 1990.

Davies, Oliver. *The Mystical Tradition of Northern Europe*. London: Darton, Longman and Todd, 1988.

Dinzelbacher, Peter, and Dieter R. Bauer, eds. *Frauenmystik im Mittelalter*. Ostfildern bei Stuttgart: Schwabenverlag, 1985.

McGinn, Bernhard. *The Flowering of Mysticism: Men and Women in the New Mysticism (1200–1350)*. New York: Crossroad Publishing Company, 1998.

———. "The Four Female Evangelists of the Thirteenth Century. The Invention of Authority." In *Deutsche Mystik im abendländischen Zusammenhang: Neu erschlossene Texte, neue methodische Ansätze, neue theoretische Konzepte*, ed. Walter Haug and Wolfram Schneider-Lastin. Tübingen: Niemeyer, 2000, 175–94.

Newman, Barbara. *From Virile Woman to Woman Christ: Studies in Medieval Religion and Literature*. Philadelphia: U of Pennsylvania P, 1995.

Phillips, Dayton. *Beguines in Medieval Strasburg: A Study of the Social Aspects of Beguine Life*. Ann Arbor: Beck, 1963.

Ruh, Kurt. *Geschichte der abendländischen Mystik*. 4 Volumes. Munich: C. H. Beck, 1993–99.

Simons, Walter. *Cities of Ladies: Beguine Communities in the Medieval Low Countries, 1200–1565*. Philadelphia: U of Pennsylvania P, 2001.

Szarmach, Paul, ed. *An Introduction to the Medieval Mystics of Europe*. Albany: SUNY Press, 1984.

Romances

Green, D. H. *The Beginnings of Medieval Romance: Fact and Fiction, 1150–1220*. Cambridge: Cambridge UP, 2002.

Ruh, Kurt. *Höfische Epik des deutschen Mittelalters*. Berlin: E. Schmidt, 1967.

Schmolke-Hasselmann, Beate. *The Evolution of Arthurian Romance: The Verse Tradition from Chrétien to Froissart*. Trans. Roger and Margaret Middleton. With an introduction by Keith Busby. Cambridge: Cambridge UP, 1998.

Simon, Ralf. *Einführung in die strukturalistische Poetik des mittelalterlichen Romans: Analysen zu deutschen Romanen der matière de Bretagne*. Würzburg: Königshausen & Neumann, 1990.

Sangsprüche und Meisterlieder

Kleinere mittelhochdeutsche Erzählungen, Fabeln und Lehrgedichte. III: Die Heidelberger Handschrift cod. Pal. germ. 341. ed. Gustav Rosenhagen. Berlin: Weidmann, 1909.

Schönbach, Anton E. *Beiträge zur Erklärung altdeutscher Dichtwerke, III–IV: Die Sprüche des Bruder Wernher I–II*. Vienna: Gerold, 1904.

Sowinski, Bernhard, ed. *Lehrhafte Dichtung des Mittelalters*. Stuttgart: Metzler, 1971.

Authors and Works

Das Alexanderlied

Buntz, Herwig. *Die deutsche Alexanderdichtung des Mittelalters*. Stuttgart: Metzler, 1973.

Carey, George. *The Medieval Alexander*. Cambridge: Cambridge UP, 1956.

Fischer, Wolfgang. *Die Alexanderkonzeption des Pfaffen Lambrecht*. Munich: Eidos, 1964.

Green, Dennis H. "The Alexanderlied and the Emergence of the Romance." *German Life and Letters* 28 (1975): 246–62.

Kratz, Dennis M. *The Romances of Alexander*. New York: Garland, 1991.

Beatrijs van Nazareth

Bradley, Ritamary. "Beatrice of Nazareth (C. 1200–1268): A Search for Her True Spirituality." In *Vox Mystica: Essays on Medieval Mysticism in Honor of Professor Valerie M. Lagorio*, ed. Anne Clark Bartlett. Cambridge: D. S. Brewer, 1995, 57–74.

Hollywood, Amy. "Inside Out: Beatrice of Nazareth and Her Hagiographer." In *Gendered Voices: Medieval Saints and Their Interpreters*, ed. Catherine M. Mooney. Philadelphia: UP, 1999, 78–98.

The Life of Beatrice of Nazareth 1200–1268, Cistercian Fathers Series 50. ed. Roger De Ganck. Kalamazoo, MI: Cistercian Publications, 1991.

Newman, Barbara. "*La Mystique Courtoise*: Thirteenth Century Beguines and the Art of Love." In *From Virile Woman to Womanchrist: Studies in Medieval Religion and Literature*, ed. Barbara Newman. Philadelphia: U of Pennsylvania P, 1995, 137–67.

Elizabeth von Schönau

Clark, Anne L. *Elisabeth of Schönau. A Twelfth Century Visionary*. Philadelphia: U of Pennsylvania P, 1992.

———. "Holy Woman or Unworthy Vessel? The Representations of Elisabeth of Schönau." In *Gendered Voices: Medieval Saints and Their Interpreters*, ed. Catherine M. Mooney. Philadelphia: U of Pennsylvania P, 1999, 35–51.

Köster, Kurt. "Das visionäre Werk Elisabeths von Schönau: Studien zu Entstehung, Überlieferung und Wirkung in der mittelalterlichen Welt." *Archiv für Mittelrheinische Kirchengeschichte* 4 (1952): 79–119.

Newman, Barbara. "Preface," in Elisabeth of Schönau, *The Complete Works*. Trans. Anne L. Clark. New York: Paulist Press, 2000.

Gottfried von Strassburg

de Boor, Helmut. "Die Grundauffassung von Gottfrieds Tristan." In *Gottfried von Straßburg*, ed. Alois Wolf. Darmstadt: Wissenschaftliche Buchgesellschaft, 1973, 25–73.

Chinca, Mark. *Gottfried von Strassburg, Tristan*. Cambridge: Cambridge UP, 1997.

Dietz, Reiner. *Der Tristan Gottfrieds von Straßburg: Probleme der Forschung (1902–1970)*. Göppingen: Kümmerle, 1974.

Ernst, Ulrich. "Gottfried von Straßburg in komparatistischer Sicht: Form und Funktion der Allegorese im Tristanepos." *Euphorion* 70 (1976): 1–72.

Fritsch-Rößler, Waltraud. *Der "Tristan" Gottfried's von Straßburg in der deutschen Literaturgeschichtsschreibung (1785–1985)*. Frankfurt am Main: Lang, 1989.

Fromm, Hanns. "Gottfried von Straßburg und Abaelard," In *Arbeiten zur deutschen Literatur des Mittelalters*, ed. H. Fromm. Tübingen: Niemeyer, 1989, 173–90.

Hasty, Will, ed. *A Companion to Gottfried von Strassburg's "Tristan."* Rochester, NY: Camden House, 2003.

Huber, Christoph. *Gottfried von Straßburg: Tristan*. Berlin: E. Schmidt, 2000.

Jaeger, C. Stephen. *Medieval Humanism in Gottfried von Strassburg's "Tristan und Isolde."* Heidelberg: Winter, 1977.

Krohn, Rüdiger. "Erotik und Tabu in Gottfrieds *Tristan*: König Marke." In *Stauferzeit: Geschichte, Literatur, Kunst*. ed. Rüdiger Krohn, et al. Stuttgart: Klett-Cotta, 1979.

Krohn, Rüdiger. "Gottfried von Strassburg." In *Deutsche Dichter: Leben und Werk deutschsprachiger Autoren*, vol. 1: *Mittelalter*, ed. Gunter E. Grimm and Frank Rainer Max. Stuttgart: Reclam, 1989.

Langer, Otto. "Der 'Künstlerroman' Gottfrieds — Protest bürgerlicher 'Empfindsamkeit' gegen höfisches 'Tugendsystem'?" *Euphorion* 68 (1974): 1–41.

McCann, W. J. "Tristan: The Celtic Material Re-examined." In *Gottfried von Strassburg and the Medieval Tristan Legend*. ed. Adrian Stevens and Roy Wisbey. London: Institute of Germanic Studies, 1990, 19–28.

Ranke, Friedrich. "Die Allegorie der Minnegrotte in Gottfrieds Tristan." In *Gottfried von Straßburg*, ed. Alois Wolf. Darmstadt: Wissenschaftliche Buchgesellschaft, 1973, 1–24.

Rocher, Daniel. "Denis de Rougemont, la 'légend' de Tristan et le roman de Gottfried von Strassburg." In *La Légend de Tristan au Moyen Âge*, ed. Danielle Buschinger. Göppingen: Kümmerle, 1982, 139–50.

Schausten, Monica. *Erzählwelten der Tristangeschichte im hohen Mittelalter: Untersuchungen zu den deutschsprachigen Tristanfassungen des 12. und 13. Jahrhunderts*. Munich: Fink, 1999.

Schirok, Bernd. "Zu den Akrosticha in Gottfrieds *Tristan*. Versuch einer kritischen und weiterführenden Bestandsaufnahme." *Zeitschrift für deutsches Altertum und deutsche Literatur* 113 (1984): 188–213.

Schoepperle, Gertrude. *Tristan and Isolt: A Study of the Sources of the Romance*. Vol. 2. New York: Franklin, 1960.

Schröder, Werner. "Zur Kunstanschauung Gottfrieds von Straßburg und Konrads von Würzburg nach dem Zeugnis ihrer Prologe." In *Über Gottfried von Straßburg, Kleinere Schriften*, ed. Werner Schröder. Vol. 4. Stuttgart: Hirzel, 1994, 104–77.

Schwietering, Julius. "Der Tristan Gottfrieds von Strassburg und die Bernhardinische Mystik." In *Philologische Schriften*. ed. Friedrich Ohly and Max Wehrli. Munich: Fink, 1969, 338–61.

Spiewok, Wolfgang. "Varianten der Waldleben-Episode in der *Tristan*-Rezeption." In *Tristan-Studien: Die Tristan-Rezeption in den europäischen Literaturen des Mittelalters*, ed. Danielle Buschinger. Greifswald: Reineke-Verlag, 1993.

Steinhoff, Hans-Hugo, ed. *Gottfried von Straßburg, Tristan: Ausgewählte Abbildungen zur Überlieferung*. Göppingen: Kümmerle, 1974.

Strohschneider, Peter. "Gotfrid-Fortsetzungen, Tristans Ende im 13. Jahrhundert und die Möglichkeit nachklassischer Epik." *Deutsche Vierteljahrschrift für Literaturwissenschaft und Geistesgeschichte* 65 (1991): 70–98.

Tomasek, Tomas. *Die Utopie im "Tristan" Gotfrids von Straßburg*. Tübingen: Niemeyer, 1985.

Wachinger, Burghart. "Zur Rezeption Gottfrieds von Straßburg im 13. Jahrhundert." In *Deutsche Literatur des 13. Jahrhunderts*, ed. Wolfgang Harms and Leslie Peter Johnson. Berlin: E. Schmidt, 1975, 56–82.

Weber, Gottfried. *Gottfried von Straßburg: Tristan und die Krise des hochmittel-alterlichen Weltbildes um 1200.* 2 vols. Stuttgart: Metzler, 1953.

Wetzel, René. *Die handschriftliche Überlieferung des "Tristan" Gottfrieds von Strassburg: Untersucht an ihren Fragmenten.* Freiburg, Switzerland: Germanistica Friburgensia, 1992.

———. "Der Tristanstoff in der Literatur des deutschen Mittelalters. Forschungsbericht 1969–1994." In *Forschungsberichte zur germanistischen Mediävistik* 5/1, ed. Hans-Jochen Schiewer. Frankfurt am Main: Lang, 1996.

Wolf, Alois. *Gottfried von Straßburg und die Mythe von Tristan und Isolde.* Darmstadt: Wissenschaftliche Buchgesellschaft, 1989.

Hadewych

Kadt, Elizabeth Wainwright-De. "Courtly Literature and Mysticism: Some Aspects of Their Interaction." *Acta Germanica* 12 (1980): 41–60.

McGinn, Bernard. "The Four Female Evangelists of the Thirteenth Century. The Invention of Authority." In *Deutsche Mystik Im Abendländischen Zusammenhang: Neu erschlossene Texte, neue methodische Ansätze, neue theoretische Konzepte (Kolloquium Kloster Fischingen 1998),* ed. Walter Haug and Wolfram Schneider-Lastin. Tübingen: Niemeyer, 2000, 175–94.

Murk-Jansen, Saskia M. "The Use of Gender and Gender-Related Imagery in Hadewijch." In *Gender and Text in the Later Middle Ages,* ed. Jane Chance. Gainesville: UP of Florida, 1996, 52–68.

Hartmann von Aue

Clark, Susan. *Hartmann von Aue: Landscapes of Mind.* Houston: Rice UP, 1989.

Cormeau, Christoph, and Wilhelm Störmer. *Hartmann von Aue: Epoche–Werk–Wirkung.* 2nd ed. Munich: Beck, 1993.

Cramer, Thomas. "Saelde und êre in Hartmanns *Iwein.*" *Euphorion* 60 (1966): 30–47.

Duckworth, David. "Heinrich and the Godless Life in Hartmann's Poem." *Mediaevistik* 3 (1990): 71–90.

Ernst, Ulrich. "Der Antagonismus von *vita carnalis* und *vita spiritualis* im *Gregorius* Hartmanns von Aue." *Euphorion* 72 (1978): 160–226 and 73 (1979): 1–105.

Fischer, Hubertus. *Ehre, Hof und Abenteuer in Hartmanns "Iwein": Vorarbeiten zu einer historischen Poetik des höfischen Epos.* Munich: Fink, 1983.

Fisher, Rodney W. "Aspects of Madness in Hartmann's *Erec.*" *Seminar* 34 (1998): 221–34.

———. "The Courtly Hero Comes to Germany: Hartmann's *Erec* and The Concept of Shame." *Amsterdamer Beiträge zur älteren Germanistik* 46 (1996): 119–30.

Gentry, Francis G., ed. *A Companion to the Works of Hartmann von Aue.* Rochester, NY: Camden House, 2005.

Gewehr, Wolf. *Hartmanns Klage-Büchlein im Lichte der Frühscholastik.* Göppingen: Kümmerle, 1975.

Haase, Gudrun. *Die germanistische Forschung zum "Erec" Hartmanns von Aue.* Frankfurt am Main: Lang, 1988.

Hallich, Oliver. *Poetologisches, Theologisches: Studien zum Gregorius Hartmanns von Aue.* Frankfurt am Main: Lang, 1995.

Hasty, Will. *Adventures in Interpretation: The Works of Hartmann von Aue and Their Critical Reception.* Columbia, SC: Camden House, 1996.

Hörner, Petra, ed. *Hartmann von Aue: Mit einer Bibliographie 1976–1997.* Frankfurt am Main: 1998.

Jackson, W. H. *Chivalry in Twelfth-Century Germany: The Works of Hartmann von Aue.* Cambridge: Brewer, 1994.

Kuhn, Hugo. "Erec." In *Dichtung und Welt im Mittelalter.* By H. K. Stuttgart: Metzler, 1959, 130–50.

McFarland, Timothy, and Silvia Ranawake, eds. *Hartmann von Aue: Changing Perspectives.* Göppingen: Kümmerle, 1988.

Mertens, Volker. *Gregorius Eremita: Eine Lebensform des Adels bei Hartmann von Aue in ihrer Problematik und ihrer Wandlung in der Rezeption.* Munich: Artemis, 1978.

Nobel, Hildegard. "Schuld und Sühne in Hartmanns Gregorius und in der frühscholastischen Theologie." *Zeitschrift für deutsche Philologie* 76 (1957): 42–79.

Pastré, Jean Marc. "Le Gregorius, la croisade et la chronologie des oeuvres de Hartmann von Aue." In *La croisade: realités et fictions; notes du colloques d'Amiens, 18–22 mars 1987,* ed. Danielle Buschinger. Göppingen: Kümmerle, 1989, 183–92.

Spaarnay, Hendrik. *Hartmann von Aue: Studien zu einer Biographie.* 2 vols. Halle, 1933, 1938; reprint Darmstadt: Wissenschaftliche Buchgesellschaft, 1975.

Tobin, Frank. "Fallen Man and Hartmann's Gregorius." *Germanic Review* 50 (1975): 85–98.

Wapnewski, Peter. *Hartmann von Aue.* 7th ed. Stuttgart: Metzler, 1979.

Heinrich von dem Türlin

Andersen, Elizabeth. "Heinrich von dem Türlîn's *Diu Crône* and the Prose *Lancelot*; An Intertextual Study." *Arthurian Studies* 7 (1987): 23–49.

Buschinger, Danielle. "Un roman arthurien post-classique: *La Couronne* de Heinrich von dem Türlin." *Le Moyen Âge* 89 (1983): 381–95.

Jillings, Lewis. *"Diu Crône" of Heinrich von dem Türlein: The Attempted Emancipation of Secular Narrative.* Göppingen: Kümmerle, 1980.

Kratz, Bernd. "Zur Biographie Heinrichs von dem Türlin." *Amsterdamer Beiträge zur älteren Germanistik* 11 (1977): 123–67.

Read, Ralph. "Heinrich von dem Türlin's *Diu Krône* and Wolfram's *Parzival*." *Modern Language Quarterly* 35 (1974): 129–39.

Thomas, Neil. *"Diu Crône" and the Medieval Arthurian Cycle.* Woodbridge, UK: D. S. Brewer, 2002.

Zach, Christine. *Die Erzählmotive der "Crône" Heinrichs von dem Türlin und ihre altfranzösischen Quellen: Ein kommentiertes Register.* Passau: Richard Rothe, 1990.

Heinrich von Freiberg

Sedlmeyer, Margarete. *Heinrichs von Freiberg Tristanfortsetzung im Vergleich zu anderen Tristandichtungen.* Bern: Herbert Lang, 1976.

Heinrich von Veldeke

Brandt, Wolfgang. *Die Erzählkonzeption Heinrichs von Veldeke in der "Eneide": Ein Vergleich mit Vergils "Aeneis."* Marburg: Elwert, 1969.

Dittrich, Marie-Luise. *Die "Eneide"Heinrichs von Veldeke: I. Teil: Quellenkritischer Vergleich mit dem "Roman d'Eneas" und Vergils "Aeneis."* Wiesbaden: Steiner, 1966.

Fisher, Rodney W. *Heinrich von Veldeke: "Eneas." A Comparison with the Roman d'Eneas, and a Translation into English.* Frankfurt am Main: Lang, 1992.

Groos, Arthur. " 'Amor and His Brother Cupid': The 'Two Loves' in Heinrich von Veldeke's Eneit." *Traditio* 32 (1976): 239–55.

Kaplowitt, Stephen J. "Heinrich von Veldeke's Song Cycle of *Hohe Minne.*" *Seminar* 11 (1975): 125–40.

Kasten, Ingrid. "Herrschaft und Liebe: Zur Rolle und Darstellung des 'Helden' im *Roman d'Eneas* und in Veldekes *Eneasroman.*" *Deutsche Vierteljahresschrift für Literaturwissenschaft und Geistesgeschichte* 62 (1988): 227–45.

Kistler, Renate. *Heinrich von Veldeke und Ovid.* Tübingen: Niemeyer, 1993.

Klein, Thomas. "Heinrich von Veldeke und die mitteldeutschen Literatursprachen. Untersuchungen zum Veldeke-Problem." In *Zwei Studien zu Veldeke und zum Strassburger Alexander.* By Thomas Klein and Cola Minis. Amsterdam: Rodopi, 1985, 1–121.

Lieb, Ludger. "Modulationen: Sangspruch und Minnesang bei Heinrich von Veldeke." *Zeitschrift für deutsche Philologie* 119 (2000): 38–49.

Sacker, Hugh. "Heinrich von Veldeke's Conception of the Eneid." *German Life and Letters* 10 (1956/57): 210–18.

Schieb, Gabriele. *Henric van Veldeken: Heinrich von Veldeke.* Stuttgart: Metzler, 1965.

Sinnema, John R. *Hendrik van Veldeke.* New York: Twayne Publishers, 1972.

Weicker, Tina Sabine. *"Do wart daz buch ze Cleve verstolen:* Neue Überlegungen zur Entstehung von Veldekes *Eneas.*" *Zeitschrift für deutsches Altertum und deutsche Literatur* 130, 1 (2001): 1–18.

Helmbrecht

Brackert, Helmut. "Helmbrechts Haube." *Zeitschrift für deutsches Altertum und deutsche Literatur* 103 (1974): 166–84.

Fischer, Hanns. "Gestaltungsschichten im *Meier Helmbrecht*." *Beiträge zur Geschichte der deutschen Sprache und Literatur* 79 (1957): 85–109.

Jackson, William E. "Das Märe von Helmbrecht als Familiengeschichte." *Euphorion* 68 (1974): 229–51.

Keinz, Friedrich. *Helmbrecht und seine Heimat*. Leipzig: Hirzel, 1887.

Knapp, Fritz Peter. "Standesväter und Heimatverächter in der bayrisch-österreichischen Literatur des Spätmittelalters." In *Wernher der Gärtner "Helmbrecht": Die Beiträge des Helmbrecht-Symposions in Burghausen 2001*, ed. Theodor Nolte and Tobias Schneider. Stuttgart: Hirzel, 2001.

Langbroek, Erika. "Warnung und Tarnung im *Helmbrecht*. Das Gespräch zwischen Vater und Sohn Helmbrecht und die Haube des Helmbrecht." *Amsterdamer Beiträge zur älteren Germanistik* 36 (1992): 141–68.

Menke, Petra. *Recht und Ordo-gedanke im Helmbrecht*. Frankfurt am Main: Lang, 1993.

Seelbach, Ulrich. *Späthöfische Literatur und Rezeption: Studien zum Publikum des "Helmbrecht" von Wernher der Gartenaere*. Berlin: Schmidt, 1987.

Sowinski, Bernhard. "Parzival und Helmbrecht: Höfische Kalokagathie und bäurische Usurpation." In *Von Wyssheit würt der Mensch geert: Festschrift für Manfred Lemmer zum 65. Geburtstag*, ed. Ingrid Kühn and Gotthart Lerchner. Frankfurt am Main: Lang, 1993, 117–27.

———. *Wernher der Gartenaere, Helmbrecht: Interpretation*. Munich: Oldenbourg, 1971.

Hildegard von Bingen

Ferrante, Joan. "*Scribe quae vides et audis*. Hildegard, Her Language, and Her Secretaries." In *The Tongue of the Fathers: Gender and Ideology in Twelfth-Century Latin*, ed. David Townsend and Andrew Taylor. Philadelphia: U of Pennsylvania P, 1998, 102–35.

Flanagan, Sabina. *Hildegard of Bingen, 1098–1179: A Visionary Life*. 2nd ed. New York: Routledge, 1998.

Newman, Barbara. *Sister of Wisdom: St Hildegard's Theology of the Feminine*. Berkeley: U of California P, 1987.

Konrad von Würzburg

Bleck, Reinhard. *Überlegungen zur Entstehungssituation der Werke Konrads von Würzburg, in denen kein Auftraggeber genannt wird*. Vienna: Halosar, 1987.

Brandt, Rüdiger. *Konrad von Würzburg*. Darmstadt: Wissenschaftliche Buchgesellschaft, 1987.

———. *Konrad von Würzburg: Kleinere epische Werke*. Berlin: E. Schmidt, 2000.

———. "Literatur zu Konrad von Würzburg 1987–1996." *Archiv für das Studium der neueren Sprachen und Literaturen* 236 (1999): 347–49.

Brunner, Horst. "Genealogische Phantasien. Zu Konrads von Würzburg *Schwanritter* und *Engelhard*." *Zeitschrift für deutsches Altertum und deutsche Literatur* 110 (1981): 274–99.

Cain van D'Elden, Stefanie. "Does Might make Right? The *Schwanritter* by Konrad von Würzburg." In *Courtly Literature, Culture and Context*, ed. Keith Busby and Erik Kooper. Amsterdam: Benjamins, 1990, 549–59.

Cramer, Thomas. "Minnesang in der Stadt. Überlegungen zur Lyrik Konrads von Würzburg." In *Literatur, Publikum, historischer Kontext*, ed. Gert Kaiser. Frankfurt am Main: Lang, 1977, 91–108.

Dahnke-Holtmann, Dagmar. "Die dunkle Seite des Spiegels. Das Verneinen in der *Goldenen Schmiede* Konrads von Würzburg." *Jahrbuch der Oswald von Wolkenstein-Gesellschaft* 5 (1988/89): 157–68.

Dobozy, Maria. "Der Alte und der Neue Bund in Konrads von Würzburg *Heinrich von Kempen*." *Zeitschrift für deutsche Philologie* 107 (1988): 386–400.

Essen, Erika. *Die Lyrik Konrads von Würzburg*. Marburg: Bauer 1938.

Fischer, Hubertus, and Paul Gerhard Völker. "Konrad von Würzburg: Heinrich von Kempten. Individuum und feudale Anarchie." In *Literaturwissenschaft und Sozialwissenschaften*. Vol. 5: *Literatur im Feudalismus*, ed. Dieter Richter. Stuttgart: Metzler, 1975, 83–130.

Leipold, Inge. *Die Auftraggeber und Gönner Konrads von Würzburg: Versuch einer Theorie der "Literatur als soziales Handeln."* Göppingen: Kümmerle, 1976.

Lienert, Elizabeth. *Geschichte und Erzählen: Studien zu Konrads von Würzburg "Trojanerkrieg."* Wiesbaden: Reichert, 1996.

Oettli, Peter. *Tradition and Creativity: The Engelhard of Konrad von Würzburg. Its Structure and Sources*. Frankfurt am Main: Peter Lang, 1986.

Rikl, Susanne. *Erzählen im Kontext von Affekt und Ratio: Studien zu Konrads von Würzburg "Partonopier und Meliur."* Frankfurt am Main: Lang, 1996.

Schnell, Rüdiger. "Die *Wahrheit* eines manipulierten Gottesurteils. Eine rechtsgeschichtliche Interpretation von Konrads von Würzburg *Engelhard*." *Poetica* 16 (1984): 24–60.

Strohschneider, Peter. "Ursprünge: Körper, Gewalt und Schrift im *Schwanritter* Konrads von Würzburg." In *Gespräche-Boten-Briefe: Körpergedächtnis und Schriftgedächtnis im Mittelalter*, ed. Horst Wenzel. Berlin: E. Schmidt, 1997, 127–53.

Kudrun

Campbell, Ian R. *Kudrun: A Critical Appreciation*. Cambridge: Cambridge UP, 1978.

Hoffmann, Werner. "Kudrun." In *Mittelhochdeutsche Romane und Heldenepen*, ed. Horst Brunner. Stuttgart: Reclam, 1993, 293–310.

Huber, Eduard. "Die Kudrun um 1300." *Zeitschrift für deutsche Philologie* 100 (1981): 357–81.

McConnell, Winder. *The Epic of Kudrun: A Critical Commentary.* Göppingen: Kümmerle, 1988.

———. "The Passing of Old Heroes: The Nibelungenlied, Kudrun, and the Epic Spirit." In *Genres in Medieval German Literature*, ed. Hubert Heinen and Ingeborg Henderson. Göppingen: Kümmerle, 1986, 103–13.

Murdoch, Brian. "Interpreting Kudrun: Some Comments on a Recent Critical Appreciation." *New German Studies* 7 (1979): 113–27.

Rupp, Heinz, ed. *Nibelungenlied und Kudrun.* Darmstadt: Wissenschaftliche Buchgesellschaft, 1976.

Schmidt, Klaus. *Begriffsglossar und Index zur Kudrun.* Tübingen: Niemeyer, 1994.

Schmitt, Kerstin. *Poetik der Montage: Figurenkonzeption und Intertexualität in der "Kudrun."* Berlin: E. Schmidt, 2002.

Wisniewski, Roswitha. *Kudrun.* 2nd ed. Stuttgart: Metzler, 1969.

Der Marner

Haustein, Jens. *Marner-Studien.* Tübingen: Niemeyer, 1995.

Mechthild von Magdeburg

Andersen, Elizabeth A. *The Voices of Mechthild von Magdeburg.* New York: Lang, 2000.

Hollywood, Amy. *The Soul as Virgin Wife: Mechthild of Magdeburg, Marguerite Porete, and Meister Eckhart.* Notre Dame, IN: U of Notre Dame P, 1995.

Peters, Ursula. *Religiöse Erfahrung als literarisches Faktum: Zur Vorgeschichte und Genese frauenmystischer Texte des 13. und 14. Jahrhunderts.* Tübingen: Niemeyer, 1988.

Poor, Sara S. "Cloaking the Body in Text: Mechthild von Magdeburg and the Question of Female Authorship." *Exemplaria* 12.2 (2000): 417–53.

———. *Mechthild of Magdeburg and Her Book: Gender and the Making of Textual Authority.* Philadephia: U of Pennsylvania P, 2004.

Tobin, Frank. *Mechthild von Magdeburg: A Medieval Mystic in Modern Eyes.* Columbia, SC: Camden House, 1995.

Das Nibelungenlied/Klage

Andersson, Theodore M. *A Preface to the Nibelungenlied.* Stanford: Stanford UP, 1987.

Ehrismann, Otfried. *Nibelungenlied. Epoche–Werk–Wirkung.* Munich: Beck, 1987.

———. *Das Nibelungenlied in Deutschland: Studien zur Rezeption des Nibelungenliedes von der Mitte des 18. Jahrhunderts bis zum ersten Weltkrieg.* Munich: Fink, 1974.

Frakes, Jerold C. *Brides and Doom: Gender, Property, and Power in Medieval German Women's Epic.* Philadelphia: U of Pennsylvania P, 1994.

Gentry, Francis G. "Die Rezeption des *Nibelungenliedes* in der Weimarer Republik." In *Das Weiterleben des Mittelalters in der deutschen Literatur*, ed. James F. Poag and Gerhild Scholz-Williams. Königstein/Ts: Athenäum, 1983.

Gillespie, George T. "Die Klage as a Commentary on Das Nibelungenlied." In *Probleme mittelhochdeutscher Erzählformen: Marburger Colloquium 1969*, ed. Peter Ganz and Werner Schröder. Berlin: Schmidt, 1972.

Haymes, Edward R. *The Nibelungenlied: History and Interpretation*. Urbana: U of Illinios P, 1986.

————— "A Rhetorical Reading of the *Hortforderungszene* in the *Nibelungenlied*." In *"Was sider da geschach.": American-German Studies on the Nibelungenlied Text and Reception*, ed. Werner Wunderlich and Ulrich Müller. Göppingen: Kümmerle, 1992.

Heinzle, Joachim. *Das Nibelungenlied: Eine Einführung*. Munich: Artemis, 1987.

Heinzle, Joachim, and Anneliese Waldschmidt, eds. *Die Nibelungen: Ein deutscher Wahn, ein deutscher Alptraum. Studien und Dokumente zur Rezeption des Nibelungenstoffs im 19. und 20. Jahrhundert*. Frankfurt am Main: Suhrkamp, 1991.

Hoffmann, Werner. *Das Nibelungenlied*. Frankfurt am Main: Diesterweg, 1987.

—————. *Das Nibelungenlied: Interpretation von Werner Hoffmann*. Munich: Oldenbourg, 1969.

Körner, Josef. *Nibelungenforschungen der deutschen Romantik*. Darmstadt: Wissenschaftliche Buchgesellschaft, 1968.

Krüger, Peter. "Etzels Halle und Stalingrad: Die Rede von Göring vom 30.1.1943." In *Die Nibelungen: Ein deutscher Wahn, ein deutscher Alptraum*, ed. Joachim Heinzle and Anneliese Waldschmidt. Frankfurt am Main: Suhrkamp, 1991.

Mackwitz, Walter. *Die Nibelungen: ihr Schicksal, ihr Gold und ihr Untergang*. Bremen: Donat, 2002.

McConnell, Winder. *The Nibelungenlied*. Boston: Twayne, 1984.

Mowatt, D. G., and Hugh Sacker. *The Nibelungenlied: An Interpretive Commentary*. Toronto: U of Toronto P, 1967.

Müller, Jan-Dirk. *Spielregeln für den Untergang: Die Welt des Nibelungenliedes*. Tübingen: Niemeyer, 1998.

Nagel, Bert. *Das Nibelungenlied: Stoff — Form — Ethos*. Frankfurt am Main: Hirschgraben Verlag, 1965.

Panzer, Friedrich. *Studien zum Nibelungenlied*. Frankfurt am Main: Diesterweg, 1945.

Sattel, Sabine B. *Das Nibelungenlied in der wissenschaftlichen Literatur zwischen 1945 und 1985: Ein Beitrag zur Geschichte der Nibelungenforschung*. Frankfurt am Main: Lang, 2000.

Schröder, Werner. *Nibelungen-Studien.* Stuttgart: Metzler, 1968.

Thomas, Neil. *Reading the "Nibelungenlied."* Durham: University of Durham, 1995.

Weber, Gottfried. *Das Nibelungenlied: Problem und Idee.* Stuttgart: Metzler, 1963.

Wunderlich, Werner, and Ulrich Müller. *"Waz sider da geschach": American-German Studies on the Nibelungenlied. Text and Reception. With Bibliography 1980–1990/91.* Göppingen: Kümmerle, 1992.

Das Rolandslied

Ashcroft, Jeffrey. "Konrads *Rolandslied,* Henry the Lion and the Northern Crusade." *Forum for Modern Language Studies* 22:2 (1986): 184–208.

———. "Miles dei — gotes ritter: Konrad's *Rolandslied* and the Evolution of the Concept of Christian Chivalry." *Forum for Modern Language Studies* 17: 2 (1981): 146–66.

Backes, Herbert. *Bibel und Ars Praedicandi im "Rolandslied" des Pfaffen Konrad.* Berlin: Schmidt, 1966.

Bertau, Karl. "Das deutsche *Rolandslied* und die Repräsentationskunst Heinrichs des Löwen." *Der Deutschunterricht* 20/2 (1968): 4–30.

Buschinger, Danielle, and Wolfgang Spiewok. *Das "Rolandslied" des Konrad: Gesammelte Aufsätze.* Greifswald: Reineke-Verlag, 1996.

Ernst, Ulrich. "Kollektive Aggression in der *Chanson de Roland* und im *Rolandslied* des Pfaffen Konrad." *Euphorion* 82:2 (1988): 211–25.

Kartschoke, Dieter. *Die Datierung des deutschen "Rolandsliedes."* Stuttgart: Metzler, 1965.

Lejeune, Rita, and Jacques Stiennon. *The Legend of Roland in the Middle Ages.* New York: Phaidon, 1971.

Ott-Meimberg, Marianne. *Kreuzzugsepos oder Staatsroman? Strukturen adeliger Heilsversicherung im deutschen "Rolandslied."* Zurich: Artemis, 1980.

Rudolf von Ems

Brackert, Helmut. *Rudolf von Ems: Dichtung und Geschichte.* Heidelberg: Winter, 1968.

Ehlert, Trude. "Der Alexanderroman." In *Interpretationen: Mittelhochdeutsche Romane und Heldenepen,* ed. Horst Brunner. Stuttgart: Reclam, 1993, 21–42.

Ehrismann, Gustav. *Studien über Rudolf von Ems: Beiträge zur Geschichte der Rhetorik und Ethik im Mittelalter.* Heidelberg: Winter, 1919.

Elsperger, Adolf. *Das Weltbild Rudolfs von Ems in seiner Alexanderdichtung.* Erlangen: Palm & Enke, 1939.

Ertzdorff, Xenia von. *Rudolf von Ems: Untersuchungen zum höfischen Roman im 13. Jahrhundert.* Munich: Fink, 1967.

Green, Dennis. "On the Primary Reception of the Works of Rudolf von Ems." *Zeitschrift für deutsches Altertum* 115 (1986): 151–80.

Haug, Walter. "Rudolfs 'Willehalm' und Gottfrieds 'Tristan': Kontrafaktur als Kritik." In *Deutsche Literatur des späten Mittelalters (Hamburger Colloquium 1973)*, ed. Wolfgang Harms and L. Peter Johnson. Berlin: E. Schmidt, 1975, 83–98.

Jaurant, Danielle. *Rudolfs "Weltchronik" als offene Form: Überlieferungsstruktur und Wirkungsgeschichte.* Tübingen: Francke, 1995.

Kahn, Ludwig. "Rudolf von Ems: Der gute Gerhard. Truth and Fiction in Medieval Epics." *Germanic Review* 14 (1939): 208–14.

Odenthal, Angelika. *Rudolf von Ems: Eine Bibliographie.* Cologne: G. Gabel, 1988.

Schnell, Rüdiger. *Rudolf von Ems: Studien zur inneren Einheit seines Gesamtwerkes.* Bern: France, 1969.

Stevens, Adrian, "Zum Literaturbegriff bei Rudolf von Ems." In *Geistliche und weltliche Epik des Mittelalters in Österreich.* Göppingen: Kümmerle, 1987, 19–28.

Tippelskirch, Ingrid von. *Die Weltchronik des Rudolf von Ems: Studien zur Geschichtsauffassung und politischer Intention.* Göppingen: Kümmerle, 1979.

Walliczek, Wolfgang. "Rudolf von Ems: Der guote Gêrhart." In *Mittelhochdeutsche Romane und Heldenepen*, ed. Horst Brunner. Stuttgart: Reclam, 1993, 255–70.

Wisbey, Roy A. *Das Alexanderbild Rudolfs von Ems.* Berlin: Schmidt, 1966.

Wyss, Ulrich. "Rudolfs von Ems 'Barlaam und Josaphat' zwischen Legende und Roman." In *Probleme mittelhochdeutscher Erzählformen*, ed. Peter Ganz and Werner Schröder. Berlin: E. Schmidt, 1972.

Zoeller, Sonja. *Kaiser, Kaufmann und die Macht des Geldes: Gerhard Unmaze von Köln als Finanzier der Reichspolitik und der "Gute Gerhard" des Rudolf von Ems.* Munich: Fink, 1993.

Der Stricker

Brall, Helmut. "Strickers Daniel von dem blühenden Tal. Zur politischen Funktion späthöfischer Artusepik im Territorialisierungsprozeß." *Euphorion* 70 (1976): 222–57.

Brandt, Rüdiger. *"Erniuwet": Studien zu Art, Grad und Aussagefolgen der Rolandsliedbearbeitung in Strickers "Karl."* Göppingen: Kümmerle, 1981.

Classen, Albrecht. "Misogyny and the Battle of Genders in the Stricker's Maeren." *Neuphilologische Mitteilungen* 92 (1991): 105–22.

Hofmann, Klaus. *Strickers "Frauenehre": Überlieferung — Textkritik — Edition — literaturgeschichtliche Einordnung.* Marburg: Elwert, 1976.

Kern, Peter. "Rezeption und Genese des Artusromans. Überlegungen zu Strickers *Daniel vom blühenden Tal.*" Special Issue of *Zeitschrift für deutsche Philologie* 93 (1974): 18–42.

Ragotzky, Hedda. *Gattungserneuerung und Laienunterweisung in Texten des Strickers.* Tübingen: Niemeyer, 1981.

Reisel, Johanna. *Zeitgeschichte und theologisch-scholastische Aspekte im "Daniel von dem blühenden Tal" des Stricker*. Göppingen: Kümmerle, 1986.

Resler, Michael. "Zur Datierung von Strickers *Daniel von dem Blühenden Tal.*" *Euphorion* 78 (1984): 17–30.

Wailes, Stephen. "Stricker and the Virtue *Prudentia*: A Critical Review." *Seminar* 13 (1977): 136–53.

———. *Studien zur Kleindichtung des Strickers*. Berlin: Schmidt, 1981.

Ulrich von Liechtenstein

Dopsch, Heinz. "Zwischen Dichtung und Politik: Herkunft und Umfeld Ulrichs von Lichtenstein." In *Ich — Ulrich von Liechtenstein: Literatur und Politik im Mittelalter*, ed. Franz Viktor Spechtler and Barbara Maier. Klagenfurt: Wieser, 1999, 49–104.

Händl, Claudia. *Rollen und pragmatische Einbindung: Analysen zur Wandlung des Minnesangs nach Walther von der Vogelweide*. Göppingen: Kümmerle, 1987.

Heinen, Hubert. "Ulrich's von Liechtenstein Sense of Genre." In *Genres in Medieval German Literature*, ed. Hubert Heinen and Ingeborg Henderson. Göppingen: Kümmerle, 1986, 16–29.

Kartschoke, Dieter. "Ulrich von Liechtenstein und die Laienkultur des deutschen Südostens im Übergang zur Schriftlichkeit." In *Die mittelalterliche Literatur in Kärnten*. Vienna: Halosar, 1981, 103–43.

Kühnel, Jürgen. "Zu den Tageliedern Ulrichs von Liechtenstein." *Jahrbuch der Oswald von Wolkenstein-Gesellschaft* 1 (1980/1): 99–138.

Müller, Ulrich. "Männerphantasien eines mittelalterlichen Herren: Ulrich von Lichtenstein und sein 'Frauendienst.'" In *Variationen der Liebe: Historische Psychologie der Geschlechterbeziehung*, ed. Thomas Kornbichler and Wolfgang Maaz. Tübingen: edition discord, 1995, 27–50.

———. "Ulrich von Liechtenstein und seine Männerphantasien: Mittelalterliche Literatur und moderne Psychologie." In *Ich — Ulrich von Liechtenstein: Literatur und Politik im Mittelalter*, ed. Franz Viktor Spechtler and Barbara Maier. Klagenfurt: Wieser, 1999, 297–317.

Schmidt, Klaus, et al., eds. "Bibliographie zu Ulrich von Lichtenstein." *Ich — Ulrich von Liechtenstein: Literatur und Politik im Mittelalter*, ed. Franz Viktor Spechtler and Barbara Maier. Klagenfurt: Wieser, 1999, 495–509.

Spechtler, Franz Viktor. "Ulrich von Liechtenstein bei Gerhart Hauptmann und Hugo von Hofmannsthal." In *Mittelalter-Rezeption*, ed. Jürgen Kühnel, et al. Göppingen: Kümmerle, 1979, 347–64.

———. "Die Urkunden-Regesten zu Ulrich von Liechtenstein. Bemerkungen zu den Urkunden und zu einer Biographie Ulrichs von Liechtenstein." *Ich — Ulrich von Liechtenstein: Literatur und Politik im Mittelalter*, ed. Franz Viktor Spechtler and Barbara Maier. Klagenfurt: Wieser, 1999, 441–93.

Spechtler, Franz Viktor, and Barbara Maier, eds. *Ich — Ulrich von Liechtenstein: Literatur und Politik im Mittelalter.* Klagenfurt: Wieser, 1999.

Ulrich von Türheim

Grubmüller, Klaus "Probleme einer Fortsetzung: Anmerkungen zu Ulrich's von Türheim Tristan-Schluß." *Zeitschrift für deutsches Altertum und deutsche Literatur* 114 (1985): 338–48.

Ulrich von Zatzikhoven

Chamberlin, Rick. *"Got hât liut unde lant von manegem wunder gemaht:* An Example of the Marvellous as Allegory in Ulrich von Zatzikhoven's *Lanzelet." Michigan Germanic Studies* 24 (1999): 8–17.

Combridge, Rosemary. "Der Lanzelet Ulrichs von Zatzikhoven im Kreuzfeuer der Editionsprinzipien." In *Methoden und Probleme der Edition mittelalterlicher Texte* (Beiheft zu *Editio*), ed. Rolf Bergmann and Kurt Gärtner. Tübingen: Niemeyer, 1993, 40–49.

Jackson, W. H. "Ulrich von Zatzikhoven's *Lanzelet* and the Theme of Resistance to Royal Power." *German Life and Letters* 28 (1974–75): 285–97.

McLelland, Nicola. *Ulrich von Zatzikhoven's Lanzelet: Narrative Style and Entertainment.* Cambridge: Brewer, 2000.

Meyer, Kathleen J. *"Lanzelet* and the Enclosure of Female sexuality." In *New Texts, Methodologies, and Interpretations in Medieval German Literature.* ed. Sibylle Jefferis. Kalamazoo Papers 1992–1995. Göppingen: Kümmerle, 1999, 159–72.

Pérennec, René. "Artusroman und Familie: *daz welsche buoch von Lanzelete." Acta Germanica* 11 (1979): 1–51.

Ruh, Kurt. "Der Lanzelet Ulrichs von Zatzikhoven, Modell oder Kompilation?" In *Deutsche Literatur des späten Mittelalters,* ed. Wolfgang Harms and L. Peter Johnson. Berlin: E. Schmidt, 1975, 47–55.

Schmid, Elizabeth. "Mutterrecht und Vaterliebe: Spekulationen über Eltern und Kinder im Lanzelet des Ulrichs von Zatzikhoven." *Archiv für das Studium der neueren Sprachen und Literaturen* 229 (1992): 241–54.

Schultz, James. "Lanzelet: A Flawless Hero in a Symmetrical World." *Beiträge zur Geschichte der deutschen Sprache und Literatur* 102 (1980): 160–88.

Soudek, Ernst. "Die Funktion der Namensuche und der Zweikämpfe in Ulrich von Zatzikhovens *Lanzelet." Amsterdamer Beiträge zur älteren Germanistik* 2 (1972): 173–85.

Zellmann, Ulrike. *Lanzelet: Der biographische Roman als Auslegungsschema dynastischer Wissensbildung.* Düsseldorf: Droste, 1996.

Walther von der Vogelweide

Beyschlag, Siegfried, ed. *Walther von der Vogelweide.* Darmstadt: Wissenschaftliche Buchgesellschaft, 1971.

Bumke, Joachim. "Walther von der Vogelweide," In *Kindlers Neues Literatur Lexikon*, vol. 17, ed. Walter Jens. Munich: Kindler Verlag, 1988, 398–403.

Ehlert, Trude. *Konvention — Variation — Innovation: Ein struktureller Vergleich von Liedern aus "Des Minnesangs Frühling" und Walther von der Vogelweide*. Berlin: Schmidt, 1980.

Heinen, Hubert. "Walther von der Vogelweide." In *Dictionary of Literary Biography*, vol. 138: *German Writers and Works of the High Middle Ages*, ed. James Hardin and Will Hasty. Detroit: Gale, 1994, 158–69.

Jones, George F. *Walther von der Vogelweide*. New York: Twayne, 1968.

McFarland, Timothy, and Silvia Ranawake, eds. *Walther von der Vogelweide: Twelve Studies*. Oxford: Meeuws, 1982.

Mück, Hans-Dieter, ed. *Walther von der Vogelweide: Beiträge zu Leben und Werk*. Stuttgart: Stöffler & Schütz, 1989.

Nolte, Theodor. *Walther von der Vogelweide: Höfische Idealität und konkrete Erfahrung*. Stuttgart: Hirzel, 1991.

Reichert, Hermann. *Walther von der Vogelweide für Anfänger*. 2nd ed. Vienna: WUV-Universitätsverlag, 1998.

Scholz, Manfred Günter. *Walther von der Vogelweide*. Stuttgart: Metzler, 1999.

Wernher der Gärtner

Fischer, Hanns. "Gestaltungsschichten im *Meier Helmbrecht*." PBB 79 (1957): 85–109.

Keinz, Friedrich. *Helmbrecht und seine Heimat*. Leipzig: Hirzel, 1887.

Knapp, Fritz Peter. "Standesväter und Heimatverächter in der bayrisch-östterreichischen Literatur des Spätmittelalters." In *Wernher der Gärtner "Helmbrecht": Die Beiträge des Helmbrecht-Symposions in Burghausen 2001*, ed. Theodor Nolte and Tobias Schneider. Stuttgart: Hirzel, 2001.

———. "Wernher der Gärtner." In *Die deutsche Literatur des Mittelalters: Verfasserlexikon*, vol. 10, ed. Burghart Wachinger. Berlin: de Gruyter, 1999.

Langbroek, Erika. "Warnung und Tarnung im *Helmbrecht*. Das Gespräch zwischen Vater und Sohn Helmbrecht und die Haube des Helmbrecht." *Amsterdamer Beiträge zur älteren Germanistik* 36 (1992): 141–68.

Menke, Petra. *Recht und Ordo-gedanke im Helmbrecht*. Frankfurt am Main: Lang, 1993.

Seelbach, Ulrich. *Bibliographie zu Wernher der Gartenaere*. Berlin: E. Schmidt, 1981.

———. "Hildemar und Helmbrecht: Intertextuelle Bezüge des *Helmbrecht* zu den Liedern Neidharts." In *Wernher der Gärtner: "Helmbrecht": Die Beiträge des Helmbrecht-Symposions in Burghausen*, ed. Theodor Nolte and Tobias Schneider. Stuttgart: Hirzel, 2001, 45–69.

———. *Späthöfische Literatur und ihre Rezeption im späten Mittelalter: Studien zum Publikum des "Helmbrecht" von Wernher dem Gartnaere*. Berlin: E. Schmidt, 1987.

Sowinski, Bernard. "Parzival und Helmbrecht. Höfische Kalokagathie und bäurische Usurpation." In *Von Wyssheit würt der Mensch geert: Festschrift für Manfred Lemmer zum 65. Geburtstag*, ed. Ingrid Kühn and Gotthart Lerchner. Frankfurt am Main: Peter Lang. 117–27.

Wirnt von Grafenberg

Cormeau, Christoph. *"Wigalois" und "Diu Crône": Zwei Kapitel zur Gattungsgeschichte des nachklassischen Aventiureromans.* Munich: Artemis, 1977.

Eming, Jutta. "Aktion und Reflexion: Zum Problem der Konfliktbewältigung im Wigalois am Beispiel der Namurs-Episode." In *Spannungen und Konflikte menschlichen Zusammenlebens in der deutschen Literatur des Mittelalters*, ed. Kurt Gärtner, Ingrid Kasten, and Frank Shaw. Tübingen; Niemeyer, 1996, 91–101.

———. *Funktionswandel des Wunderbaren: Studien zum "Bel Inconnu," zum "Wigalois" und zum "Wigoleis vom Rade."* Trier: Wissenschaftlicher Verlag, 1999.

Lohbeck, Gisela. *Wigalois: Struktur der "bezeichnunge."* Frankfurt am Main: Lang, 1991.

Mitgau, Wolfgang. "Nachahmung und Selbständigkeit Wirnts von Gravenberc in seinem *Wigalois.*" *Zeitschrift für deutsche Philologie* 82 (1963): 321–37.

Neumann, Friedrich. "Wann verfaßte Wirnt den Wigalois?" *Zeitschrift für deutsches Altertum* 93 (1964): 31–62.

Schröder, Werner. "Der synkretische Roman des Wirnt von Gravenberg. Unerledigte Fragen an den *Wigalois.*" *Euphorion* 80 (1986): 235–77.

Thomas, Neil. *A German View of Camelot: Wirnt von Gravenberg's "Wigalois" and Arthurian Tradition.* Frankfurt am Main: Lang, 1987.

———. *Wirnt von Gravenberg's "Wigalois": Intertextuality and Interpretation.* Cambridge: D. S. Brewer, 2005.

Wehrli, Max. "Wigalois." *Der Deutschunterricht* 17/2 (1965): 18–35.

Wolfram von Eschenbach

Borck, Karl Heinz. "Wolframs Tagelied 'den morgenblic bi wahtaers sange erkos.' Zur Lyrik eines Epikers." In *Studien zur deutschen Literatur: Festschrift für Adolf Beck zum 70. Geburtstag*, ed. Ulrich Fülleborn and Johannes Krogoll. Heidelberg: Winter, 1979.

Brunner, Horst. *"Artus der wise höfsche man.* Zur immanenten Historizität der Ritterwelt im *Parzival* Wolframs von Eschenbach." In *Germanistik in Erlangen: Hundert Jahre nach der Gründung des deutschen Seminars*, ed. Dieter Peschel. Erlangen: Universitätsbund Erlangen-Nürnberg, 1983.

Bumke, Joachim. *Die Blutstropfen im Schnee: Über Wahrnehmung und Erkenntnis im "Parzival" Wolframs von Eschenbach.* Tübingen: Niemeyer, 2001.

———. *Wolfram von Eschenbach.* 8th ed. Stuttgart: Metzler, 2004.

Bumke, Joachim. *Wolframs Willehalm: Studien zur Epenstruktur und zum Heiligkeitsbegriff der ausgehenden Blütezeit*. Heidelberg: Winter, 1959.

Fuchs, Stephan. *Hybride Helden: Gwigalois und Willehalm. Beiträge zum Heldenbild und zur Poetik des Romans im frühen 13. Jahrhundert*. Heidelberg: Winter, 1997.

Gibbs, Marion E. "Fragment and Expansion: Wolfram von Eschenbach, *Titurel* and Albrecht, *Jüngerer Titurel*." In *The Arthur of the Germans: The Arthurian Legend in Medieval German and Dutch Literature*, ed. W. H. Jackson and Silvia Ranawake. Cardiff: U of Wales P, 2000, 69–80.

Green, Dennis Howard. "Homicide and *Parzival*." In *Approaches to Wolfram von Eschenbach*, ed. Dennis Howard Green and Leslie Peter Johnson. Frankfurt am Main, 1978, 11–82.

Greenfield, John. *Vivianz: An Analysis of the Martyr Figure in Wolfram von Eschenbach's "Willehalm" and in his Old French Source Material*. Erlangen: Palm & Enke, 1991.

Greenfield, John, and Lydia Miklautsch. *Der "Willehalm" Wolframs von Eschenbach. Eine Einführung*. Berlin: de Gruyter, 1998.

Hasty, Will. *A Companion to Wolfram's "Parzival."* Columbia, SC: Camden House, 1999.

Heinzle, Joachim. *Stellenkommentar zu Wolframs Titurel: Beiträge zum Verständnis des überlieferten Textes*. Tübingen: Niemeyer, 1972.

Johnson, L. Peter. "*Sîne klâwen*, An Interpretation." In *Approaches to Wolfram von Eschenbach*, ed. Dennis Green and L. Peter Johnson. Frankfurt am Main: Peter Lang, 1978.

Jones, Martin H., and Timothy McFarland, eds. *Wolfram's "Willehalm": Fifteen Essays*. Rochester, NY: Camden House, 2002.

Kiening, Christian. *Reflexion-Narration: Wege zum "Willehalm" Wolframs von Eschenbach*. Tübingen: Niemeyer, 1991.

Lofmark, Carl. *Rennewart in Wolfram's "Willehalm": A Study of Wolfram von Eschenbach and his Sources*. Cambridge: Cambridge UP, 1972.

McFarland, Timothy. "The Emergence of the German Grail Romance: Wolfram von Eschenbach, *Parzival*." In *The Arthur of the Germans: The Arthurian Legend in Medieval German and Dutch Literature*, ed. W. H. Jackson and Silvia Ranawake. Cardiff: U of Wales P, 2000, 54–68.

Parshall, Linda B. *The Art of Narration in Wolfram's "Parzival" and Albrecht's "Jüngerer Titurel."* Cambridge: Cambridge UP, 1981.

Read, Ralph. "Heinrich von dem Türlin's *Diu Krône* and Wolfram's *Parzival*." *Modern Language Quarterly* 35 (1974): 129–39.

Sowinski, Bernhard. "Parzival und Helmbrecht. Höfische Kalokagathie und bäurische Usurpation." In *Von Wyssheit würt der Mensch geert: Festschrift für Manfred Lemmer zum 65. Geburtstag*, ed. Ingrid Kühn and Gotthart Lerchner. Frankfurt am Main: Lang, 1993, 117–27.

Thomas, Neil. "Sense and Structure in the Gawan Adventures of Wolfram's Parzival." *Modern Language Review* 76 (1981): 848–56.

Unzeitig-Herzog, Monika. "*Artus mediator*. Zur Konfliktlösung in Wolframs *Parzival* Buch XIV." *Frühmittelalterliche Studien* 32 (1998): 196–217.

Wapnewski, Peter. *Die Lyrik Wolframs von Eschenbach: Edition, Kommentar, Interpretation.* Munich: Beck, 1972.

Wolff, Ludwig. "Wolframs *Schionatulander und Sigune*": *Studien zur deutschen Philologie des Mittelalters. Friedrich Panzer zum 80. Geburtstag am 4. September 1950 dargebracht*, ed. R. Kienast. Heidelberg: Winter, 1950, 116–30.

———. "Der *Willehalm* Wolframs von Eschenbach." *Deutsche Vierteljahrsschrift* 12 (1934): 504–39.

Young, Christopher. *Narrativische Perspektiven in Wolframs "Willehalm."* Tübingen: Niemeyer, 2000.

Contributors

ELIZABETH A. ANDERSEN is Senior Lecturer at the University of Newcastle, UK. She works on German literature of the twelfth and thirteenth centuries, in particular on Arthurian courtly romances and women's mystical writing. Her principal focus in the former has been the *Prosa-Lancelot* and in the latter Mechthild von Mageburg's *Das fliessende Licht der Gottheit*, about which she has written a monograph (2000). She has also produced a translation of selected passages from Mechthild's writings (2003). Currently she is working on the influence of hagiography on secular courtly literature.

CHARLES R. BOWLUS is Professor of History at the University of Arkansas at Little Rock. He has published widely on Central European history in the Middle Ages. His most important book is *Franks, Moravians, and Magyars, The Struggle for the Middle Danube* (788–907) (1995). He has recently completed a monograph on the battle of Lechfeld that is currently in press. His next project is a study of German imperial-Byzantine rivalries in Central Europe.

RÜDIGER BRANDT is Professor of Medieval German Language and Literature at the University of Duisburg-Essen. He is editor of *Lateres* (with D. Lau and K. O. Seidel) and *Perspicuitas* (with J. Fröhlich and K. O. Seidel). He has written widely on Konrad von Würzburg, and other main themes of his books and articles are literary sociology, rhetoric, media history, and lexicology.

ALBRECHT CLASSEN is University Distinguished Professor of German at the University of Arizona, Tucson. He has written books on Oswald von Wolkenstein, Wolfram von Eschenbach, the German chapbook, German women writers, the role of violence in courtly literature, on medieval alterity, on the discourses of love, marriage, and transgression, on communication in the Middle Ages, and on childhood. A book on marriage tracts, sermons, and songs appeared in 2005, and also an edition and translation of *Mai und Beaflor* is forthcoming. He is the recipient of the Bundesverdienstkreuz am Band, and serves as the editor of *Tristania*.

RODNEY FISHER was Associate Professor of German and then Adjunct Fellow at the University of Canterbury in New Zealand until 2004. His major interest and most of his publications are in the field of medieval

German literature, with interpretations and translations of the works of Heinrich von Veldeke, Walther von der Vogelweide, Hartmann von Aue, and Heinrich von Morungen. Other research interests have been translation theory, and the former East German writer Stefan Heym.

MARION E. GIBBS is Emeritus Reader in German at the University of London. Having graduated from Bedford College, she spent the major part of her career at Royal Holloway College, where she taught principally Middle High German language and literature. Her publications are primarily in the medieval period, with books on Wolfram von Eschenbach and, with Sidney M. Johnson, translations of *Willehalm, Titurel,* and Wolfram's Songs, and of *Kudrun.* Also with Sidney Johnson she published, in 1997, *A Companion to Medieval German Literature.* She is currently working on *Der Wälsche Gast.*

NIGEL HARRIS is Senior Lecturer at the University of Birmingham, UK. He is the author of *The Latin and German 'Etymachia'* (1994), and is close to completing a major edition of the *Lumen anime C* and Ulrich Putsch's *Das liecht der sel.* He has also written widely on narrative literature of the Middle High German *Blütezeit,* and on the role of animals in medieval literature and culture.

WILL HASTY is Professor of German Studies at the University of Florida. He has published widely on medieval and early modern German literature, particularly on the Arthurian romances. He is editor of *A Companion to Wolfram von Eschenbach's 'Parzival'* (1999), *A Companion to Gottfried von Strassburg's 'Tristan'* (2003), and author of *Art of Arms: A Study of German Court Poetry* (2002).

WILLIAM H. JACKSON was formerly Senior Lecturer in German at the University of St. Andrews. He has published widely on medieval German literature and written also on aristocratic culture from the twelfth to the sixteenth century. His publications include *Chivalry in Twelfth-Century Germany: The Works of Hartmann von Aue* (1994) and *The Arthur of the Germans: The Arthurian Legend in Medieval German and Dutch Literature* (co-edited with Silvia Ranawake, 2000).

SIDNEY M. JOHNSON was a highly regarded medievalist, continuing to publish up to his death in 2003. He had retired some years earlier as Professor of Germanic Studies at The University of Indiana in Bloomington. His principal enthusiasm, from his doctoral dissertation on *Willehalm,* was Wolfram von Eschenbach, but he wrote widely on other aspects of medieval German literature. He published, with Marion Gibbs, translations of Wolfram's work and of *Kudrun,* as well as a wide-ranging *Companion to Medieval German Literature.*

RÜDIGER KROHN is Professor of Medieval and Early Modern German Literature at the University of Chemnitz. He has published extensively on the German literature of the High and Late Middle Ages, on modern reception of medieval literature, and on drama, as well as on the history of German Studies. His critiques of modern literature and the theater appear regularly on radio, television, and in newspapers.

NICOLA MCLELLAND is Lecturer in German at the University of Nottingham, UK. Her book, *Ulrich von Zatzikhoven's 'Lanzelet': Narrative and Entertainment* appeared in 2000. Besides her interest in medieval literature, she has also written widely on the history of linguistic thought in Germany, particularly the Early Modern Period, and is currently preparing a book on the seventeenth-century grammarian Justus-Georg Schottelius.

ULRICH MÜLLER is Professor at the University of Salzburg, Austria. He has published facsimile editions, books, and articles on Medieval German Literature (especially lyric poetry, including that of Walther von der Vogelweide, Neidhart, Ulrich von Liechtenstein, and Oswald von Wolkenstein), the modern reception and performance of medieval literature, and musical theater (Mozart, Wagner, musicals, etc., including collaboration with opera houses in Salzburg, Bayreuth, and Vienna). Together with Ingrid Bennewitz and Franz V. Spechtler, he is currently finishing a complete edition of Neidhart's songs.

SARA S. POOR is Assistant Professor in the German Department at Princeton University. Her work and teaching focus on gender studies in conjunction with medieval devotional literature, manuscript studies, and courtly epic and romance. She is the author of *Mechthild of Magdeburg and Her Book: Gender and the Making of Textual Authority* (2004) and co-editor of *Women and Medieval Epic*, forthcoming from Palgrave Press. She has also recently completed a year's term as General Editor of *Medieval Feminist Forum* (2004–5).

MICHAEL RESLER is Professor of German Studies and longtime department chair at Boston College. His fields of interest are medieval German literature (in particular Middle High German Arthurian romance) and Germanic philology. Among his chief publications are a critical edition of Der Stricker's *Daniel von dem Blühenden Tal* and annotated English translations of *Daniel* and of Hartmann von Aue's *Erec*. He is presently working on a new translation of Hartmann's *Iwein*.

SUSANN SAMPLES is Professor of Modern Languages at Mount Saint Mary's University (Maryland). She has published on medieval German literature, in particular on the heroic narratives and the Arthurian romances. She has also published on the Afro-Germans. She is co-author of *Heroic Legends of the North,* and she is working on a book on Heinrich von dem Türlin's *Diu*

Crône. She is currently president of the North American Branch of the International Arthurian Society.

FRANZ VIKTOR SPECHTLER is Professor at the University of Salzburg. He has published editions, facsimiles, books, and articles on Medieval German Literature, on topics including Walther von der Vogelweide, Ulrich von Liechtenstein, Mönch von Salzburg; medieval romances, medieval theater, medieval legal texts, the modern reception of medieval literature, and German orthography. Together with Ingrid Bennewitz and Ulrich Müller he is currently finishing a complete edition of Neidhart's songs.

NEIL THOMAS is Reader in the Department of German at Durham University. He has published a number of monographs on the heroic epic and romance genres: *Reading the Nibelungenlied* (1995), *Diu Crone and the Medieval Arthurian Cycle* (2002), *Wirnt von Gravenberg's Wigalois: Intertextuality and Interpretation* (2005). He is writing up an interdisciplinary monograph on Chrétien de Troyes, Wolfram von Eschenbach, and *Sir Gawain and the Green Knight.*

RUTH WEICHSELBAUMER is a project assistant in the Department of German Studies at the University of Salzburg. She is currently working on the Salzburg Neidhart Edition. She has published articles on various topics in medieval German, and has recently published a book about medieval studies on the Internet.

Index